PUBLIC RIGHTS,
PUBLIC RULES

I0130663

STUDIES IN STATES AND SOCIETIES
VOLUME I
GARLAND REFERENCE LIBRARY OF SOCIAL SCIENCE
VOLUME 1065

STATES AND SOCIETIES

DULA J. ESPINOSA, *Series Editor*

PUBLIC RIGHTS, PUBLIC RULES
*Constituting Citizens in the
World Polity and National Policy*
edited by Connie L. McNeely

PUBLIC RIGHTS, PUBLIC RULES

CONSTITUTING CITIZENS IN THE WORLD POLITY AND NATIONAL POLICY

EDITED BY
CONNIE L. McNEELY

Routledge
Taylor & Francis Group

LONDON AND NEW YORK

First published 1998 by Garland Publishing, Inc.

2 Park Square, Milton Park, Abingdon, Oxon OX14 4RN
711 Third Avenue, New York, NY 10017, USA

Routledge is an imprint of the Taylor & Francis Group, an informa business

First issued in paperback 2016

Library of Congress Cataloging-in-Publication Data

Public rights, public rules : constituting citizens in the world polity and national
    policy / edited by Connie L. McNeely.
        p.   cm. — (States and societies ; v. 1) (Garland reference library
    of social science ; v. 1065.)
        Includes index.
        1. Citizenship.   2. Political sociology.   I. McNeely, Connie L.
    II. Series.   III. Series: Garland reference library of social science. States and
    societies ; v. 1.
    JF801.P83   1998
    323.6—dc21   98–35377
                                                                                    CIP

ISBN 13: 978-0-8153-2126-2 (hbk)
ISBN 13: 978-1-138-98427-1 (pbk)

Contents

Series Editor's Foreword

Recent dramatic changes in the modern world and in human relations at all levels of interaction have led to important questions about the basic sociopolitical, economic, and cultural relationships and concepts that have been the focus of scholarly and public debates. Accordingly, sociological arguments surrounding such topics as democracy and markets, sovereignty, citizenship, nationalism, diversity, and political and legal cultures are being discussed as part of a broader social and intellectual agenda. These are the kinds of issues that the books in the "States and Societies" series address. Principally concerned with issues in political sociology, broadly defined, they also speak to related topics in public policy, organizations, culture, and law and society, highlighting and examining how individuals, groups, and other social actors are defined and given meaning and the ways in which their interrelations are determined and controlled in this world of shifting realities. While focusing on contemporary concerns and debates, the books in the series generally employ an overall comparative and historical perspective to explore the underlying processes and developments affecting states and societies in the world today.

This current volume, *Public Rights, Public Rules: Constituting Citizens in the World Polity and National Policy,* unites several important contributors whose work reflects new development and insights in theoretical and empirical research. It brings together studies of global and comparative issues, as well as investigations considering local and national context, to offer a comprehensive understanding of the interplay of global and local forces in the conceptualization of citizenship, as they contribute to and are affected by the extension of both rights and rules in the public sphere. Several prominent themes in political sociology are addressed, including race, class, and gender; institutional sites, processes, and resources; and relationship between public and private definitions, concepts, structures, and practices. each chapter presents its own unique contribution set of concerns, while also addressing complementary issues through overlapping questions about citizenship and membership and sociopolitical, legal, and cultural structures, practices, and transformations. This volume provides a balance between diversity and thematic continuity, specificity and generality, and empirical study and theoretical reflection on citizenship in the contemporary world.

Dula J. Espinosa
University of Colorado
at Colorado Springs

Contributors

NITZA BERKOVITCH
Ben Gurion University

JOHN BOLI
Emory University

DULA J. ESPINOSA
*University of Colorado
Colorado Springs*

T. RYKEN GRATTET
*University of California
Davis, California*

BARBARA HOBSON
Stockholm University

DAVID JACOBSON
Arizona State University

LARS BO KASPERSEN
Aarhus University

ANTHONY W. MARX
Columbia University

CONNIE L. MCNEELY
George Mason University

JOHN W. MEYER
Stanford University

JOHN MOHR
*University of California
Santa Barbara*

ANN ORLOFF
*University of Wisconsin
Madison, Wisconsin*

FRANCISCO O. RAMIREZ
Stanford University

MARY RAUNER
Stanford University

MARGARET R. SOMERS
University of Michigan

Public Rights,
Public Rules

PART I
INTRODUCTION

1 CONSTITUTING CITIZENS

RIGHTS AND RULES

Connie L. McNeely

The dramatic changes that have occurred throughout the modern nation-state system, especially since the end of World War II and more recently, have engendered a renewed and increasing interest in issues of citizenship and rights. Public rights and responsibilities, rules and constraints, in terms of citizenship, national identity, and resources, are being renegotiated and recast everywhere in response to world-level pressures and local developments. Indeed, interest in these concepts as political and cultural formations, in their institutional and organizational determinants and effects, and in related transnational processes have brought into question the fundamental nature of nation, state, polity, and individual membership in the broadest sense. More to the point, changing notions of citizenship and rights have again been placed squarely on the sociological agenda, leading to explorations of related forms, legitimacy, jurisdiction, and practice in the contemporary world.

A central problem that cuts across much of this renewed interest in citizenship and polity membership, and related rights and rules, is the shifting nature of these social constructs in various settings and periods. Another emerging concern questions the usefulness of the concept of "citizen" itself, in light of its definition in relation to the nation-state and debates on the transformation of the nation-state and challenges to its authority—indeed, challenges to its very existence. In addition, the idea that citizenship and membership can be analyzed in terms of fixed homogeneous, stable social groupings and national polities is being soundly rejected as increasing numbers of studies and current events demonstrate the implausibility of such views. Such considerations suggest that traditional concepts of citizenship might themselves be problematic, and even inadequate in the face of new questions raised in recognition of global processes and effects in national arenas, and vice versa. What is at stake in these new debates surrounding membership and rights is the need for approaches that take into consideration the interplay of international and domestic sociopolitical, economic, and cultural contexts. Thus, it seems clear that we must engage an overall comparative and historical perspective to address these concerns in light of changing national and international interactions, conditions, and relations.

In adopting such a perspective, we must consider new developments and insights in theoretical and empirical research on this highly important issue of rights and rules in the public sphere, broadly defined, and affecting individuals and groups in a variety of settings. In other words, bringing together theoretical and empirical research on global and comparative issues, as well as investigations from local and national contexts of interest, can help us gain a more comprehensive understanding of the interplay of global and local forces in the conceptualization of citizenship, as they contribute to the extension of both rights and rules in the public sphere. This means addressing several prominent questions and themes in political sociology and related disciplines, including race, class, gender, and other forms of social diversity and stratification; institutional sites, processes, and resources; and relationships between public and private definitions, concepts, structures, and practices.

It also means understanding and forging links between micro and macro processes, and between more focused studies and larger problems of theory, ideology, and societal relations and discourses. While drawing upon unique contributions and sets of concerns, we can also address and probe complementary issues through overlapping questions about citizenship and membership, and about sociopolitical, legal, and cultural structures, practices, and transformations. Thus, the point is to achieve a balance between diversity and thematic continuity, specificity and generality, and empirical study and theoretical reflection.

Here, while introducing the basic notion of public rights, rules, and citizenship in terms of a changing international system, I consider the broad implications of recent scholarly research that has addressed related issues from various theoretical and empirical perspectives. Delineating fundamental issues and questions that are raised in this arena, I discuss the various aspects of citizenship that form the core of related debates. I also specify an overall, comprehensive approach for exploring conceptual schemes and the construction of public boundaries, reflecting changes in the rules defining citizenship roles, identities, and rights in different polity contexts. The task of describing and explaining the formation and transformation of citizenship involves consideration of such complex issues as sovereignty, jurisdiction, legal culture, diversity, welfare, and related state norms, structures, practices, and resources. More to the point, it means addressing basic ques-

tions of citizenship in light of contemporary events and historical antecedents and consequences.

Conceptual Issues and Debates

The first and most basic questions that arise here pertain to the general concept and meaning of citizenship itself: How has citizenship been defined? What
are the origins, nature, and destiny of citizenship? What are the limits, similarities, and differences of respective citizenship definitions and concepts?

Citizenship is typically described as a relationship between an individual and a nation-state involving the individual's full political membership
in the nation-state and permanent allegiance to it; the status of citizen is official recognition of the individual's integration into the political system.[1]
Indeed, citizenship is a *legal status*, regulated and defensible by law, bestow-
ing upon individuals equal rights and duties, liberties and constraints, powers and responsibilities (Marshall 1973:84). In the pure sense, the citizen
enjoys certain rights and privileges—certain protections and guarantees that
cannot be overridden—underwritten by the state; protection of person and
property is the prime function of the state on behalf of its citizens. In other
words, the notion of citizenship and rights encompasses responsibilities of
the state to "the people," to its citizens.

However, in return, citizens have certain duties and obligations to the
state. Historically, the development of citizenship, along with modern democracy, is linked to the notion and expansion of nation-state sovereignty
and the growth and extension of administrative power from the sixteenth
century (Kaspersen, chapter 6, this volume). This development was made
possible largely by the extension of the state's capacity for surveillance, that
is, the collection and storing of information about members of society and
the related ability to supervise subject populations (Giddens 1981; Held
1989:196). The relationship between the duties of citizenship and the preservation of rights is the key issue here. Although legal requirements of citizenship have varied according to context, both temporally and spatially, four
basic duties have been commonly delineated (Heater 1990): (1) participation in the political process; (2) involvement in the administration of law;
(3) enrollment in military service; and (4) the payment of taxes.[2]

This idea of citizenship is based on the assumption of the capacity of
a population to be self-organized and self-recognized as a polity, that is, as
a people in a fully functioning community and in relation to a state, as a
condition or result of that state. It is also based on the idea of citizen loyalty and identification with the state (Kaspersen, chapter 6). This means, of
course, that we are faced with fundamental questions about the meaning of

citizenship and polity in different settings: In what ways has the concept of citizenship changed over time? Do models of citizenship vary according to context? In addition, this means that, in order to understand citizenship as a basic relationship of polity and state, we must also consider the alternative: the existence of an organized society that is not identical with or defined by the state. The association of a society, or its lack thereof, with its official political organization—the state—is clearly an issue of polity and polity formation. In fact, the argument that the realm of civil society is constituted as that of citizenship is a point which, in and of itself, has constituted a contested terrain.[3]

However, for our purposes here, rather than adopting one model or theory, I follow Somers (1995:241–242) and refer to citizenship in terms of more fundamental common attributes shared by those attempting to provide accounts of the conditions for both public and private rights, for both individual protection by the state and individual freedom from the state. Here, the term citizenship encompasses the somewhat generic problem of the freedoms, rights, duties, and rules between "the people" of a territorially bounded polity, and of that polity's institutions of rule. The dichotomy of state and society becomes blurred in this instance to the extent that they are not mutually exclusive categories; rather, they are *mutually dependent*.

As Held (1989:199) points out, throughout history, from the ancient world to the present day, all forms of citizenship have had certain common attributes: citizenship entails *membership* in a *community*, and membership implies social *participation*. This follows Marshall's (1963, 1973:70) classic treatment in which citizenship refers to "full membership of a community," where membership involves participation by individuals in determining the conditions of their association. In general, citizenship has meant a certain *reciprocity* of rights against, and duties towards, the community. It has entailed membership in the community in which one lives one's life, with membership involving degrees of participation in that community. Fundamental to that notion is the question of *who should or may participate* and at what level, distinguishing between those who are members and those who are "others." In other words, what are the determinants and defining features of community membership and participation? What defining characteristics are applied in the recognition of citizens, as opposed to "others"?

While citizenship has been defined in broad categorical terms, referring to people who are included in a state's circle of *full political participation* (Lipset 1963), we also know that, over time, there have been dramatic shifts in the boundaries—and barriers—that are drawn around that "full" participation. At various points in history, there have been attempts to restrict the extension of citizenship along various lines to various categories and groups of people: "among others, owners of property, white men, educated men, men, those with particular skills and occupations, adults," etc. People have been barred from citizenship on grounds of gender, race, class, age, religion, and a variety of other factors.[4] The construction of a national citizenry represents an uneven and gradual process over time, with incorporation and accordance of rights and privileges taking longer for some groups than others (Marshall 1964), raising an additional question: How and through what process have citizenship rules and principles emerged from specific historical contexts?

While the French Revolution is typically recognized as instituting national citizenship as the modern mode of polity membership, full citizenship and membership—that is, participation of the "masses"—has come about (and is still doing so) through incremental, step-by-step abolishment of restrictive qualifications, such as property ownership, race, literacy, gender, and so forth. Many western "developed" countries, for example, had not granted full rights to women even well into the twentieth century. As Berkovitch's (chapter 4) description and analysis of the global discourse surrounding women and women's rights from the turn of the century to the present reveal, it was only in the later period, in the mid-twentieth century, that there was even a change in the related discourse, and women were "granted" rights as individuals and citizens. This gendered process has taken place on an international level, and has had major consequences for our understanding of the dynamics affecting the rights of women and of other socially defined groups in various national contexts (Orloff, chapter 9; Hobson, chapter 10; *also see* Ramirez and Meyer, chapter 3).

Citizen Identity: Specifying National Membership

The quintessential form of national membership in the modern period is that of citizenship. Yet, as mentioned above, citizenship and all its associated rights and meanings cannot be assumed by all specified populations at all times in a nation-state. Different groups display different types and degrees of incorporation into the institutionalized social order of the broader society and nation. Indeed, the concept of the nation is based on the construction of social boundaries that serve to designate societal membership for some groups as opposed to "others," and includes the notion that this designation is primary and fundamental to social identity itself.

Moreover, citizenship, membership, and incorporation in a national society key components and goals of nation-building, reflecting the identity of the modern nation-state. Indeed, usage of the term "nation" itself often encompasses both ethno-cultural and politico-legal meanings. On the one hand, it can refer to membership in a distinct *cultural community* with shared values and behavioral customs; on the other hand, it can refer to *political membership*, denoting a legally and normatively defined *community* with mutual rights and responsibilities (Gellner 1983). It is these different aspects of nation and community membership that allow conception of a single national polity that is composed of different ethno-cultural groups—and of citizens as constituting a nation. Accordingly, another question arises: What identities are appropriate for and appropriated by various politics and political action in determining and enacting citizenship? In short, how do citizen identity formation and public rights, rules, and obligations relate to the conceptualization of the nation-state?

While for some purposes we might also posit cultural similarity of the members of a political community, stress is placed here on the idea of a nation in terms of *common citizenship in a specific state*. Thus, the identity of the nation is found, not in ethno-cultural commonalties, but in *political* (democratic) procedures, discourse, and decision making (Habermas 1992). In this sense, the nation-state and citizenship are disengaged from more "primordial" definitions and requirements of common ethno-cultural descent. A similar issue is raised in Brubaker's (1992) comparison of nineteenth century German emphasis on descent as a qualification for citizenship and of French openness to naturalization for "permanent" residents, demonstrating the distinction between descent *(jus sanguinis)* and residence *(jus solis)* as defining principles of citizenship.

Moreover, citizenship as we know it would have no meaning without the existence of the state; the key structural change that allows the conception of the nation as unitary is the rise of the modern state (Giddens 1985), with states imposing pressures for various forms of cultural *loyalty* and *participation*. Again, the focus here is on what constitutes a *political community*, reflected in institutions and networks that operate *across* lines of diversity internal to nations and states (Calhoun 1993). After all, the role of the modern state is constituted by "continuous administrative, legal, bureaucratic, and coercive systems that attempt not only to structure relationships between civil society and public authority in a polity, but also to structure many crucial relationships within civil society as well" (Stepan 1978:xii).

Indeed, as Boli (1993, 1987:146) points out, a state is always associated with a polity, or the social unit constituted by a body politic, implying the structures by which central authority are organized within that unit. More to the point, it is the construction of citizenship, along with the inventory of citizen rights and national institutions, that defines the individual as a member of the nation. In other words, we can think of the nation-state as a project in which society is constituted as the nation and the individual as a citizen.

The idea of the modern nation-state includes an expectation of states to incorporate people as individual citizens, to educate and mobilize them around goals of economic and social progress and development, and to provide for and promote their welfare through public programs (Ramirez and Thomas 1987). Thus, citizenship locates both rights and national institutions within the jurisdiction of the state: "Citizenship defines individuals vis-à-vis national institutions and thereby incorporates them into national state authority" (Thomas et al. 1987:131–132). The concern here is with society constituted as a modern nation-state in which nations and states are linked together through ideas of citizenship and state-directed national development. Along with the expansion of the state comes an increase in the rights of individuals as members of the nation-state—as citizens.

Citizen Rights and Privileges

As we can see, citizenship is a multifaceted concept. However, by far the most fundamental defining issue is that of *rights*. The idea of citizenship has always been tied to the idea of rights, and the civil and legal condition of citizenship is indistinguishable from the rights defined by it as a status (Heater 1990). In fact, citizenship has even been described as *the right to have rights*.[5]

Given the centrality of the idea of rights here, we must first try to clarify its meaning in order to better understand citizenship itself. What do we mean by rights? How are rights related to issues of membership and national incorporation? What is meant by the idea that an individual has rights? What is meant by the idea that a socially defined group has rights?

One way in which rights can be conceptualized is as legitimate spheres of independent action or inaction.[6] More to the point, a right is a legitimate or socially recognized moral or legal justification for individuals to be allowed specified behavior or to demand specified behavior from others with regard to themselves. In general, citizen rights encompass the domain in which individuals look to pursue their own activities within the constraints of community, a point that requires specific consideration: In what ways do the creation and expansion of citizen rights extend or restrict the action of individuals and groups? Also, keep in mind that rights are *situational* and individual or group rights are constantly being redefined, extended, or withdrawn.[7] "All rights are limited or enlarged by obligations entailed in group membership, particular social situations, and social roles that are associated with the exercise of the particular right" (Theodorson and Theodorson 1979:350).

Moreover, as noted above, citizenship is a multidimensional concept, inscribed with a multitude of different types of rights. We might think of it as "represented by that bundle of rights that individuals can enjoy as a result of their status as 'free and equal' members of society. And to unpack the domain of rights is to unpack both the rights citizens formally enjoy and the conditions under which citizens' rights are actually realized or enacted. Only this 'double-focus' makes it possible to grasp the degrees of autonomy, interdependence, and constraint that citizens face in the societies in which they live" (Held 1989:201). Thus, additional questions are posed for exploring and specifying the characteristics of rights in order to understand the nature of citizenship: What types and features of rights exist? How do the various types and features of rights operate to define various aspects of citizenship?

Here, we turn to Marshall's (1950, 1964) classic treatment in which citizenship is identified as a set of three basic types of rights: civil, political, and social. While this typology is clearly open to criticism (Orloff, chapter 9; Somers, chapter 7),[8] it can still provide a useful analytical basis and starting point for categorizing and understanding citizen rights in general. *Civil (civic) rights* comprise, for example, freedom of speech and equality before the law; they refer to "rights necessary for individual freedom," including liberty of the person, freedom of speech, thought, and faith, the right to own property and enter into contracts, and the rights to be treated equally with others before the law. Civil rights in many ways represent limits on both the state and society; they protect individuals from arbitrary or excessive intrusion by the state and society. *Political rights* include the right to vote and to organize politically; moreover, political rights presume the existence of a collectivity; political rights are those elements of rights that create the possibility of participation in the exercise of political power "as a member of a body invested with political authority or as an elector of the members of such a body." *Social (socioeconomic) rights,* which include economic welfare and social security, are broadly defined as involving a whole range of rights "from the right to a modicum of economic welfare and security to the right . . . to live the life of a civilized being according to the standards prevailing in . . . society" (Marshall 1963; 1973:71–72).[9]

In general, the concept of citizenship denotes a status that provides *access* to special rights and powers. Thus, access to these rights is a defining issue of citizenship, basic to determining membership and polity formation and participation, recognition of which allows us to address basic issues of citizenship. For example, what role does access to rights play in incorporating individuals as members in the nation-state? What characteristics of rights are determinant of polity formation? The extension to the "masses" of civil and political rights, previously confined to narrow elites, serves an *integrative* function, incorporating "the people," more broadly defined, into society and polity.

Similarly, the extension of social rights (reflected, for example, in trade unionism, collective bargaining, and the rise of the welfare state) has been particularly viewed in *integrative* terms for the modern working class and, again, for the "masses" in general. The social rights associated with citizenship have seen expression in the belief that the nation-state has a duty to ensure *social justice* and an adequate level of welfare for its citizens.

Indeed, as Mohr (chapter 8) notes, the idea of social rights forms the conceptual foundation of the modern welfare state. The general argument underlying this idea is that a defining feature of citizenship is the recognition of *reciprocal* rights and responsibilities. Thus, the notion of social rights obliges the nation-state to provide basic welfare to its citizens. Moreover, the notion of social rights implies that all citizens generally have an obligation to support social welfare, typically through the contribution of funds; and the beneficiaries of that welfare are obliged not to abuse these rights and associated services.

Accordingly, this argument also posits that gross social and economic inequalities and inequities are incompatible with the civic and political egalitarianism inherent in citizenship status (Heater 1990:266),[10] and we are faced with another essential question: What is the relationship between notions of rights and notions of equality and equity? As Heater (1990:267) explains, social rights reflect the belief that,

> since all citizens are assumed to be fundamentally equal in status and dignity, none should be so depressed in economic or social condition as to mock this assumption. Therefore, in return for the loyalty and virtuous civic conduct displayed by the citizen, the state has an obligation to smooth out any gross inequalities by the guarantee of a basic standard of living in terms of income, shelter, food, health, and education. Essential standards in these facets of life should be enjoyed as rights of citizenship irrespective of wealth, bargaining power, sex, age, or race. Furthermore, no stigma should attach to the communal source of provision.[11]

While these assertions have at times been quite controversial, we can say in general that they reflect an issue of *balance*: balance between *the right to receive* welfare support and *the responsibility to give*. In other words, in principle, "the recipient of welfare benefits must not abuse this redistribution of wealth; and the contributor must willingly assist in the relief of want and suffering" (Heater 1990:275), such that the quality and dignity of citizenship is preserved.

In general, citizenship rights and liberties are principally those that citizens are deemed to enjoy without interference or oppression by the state (e.g., the right of assembly and freedom of speech) and, also, as a means to improvement of self and condition (e.g., the right of association and to own property).[12] Yet, we must ask some obvious questions, especially in light of recent restrictions and withdrawals of social entitlements (e.g., welfare, unemployment compensation, health care, public education, etc.) in some nation-states: How do restrictions and withdrawals of social rights affect the meaning of citizenship? Under what conditions do restrictions and withdrawals of social rights tend to occur? Are there differential effects of social rights and restrictions and withdrawals on different social groups and, thus, on the exercise of citizenship?

The idea of social rights or social welfare in particular is intrinsic to the very purpose of polity formation. On the one hand, political and social rights, including the expansion of national institutions such as education and welfare, derive principally from an ideology of state authority. Social rights "incorporate the individual in the collective body of the state, signal state jurisdiction over important areas of social life, and in general reconstitute and rationalize society" (Boli 1987:147).

On the other hand, it is people who come together and organize politically to advance their collective economic, cultural, and security interests, and to claim rights against the exigencies of life and existence (Hobson, chapter 10; Marx, chapter 13). So, how do the organizational capacities of collectivities shape political identities? What role have social movements, coalition formation, and various organizations played in definitions of citizens? Struggles to modify citizenship rules, such as in the women's movement, can take place in numerous sites and contexts, including development projects, voluntary associations, and international organizations. For example, Hobson (chapter 10) applies a "gendered lens" to citizenship as part of a broader research agenda to redefine and extend the conceptual boundaries of membership, analyzing collective identity formation, structure, and agency in the construction of citizenship rights.

Polity Participation and Citizenship

The term *polity* is typically used as a generic reference to the political institutions or political organization of a society. However, sociological references also include notions of polity as *a system of creating value* through the collective conferral of authority (Meyer 1987). Here, polity is used in this broad cultural sense, with clear implications for explaining membership and community participation, and for raising related questions: In what ways and to what extent does citizenship imply and attribute value to individuals and groups? In what ways and to what extent do polity formation and incorporation mean the extension of citizenship? The concept of polity includes political state action and other forms of collective action; related rules are formed and located in cultural processes, along with state action. In other words, binding and integrative principles and rules are constructed as part of the nation-state, locating, organizing, and *attributing value* to individuals and various collectivities as part of society as a whole.

Citizenship gives rise to a kind of conceptual ordering inherent in distinctions between members and "others," between insiders and outsiders, between "us" and "them"—distinctions that typically carry with them notions of hierarchical social and personal value and legitimacy for members and of devaluation and illegitimacy for "others." Constructed as members of a broader polity, various individuals are "assigned" or recognized as having value, and that value is expressed through extensions of rights, privileges, and obligations. Moreover, the rights and privileges of citizenship have historically expanded in waves, reflecting certain *classificatory logics* (Mohr, chapter 8) and *definitional transitions* in relation to, among other things, race, class, gender, and age,[13] and reflecting expansion in polity participation. Over time, various segments of nation-state populations, such as workers, women, and children, have been incorporated into the related polities. They have gained recognition as having value—as having the right to have rights—and gaining inclusion in definitions of citizenship.[14]

HUMAN RIGHTS AND INTERNATIONAL EFFECTS

Historically, expansion and extension of citizenship tended to be primarily based on internally ordained changes in which the rights of individuals were defined only in respect to their particular nation-state membership. However, in contrast, the postwar period has seen an increased discourse of *human rights* that has both transcended and penetrated the boundaries of the nation-state in which value has been attributed to all human beings, imbuing them with rights on the basis of their "personhood" over and above national affiliation. Again, we must ask fundamental questions: What are the implications of human rights for issues of national identity and participation? So, how does the notion of human rights transform and change the meaning of citizenship? Indeed, the effects and implications of human rights form a central debate on the recognition and determination of citizenship in the broad sense of polity membership. Along with other forces, proclamations of *universal* human rights have been a critical force in the mobilization and demand for recognition of *equal value* and social worth for all "others"—the extension of polity—providing a direct sense of *community membership* and the goal of *equal membership* for all peoples in the community (Marshall 1973). Note the expanded notion of community to include all nationals and nationalities, as opposed to reflecting only a unidimensional or monolithic membership composition. Moreover, this translates into principles of *equal membership* for all in the *community of human beings* and the extension of rights accordingly.

This idea presents a fundamental problem in both theory and practice. On the one hand, citizenship defines bounded populations, with specific rights and duties, detailing membership for some while excluding "others" on the basis of nationality. However, on the other hand, there are situations in which these "others" are granted rights and protections—and, thus, a kind of membership—by a state in which they are officially classified as foreigners and aliens.[15] For example, in numerous developed countries, migrant populations formally defined as outside the national polity have been extended rights previously accorded only to nationals, thus transforming and challenging the basis of national citizenship (Soysal 1994).

Thus, the issue that we see increasingly raised today is that of rights *within* versus rights *across* groups, across communities, across nation-states. Here again some basic questions arise (Heater 1990): What is the distinction between rights that a person has as a human being and rights enjoyed as a citizen over time? More to the point, if certain rights are considered universally applicable, how does this idea relate to the idea of the privileged status of citizenship? Much of the recent discourse surrounding notions of rights reflects developments at the international—or, rather, transnational—level. Indeed, we have seen the development of a *human rights regime* that transcends the nation-state; there is an institutionalized framework shaping relations between these groups and associated states and governments.

Moreover, there exists an *international regime of legal standards* addressing rights of noncitizens, and of "marginalized" groups or "others" in general, even if formally citizens. While different states have developed different laws, policies, and legal and organizational structures (Marx, chapter 13), there is also an overarching body of formal international law and policy addressing related issues. In general, the point is that we must raise and attend questions about international influence and diffusion, indicating linkages between national and international criteria for the relationship between nation-states and various peoples, based on international law and other international structures and institutions: How do legal cultures affect patterns of incorporation in general? What affect do international law and institutions have on internal conceptions of rights and membership, in theory and practice?

Rights and duties have found expression in international law, elaborated in a legal framework that is deliberately set above any individual nation-state in the community of nation-states.[16] Thus, we find a contested terrain on which citizenship is subject to both national sovereignty and world level values and beliefs. It was in the post–World War II period that the treatment by a state of persons within its jurisdiction came to be generally considered a legitimate province of international law and, more to the point, of transnational concern.[17] Indeed, the post–1945 development of a formal international regime of human rights is one of the most significant aspects of the world institutional order.

> Prior to World War II human rights were almost universally viewed as the exclusive preserve of the state . . . there was not even a weak declaratory international human rights regime. With few exceptions, as recently as fifty years ago, human rights were not even considered to be a legitimate international concern. . . . World War II marks a decisive break: . . . human rights became for the first time a recognized international issue area. (Donnelly 1986)

To be sure, the idea of human or "natural" rights has not been without criticism and controversy, as expressed in Bentham's unequivocal dismissal of the concept: "Natural rights is simple nonsense, natural and imprescritable rights, rhetorical nonsense—nonsense upon stilts."[18] This kind of criticism reflects objection to two basic assumptions (Heater 1990): the idea that rights can be viewed as "natural" rather than acquired pragmatically through political pressure and concession; and the idea that these rights could be so entrenched as never to be overridden, even in dire crises. However, criticisms notwithstanding, notions of human rights have been codified at the world level and adopted in the discourse, structures, and operations of nation-states throughout the world.

The International Institutional Order

Accordingly, we must ask certain basic questions: How have rights been specified at the international level? Through what institutional processes are internationally defined rights mobilized and disseminated? In what ways and to what extent have internationally defined rights been incorporated at the national level? Following the discussion above, we can delineate two crucial developments effecting a conceptual shift or reconfiguration of citizenship: (1) "the emergence of universalistic rules and conceptions regarding the rights of the individual"; and (2) a transformation in the organization of the international state system, reflecting "an increasing interdependence and connectedness, intensified world-level interaction and organizing, and the emergence of transnational political structures" (Soysal 1994:144–145). The *intensified international system* has confounded and complicated issues of nation-state sovereignty and jurisdiction, with an increasing number of aspects of the public domain, which had been exclusively under the jurisdiction of the nation-state, becoming legitimate concerns of international discourse and action. Individual rights are formalized and legitimated in numerous international codes, conventions, and laws, ascribing universal rights to persons regardless of nation-state membership status. Moreover, states are given the responsibility of respecting and ensuring the rights of all individuals—not just formal citizens—within their territory and jurisdiction. Indeed, related provisions have been incorporated into the constitutions and laws of several countries, with some also including protection against the collective expulsion of aliens.

Also, codes on rights and the status of migrants, foreigners, minorities, women, and other "others"—and on human beings in general—have been elaborated and regularized through a complex of international treaties, conventions, charters, and other instruments of intergovernmental organizations, supported by numerous nongovernmental organizations.[19] These codes encompass such issues as entry and residence, choice and security of employment, collective bargaining, working conditions, social security, education of children, associative rights, and so forth, along with individual and collective freedoms and nondiscrimination on the basis of race, religion, or gender.

In addition, the scope of several international instruments cover not only the membership-conferred civil, political, and social rights of individuals, but also the rights of certain groups or categories of persons as *collectives*. What is meant by the idea that a specified collection of individuals has rights, and how do they compare with overall notions of citizen rights? Rights that apply to groups as collectives are typically *cultural rights*, such as the right to an ethnic identity, culture, language, and so forth. Indeed, the cultural rights of collectives, or specific status groups, have emerged as a locus of national and international legal action and contention (Soysal 1994; Blaustein et al. 1987).

In general, there exists a wide range of international instruments that aim to set standards for "equitable" treatment and the elimination of disparities between nationals, aliens, and other categories of people, based on their overriding recognition and identity as human beings. It is interesting to note that these ideas have also been incorporated into the curricula of various education systems, and are particularly reflected in civics courses (Rauner, chapter 5). While highly consequential in the generation of inequalities—whether local, national, or global—schools have also included formal goals aimed at the creation of attitudes of tolerance as opposed to discrimination, of universalism as opposed to localism.

Education has been considered a crucial component in the establishment of democracy and human rights and of moral and ethical behavior, with ideological foundations contributing to a sense of belonging, participation, and inclusion, as opposed to fragmentation and exclusion. Schools are one of the primary arenas in which selected "knowledge" is labeled, prescribed, and transmitted, with broad social implications (Meyer et al. 1992a). Indeed, educational efforts to deter discrimination and augment the capacity for meaningful participation among various sectors have been proclaimed in ideology and policy (McNeely 1995).

Crossing Boundaries/Sharing Space

Citizen rights have developed in the international context to the extent that they also pose questions of nation-state boundary maintenance and jurisdiction, of a nation-state's right to autonomy and sovereignty. Importantly, nation-state claims to citizen loyalty are often posed as a means of sustaining claims to sovereignty (cf. Kaspersen, chapter 6). However, as international actors, modern nation-states are affected by patterns of immigration and other transnational forces, and they typically contain highly diverse—including noncitizen—populations, with demands for group identity and recognition becoming more common.

As discussed here, much of the modern notion of citizenship and rights is constructed in the transnational arena, and rights and privileges once reserved for citizens of a nation-state, in the traditional sense, are codified and expanded as personal, human rights, undermining traditional models of limited citizenship. Indeed, the usefulness of the concept of citizen has come into question, itself serving only as an end in a sphere of contention over rights and responsibilities. However, if sovereignty is tied to citizen loyalty and identity, the issue becomes even more fundamental for the existence of the nation-state. Indeed, what happens to sovereignty when the nation-state is inhabited by significant numbers of noncitizens? While sovereignty has always been a relative term based on mutual recognition and legitimation, this question reflects a fundamental dialectic and shift among principles constructed and maintained in world-level discourses and structures (Jacobson, chapter 2).

Overall, we can posit a *shift in global discourse* and approaches to citizenship. This shift has accompanied various phases of immigration in this century. Whereas applications of citizenship anchored in territorialized notions of cultural belonging were previously dominant, more recent experience reflects a process in which "national citizenship is losing ground to a more universal model of membership, anchored in deterritorialized notions of persons' rights." Soysal (1994:3) has called this a "postnational" model of citizenship, reflecting "a different logic and praxis: what were previously defined as national rights become entitlements legitimized on the basis of personhood." The basic premise of this argument is that national citizenship is no longer the main determinant of individual rights and privileges, that these rights are now codified in a scheme that emphasizes universal personhood rather than nationality. The normative framework and legitimacy of this postnational citizenship derive from transnational discourse and structures that celebrate human rights as world-level organizing rules or principles, conferring upon every individual "the right and duty of participation in the authority structures and public life of a polity, regardless of historical or cultural ties to that community."[20]

However, this situation flies in the face of a bounded and privileged national identity, defined by community and participation limited to selected individuals. This leads to a particularly important question for theoretical and empirical research that is a principal issue in political debates today: What are the implications of universal human rights for conceptions of citizenship that rely on a sense of common identity to generate a loyal commitment to the nation-state and fellow citizens? Thus, we can see how disagreement on rights, participation, and identity can derive from problems of incorporation into a complex society for development into a unitary polity. The whole notion of human rights implies an inclusionary approach, applying to individuals within and across groups, and how this works in practical terms leads to important questions for research: How do noncitizens exercise citizenship and human rights? In what ways do noncitizens gain access to and participate in the polity, and what are the implications of their participation for conceptions of national citizenship and identity?

As Somers (chapter 7) suggests, our notions of citizenship and participation must include considerations of relationships among public spheres, community associational life, and patterns of political culture—and they must do so at every level of analysis. Indeed, historically, to act as a citizen has meant to act in the *public sphere* (Jacobson, chapter 2), and citizenship has been defined in terms of a *public culture.* As is that of traditional formal citizens, the polity participation and claims of "others," including "foreign" populations without formal citizenship, is grounded in notions of a *shared public space*; in a set of abstract principles and responsibilities (such as human rights, desire for "justice," desire for a "better life," etc.); and in the organization and routine of everyday life (they pay taxes, have businesses, work in factories and services, rent apartments, join unions and political parties, formulate platforms, advance claims, etc.). In other words, they share the public space, participating in the polity alongside privileged national citizens. Thus, the broad participation of these "others" challenges traditional exclusionary accounts of membership. This trajectory of polity participation precludes national fixities and allows for shifting categories of citizenship (Soysal 1994:166). Moreover, complex patterns of migration and international relations, resulting in "non-national" populations residing and taking part in various aspects of social, political, and economic life in nation-states other than "their own," can raise additional complex questions.[21] What has been the course of social participation for different groups? What factors have facilitated or inhibited social participation for different groups? What are the factors and processes that cut across the dimensions that allow, include, or exclude polity participation in the nation-state?

Our increasingly interconnected and interdependent world is one in which transnational discourses and structures are increasingly intertwined with and reverberate through national-level policies and institutional arrangements that reflect the rights and rules that constitute citizenship and determine membership, *defined in terms of participation,* in contemporary polities. Thus, "a new and more universal concept of citizenship has unfolded in the postwar era, one whose organizing principles are based on universal personhood rather than national belonging" (Soysal 1994:1). Yes, classifications of citizen and alien, of citizen and "other," still persist, and are points of contention in many nation-states and in the international system. Yet, even in their maintenance we can see that the foundation of national citizenship has been reconfigured, and rules of membership and polity formation and participation have shifted accordingly.

Human Rights, Democracy, and Equality

How do conceptions of human rights transform traditional models of citizenship? On the one hand, as Heater (1990:251–252) argues, we have a world in which general human rights "(as opposed to any specific political enfranchisement) can and do exist independently of the concept or institution of citizenship." However, on the other hand, insofar as human rights are *"equal and inalienable rights of all members of the human family,"*[22] perhaps the status of citizenship in the traditional sense may have become relevant only in a watchdog capacity. Whether or not one agrees with this characterization, a fundamental question still lingers: How do conceptions of human rights shape the meaning and extension of equality, and what does this mean for applications of citizenship? Inasmuch as the individual has a relationship with the world at large, *ideal* citizenship is expressed as a *moral* duty of *reciprocal* recognition of the dignity and rights of other human beings.

However, we must also note that several citizenship ideals are regularly transgressed.[23] What do rights mean in terms of principle versus practice? What do citizen and human rights mean in actual "lived" reality? What are the formal rights that people enjoy versus the actual capacities they have to enact them? How and to what extent are different groups affected by changes in citizen rights, and what are the broader implications of those changes in terms of social relations? The development and implementation of citizenship rights depends on the nexus of the legal infrastructure and varying capacities for participation (Somers, chapter 7; Hobson, chapter 10; Marx, chapter 13).

Of course, interests and power relations also frame capacities to exercise rights and realize identities defined through membership and participation. While, as Orloff (chapter 9) argues, they can vary qualitatively according to context, political interests figure largely in shaping citizenship policies and rules, associated privileges, and, significantly, the very ideas that they either mobilize or suppress (Tilly 1995). Multiple identities, associated with multiple interests, and the ways in which power affects related principles must also be considered in determining the process through which citizenship is constructed. In short, what are the rule-making politics of citizenship? How does power operate through the rules of citizenship? What kinds of institutional structures have been created in support of various interests and visions of citizenship?

As noted earlier, until relatively recently in human history, the status of citizenship was typically limited to white male property-owners, bound together by social, economic, and cultural affinities. However, in the modern period, all individuals have increasingly been defined in terms of citizenship, and human rights have increasingly been translated into citizen rights, and vice versa. Related "democratic" developments have included broader conceptions of nations, with demands that there be a less exclusionary approach to membership and participation, leading to an expanded composition of citizenship. Citizen rights have become more integrative and incorporative, bringing various individuals "fully into the arena of state action and control" (Boli 1987:147).

However, how is citizenship related to forms of democratic action, and to what does democratic action refer in light of notions of citizenship? In theory, citizenship entails *equal legal and political incorporation*: citizens are *equal* before the law; their votes are *equal;* they have *equal* opportunities for political office. However, many "citizens" are decidedly *more equal* than others (and "others")—as are some noncitizens. For example, in the United States, until World War I, white male aliens could vote in local, state, and national elections in twenty-two states, exercising political rights that many "citizens"—Black and female—did not have (Raskin 1993). Also, as Marx's (chapter 13) analysis of race as a political and social identity in Brazil, South Africa, and the United States demonstrates, state creation or incorporation of racial labels and categories, institutionalizes racial politics and discrimination over time, and is an important aspect of organized repression.[24] In general, minority populations have typically been denied full citizenship rights, irrespective of formal equal citizenship status.

Remember that, even with the recognition of universal human rights and transnational effects, the notion of citizenship is still inextricably tied to membership in the nation-state: the individual has legal status as a citizen of a nation-state.[25] Thus, we must still pose questions in keeping with that consideration, not only about citizenship per se, but about the state itself: What are the changing roles of the state in relation to its citizens and citizenship in general? Even international organizational human rights documents, as mentioned earlier, such as those of the United Nations providing criteria for judging the way that people should be treated in their capacity as human beings, express those criteria in terms of how they should be treated *by their own nation-states.* In the international institutional order, definitions, rules, and principles may be laid out in the larger system, but it is nation-states that are charged with the responsibility of upholding and implementing them (Meyer 1987); citizenship is enacted at the nation-state level. However, having said that, although nation-states remain the primary agents of that citizenship, the parameters of citizenship appear increasingly determined at the global level and affected by global processes.

INSTITUTIONS, PROCESSES, AND CHANGE

Previously dominant arguments about citizenship have concentrated principally on national or subnational interests and needs as explanatory factors, but they do not easily account for the worldwide expansion and diffusion of similar citizenship principles and their transformation into general human rights, and vice versa (Boli 1987). They appear especially unable to make sense of the worldwide extension of citizenship principles and human rights to women, minorities, and foreigners, among "others," despite exclusionary efforts. The continued reification of state interests, reflecting assumptions that consider only their primacy in shaping national adherence to world-level accounts, can obscure effects of globalization processes and national enactments of world standards or accounts. A more "balanced" outlook would seem more in keeping with historical shifts in the rights and rules constituting citizenship and polity formation, and our related questions must reflect broader considerations: What is the impact of both international and national economic, political, and social development on the adoption of individual rights and their elaboration for "others"? What is the effect of national-level factors relative to transnational ones in the adoption of individual rights over time? How do world emphases on citizenship and human rights affect rates of adoption of related legal policies in individual countries? An understanding of citizenship means developing an understanding of the relationships between the dynamics of global and local forces, considering varying social, political, economic, and cultural conditions in the world and in different countries and contexts, during different periods, and how they affect each other.

What are the implications of global relations and processes for nation-states and citizenship? Changes in the global cultural, economic, and political system and in individual countries have led to challenges to the assumption that citizenship must be defined particularly as a status. It might be more useful if we reconceptualize citizenship, not as a status, but as an "instituted process" (cf. Somers 1993), thus capturing the conceptual shifts and empirical transformations of the modern period.

A World Polity Perspective

In order to determine this process, we must examine the institutions themselves in which citizenship is framed and constituted. Here, I refer to the sociological perspective on institutions as codified cultural constructions; institutions are sets of cultural rules giving collective meaning and value to particular actors and activities (Meyer and Scott 1983; Powell and DiMaggio 1991). An institutionalist approach in this case emphasizes the existence of a *world polity* in order to make sense of transformations in citizenship. Such an approach can address the complex formations, transformations, questions, and problems presented by and in relation to citizenship at various levels of social interaction. This world polity perspective is grounded in the idea of a world political culture that has increasingly privileged the nation-state, along with a universalistic vision of persons as individuals and citizens. This basic idea leads to arguments positing that changes in national societies reflect not only *endogenous,* but also, significantly, *exogenous* institutional processes.

Ramirez and Meyer (chapter 3) suggest several ways in which these institutionally framed changes can be revealed. For one thing, exogenous rules of sovereignty legitimate the construction of modern societies as nation-states, which, in turn, increases the likelihood that they will adopt the policies and structures of "standard" nation-state entities (Giddens 1984; Jackson and Rosberg 1982; McNeely 1995; Meyer 1987). Also, models of these policies are codified and legitimated, often in international organizations, such that conformity to them appears rational and even necessary to definitions of nation-states (McNeely 1995). In addition, exogenous ideological changes in issues central to nation-state structure, such as definitions of progress or justice, or the means to attain them, will influence internal rules regarding citizenship rights and the social categories to which they apply. Moreover, alternative models of organizing society and their related practices are delegitimated over time.

Thus, an institutionalist world polity perspective has implications for a number of issues related to the rights and rules through which citizenship is constructed, especially in light of relations and developments in the international system. Analyses must be aimed at several basic questions (Ramirez and Meyer, chapter 3). For example, what types of rights become defined transnationally as human rights? Do international rights regimes expand with economic expansion? Do international rights regimes expand with the expansion of the nation-state system? Are there core citizenship rights that diffuse more successfully, impeding the establishment of alternative principles and types of rights? How much do the types of rights stressed in given time periods reflect the national characteristics of the dominant powers? What types of rights are more likely to be extended to specific groups or classifications of persons, and in what capacity will those persons be recipients?

Analyzing of trends in citizenship means focusing on the nature of global processes, and on linkages between nation-states and the global institutional context. Part of the power of the world polity approach is that it allows for consideration of both national and international factors and effects. Changes in the international system—including, for example, the changed defense structure in western Europe, the development of the European Community and the European Union, the end of the Cold War, and political upheavals around the world—have involved redefinitions of citizen roles and citizen obligations, ranging from conscription to payment of taxes, from welfare rights to mass education (Kaspersen, chapter 6). An understanding of citizenship, with all of its contemporary reconfigurations, requires an appreciation of the modern nation-state in relation to both internal and external institutional bases (cf. Evans et al. 1985).

As discussed above, several recent studies show the significance of transnational regimes and global institutions in the rise and diffusion of citizenship principles, which are often normatively set forth as universal human rights (e.g., McNeely 1995; Meyer et al. 1992b; Ramirez 1989; Soysal 1994; Thomas et al. 1987; Ventresca 1995). Ramirez and Meyer (chapter 3) extend this point, calling for research that must, among other things, look to further question, describe, and analyze the worldwide expansion of rights and the extension of those rights to individuals as both citizens and persons, and the application of those rights to "others," such as women, minorities, and foreigners; to investigate the development and activities of international organizations as carriers of those rights; to assess the impact of world ideological and structural developments on the national adoption of citizenship and human rights principles, especially in regard to the determination and identification of "others"; to compare the impact of global factors on legal norms with the effects of variations in linkages between a nation-state and the wider world order, and with the effects of variations in internal national economic, political, and social structures; and to determine the extent to which effects of linkage factors increase and internal factors decrease in relation to the degree to which world ideological and organizational factors favor universal, expanded human rights in different historical periods. Similarly, Jacobson's (chapter 2) analysis of historical shifts in conceptions of state and society also leads us to explore various levels of interaction—international, state, and nonstate—in order to understand citizenship across various perspectives.

Polity Participation and Expansion

In describing global and national changes, several issues arise that reflect trends toward increasingly expanded notions of membership and participation. For example, we can look to how women increasingly gained suffrage, reproductive rights, and family leave benefits (Berkovitch, chapter 4); or how former national social rights, such as workers' compensation or healthcare, become framed as citizen and human rights (Grattet, chapter 11; Espinosa, chapter 12). However, Ramirez and Meyer's (chapter 3) discussion also leads us to another important question that must be addressed to understand the impact of institutional processes on participation, equality, and citizenship in general: What citizenship principles and human rights emerge, but fail to become globalized or continue to be expressed or applied in ways that are antithetical to equity and equality, that is, in ways that typically favor dominant groups? A prominent example of this issue is that of social benefits for only full-time workers in the paid labor force which, on the face of things, may seem neutral and universally applicable, but in practice tends to favor males (Orloff, chapter 9), reflecting gendered institutional processes.

Issues of labor and worker rights have often dominated the political discourse and dynamics of citizen rights in general. Analyses by Espinosa (chapter 12) and by Grattet (chapter 11) demonstrate issues of empowerment and incorporation within a market economy, coopting and extending rights to workers.[26] In fact, worker demands have typically been couched in a discourse of rights and obligations—in other words, in a discourse of citizenship. Another issue that also arises in consideration of labor and market relations in citizenship developments is that, as Tilly (1995) points out, during the twentieth century, states have greatly stressed labor force position and market ties in determining qualifications for citizenship, with preference to those in nationally-based organizations or with valuable skills. This criterion has often been used as a status differentiator in determining "preferred" immigrant "value" for polity exclusion or inclusion. Moreover, the racialized and gendered character of social provisions has come particularly into question in this regard, with calls for more detailed and attentive theoretical and empirical analyses. Indeed, Orloff (chapter 9), and also Mohr (chapter 8), reflecting on gender and the analytic categories that have informed most research on the welfare state, offer frameworks that reach across various approaches for more comprehensive consideration of the issues at hand.

Institutional Dialectics and Contradictions

The world institutional order, by definition, reflects a great deal of structural and ideological homogeneity and isomorphism (McNeely 1995; Thomas et al. 1987). Yet, we know that human society also reflects idiosyncrasies and conflicts; within the broader institutional framework, enormous differences and dialectical relationships are played out. Thus, while we can posit the transnational development of universal human rights and their incorporation into national conceptions of membership and polity participation, this does not necessarily imply a consensual, universally internalized value system. Postulating effects of transnational forces on nation-state structure, discourse, and practice does not mean that they will result in a unified or homogeneous world institutional order. Rather, as Thomas and Boli (1993) explain, world-level consensus is more concerned with world-level rules and principles that define entities and related characteristics, structures, and practices. The fundamental nature of the world polity, or global institutional order, reflects an underlying homogeneity, but it is an homogeneity on which enormous differences and distinctions are constructed.

In other words, the world polity is not necessarily a consistent and conflict-free system. Rather, we should think of it as a complex of values, interests, and ideologies overlying a set of ontological assumptions, collective purposes, ideological claims, and prescriptions (Thomas and Boli 1993). Indeed, the global system enacts multiple institutionalized discourses and modalities of legitimate action that may or may not operate in agreement with each other, demonstrating the need for further comparative study.

State actions, policies, and identities may reflect multiple sets of norms and institutions, and global precepts may simultaneously constrain and enhance the scope of nation-state and individual action. It is in recognition of these dialectical processes that the utility of an institutionalist approach becomes particularly apparent. While the sociological institutionalist approach has typically been employed to explain isomorphic organizational outcomes and symbolic conformity to external standards, it can be extended to help us unravel and understand the institutional framing and discourse surrounding dialectical relationships and paradoxes reflected in conceptions and practice of citizenship. Given the relational nature of citizenship itself, this kind of approach is particularly appealing.

For example, recent events in domestic and world politics over the last decade may seem at first glance to contradict claims to the declining significance of models of nationally exclusive citizenship. Here, we must look to the dialectical relationship of national sovereignty and universal human rights, both of which are constructed and supported in the world institutional context (McNeely 1995; Soysal 1994; Jacobson, chapter 2). What we have here is a dialectic that reflects both the closure and restriction of national polities and their expansion beyond national limitations and definitions. On the one hand, we have boundary construction and exclusion; on the other, we have increased penetration, extension, and inclusion.

How do we explain polity inclusion and exclusion within the same institutional framework? How do we explain the presence of contradictory citizenship relations given arguments for transnational effects and institutional conformity? In order to understand this seeming institutional contradiction, we *must*, in fact, consider and give currency to world-level institutional processes and structures. The same world-level processes and institutional structures that foster Soysal's (1994) postnational model of citizenship also reify the nation-state and sovereignty; both are constructed at the world level. While human rights ascribe a universal status to individuals and their rights, undermining the boundaries of the nation-state, institutionalized notions of sovereignty reinforce national boundaries and invent new ones. Moreover, in practical terms, this means that, while rights may be increasingly transnational in character, they remain organized at the national level; "the exercise of universalistic rights is tied to specific states and their institutions" (Soysal 1994:157). This paradox, "the universalization of particularism and the particularization of universalism" (Robertson 1992:100), is the hallmark of postwar membership and polity determination.

How can we depict the interplay of globalizing and localizing forces in the conception of citizenship, as they contribute to the (ex)tension of rights and rules in the public sphere? A world polity approach allows us to examine the (shifting) structural outcomes of the contradictions of global and national citizenship rights and rules, within which we can also consider the antagonisms and conflict over rights discourse itself. Citizenship, pertaining to membership and participation in the overall polity, is intimately linked to the "politicization" of social relations and activities (Giddens 1985), with a potential for conflict, antagonism, and instability threatening any period of social equilibrium, but also with a potential for harmonization and the diffusion of egalitarian principles. Again, we are presented with a paradox: How do the same citizenship principles support contradictory processes within the world institutional order? How does the institutional framework of citizenship support both fragmentation and unity in polity relations? How does the institutional framework of citizenship support both exclusion and inclusion in polity relations?

The right to self-determination has often been raised as an issue of membership and identity in the contemporary period and provides us with an important instance here. Ethnonationalist and religious affiliations have been increasingly raised as exclusionary bases for citizenship and recognition in recent times. Contemporary ethnonationalist struggles, for example, in attempts to assert and construct boundaries, draw upon world institutionalized claims of rights to self-determination and cultural identity to legitimate exclusionary delineations between those with membership and "others." Self-determination has been framed as a universal human right, supporting claims to cultural distinctiveness and identity as inalienable rights. More explicitly, recent claims to self-determination and cultural rights have focused on assertions of connectedness of citizenship with ethnicity and nation-state. These claims can be turned against, not only other nations and states, but particularly against "internal others"—minorities, aliens, and strangers (Walzer 1992).[27] Democratic citizenship, as discussed earlier, is conceptualized as less exclusionary than citizenship based on ethno-nationalism. Yet, assertions of (ethnonationalist) self-determination have typically employed a discourse framing it as a universal human right, and as a right to democratic establishment. Indeed, related movements have been counted as part of the recent wave of democracy. Thus, we can have instances of "globalism producing tribalism."

So, on the one hand, there is evidence supporting arguments that conceptualizations of membership emphasizing "primordial," more ascriptive bases of social solidarity (e.g., race, ethnicity, language, religion, nationality, etc.) have been increasingly supplanted over time by categories and classifications that highlight state-mandated citizenship and membership, as in school participation, mandatory military service, and the like. For example, Ventresca's (1995) analysis of population censuses from the late nineteenth century to the present supports these arguments. On the other hand, we have also seen a resurgence of publicly defined categories embodying more "traditional" forms of social solidarity, mobilization, and discrimination. However, note that,

> If self-determination and human rights are to contribute to a better life for a greater number of people in the twenty-first century, it will be as joint guarantors of tolerance and justice. These two principles, reflecting to some extent the inherent tension between minority rights and majority rule, must guide society's constant attempts to find an appropriate balance among the interlocking identities of the individual, the group, and the state. (Hannum 1990:477)

We can also look to how "nation-states are charged with expanding 'responsibilities,' on the basis of human rights, with respect to the foreign populations living within their borders." At the same time, however, "they are expected to regulate immigration and exercise border controls as a fundamental expression of their sovereignty. . . . These apparent contradictions precipitate around the constructs of the bounded, territorialized nation-state and universal, deterritorialized rights, creating a dialectical tension" (Soysal 1994:7–8).[28] Thus, we have citizenship conceived as a set of mutual, contested claims between states and members of socially constructed and defined groups or categories (cf. Tilly 1995).[29]

In addition, research has also revealed contradictory shifts in definitions of citizen rights themselves. "Rights are increasingly defined as alienable, as deriving from and subject to restriction by the state, rather than inalienable, or inherent in the individual without restriction" (Boli 1987:134)—as are human rights by definition. They are inalienable only to citizens. This dialectic is reflected in the categories of rights delineated in definitions of citizenship, expressing a contradiction that is the crux of numerous contemporary political debates.[30]

Let us be clear here: "When the Greeks developed the institution of citizenship, it was never intended to embrace so many people claiming so many rights as today" (Heater 1990:288). Indeed, it began (and, some would argue, remains) as a means for status differentiation and exclusion between those who "belong" and "others." Therein lies the problem: *citizenship fluctuates between being an agent of segregation and being an agent of association.* Within the nation-state, citizenship began as a means of differentiating between inhabitants, as a status differentiator. However, contemporary conceptions of democracy have led to its interpretation as a status equalizer. Internationally, and in multiracial and multiethnic nation-states, we can conceptualize citizenship, on the one hand, as a device for recognizing the commonality and universal aspects of human beings; on the other hand, citizenship is a means for constructing boundaries and distinguishing members from "others." Thus, it seems that there are different "modes" of citizenship that can either complement or contradict each other.

We can identify at once the paradox of the development of citizenship as a process of extending and deepening citizenship, or *inclusionary citizenship,* in the face of struggles by many to prevent the broadening of membership, or *exclusionary citizenship.* The rules and principles of citizenship involve the distribution of rights and privileges, simultaneously constraining and enabling the practice of citizenship. This dual character of citizenship rules, their constraining and enabling effects, is a crucial element of its institutionalization. This has led to internal tension and conflict over redefining and reconfiguring the boundaries of membership, and thus of the nation-state itself.

While transnational discourses and models may increasingly penetrate national frameworks, inducing greater polity incorporation of "others," there are still variations and polity-specific modes of membership that can differentially affect the patterns of incorporation in individual countries (Soysal 1994). Nationally specific forms of membership determine state rhetorics, policies, programs, and budgets that affect associated populations, and determine related organizational activities and polity participation. Indeed, differences in national contexts can affect the adoption and interpretation of global norms, producing different outcomes in different national settings, as demonstrated in Sikkink's (1991) comparative account of the institution-alization of human rights in state bureaucratic structures and laws in Europe and the United States.[31]

Discursive claims and accounts of human rights now appear in a great deal of contemporary national policy language and debates pertaining to citizen and noncitizen rights, and to issues of primacy of one versus the other (and the "other"). Official rhetorics today often include references t multiculturalism and diversity, and claims for rights are typically posed in terms of inalienable rights of personhood. As Soysal (1994:155) observes,

> Membership rights are recast as human rights; governments, organi-zations, and individuals recurrently appeal to this 'higher-order' principle. . . . The dominance of human rights discourse, and the defi-nition of individuals and their rights as abstract universal categories, license even foreign populations to push for further elaboration of their rights. The fact that rights, and claims to rights, are no longer confined to national parameters, supports the premise of a postnational model of membership.

Note, however, that in cases "where the nation-building efforts are still underway, or are contested by alternative groups or ideologies, national citizenship constitutes a significant category and important organizational consequences . . . boundaries between citizens and noncitizens are sharply constructed, without much space for ambiguity" (Soysal 1994:156). Foreigners in such systems are generally excluded from most forms of participatory rights and entitlements.

Moreover, although it is now relatively rare for explicit discrimination still to be legally sanctioned,[32] "throughout the world civil rights enjoyed by the dominant sectors of any given society are denied to an equal degree to others by discrimination and prejudice" (Heater 1990:256). There exists an institutional framework of principles, norms, rules, procedures, and values that operate to effectively include, exclude, or ignore certain categories and identities as citizens. Indeed, citizenship rules, discourses, and structures contain implicit and explicit messages and valuations about member characteristics. Ascriptive characteristics that ostensibly belong to the individual level, are realized as a differentiating regime and discourse associated and enacted within those characteristics. This issue of de jure versus de facto discrimination reflects a deep contradiction and paradox of citizenship in ideology and practice, and it is bound in overall power relations in society.

As do rights and rules internally defined as applicable to all citizens equally, the codification of human rights has a twofold role—first, as a restraint on government from too much abuse of its power and, second, as a deterrent of discrimination against the numerous categories of "second-class" citizens and "others" in a society (Heater 1990). This role is grounded in the paradoxes of membership in the contemporary world, requiring research on the extent to which notions of universal human rights and personhood influence nation-state policy and practice, and the extent to which they influence the (legitimated) claims that can be made by individuals on the nation-state and polity, and vice versa. Moreover, it requires specification of the types of rights that are complementary and those that conflict with each other. Institutional structures, determining membership privilege, rights, and participation, are historically produced and determined (Marx, chapter 13). While struggles for citizenship involve contesting institutional structures and rules, they also draw on them for definition.

Conclusion

Citizenship has been one of the great driving forces of the modern era (Marshall 1973) and, in many ways, it is considered the ultimate form of membership in a world comprised of nation-states. Indeed, the modern nation-state developed and is maintained partly in response to demands to articulate and protect a wide range of citizenship rights and interests. Thus, any treatment of rights—and of the relationship between their formal expression and the actual possibilities of their realization—requires a substantial account of the nation-state and, more, of the nation-state as part of the world institutional order (Jacobson, chapter 2; Kaspersen, chapter 6).

The modern egalitarian version of citizenship, with equal rights and obligations for all, has defined and assigned the affiliation of the individual—the citizen—to a specific state. However, as discussed here, especially since the end of World War II, this connection between nation-state and citizenship has been going through a fundamental process of change. Indeed, citizenship is a flexible concept with changing content and implications dependent on context and level and unit of analysis.

More to the point, dramatic changes in the overall global system, including regional relations, make it exceedingly clear that citizenship rights can no longer be addressed as if solely determined by processes internal to nation-states. Globalization has produced a context in which the development of citizenship rights, and the policies elaborating them, is increasingly related to a world-level normative culture that fosters the adoption of human rights as citizenship principles. The global elaboration and codification of these rights are an expression of an intensified world culture and international linkages.

However, of course, we must also look to practical capacities to realize these principles (or not) in order to determine the depth of their institutionalization. We know that inequalities of race, class, and gender, among others, persist. We know that the definition and exclusion of "others" persist. We know that the denial and undermining of rights, reflecting sociopolitical, economic, and cultural dynamics and inequality, persist. We know that exclusion and discrimination against various noncitizens, as well as citizens—against migrant workers and their families, against people of color, against women—persist. However, we also know that change has occurred over time.

The boundaries of citizenship ultimately define membership of individuals and of social groups or collectivities, and citizenship rights have been established and changed in light of social movements aiming to either expand or defend definitions of social membership and participation (Turner 1986a). Indeed, "the struggle over the nature and extent of citizenship has *itself* been a, if not the, central medium of social conflict—the medium through which various classes, groups, and movements strive to enhance and protect their rights and opportunities" (Held 1989:200). Persons, who once were not even legally defined as persons,[33] have over time been incorporated as citizens. The transformation of national rights into universalistic human rights and entitlements have allowed those defined as "others"—whether citizens or noncitizens—to make claims on the state and participate in the wider polity, even while debates over their membership are accentuated. Claims may be challenged and contested, but the point is that the very discourse, the fact that these rights are debated as such in the first place, reflects political and cultural shifts in the structure and meaning of citizenship.

There are many active, competing, and complementary factors that together constitute contemporary models of community membership and polity participation. The series of interrelated and overlapping issues and questions presented here represent different ways of expressing or viewing the complex problems that must be addressed if we are to gain understanding about the rights and rules that constitute citizens and polity relations in general. Accordingly, a world polity and institutional framework can afford us insight on the changing concept of citizenship in the world today. The world is becoming increasingly interconnected, reflecting intensified processes of globalization. Paradoxically, however, that globalization is exerting simultaneous pressures toward both unity and fragmentation. Approaching this issue from an institutionalist world polity perspective will allow us to delineate the implications of this and related paradoxes for citizenship and polity formation.

Studying the relationship between citizenship and nation-states will extend our understanding of the complexities of national definition and meaning, and will allow us to scrutinize institutionalized models of incorporation and membership, and of group relations in individual polities. However, in today's world of interconnections, interdependence, and globalization, we can no longer address the notion of citizenship only in relation to the nation-state. While the nation-state is still the key context in which citizenship is implemented, the intimate bond between rights and definitions of citizenship also requires consideration of new and changing global realities and related processes—realities and processes that, indeed, affect the definition and existence of the nation-state itself and the individuals constituting it as citizens. By positioning the overall problem in consideration of world level processes, we can engage in a more informed debate on the general questions of citizenship, rights, and polity. By placing the overall problem in a comparative and historical context, we can lay the foundation for understanding the basic issue of citizenship and polity formation in the contemporary world order.

NOTES

1. M.C. Havens in Heater (1990:246).

2. Of course, the first two of these may also be viewed as rights to be protected.

3. *See* Alexander (1993), Taylor (1990), and Calhoun (1993) for discussions on the multiplicity of meanings of the term.

4. *See* general discussion in Held (1987).

5. U.S. Chief Justice Earl Warren, in Perez v. Brownell, 1958, cited in Heater (1990).

6. Held (1989) presents this as the type of rights central to the Marshall-Giddens debate on citizenship.

7. In fact, many rights are given up voluntarily when people join groups that demand special discipline, sacrifice, and conformity. Thus, a group may recognize a general right of an individual but sanction that individual for exercising the right in an immediate situation. (For example, the right of free speech may not be equally the same for an individual depending on various social roles and identifications, such as limiting speech about "classified" information by a government agent.)

8. *Also see* Mann (1987); Giddens (1982, 1984); Orloff (1993); Held (1989).

9. Of course, some kinds of rights are contained in and cross over more than one of these broad categories. For example, reproductive rights can, arguably, reflect all three.

10. However, it has also been argued that state provision of welfare is unrelated to citizenship status. Other justifications for state provided social welfare include the principle of distributive justice and "the cynical/realist belief that some state relief of poverty is necessary to ward off an insurrectionary response of the downgraded to their condition" (Heater 1990:266).

11. Of course, in the United States—which, while displaying some related fea-

tures, is not a welfare state—a basic practice associated with the provision of welfare is the attachment of stigma, which has proven a powerful force for political, economic, and cultural manipulation (Tronto 1993). These aspects of social rights and citizenship are in general not without controversy, reflecting a conflict of ideals and differing interpretations among various groups. Other arguments also posit that citizenship and social rights, as here described, are incompatible with capitalism, by its very nature and definition, representing a conflict of ideals. See discussion and references in Heater (1990, especially pp. 267–272).

12. The right of freedom from interference or oppression by the state is often cited as the distinguishing mark of a citizen from a subject.

13. *See* Ramirez (1989); Marshall (1973); Turner (1986b).

14. Indeed, these waves have represented an overall shift in which most ascriptive criteria have been formally, in legal terms, denied as institutional bases for citizenship (Turner 1986a).

15. This situation is characterized by a variety of status designations, including, for example, legal temporary migrants, permanent residents, political refugees, illegal aliens, ex-colonial citizens, etc.

16. For example, for the first time in history, the International Tribunal at Nuremberg in 1945 held that—except when there is no room for "moral choice"—when international rules protecting "basic humanitarian values" are in conflict with state laws, the international rules take precedence and the individual must transgress the state law.

17. With the exception of doctrines of humanitarian intervention and state responsibility for injuries to aliens.

18. In Stewart (1984:14).

19. *See,* for example, the Universal Declaration of Human Rights, the International Covenant on Civil and Political Rights, and the European Convention on Human Rights, along with a multitude of other related universal and regional instruments. For further discussion, *see* Wronka (1992); Donnelly (1986); and Blaustein et al. (1987).

20. Other recent studies have addressed the difference between the national and postwar membership models primarily in terms of residence, rather than citizenship. For example, Hammar (1990) proposes the term "denizen" for long-term resident foreigners who possess substantial rights and privileges. Brubaker (1989) posits a model of dual membership comprised by an inner circle of citizenship, based on nationality, and an outer circle of denizenship, based on residency. Models such as these are still determined within the confines of the nation-state, still construing changes in citizenship as territorial. However, Soysal (1994:139) argues that, by overlooking the changing basis and legitimacy of membership and fundamental changes in the relationship between the individual, nation-state, and world order, they fail to recognize "a profound transformation in the institution of citizenship, both in its institutional logic and in the way that it is legitimated. To locate the changes, we need to go beyond the nation-state."

21. Soysal's (1994:2) study of guestworkers in various European nation-states exemplifies how "foreign" communities, without formal citizenship status, have been incorporated into various aspects of the social and institutional order of the nation-states in which they reside.

22. UN Universal Declaration of Human Rights, preamble, emphasis added.

23. For example, the concept of social rights in citizenship presupposes at least some minimum standard of living, including health care and education, below which no one should be allowed to fall; these rights are regularly transgressed, particularly in the highly stratified nonwelfare states. They are also posed as the basis of much current political conflict and debates on membership and privilege defined in terms of access to resources.

24. However, he also discusses how, ironically, the institutionalization of po-

litically-supported and ratified discriminatory categories can be used to facilitate later mobilization against discrimination.

25. Heater (1990:258–260) notes that, in practical terms, neither international theory nor international law recognizes the status of "world citizen." At times, the term has been applied to formally recognized refugees, or stateless persons, and to other circumstances in which the "individual can be deemed to be appealing to his rights *qua* world citizen when his rights *qua* nation citizen have been circumscribed by his own state." Heater also notes a few other exceptions.

26. As opposed to the transformation of dominant economic structures; while the terrain of rights may change, the market is still maintained.

27. As in excuses for "ethnic cleansing."

28. Another irony is reflected in the fact that while nation-states are charged with protecting the rights of citizens, it is also nation-states that are often identified as violators of those rights.

29. *See* references in Tilly (1995:6,fn.7).

30. Similarly, Heater (1990:252) makes an even deeper distinction when he asks if there is a difference, for example, between the negative freedom of not being unjustly imprisoned for any reason and the positive freedom of a citizen to speak and write in criticism of the law or government—in short, between those rights of the person as a person, versus those civil and political rights of the citizen (e.g., freedom of speech) enjoyed in concert with fellow citizens, that is, as part of the "community." This issue speaks to an essential element of a citizen-based polity: the balance (tension) between the honoring of rights of the citizen by the nation-state and the ability of the nation-state to wield authority over its citizenry.

31. As I discuss elsewhere (McNeely 1996), the case of indigenous peoples and rights provides another example in which issues of membership, and related regimes themselves, represent antagonistic processes and outcomes. On the one hand, constitutional provisions, treaties, laws, regulations, and other formal policies, constituting a legal framework and rights regime, often include formal national recognition, with guarantees of indigenous self-determination and collective rights, providing a foundation for legal protections and claims. Yet, on the other hand, states frequently have invoked a legal basis for contravening and abrogating the rights of indigenous peoples. Indeed, the legal record is filled with such contradictions (Shattuck and Norgren 1991).

32. *See* Heater (1990:256–257) for examples of exceptions to this point.

33. In fact, who at times were explicitly defined in law as not being persons, as not being human beings.

REFERENCES

Alexander, J.C. 1993. "The Return to Civil Society." *Contemporary Sociology* 22 (6):797–803.

Berkovitch, N. 1994. "From Motherhood to Citizenship." Dissertation, Department of Sociology, Stanford University.

Blaustein, A.P., R.S. Clark, and J.A. Sigler, eds. 1987. *Human Rights Sourcebook*. New York: Paragon House.

Boli, J. 1987. "Human Rights or State Expansion? Cross-National Definitions of Constitutional Rights, 1870–1970." Pp. 133–149 in Thomas et al.

Boli, J. 1993. "Sovereignty from a World Polity Perspective." Presented at the annual meeting of the American Sociological Association, Miami.

Brubaker, W.R., ed. 1989. *Immigration and Politics of Citizenship in Europe and North America*. Lanham, MD: University Press of America.

Brubaker, R. 1992. *Citizenship and Nationhood in France and Germany*. Cambridge: Cambridge University Press.

Calhoun, C. 1993. "Nationalism and Civil Society: Democracy, Diversity, and Self-Determination." *International Sociology* 8(4):387–411.

Donnelly, J. 1986. "International Human Rights: A Regime Analysis." *International Organization* 40:559–642.

Evans, P.B., D. Rueschemeyer, and T. Skocpol, eds. 1985. *Bringing the State Back In.* Cambridge: Cambridge University Press.

Gellner, E. 1983. *Nations and Nationalism.* Ithaca: Cornell University Press.

Giddens, A. 1981. *A Contemporary Critique of Historical Materialism.* London: Macmillan.

Giddens, A. 1982. *Profiles and Critiques in Social Theory.* London: Macmillan.

Giddens, A. 1984. *The Constitution of Society.* Berkeley: University of California Press.

Giddens, A. 1985. *The Nation-State and Violence.* Cambridge: Polity Press.

Habermas, J. 1992. *Faktizität und Geltung.* Frankfurt: Suhrkamp.

Hammar, T. 1990. *International Migration, Citizenship, and Democracy.* Aldershot: Gower.

Hannum, H. 1990. *Autonomy, Sovereignty, and Self-Determination: The Accommodation of Conflicting Rights.* Philadelphia: University of Pennsylvania Press.

Heater, D. 1990. *Citizenship: The Civic Ideal in World History, Politics, and Education.* New York: Longman.

Held, D. 1987. *Models of Democracy.* Cambridge: Polity Press.

Held, D. 1989. *Political Theory and the Modern State.* Stanford: Stanford University Press.

Jackson, R.H., and C.G. Rosberg. 1982. "Why Africa's Weak States Persist: The Empirical and the Juridical in Statehood." *World Politics* 35(1):1–24.

Krasner, S.D., ed. 1983. *International Regimes.* Ithaca: Cornell University Press.

Lipset, S.M. 1963. *Political Man: The Social Bases of Politics.* Garden City, NY: Doubleday.

Mann, M. 1987. "Ruling Class Strategies and Citizenship." *Sociology* 21:339–354.

Marshall, T.H. 1950. *Citizenship and Social Class.* Cambridge: Cambridge University Press.

Marshall, T.H. 1963. *Sociology at the Crossroads.* London: Heinemann Educational Books.

Marshall, T.H. 1964. *Class, Citizenship, and Social Development.* Garden City, NY: Doubleday.

Marshall, T.H. 1973. "Citizenship and Social Class." In *Class, Citizenship, and Social Development,* edited by T.H. Marshall. Westport, CT: Greenwood Press.

McNeely, C.L. 1995. *Constructing the Nation-State: International Organization and Prescriptive Action.* Westport, CT: Greenwood Press.

McNeely, C.L. 1996. "Intergroup Dynamics and Relations: Analyzing Nations Within Nations." Presented at the annual meeting of the Social Science History Association, New Orleans.

Meyer, J.W. 1987. "The World Polity and the Authority of the Nation-State." Pp. 41–70 in Thomas et al.

Meyer, J.W., D. Kamens, and A. Benavot. 1992a. *School Knowledge for the Masses: World Models and National Curricula in the Twentieth Century.* Philadelphia: Falmer Press.

Meyer, J.W., F.O. Ramirez, and Y. Soysal. 1992b. "World Expansion of Mass Education, 1870–1980." *Sociology of Education* 63:128–149.

Meyer, J.W., and W.R. Scott. 1983. *Organizational Environments: Ritual and Rationality.* Beverly Hills, CA: Sage.

Orloff, A.S. 1993. "Gender and the Social Rights of Citizenship: The Comparative Analysis of Gender Relations and Welfare States." *American Sociological Review* 58:303–328.

Powell, W.W., and P.J. DiMaggio, eds. 1991. *The New Institutionalism in Organizational Analysis.* Chicago: University of Chicago Press.

Ramirez, F.O. 1989. "Reconstituting Children: Extension of Personhood and Citizenship." Pp. 143–165 in *Age Structuring in Comparative Perspective,* edited by D. Kertzer and K.W. Schaie. Hillsdale, NJ: Erlbaum.

Ramirez, F.O., and J.W. Meyer. 1994. "Citizenship Principles, Human Rights, and the National Incorporation of Women, 1870–1990." Unpublished paper, Department of Sociology, Stanford University.

Ramirez, F.O., and G.M. Thomas. 1987. "Structural Antecedents and Consequences of Statism." Pp. 111–129 in Thomas et al.

Raskin, J.B. 1993. "Time to Give Aliens the Vote (Again)." *The Nation,* 5 April.

Robertson, R. 1992. *Globalization: Social Theory and Global Culture.* London: Sage.

Shattuck, P.T., and J. Norgren. 1991. *Partial Justice: Federal Indian Law in a Liberal-Constitutional System.* New York: Berg.

Sikkink, K. 1991."The Political Power of Foreign Policy Ideas: The Origins of Human Rights Policy in the U.S. and Western Europe." Presented at the annual meeting of the American Political Science Association, Washington, DC.

Somers, M.R. 1993. "Citizenship and the Place of the Public Sphere: Law, Community, and Political Culture in the Transition to Democracy." *American Sociological Review* 58:587–620.

Somers, M.R. 1995. "Narrating and Naturalizing Civil Society and Citizenship Theory: The Place of Political Culture and the Public Sphere." *Sociological Theory* 13(3):229–274.

Soysal, Y.N. 1994. *Limits of Citizenship: Migrants and Postnational Membership in Europe.* Chicago: University of Chicago Press.

Stepan, A. 1978. *The State and Society: Peru in Comparative Perspective.* Princeton: Princeton University Press.

Stewart, R. 1984. *A Dictionary of Political Quotations.* London: Europa Publications.

Taylor, C. 1990. "Modes of Civil Society." *Public Culture* 3:95–118.

Theodorson, G.A., and A.G. Theodorson. 1979. *A Modern Dictionary of Sociology.* New York: Barnes and Noble Books.

Thomas, G.M., and J. Boli. 1993. "World Culture/World Polity Context of International Non-Governmental Organizations." Presented at the annual meeting of the American Sociological Association, Miami Beach.

Thomas, G.M., J.W. Meyer, F.O. Ramirez, and J. Boli. 1987. *Institutional Structure: Constituting State, Society, and the Individual.* Newbury Park, CA: Sage.

Tilly, C. 1995. "Citizenship, Identity, and Social History." *International Review of Social History* 40, Supplement 3:1–17.

Tronto, J. 1993. *Moral Boundaries: A Political Argument for an Ethic of Care.* New York: Routledge.

Turner, B.S. 1986a. *Citizenship and Capitalism: The Debate over Reformism.* London: Allen and Unwin.

Turner, B.S. 1986b. "Personhood and Citizenship." *Theory, Culture, and Society* 3:1–16.

Ventresca, M.J. 1995. "When States Count." Dissertation, Department of Sociology, Stanford University.

Walzer, M. 1992. "The Civil Society Argument." Pp. 89–107 in *Dimensions of Radical Democracy,* edited by C. Mouffe. London: Verso.

Wronka, J. 1992. *Human Rights and Social Policy in the 21st Century.* New York: University Press of America.

PART II

THE WORLD POLITY

GLOBAL PROCESSES AND TRANSNATIONAL EFFECTS

2 STATE AND SOCIETY IN A WORLD UNBOUND

David Jacobson

The duality of state and society, authority and liberty, or public and private is embedded in the vocabulary and in the constitutions of countries in the West and, increasingly, in the rest of the world as well. Modern society and politics cannot be intelligently understood without reference to the terms state and society, public and private. The rise of the modern state sharpened the public-private distinction. The public character of the modern state is implicit in the rules and regulations limiting the exercise of state power. Deliberations in the government must be publicly accountable and open to general participation—at least formally. When citizens view their churches, businesses and other civic associations as lying in the private sphere, they are claiming limits to the power of the state. The limits are not absolute but any state intervention in the private sector must meet the test of public interest (Starr 1989). The terms public and private capture the quintessence of political and social life, at least in the West, since the seventeenth century. Issues from pacifism to abortion, urban planning to medical insurance have been caught up in the discourse of public obligations and private rights.

If duality of state and society has been the organizing frame of political debate and practice since, arguably, the Peace of Westphalia in 1648, then there are signs that we are reaching another "Westphalian moment." In other words, the notions of state and society, public and private, decreasingly reflect the political and social "architecture" of life "out there." If so, we can begin the process of distilling and discovering the emerging "organizing principle(s)"—the new axes—of politics and "society" (the later concept itself now coming into question).

The signs of such change are in the fraying of the linkages between state and society. The growing foreign populations in Western Europe and in the United States; the declining interest in naturalization of those populations (even when it is possible); the growing proportion of persons with dual citizenship and multiple state membership; and even the increase in cross-national marriages indicate that traditional models of the melting pot, of a unitary and bounded civil society, are, at best, in question.[1] For many Turks in Germany and Mexicans in the United States home, in the metaphoric as well as in the literal sense, is somewhere else. Even "nationals," classically understood, increasingly fear that they will become foreigners in their own countries as the cultural, ethnic, and religious hues of "their homeland" become ever more nuanced. Living in a diaspora is becoming the common experience. Similarly, domestic society has become a microcosm of the world-at-large: North-South divisions have been domesticated (*see* Appadurai 1993; Jacobson 1996; and Rouse 1991).

In this chapter, I sketch out the classical notions of the civil society and how it has been anchored in ideas of nationhood, sovereignty, and in the international system. Against this canvas, I make some suggestion as to the evolution of state and society in a changing international order.

CIVIC POLITICS

The historian Joseph Strayer (1970) noted that there was a time when a man without a family and a lord, a local community and a church, was socially of little worth. Sacrifices of life and property were made for that same family, lord, community, and religion. The state, such as it was, was generally remote and of little importance. Today, one can get on reasonably well without a family, a local community, or religious affiliation. But to be stateless is a bleak prospect: no rights, little security, and little likelihood of regular employment. The state and the citizen, caught in a dialectic of mutual support and opposition, define and organize the available forms of social, economic, and political activity.

Medieval society provides a striking conceptual (and historical) foil to elicit the nature of the modern state. Medieval society was made up of inactive persons, of nonparticipants. Medieval political life was radically fragmented and decentralized. Social horizons usually did not extend beyond the family, manor, or shire; very rarely did politics extend to the level of public concern. Indeed, feudalism almost precluded political relations. Relations were based on family and private treaty, and were personal, patriarchal, and affective. Bonds of personal allegiance were hierarchically arranged. Kinship and fealty precluded civic association. Dynastic ambition ruled out programmatic ideologies. Medieval life, devoid of public vision, or a self-conscious citizenry, consisted of *subjects* who obeyed. In a hierarchical and deferential world, independent, civil politics were inconceivable (Bloch 1961; Hanson 1970; Lerner 1958). Only in the Italian City Republics were civil politics evident.

The "diplomacy" of medieval Europe reflected its feudal makeup. Diplomats were messengers for a myriad of private parties. Kings made treaties with vassals; vassals made treaties with vassals. Kings received ambassadors from their subjects, or from the subjects of *other* princes. Diplomacy was, in effect, simply a formal means of communication in a hierarchically organized society. It carried none of the trappings that signified sovereignty, such as resident embassies or diplomatic immunities. Ambassadors were termed "public officials," but the public to be served was a unified *Republica Christiania*. (Similarly, the prince was expected to enforce not only his own municipal law, but also the common law of the whole community.) The reception or sending of envoys was not considered to be a sign of sovereignty or respect. In the Italian City Republics, however, diplomacy became an expression of shifting political loyalties and the rise of civil politics. Significantly, in parts of Italy organized foreign offices and permanent diplomatic agents were established (Mattingly 1955).

The curious aspect of feudal Europe, however, was that nearly all political communication was of a private diplomatic sort—a means of upholding the personal and contractual ties that bound the princes with his vassals. Thus, Donald Hanson (1970) points out, central political institutions were akin to diplomatic meetings rather than to practices of representation and government. Similarly in diplomacy or war, a ruler might find that one of his men had switched loyalties to a rival. It was as if, Hanson notes, a state governor in the United States chose to change loyalties from the President to, say, the Mexican government. A notion inconceivable in the nation-state was not uncommon in the Middle Ages. The transformation that the modern state has brought about is all the more dramatic when posed against its medieval setting. Perhaps the most important aspect of the modern state is that it is a distinct, discrete, and separate entity in the broader social structure. The patrimonial state, in contrast, was fully identified with the prince. He had judicial powers and was concerned primarily with upholding the pattern of customary rights of his subjects. The prince's authority, however, was woven into an almost seamless social tapestry (Shennan 1974). There was no seam marking the divide between public and private. The modern state is specifically political, both as the embodiment of the nation and as a bureaucracy, with political personnel and functions (Poggi 1978). The discrete and public character of the state was a product of the separation of politics from the household, and the appearance of formally free men (Arendt 1958; Walzer 1965).

The very distinctive and discrete character of the state, however, could be defined only in terms of its antithesis—society. The state was now a public arena, where private associations and individuals purposefully shaped political and social relations. Yet the duality and mutual distinctiveness of state and society posed an insidious challenge to the state, and diluted its role as the embodiment of *Res Publica*. In other words, society could be, and was in some cases, described and understood to be an autonomous body capable of acting almost on its own. The state, likewise, was reduced to its bureaucratic and administrative essentials. It ceased to be a nation-state, an expression of nationalism. The glory of the state faded into the humdrum task of government.

The public dimension that came to characterize the state focused attention on the central government. Loyalties were not exclusive to the family, but were also directed to the civic order. The limited horizons of village and shire broadened to the state and, indeed, to the international level. The state was public in the sense that it was situated at the center of political activity of general concern to the country. Problems of authority were public in scope, not simply personal and local (Hanson 1970). The state as an abstract entity, not the person of the ruler, became the basis of authority. The state, accessible to its citizens, was publicly accountable (Shennan 1974). The state became the embodiment of the national community.

The emergence of the citizen signalled the integration and participation of private men in the political order (Walzer 1965). Politics was a "conscientious labor"; politics was the activity of constructing and defining the very character of social and political relations. Even more striking, however, was how the public character of the state insinuated the dialectic of state and society, of a public sphere and private association, into the language of modern history. In constructing, forming, and shaping the political order, citizens made public presentations of their demands. And to make those demands groups were formed; civil associations were born, united voluntarily on the basis of ideas, not blood. The rise of the state witnessed the rapid spawning of new organizations, political parties, and organizational initiative. Political activity demanded organization and programmatic expression of purposes.

The ideal of civic politics, going back to and drawing on the City Republics of Renaissance Italy, was that of an active citizenry. Citizens, in their civic associations and as individuals, are constantly involved in the making of public decisions. Life is given over to civic concerns. Private life, and a life of introspection (which was contrasted with *vivere civile*), could be "corrupting," a threat to the Republic, if enjoyed at the expense of civic duty. Private interests had to be pursued from a civic perspective. Such interests, however, were not forsaken—normatively as well as practically.

People, political theorists reasoned, were social in that their lives were pursued in association with others. Political activity represented the general association within which all particular associations met and united. Political society, then, is a society of active and self-conscious beings. Political activity constructs relations to the point of creating the polity's own morality (Pocock 1975; Skinner 1978). Society, in contrast to the integrated character of the state, appears as a "multitude of discrete, self-interested, and self-activated individuals relating to one another primarily through private choice" (Poggi 1978). For this reason, the modern state also ushers in the age of ideology, the programmatic propagation of a set of ideals. Similarly, the citizen, necessarily independent in order to act in the public arena, is bestowed with the "rights of conscience"; to think independently of the state in order to participate in constituting the body politic.

The distinctiveness of the state makes it vulnerable to criticism; it is not part of a seamless social fabric. The state, the political society, is thus an object of reform. Indeed, the state, as government, is now potentially an object to be resisted, even overthrown. The age of ideology, in turn, is the harbinger of the age of revolutions (unprecedented in Europe prior to the rise of the modern state in the sixteenth and seventeenth centuries). Consequently, a dynamic sense of future possibilities, of progress, imbues politics. Conversely, history and historical precedents become ideologically salient, as the legal authorities seek customary legal roots in place of laws of nature. The political community is, then, rooted in the past and in the promise of the future. The nation thus has a mythological presence for citizens that borders on the eschatological (Skinner 1978).[2] The state, as the political embodiment of the community, consequently represents the nation vis-a-vis other nation-states, a function carrying with it the mythic national persona.

The state, on the one hand, is the political expression of the nation. The state, however, also has the less grand role as the administrative bureaucracy. But it is on such a level that the jurisdiction of private individuals and groups can be mapped (and compared cross-nationally). Institutionally, the public dimension of the state is manifest in the centrality of representative bodies. The degree of centrality is, so to speak, an open question. The British Parliament has traditionally had a greater untrammeled jurisdictional reach than the United States Congress. Similarly, the government of France has more extensive authority than the Federal Government. (Conversely, authority historically has been more decentralized, and devolves more readily into local government and civil and economic groups in the United States.) However, the legislature, whatever its form, is the arena where laws are crafted and where the public realm is made evident. The state, embodied in these representative bodies, is the exclusive source of law over its citizens and territory. No matter how internally differentiated, or how authority is distributed, the state is the fountainhead of decision making. In this sense, the state is a unitary entity (Poggi 1978). As an administration and bureaucracy, the state, even in its minimalist forms, looms large, impinging on all sectors and regions of a country, making its presence an integral part of daily life—a historical development of profound importance (Rabb 1975).

The centrality of lawmaking bodies leads us to another characteristic of the state. The abstract nature of the modern state—the state does not "belong" to anyone, as the patrimonial state was identified with the prince—highlights the significance of positive law. The self-conscious citizenry construct their nation, and create their own morality, enacting laws. Law is no longer a king's command but an expression of general consent (Laski 1921). (Indeed, some 19th and early 20th century theories of the state posited near identity between the state and its law [Poggi 1978].) And it is through the laws that the distinctions and jurisdictional boundaries between the state and civil, economic and other associations can be drawn. The division is explicitly recognized in the legal classifications of public law, concerning the activities of the state, and private law, which concerns the autonomous activities of individuals pursuing their personal interests. The law defines the rights and duties of the citizen, creating boundaries against state encroachment. Other laws, in an explicitly or implicitly constitutional form, guarantee the citizens direct or mediated access to participation in public decisions. Furthermore, laws in the modern state are universal and general, seek consistency, and are impersonal (Poggi 1978). Such impartiality is rooted in the egalitarian and liberal assumptions of civil politics.

So much for the dynamics and mechanics of civil politics. How is authority located and distributed between state and society, while keeping a sense of unity and nationhood intact? What does this mean in terms of international politics?

SOVEREIGNTY

Sovereignty—the notion that there is an ultimate and final authority in the political community—is not authority per se. Authority, F.H. Hinsley notes, is as old as man. People submit to authority and power, not to sovereignty. The concept of sovereignty arose with the modern state, and with the distinction between state and society. The distinction posed (and poses) the problem of multiple associations; the state is not the only agency in the community. Sovereignty is a statement on, and a response to, the problem of the duality of state and society, as entities that are "judged to be necessary to each other and sufficient unto themselves" (Hinsley 1966).

For a political community to be a community, sovereignty has to be located somewhere. Sovereignty is what distinguishes the state, the body politic, from other forms of association. A supreme authority, theorists of sovereignty held, is necessary if there is to be a community at all. "An ultimate unity of allegiance," Harold Laski (1921) writes, "was a guarantee of order." A world of purely private rights does not sanction the protection of general interests. Other associations, such as churches, trade unions or businesses, have a "will," but their wills are subject to judicial appeal. Such bodies lack, in other words, the sovereignty of the state. The state is the all-encompassing expression of the common bond that unites all on the basis of identical citizenship. The state is universal in its grasp, as it represents the one compulsory association.

It is in the nuanced meanings attributed to the state, as the embodiment of the body politic and an administrative organ, that the dilemma apparent in the state-society division can be resolved. For in internal politics sovereignty bestows upon *government* the authority to go about its business of governing. The state can govern in the age of civil politics because sovereignty, while creating a supreme power, did not create an absolute power over the community. Institutionally, this is reflected in the constitutional safeguards that uphold popular consent as the basis of government. Thus, sovereignty is exercised in such a way that government and community are knitted together. Absolutist government is free to ignore all laws and restraints. Sovereign government comprises both ruler and ruled (Hinsley 1966). In other words, the dual understandings of the state allows it simultaneously to govern on the one hand, while maintaining its legitimacy as the expression of the political community on the other. In the sovereign state a unity of state and society is realized.

The citizenry is consequently supreme, but power is necessarily delegated to the legislature and the executive branches of government. Constitutional guarantees make government accountable to the citizens, and, indeed, may devolve authority downward. Thus, as Grotius (1925) put it, sovereignty is "a unity," but it may be divided (through constitutional checks and balances and federal staggering of authority, for example). Paradoxically, however, the constitutional state, particularly in terms of the division of powers between government and society, has the potential for undermining the sovereignty of state (Hinsley 1966). Jurisdictional power can be so decentralized that civil (or other) associations become autonomous actors in their own right. In the early American Republic, for example, it was not at all clear whether federal citizenship took precedence over state citizenship—an issue that would be resolved only in the Civil War (Kettner 1978). Sovereignty is an expression of where ultimate loyalties of the citizens lie; an institutional division can dilute or redirect such loyalties. How state and society are constitutionally structured reflects the degree to which the state is sovereign.

Insofar as the state is sovereign, its internal distinctions are not reflected in foreign politics. Internationally, the state is a sovereign whole. (Similarly, while internally sovereignty designates supreme political power within the community, in interstate relations sovereignty symbolizes the antithesis: the principle that no supreme authority exists over and above the state's.) (*See* Hinsley 1966.)

Indeed, the sovereign state, as the embodiment of the body politic, takes on the attributes of a unitary personality. This is true domestically as well as externally, but domestically the personality of the state may be lost in constitutional debates and questions about the limits and scope of sovereignty (Hinsley 1966). In foreign affairs, the organic, personal quality of the sovereign state is absolute. Constitutional rights enjoyed domestically by individuals and associations "end at the water's edge." The singularity of sovereignty cannot be undermined. Precepts of international relations are rooted in the theory of corporate legal personality. Such a basis for international intercourse allows for rights and obligations similar to those of individuals to be attributed to states (Wight 1977). Formal equality, for example, exists between states as between individuals within a state. States have the right of self-defense and are held accountable for their actions (Kaplan and Katzenbach 1961).

The personality attributed to the state is also expressive of the body-politic as a nation, as a focus of common loyalties and a shared identity. The state represents the public domestically; externally, that public has a national (or even a nationalistic) color. The state becomes a nation-state (notwithstanding complications that matching state with nation involves). The state as a consequence, C.A.W. Manning (1962) writes, is viewed as expressing the "will of the community." No factual communal will, as such, exists. However, the constitutional framework and institutional process (elections, referendums, and so on) provide a notional "national will." States are thus projected as persons, with self-assertion, self-control and, above all, self-determination. From the days of the Italian City Republics liberty had a connotation not only of self-government of the citizenry, but of political independence from outsiders—of national self-determination (Skinner 1978).

The nature of the state-society division, the personality of the state and—the linchpin of all these dimensions—state sovereignty, constitute the sociological underpinning of international relations. Such relations are between *states*; the state is the sole agent through which, or at the behest of whom, cross-border activities and exchange can take place. The state represents the general interests of the nation, and it is through state sovereignty that the principle of self-determination is ensured. If other agents or associations undertake to determine international policy and practice—be it in economic or political regulation, or in alien admissions—then the sovereignty of the state is in question. (It is a different story, of course, if such associations act *through* the political center in order to affect political agendas.)

The diplomatic institutions of the modern state reflect both the sovereignty and the public dimension of the state. From the middle of the 17th century, with the emergence of the modern state, envoys were sent or received as a mark of respect and as a prerogative of sovereignty, not simply as messengers, as was previously the case. The appearance of foreign ministries and permanent diplomatic officers in this period were, Garrett Mattingly (1955) observes, an institutional expression of "a profound change in the relations of political power, and of an accompanying reorientation in the minds and hearts of men." Similarly, permanent embassies arose and became channels of official exchange. Embassies conveyed recognition and initially were conceded only to allies. Ambassadors, representing their countries, enjoyed diplomatic immunities and thus carried the sovereignty of their nations into foreign territory. The ambassador did not express any private views—he or she existed to serve the state. Countrymen and women abroad were now under the protection of their ambassadors.

The Peace of Westphalia of 1648 was the seedbed for the international institutionalization of the state system, as well as marking the demise of the Holy Roman Empire. The settlement, ending the Thirty Years War, was an unprecedented multilateral agreement among states. State sovereignty was recognized. The republican governments of the Netherlands and the Swiss Confederation were formally admitted to the family of nations. The essential institutional framework was established (Wight 1977).

Sovereignty is also the root of power politics in international relations. The state can only uphold its sovereignty through force and, as Machiavelli pointed out, force lies at the heart of the state. Force guarantees the state (Skinner 1978). Self-determination could similarly only be assured if nations could prevent others from determining their fate. (Contemporary theorists often view force as the basis of international relations and fail to observe the reasons behind it.) The concept of the balance of power thus became associated with sovereignty, since the rise of the modern state (Hinsley 1966).

In 17th century England, J.G.A. Pocock (1985) writes, it was impossible to propagate even the most radical conception of liberty without describing some form of authority at the same time. That is as true today as it was then, when the modern state first emerged. State and society are paired opposites, in opposition yet complementary, and mutually dependent. By extending the jurisdictional reach of the state, the character of private life is vitally affected—not simply because the realm of the private is contracted, but because the very character of relations within the private sphere will be changed. Conversely, expand personal liberty and contract the state and the character of social and political relations will qualitatively (and not just quantitatively) be re-formed.

Georg Simmel (1950) captures the interconnectedness of public and private realms when he notes that the boundary demarcating a private region "cannot be answered in terms of a simple principle, it leads into the finest ramifications of societal formation."

It need hardly be said that arguments were and are put forth that society can be projected as a meaningful reality apart from the state, that society has "forces of cohesion" independent of state institutions. The state, in this view, is reduced to a purely administrative role. Even then, government is viewed as coercive, at best a necessary evil that must be held in check (Hanson 1970).

Capitalism gave substance to the concept of society as a potentially autonomous entity. Marxism would inherit this capitalistic attribute (of projecting society as an autonomous entity)—the state would wither on the vine, whether publicly or privately owned.

The term *property* was a judicial term before it had a purely economic connotation; "property" and "proprietary" were interchangeable words in the 17th century (Pocock 1975). Liberty was associated with private property, because to be free one must have "a sphere of self-assertion," an area of jurisdiction closed to the external world. The problem then became how to determine the limits of private property rights in order to ensure the interests of the common good—that is, the problem of where to draw the boundary between state and society, or public and private realms (Cohen 1982). The civically active, it was reasoned, had to have a minimum land tenure. Such land defined their independence, and set the proprietor free to act in the public realm, to set forth for the commonwealth (Pocock 1975).

Capitalism as a form of social and economic relations is first perceived at the end of the 17th century in England with definite consequences for the orthodox view of civil politics. Land, like anything else, became a marketable commodity. At the very least, this raised questions about the use of land as the singular realm of the private, as the base for civic activity. Perhaps more importantly, questions arose as to the degree the "market man" could or wished to participate in the civic order: the exchange of commodities, as such, was not linked to the citizen's civic activities. In commercial society, the capitalist's world is mostly privatized and subjective, and only the whims of the market reveal to him or her the "factual basis" of his or her opinions. Since capitalism was at first viewed as fantasy rather than reality, laws of the market had to be discovered (or created) to render rational an otherwise incomprehensible universe (Pocock 1985; Pocock cites Hirschman 1976). Such laws, and concepts such as the "invisible hand," implied that society had forces of cohesion that were autonomous and apart from the state.

The idea that there was some moment that a "market man" emerged who was emancipated from politics, and who did not have to be civilly active to be a "self-satisfactory being," is strongly criticized by Pocock. While acknowledging that classic political man may have been dealt a serious blow by capitalism, Pocock notes that the dialogue between polity and economy never ended. Aside from the historical record, Pocock's criticisms make sociological sense. Shared understandings, commitments, agreements and attitudes essential to the market (or any human organization) would not be plausible in a completely privatized society. Similarly, the English theorist Ireton declared that the law—authority—must give the individual his (and later, her) social rights if property is to have any security at all (Pocock 1975). However, the market did provide a model in which civil politics was a diminished fixture, and in which active participation in the civil order—in shaping the nation—was not a first concern of the capitalist *qua* capitalist. The realm of politics may be of interest to the market man as an administrative mechanism to regulate (but not control) the market in order to ensure its smooth functioning. Political conditions that provide for optimal market activity are sought. The political center serves as a locus for interest-groups to enforce fair access to the market for "equal opportunity" or a proportional cut of the national pie.

Today, however, the duality of state and society is coming under strain under the impact of a "globalizing" world and transnational activities. Certain assumptions of the nation-state are in question. The loyalties of economic and other associations are no longer necessarily focused on the state. The state is no longer the single arbiter of cross-national ties.

THE NEW AXIS-MUNDI

The notion of society as an autonomous entity has, in one sense, become true. Economic, social, political, and other associations act inter- and trans-nationally and independently of any state involvement. The classical imagery of societies and associations being contained within the territorial confines of the state, and all activities across national borders as taking place through, or at the behest of, the state is patently untrue today (and probably only an approximate truth in the past). The vertical axis between state and society, in the West at least, has been cracked.

Capitalism's potentially problematic relationship to civic politics (and, by extension, the nation-state) is no longer a theoretical question—or a potentiality. Cross-societal ties in the global marketplace are commonplace, a truism. Transnational corporations, whose interests are genuinely multinational, are a growing phenomenon. These cross-societal, "horizontal" ties, furthermore, are not only economic. International migration, ethnic dispersion, increasing populations with multiple citizenships, an increase in marriage between nationals of different countries, transnational political and social movements, together with a global media make this phenomenon social and political as well.

With the weakening of unique, undivided loyalties that is inherent in the attenuation of the state-society link of a civil society—an attenuation which accompanies the growing "society-society" linkages—the nature of the ties of the individual and nongovernment groups vis-a-vis the state changes. Once the state could call on its citizenry to sacrifice for the collective good, while the citizen *qua* citizen could demand certain rights and benefits from his or her state. With that organic and exclusive relationship fraying (though by no means eclipsed), new rationales linking the individual and the state have come to the fore.

The dramatic rise in the significance of human rights in Western Europe and North America since the 1970s is a part of this development.[3] Human rights transcend the citizen-alien distinction and, indeed, now transcend the state itself. Human rights are anchored in international—even transnational—institutions, like the international human rights codes of the United Nations, the European Convention on Human Rights, and the Organization for Security and Cooperation in Europe (OSCE). This is significant because it means that we now have a global, transnational political and legal order that, by definition, circumscribes state sovereignty.

Thus individuals, be they citizens, foreign residents, or even tourists, can now make claims on the state on the basis of human rights. As the civic tie between state and society weakens, so human rights become all the more salient. Aside from effectively drawing in larger swaths of the population into the legal web of the state, this development changes the political and social "architecture."[4] The states-system classically is a two-tiered structure, in which nongovernment associations and citizens have agency within the state, and only the state has agency on the international stage. With the growing significance of transnational human rights legal codes and institutions, the two tiers are now one, and nongovernmental groups (NGOs) and individuals are the agents of a broader global order. (It must be stressed, however, that this framework applies primarily to Western Europe and North America, and is spreading slowly to parts of Eastern Europe. Notions of sovereignty are still vehemently asserted in many developing countries.)

The growing multifarious, transnational ties produced by multinational corporations, migration, diasporic communities, environmental movements, and the like leads to a circumstance where individuals and NGOs make cross-cutting claims on different states (particularly if those states lie in the Western orbit) on the basis of human rights. Claims can be made on one state for, say, the effects of pollution originating in that state on another country or people. Under the OSCE, an NGO in one country can make demands on a foreign government to restrain the activities of its "own" nonstate groups that may be, for example, racist or anti-Semitic (*see* Meron 1989).

States that try to exclude elements of the population from its legal protections, once an acceptable practice of self-determination, are sanctioned. For example, in 1994 Latvia legislated that the roughly 36 percent of its population that was Russian would not be eligible for Latvian citizenship. The OSCE and the Council of Europe, the parent body of the European Convention on Human Rights, intervened and demanded that Latvia include the Russian population as citizens. The Latvians complied within two months (Erlanger 1994).

Hence the state becomes the regulative mechanism of a broader (international) constitutional order. As international institutions and law come to focus on human rights, so NGOs and individuals become the agents that propagate, reproduce, and interpret the premises of the international order itself. In being able to make claims on the courts in terms of international human rights code, nonstate associations reproduce and realize those codes as the "modality" of the international order. That order exists only in virtue of being reproduced in this manner. Conversely, nonstate associations can only make such claims by presupposing the a priori existence of an international institutional order that recognizes such claims. The state, as the mediator and regulative mechanism of this order, consequently plays a critical role in facilitating and supporting this complex of "enduring relationships." (*See* Bhasker 1979; *see also* Wendt 1987.) The state, formerly *the* actor in international relations, now becomes the forum or mechanism that binds together the nonstate associations and the set of rules that make up the international order.

The state, consequently, has become a forum for competing claims and beliefs (*see* Koh 1991). The state is no longer projected as the embodiment of the "general will" of a people or nation, but is now a forum for "competing wills," often concerning transnational associations and issues. Contested issues are adjudicated on the basis of the "merits" of the case, as defined by international human rights codes, and not on the basis of "national interest" or how the state defines its scope of jurisdiction (*see* "Constructing the State Extra-Territorially" 1990).

As individuals and nongovernment associations become the object of international institutions and law, so NGOs also act on these institutions directly. A variety of Catholic, Muslim, and feminist nonstate organizations, for example, were active in the debate over abortion rights, or absence thereof, at the United Nations population conference in Cairo in 1994. This also attests to the importance of international human rights law and declarations in what once was considered a purely "domestic" domain. Defining human rights—as fluid a notion as any legal concept—becomes an important battle.

As the international relations scholar Paul Wapner has suggested, contemporary developments suggest that a "*world* civic politics" is emerging. Wapner (1995:339) writes with reference to transnational environmental groups:

> While global civil society is analytically a distinct sphere of activity, it is shaped by, and in turn shapes, the states-system. States' actions greatly influence the content and significance of economic, social and cultural practices . . . [Transnational environmental activist groups] disseminate an ecological sensibility, pressure corporations, or work to empower local communities. . . . In each instance, activist efforts intersect with the domain of the state . . . [However] transnational activism does not simply become politically relevant when it intersects with state behavior. Rather, its political character consists in the ability to use diverse mechanisms of governance to alter and shape widespread behavior.

Global civil society, one may add, tends to be less bounded than the civil society of the nation-state, with groups more devoted to single-issues causes; the metaphor of the "quilt" is more apt than the metaphor of the melting-pot.

It is reasonably clear that the binary distinctions that have guided social theory and practice—state and society, and "domestic" and "international" above all—are becoming anachronistic, at least in the West. Some propositions can be put forward, however, suggesting in part the shape of things to come:

- First, as the state-society linkage becomes more attenuated, the notion of a unitary state comes into question.
- Second, the state source of legitimacy is shifting from principle of national self-determination to international human rights.
- Third, the state is increasingly detached from its status as the embodiment of the body politic, or nation.
- Fourth, ethnic and other nongovernmental groups increasingly can act on the global stage as independent actors—they no longer need a territorial state to have agency on the international stage. This parallels the ongoing shift in international law in which individuals and nonstate groups are objects of that law (as opposed to states exclusively holding that status).
- Fifth, political agency is being "deterritorialized."
- Sixth, the "imagery" of the state is less that of the melting pot, and more that of a "multicultural" or consociational polity.

Most importantly, we need to break away from the distinctions, unfortunately embedded in our disciplinary boundaries, between state and society, and their interlocking and binary correlate, domestic and international. Instead, we should replace the duality of state and society with a *tripartite distinction* that captures the international institutional, state, and nonstate levels. In each case, or on each level, we need to continue to reconceptualize how, say, the state is distinctly different from the (nation) state antecedent. We also need to further conceptualize how these different levels intersect.

Needless to say, many questions remain. For example, how are "private" and "public" conceptualized in this new order of things? Given the shifting role of the state, what is the place of ideology? In what institutional forms will nationalism come to be expressed? How do class differences (and conflict) align in this new environment? As we reach the end of the millennium, the cartographer is not the only one who has to remap the world; sociologists, philosophers, and political scientists face that daunting task as well.

NOTES

1. Starting in early 1995, however, there was in the United States a surge of requests for naturalization. One factor in this development was a bill before Congress that would limit certain welfare benefits to citizens (excluding resident aliens). The intention of the Mexican government to legalize dual citizenship was thought likely to raise the rate of naturalization requests even further—though this, of course, would increase the phenomenon of dual citizenship as well.

2. S.N. Eisenstadt discusses the beginnings of revolution and its sources in *Revolution and the Transformation of Societies* (1978).

3. This is documented in Jacobson (1996).

4. The discussion that follows draws extensively from Jacobson (1996:117–121).

REFERENCES

Arendt, Hannah. 1958. "The Public and the Private Realm." In *The Human Condition*. Chicago: University of Chicago Press.

Appadurai, Arjun. 1993. "The Heart of Whiteness." *Callaloo*, 16(4).

Bhasker, Roy. 1979. *The Possibility of Naturalism*. Brighton, England: Harvester Press.

Bloch, Marc. 1961. *Feudal Society*, trans. L. A. Manyon. Chicago: University of Chicago Press.

Cohen, Morris R. 1982. *Law and the Social Order*. New Brunswick: Transaction Books.

"Constructing the State Extra-Territorially: Jurisdictional Discourse, the National Interest and Transnational Norms." *Harvard Law Review* 103, 1990.

Eisenstadt, S. N. 1978. *Revolution and the Transformation of Societies*. New York: Free Press.

Erlanger, Steven. 1994. "Latvia Amends Harsh Citizenship Law that Angered Russia." *New York Times*, July 24.

Grotius, Hugo. 1925. *The Law of War and Peace*. Indianapolis: Bobbs-Merrill.

Hanson, Donald W. 1970. *From Kingdom to Commonwealth*. Cambridge, MA: Harvard University Press.

Hinsley, F. H. 1966. *Sovereignty*. London: Watts.

Hirschman, Albert. 1976. *The Passions and the Interests*. Princeton: Princeton University Press.

Jacobson, David. 1996. *Rights Across Borders: Immigration and the Decline of Citizenship*. Baltimore: The Johns Hopkins University Press.

Kaplan, Morton A., and N. deB. Katzenbach. 1961. *The Political Foundations of International Law*. New York: Wiley.

Kettner, James H. 1978. *The Development of American Citizenship 1680–1870*. Chapel Hill: University of North Carolina Press.

Koh, Harold Hongju. 1991. "Transnational Public Law Litigation. *The Yale Law Journal* 100.

Laski, Harold J. 1921. *The Foundations of Sovereignty*. New York: Harcourt Brace.

Lerner, Daniel. 1966 [1958]. *The Passing of Traditional Society*. New York: Free Press.

Manning, C. A. W. 1962. *The Nature of International Society*. New York: Wiley.

Mattingly, Garrett. 1955. *Renaissance Diplomacy*. London: Jonathan Cape.

Meron, Theodor. 1989. *Human Rights and Humanitarian Norms as Customary Law*. Oxford: Clarendon Press.

Pocock, J. G. A. 1975. *The Machiavellian Moment*. Princeton: Princeton University Press.

Pocock, J. G. A. 1985. *Virtue, Commerce and History*. Cambridge: Cambridge University Press.

Poggi, G. 1978. *The Development of the Modern State*. Stanford, CA: Stanford University Press.

Rabb, Theodore. 1975. *The Struggle for Stability in Early Modern Europe*. New York:

Oxford University Press.

Rouse, Roger. 1991. "Mexican Migration and the Social Space of Postmodernism."
Diaspora 1 (1):8–23.

Shennan, J. H. 1974. *The Origins of the Modern European State*. London: Hutchinson.

Simmel, Georg. 1950. *The Sociology of Georg Simmel*. Kurt Wolff, ed. New York:
Free Press.

Skinner, Quentin. 1978. *The Foundation of Modern Political Thought*. Cambridge:
Cambridge University Press.

Starr, Paul. 1989. "The Meaning of Privatization." In Alfred Kahn and Sheila Kamer-
man, eds., *Privatization and the Welfare State*. Princeton: Princeton University Press.

Strayer, Joseph R. 1970. *On Medieval Origins of the Modern State*. Princeton:
Princeton University Press.

Walzer, Michael. 1965. *The Revolution of the Saints: A Study in the Origins of Radical Politics*. Cambridge: Harvard University Press.

Wapner, Paul. 1995. "Politics Beyond the State: Environmental Activism and World
Civic Politics." *World Politics* 47(3):311–340.

Wendt, Alex. 1987. "The Agent-structure Problem in International Theory." *International Organization* 41(3):335–370.

Wight, Martin. 1977. *Systems of States*. Leicester: Leicester University Press.

3 DYNAMICS OF CITIZENSHIP DEVELOPMENT AND THE POLITICAL INCORPORATION OF WOMEN

A GLOBAL INSTITUTIONALIZATION RESEARCH AGENDA

Francisco O. Ramirez
John W. Meyer

Throughout the world, national societies are increasingly influenced by transnational principles of citizenship. Even in societies varying in economic or political structure, standard definitions of the civil, political, and social rights of citizens are on the rise. The globalization of these principles was unanticipated in social science theories that emphasize either the functional needs of societies or the interests of dominant elites as the underlying explanations of political change. Such theories assume that internal and varying economic arrangements and political organizations play the main role in explaining the development of citizenship rights and their extension to women. These assumptions continue to underlie much of the literature on citizenship and on gender and, thus, this literature has great difficulty accounting for the rapid development of standardized citizenship principles and their ideological and organizational impact on the rights of women (Ramirez 1996). Furthermore, prevailing social theory ignores the recent shift in emphasis from standardizing citizenship principles within individual nations to articulating the human rights of all persons, independent of their membership in any national polity. The contemporary focus on human rights in both international organizations and in nation-states invites new research questions that go beyond the more conventional understanding of citizenship (Soysal 1994).

This chapter outlines a broad research agenda to study world patterns in the adoption by nation-states of formal principles of citizenship, the extension of these principles to women, and the transformation of some of these principles into transterritorial human rights This proposal is informed by a theoretical perspective that views nation-states and individuals as highly dependent on world cultural models for their core status as actors pursuing legitimated goals such as progress, justice, and equality (Meyer et al. 1996a; Thomas et al. 1987). That is, both nation-states and individuals owe their taken for granted status and the legitimacy of their agendas to these models and their organizational carriers. From this perspective, it is the triumph of world models of the nation-state and its citizenry that accounts for the proliferation of national citizenship principles and the political incorporation of women. Thus, it is not surprising that societies which may continue to vary with respect to endogenous economic and political structures may nevertheless increasingly adhere to common citizenship standards. World cultural models privilege nation-states as imagined communities of solidarity (Anderson 1991) and individuals as rights-bearing citizens (Turner 1990). These models contain recipes for both national and individual development and these recipes have been advertised throughout the world as scripts for progress.

The quest for and the desirability of progress are central features of these models as they developed in the West. It is often argued that the economic and geopolitical triumph of the West clearly enhanced the visibility and attractiveness of these scripts for progress. This thesis is accurate but incomplete. Many dominant civilizations have either hoarded their scripts for progress or imagined their lack of applicability to peoples beyond this or that "great wall." The visibility of what started as Western models of the nation-state and its citizenry was not an accident. These models were not so much pirated (Anderson 1991) as carried across the world with missionary zeal (Meyer et al. 1996b). To be sure, this voyage was riddled with inconsistencies and contradictions but the universalistic character of the scripts facilitated their increasingly worldwide use. For example, the ingredients of successful national independence movements throughout the 19th and 20th centuries clearly illustrate the Western origins of their quest for progress. Thus, while it is true that "winners" are more likely to be copied by others, the Western "winners" seemed especially eager to serve as models. Moreover, the Western models (both the liberal and socialist variants) are developed as abstract and ahistorical means/ends schemata that make it possible to retain (or even invent) local accents while veering toward a common idiom of citizenship within a standardized nation-state.

In the late 20th century, no nation-states and no individuals are presumed to fall outside the scope of this common idiom. On the contrary, all nation-states are expected to promote the development of all their individual citizens and all individual citizens are likewise expected to contribute to national development. This expectation is articulated within and between nation-states, in international governmental and in international nongovernmental organizations, and by an army of experts and consultants on a broad range of national and individual development issues. This expectation has thus become a central feature of world and national discourse on citizenship, generating similar developments in different places.

We have earlier utilized this perspective to understand the rise of mass schooling as a widespread legal right and requirement (Ramirez and Boli 1987; Ramirez and Ventresca 1992), the expansion of primary educational enrollments (Meyer, Ramirez, and Soysal 1992), and the increasingly similar subject matter emphasis in curricular content (Meyer, Kamens, and Benavot 1992). These studies show worldwide educational developments that cannot be accounted for by societal level factors. These developments are better understood, though, if one assumes that education is defined throughout the world as the key means to individual and national development. Different nation-states and different individuals seize upon similar educational goals because they are attuned to and influenced by the same world cultural models.

This perspective has also been used to interpret world patterns in the political incorporation of women as citizens (Ramirez 1987) and their increased participation in higher education (Bradley and Ramirez 1996). These studies suggest the importance of world models and their organizational carriers in the rise and spread of a series of citizenship principles applied to women. We now seek to situate these studies within a broader research agenda with the following goals:

- To describe and analyze the global-level expansion of legal rights and the extension of these rights to individuals as both citizens and persons; and to describe the subsequent application of these rights to women.

- To describe the development and activities of international organizations as carriers of these rights.

- To assess the impact of global ideological and organizational developments on the rate at which individual countries adopt citizenship and human rights principles, and especially on national policies regarding women.

- To compare the impact of global factors on legal norms with the effects of (1) variations in the linkages between a nation-state and the wider world order and (2) variations in the endogenous national economic, political, and social structures.

- To gauge the extent to which the effects of linkage factors increase and the effects of internal factors decrease as a function of the degree to which global ideological and organizational factors favor standardized, expanded human rights in different historical periods.

To illustrate the research agenda, consider equality between the sexes. The project focuses on the declaration of equality between men and women as a principle increasingly articulated in national constitutions and in state bureaucracies, the elaboration of this principle within international organizations such as the United Nations Educational, Scientific, and Cultural Organization (UNESCO) and the International Labor Organization (ILO); and the crystallization of some forms of equality between women and men as general human rights that are meaningfully discussed as such in world conferences (e.g., the 1995 World Conference on Women in Beijing). This undertaking describes worldwide and regional trends in the development of equality between the sexes as a national citizenship principle, an international norm, and a human rights standard. This descriptive data makes it possible to compare the principle of equality between the sexes in earlier periods with the current one. This project also has explanatory goals. We propose to analyze the extent to which a national adoption is influenced by the adoption policies of other nation-states, the activities of international organizations such as the United Nations (e.g., the Universal Declaration of Human Rights 1948, and the Convention on the Elimination of All Forms of Discrimination Against Women 1979), the extent to which a nation-state is linked to the wider world of nation-states and transnational organizations, and/or by internal developments within the nation-state. In both comparative sociology and in international relations, the usefulness of conceptualizing women's rights as a transnational issue has been recently emphasized (Berkovitch 1994).

The same strategy applies to a variety of other specific individual rights in many different social sectors, such as politics, education, work, and the family. We focus on both the ideological and organizational manifestations of citizenship principles, depicting their development across nation-states and, in the aggregate, across the world itself. Throughout this project, citizenship principles are conceptualized as more globally institutionalized to the degree that these principles are affirmed in (a) national constitutions or state policies and in (b) international conferences and organizations. Citizenship principles are more globally institutionalized as human rights to the extent that they are articulated as applicable to all persons (or adults, in some cases) regardless of national citizenship.

It is fashionable to decry the spreading of rules as paper doctrines unrelated to practice—and indeed, current intense commitments to the principles of human rights lead to the intensified identification of abuses. But this ignores a fundamental point to which this study calls attention: prior to 1945 no one expected a mass worldwide expansion of citizenship principles or their extension to women (Donnelly 1986). Now it is routine to discover "civil liberties violations" in all sorts of countries where such principles did not previously exist and to discuss the most elaborate rights of women in places where women until recently had no standing at all. It is our aim to analyze the process by which models of citizenship and human rights have been so widely extended. Such a study is probably a useful precursor to future studies of local practice in particular areas: our theoretical perspective supposes that world changes would affect practice even where local rules have not changed (Meyer 1980; Ramirez 1998).

In what follows, we clarify what has been called the global institutionalization perspective. Next, this theoretical perspective is translated into a concrete research agenda. First, we specify the dependent variables of interest and identify potential measures and the sources of this data. Lastly, we focus on the independent variables and outline a strategy for undertaking longitudinal cross-national analyses.

THE GLOBAL INSTITUTIONALIZATION PERSPECTIVE

Classical sociological arguments often provide functionalist explanations for the rise of citizenship. For social order theorists, increased societal complexity makes social integration more problematic. The development of citizenship solves this problem by creating a common integrative bond among increasingly differentiated individuals (Parsons 1966; Simmel 1955). For class reproduction theorists, capitalism increases inequality and results in more alienated individuals. The integrative power of citizenship is thus functional for the dominant elites and their interests rather than for the social system as a whole (for a discussion, *see* Giddens 1987). The two versions differ more in normative assessment than empirical explanation. Other lines of inquiry privilege class or state interests as an explanatory variable and generate causal imagery operating at the national societal level. Citizenship may be seen as a "deal" made with potentially troublesome populations either by state builders in exchange for tax and conscription powers (cf. Tilly 1975) or by dominant economic elites in exchange for greater labor compliance.

All these lines of argument stress the importance of national or subnational interests or needs as explanatory factors. None of these arguments accounts for the sweeping worldwide expansion of similar citizenship principles nor for their transformation into transterritorial human rights (Boli 1981). These arguments seem especially unable to make sense of the increasingly worldwide extension of citizenship principles to women (Ramirez 1996). Confronted with the increasing standardization and expansion of citizenship and human rights, functionalist and many other arguments of-

63

ten retreat into case studies that, however informative, do not shed light on the transnational trends and changes. These studies frequently result in elaborate discussions of how local forces produced change, while ignoring the fact that similar change was going on nearly everywhere in the world at the same time.

To make sense of a worldwide phenomena, the global institutionalization perspective postulates the existence of world models that historically privileged the nation-state, societal progress, and a universalistic vision of individual persons and citizens. This core idea leads us to expect that a great number of the changes in national or subnational units take place within a cultural domain that is exogenous to particular national or subnational settings. Changes in national societies reflect exogenous cultural models in several ways.

First, exogenous rules of sovereignty legitimate the constitution of modern societies as nation-states, which increases the likelihood that these will adopt the standard policies of nation-state entities (Giddens 1984; Jackson and Rosberg 1982; Meyer 1980). Second, models of these standard policies are constructed and legitimated, often in international conferences and organizations, such that conformity to them seems rational and even necessary to aspirant nation-states (McNeely 1995). Third, exogenous ideological changes in matters core to nation-state structure, such as definitions of development, justice, or the means to attain these goals, will influence internal rules regarding citizenship rights and the social categories to which these apply. Lastly, alternative models of organizing society and practices more consistent with these alternatives are delegitimated over time, as in the collapse of the apartheid regime in South Africa.

Our own work on the origins and expansion of mass education around the world illustrates the empirical viability of the global institutionalization perspective. Our analysis of the expansion of mass enrollments from 1870 to 1980 clearly shows that its growth is unrelated to the internal structures of the societies involved and is positively influenced by the triumph of any version of nation-state ideology and organization (Meyer et al. 1992). In related research, we show that the national adoption of compulsory school rules and educational ministries is also a worldwide process involving much isomorphism (Ramirez and Ventresca 1992).

Much ideological and organizational isomorphism is involved in the vast diffusion of a broad range of citizenship rights. Even if the origins of specific citizenship arrangements, such as education and welfare programs, appear to fit with the functional requirements of more complex societies, the cultural accounts involved have spread and developed as legitimating ideologies in very unlikely parts of the world. Similarly, even if the social control aims of political and economic elites plausibly explain the origins of state-orchestrated extension of rights to individuals, the diffusion of these citizenship principles across varying states, economies, and cultures requires a more parsimonious explanation than found in the country-specific interpretations.

Donnelly (1986) concretely depicts the global context of human rights development:

> Prior to Word War II human rights were almost universally viewed as the exclusive preserve of the state . . . there was not even a weak declaratory international human rights regime. In the interwar period the International Labor Organization (ILO) undertook some minor efforts in the area of workers' rights. . . . With these very few exceptions, as recently as fifty years ago, human rights were not even considered to be a legitimate international concern. . . . World War II marks a decisive break: the defeat of Germany ushered in the contemporary international human rights regime. . . . In the late 1940s human rights became for the first time a recognized international issue area.

But like many regime theorists, Donnelly nonetheless assumes that autonomous state interests shape national adherence to world standards (Krasner 1983). Why so many historically different entities should act as if they were influenced by common world standards is not well addressed in this literature. The reification of state interests obscures processes of contemporary cultural globalization and national enactment of world standards. However, alternative views assigning greater weight to global structures and international organizations and less autonomy to states and other actors are on the rise in international relations (Ashley 1987; Bull and Watson 1984; Ruggie 1987), in comparative sociology (Featherstone 1990; Robertson 1992; Thomas et al. 1987), and in the field of formal organizations (Meyer and Rowan 1977; Meyer and Scott 1983; Powell and DiMaggio 1991; Zucker 1983).

The global institutionalization perspective informs the ideas that frame our proposed investigation. These are: (1) *Elaboration*: A variety of dimensions of citizenship will be increasingly specified within world models. We shall later identify and discuss some general dimensions of citizenship rights. (2) *Consensus*: There will also be an increase in shared discourse on citizenship rights across nation-states. For example, the rights of indigenous peoples or of women of any color to be treated as citizens and persons should become the subject of parallel public commentaries in many countries. (3) *Articulation*: There will be an expansion of the international organizational carriers of these rights, as indicated by a proliferation of treaties, resolutions, and ratifications in the United Nations and its agencies (Forsythe 1991) and in regional organizations such as the Organization for Economic Cooperation and Development (OECD). Furthermore, there will be an increase in international nongovernmental human rights organizations in general, and with respect to women's rights in particular. (4) *Universalization*: There will be an increase in the classification of these rights as basic transterritorial human rights rather than as merely national citizenship rights. That is, national cultural or religious traditions will be less frequently invoked over time to circumscribe some rights or to create idiosyncratic ones (e.g., justifications of sex-based differentiation and subordination). This change implies the growing influence of transnational standards in national settings. (5) *Structuration*: Lastly, for some research purposes we treat the proportion of countries having adopted policies related to a right as itself an indicator of worldwide "peer" pressure and/or facilitation. Examples of such density arguments are found in the work of Hannan and Freeman (1989).

To summarize, we expect to show that citizenship principles undergo changes in the direction of higher levels of elaboration, consensus, and articulation. We further expect an increase in the numbers of citizenship principles set forth as universal human rights. Thus, nation-states and aspirant nation-states will find themselves situated in a world with more citizenship rights, greater international consensus as regards these rights (and their abuses), more organizational action highlighting rights-related issues, and a greater proclivity to treat these as human rights. This will also be a world where a greater number of nation-states enact the appropriate legal norms and policies. We assume that higher levels of structuration are both positively influenced by and positively influence greater degrees of elaboration, consensus, articulation, and universalization. All of these processes strongly pressure nation-states to adopt laws and policies affirming citizenship and human rights.

The global institutionalization perspective bears on a number of specific issues related to citizenship principles. A first task is a straightforward descriptive one and involves the collection of cross-national time-series information on variables characterizing many citizenship rights. These data characterize worldwide and regional trends in citizenship development and may be used to ascertain whether the direction and magnitude of these changes are consistent with the expectations set forth in the preceding paragraph. We also propose to model the evolution of citizenship rights along lines suggested in previous work. Our cross-national and longitudinal analyses will seek to answer questions such as the following: Do world-level rights regimes expand with worldwide economic expansion or the expansion of the nation-state system itself? Is there a core of citizenship rights that more successfully diffuses, out-competing alternative ideologies and types of rights? How much do the kinds of rights stressed in a given time period reflect the national characteristics of the dominant powers? More concretely, did the post–World War II decline of Germany slow worldwide expansion rates of the sorts of welfare rights associated with the corporatist model of state and society (Flora and Heidenheimer 1981)? Has American dominance since 1945 produced world emphases on rights linked to the American liberal model? Will the demise of the Soviet Union further enhance consensus on world standards of human rights? Or, alternatively, if hegemonic competition cynically promoted human rights development to make possible accusations of human rights violations, will human rights emphasis in world discourse slow down?

Corollary analyses focus on the rise of human rights violations as a global problem. One issue is to distinguish categories of rights that become stressed as human rights. A further issue is to explore the roles played by organizational carriers that monitor human rights—from the more limited Red Cross focus on violations under wartime conditions, to the more elaborated Amnesty International focus on everyday life rights violations—and to explore the extent to which these violations come to be discussed not as disruptions of national laws but as crimes against humanity (cf. Nanda, Scarritt, and Shepherd 1981). A rise in the latter discourse would be indicative of an increase in universalization. Furthermore, research will distinguish between the degree to which human rights violations are applied to women qua individual persons or as a distinctive gender-based status group (Reanda 1984).

We then propose to examine how increased emphases on citizenship and human rights in international organizations affect rates of national adoption of relevant legal policies. Adoption rates may be directly affected by organizational and communication linkages to world models, such as membership in the appropriate international organizations, and by variables indicating that a country formally fits the standard nation-state models and is thus a more likely target for rapid isomorphism in particular rights areas. The global institutionalization perspective suggests that such variables should be most important in affecting rates of formal adoption.

Finally, we propose to examine the impact of national economic, political, and social development on the adoption of individual rights and their elaboration for women. Classic arguments suggest that national-level factors are the main ones at issue. Such factors may play a strong role in the early adoption of individual rights, but effects are likely to decline over time with the rise of standardized rights at a more global level. Our own cross-national work on educational expansion (compare Meyer et al. 1977 with Meyer et al. 1992) provides a direct example of the increasing significance of world political culture in the post–World War II period. Similar findings are obtained in an analysis of the extension of the franchise to women, with endogenous factors showing less influence in the more recent time period while exogenous ones become stronger over time (Ramirez et al. 1992).

VARIABLES AND INDICATORS

Our overall goal, then, is to empirically analyze longitudinal cross-national data to demonstrate the rise of citizenship principles and their extension to women; to show the increasing impact of world models of appropriate citizenship (and linkages to their organizational carriers) on policies and rules in individual countries; and lastly, to show the corresponding decline in the influence of properties of particular economies, states, and cultures. The dependent variables analyzed are formal rights and policies rather than degrees of implementation because our research focuses on the emergence of a consensual world standard for national legal norms against which national policies are themselves evaluated.

Marshall (1964) identified three types of individual citizenship rights and saw these as having emerged in Britain in a rough historical sequence. Civil rights protect the individual from the state, for example freedom of speech and assembly. Political rights entitle the individual to act in the public realm: the right to vote and seek public office are classic illustrations. Social rights mandate that the state provide individuals with substantive benefits such as education and welfare.

Marshall's typology has been criticized for being arbitrary (Sommers 1993) and in good measure parochially British in assuming an evolutionary sequence from civil to social rights (Mann 1987). These criticisms highlight some shortcomings in the original conceptualization. But in studies linked to our own work, Boli (1981) and Hooper (1988) demonstrate that Marshall's typology may be effectively used to distinguish historical periods in the development of individualism and dramatically reflects worldwide trends from the mid-19th century to the present. The typology thus provides a reasonable basis for proceeding, and we propose to examine:

CIVIL RIGHTS

(a) It is now possible to trace the rise of constitutional and legislative guarantees protecting the individual from arbitrary mistreatment by the state. Primary data sources on national constitutions and constitutional changes over time include, for example, Dareste (1891, 1910, 1928–34), Peaslee (1950, 1956, 1965–70), and Blaustein and Franz (1971). Other studies (Boli 1981; Inkeles 1975) have developed constitutional indexes and shown dramatic worldwide extension of such rights over the past century. These codes have been utilized to characterize countries every 20 years, from 1870 to 1970. We intend to extend the constitutional index to 1990 to capture some of the most recent changes. A wider range of more specific indicators, including legislative protections, need to be collected from sources such as Duchacek (1973) and the United Nations (1946–92). We also propose to track the spread of public reporting of human rights abuses, as itself an indicator of the spread of the rules in question. Data sources include Nanda et al. (1985); Kate (1986); *Comparative Human Rights* issues; and annual reports from Amnesty International and Human Rights Watch.

(b) The extension of formal civil rights and protections to women is a long-term historical process. A core issue is the extension of state protection to women against controlling and subordinating forces built into traditional family relations. We are thus especially interested in the extension of active state protection to women in areas where patriarchal logic may have been especially dominant: rights to control their own marriage and reproduction, expanded protection against rape (including marital rape), and policy interventions in the area of spousal abuse. Cross-national data sources include Sivard (1985), Lapham and Mauldin (1985), Stepan (1979), Cook and Dickens (1979) and the United Nations (1992); *see also* Graveson and Crane (1957) for a survey of family law from 1857 to 1957. At the organizational level we propose to note and analyze the rise of national and international journals, organizations, and conferences that specifically address the relevant issues. Examples include the organization and content of the *International Directory of Women's Development Organizations* and source books on women's rights in international conventions (Langley 1991; Halberstam and Defeis 1985). At the ideological level we can examine the content of laws (e.g., *Columbia Human Rights Law Review* 1981) and resolutions. Preliminary analyses of abortion laws are underway (McEneaney and Ramirez 1996).

POLITICAL RIGHTS

(a) The classic dependent variable here is the long-term extension of the franchise to the mass population, in the 19th and early 20th centuries. Primary data sources include Mackie and Rose (1991) and country-level reports. It is also possible to analyze the spread of rules guaranteeing in one way or another the rights of individuals to organize and express their interests in the polity. Data sources and analyses of political rights development and limitation include the work of Bollen on political democracies and individual rights (1980, 1986; *see also* Diamond, Linz, and Lipset 1988).

(b) The extension of the franchise to women is a central issue that continues to generate theoretical debate among scholars (*see* Katzenstein 1984 and MacKinnon 1983 for differing points of view). As noted earlier, analyses suggest that the societal-level factors that influence early adoption may weaken over time, a process emphasized within the global institutionalization perspective (Ramirez et al. 1992). More extensive analysis is required to distinguish between processes that affect the extension of the franchise to men from those that influence its acquisition by women. It is also useful to analyze the long-term trends in female office holding in both legislative and executive positions as an indicator of changing political status. Data sources include Newland (1975) and the papers in Katzenstein and Mueller (1987), and in Shreir (1988).

Social Rights

(a) Social rights for individual persons were realized primarily in the areas of welfare and employment. The rise of formal public welfare programs has been examined extensively (Abbott and de Viney 1989; Collier and Messick 1975; Flora and Heidenheimer 1981; Orloff and Skocpol 1984). Previous work linked to our own research has attempted to tie the spread of such provisions to world standards and international organizations, particularly the ILO (McNeely 1995; Strang and Chang 1993; Thomas and Lauderdale 1989). We propose both to develop the line of causal reasoning developed in this literature and to augment it with analysis of legal and constitutional provisions for employment and related rights.

(b) The extension of equality of employment opportunity and equal wages for equal work rights to women provides a natural focus for comparative analysis. Orloff (1993) critically assesses the gendered character of social citizenship and its implications for women. Some of our prior work has involved examining women's share of the paid labor force and the upper echelon occupations (Ramirez and Weiss 1979), including the labor force status of married women relative to single women (Ramirez 1981). Related research focusing on the expansion of pre-primary enrollments and other aspects of organized childcare complement our work (O'Connor 1988). Data sources include UNESCO Yearbooks, publications from ILO, and Boulding (1976).

Our proposed analyses take two forms. First, we propose to describe and analyze the worldwide expansion and institutionalization of the citizenship principles and human rights on which we focus. Second, we propose to show the impact of the world and regional changes in changing the rates at which individual countries adopt such principles and rights as policies.

Describing and Analyzing Global Changes

A large part of our task is descriptive and involves empirically tracking (with descriptive tables and graphs) changes over time in variables described above: (1) proportions of countries adopting particular rights policies, (2) measures of the development and expanded activity of the international organizational carriers of these rights, and (3) indicators of shifts in the conception of rights from territorially grounded citizenship principles to more universalistic assertions of "human rights."

In addition, we will analyze such changes in the world as a whole, using standard time- series analysis. We propose, for instance, to analyze the expanded numbers of international organizations concerned with the rights of women. In these timeseries analyses, relevant *independent variables* include: (1) *Rates of growth in the world economy.* Periods of high growth create resources which, given the unique structure of the modern world system, tend to become invested in the expanded identity or status of the legitimated individual (as well as nation-state) members of the system (Thomas et al. 1987). Data on periods of world economic expansion and contraction may be found in *The Economist* (1982), Barr (1979), and other sources. (2) *The rise of international organization in general—that is, the formal organization of the world political system.* Political organization at the world level tends to parallel the ideological and structural currents that have obtained at lower (national) system levels. Thus, the rise in international political organization generates reaffirmations of doctrines of citizenship exactly as the earlier development of the nation-state (even in relatively absolutist forms) created similar (though often emphasizing the duties of citizenship) emphases on individual citizenship identity. Data on international treaties and networks may be found, for example, in Small and Singer (1973) and more recently in Bull and Watson (1984). (3) *The degree to which the dominant or hegemonic countries, in particular periods, have policies and organizational structures emphasizing the rights of women.* This is the classic assumption that rules articulated in wider societies tend to reflect those supported by their dominant members. In periods when liberal societies emphasizing women's rights are especially hegemonic, women's rights flourish at the world level. Data sources for periods of core hegemony versus core competition include Modelski and Thompson (1987). (4) *The overall proportions of countries which themselves have policies emphasizing the rights of women.* These data would reflect the conventional idea that world norms may be simple aggregates of policies obtained in typical nation-states.

Another set of independent variables will characterize the linkages between a nation-state and the broader world culture. We will utilize readily available indicators including: (1) the extensiveness of membership in international organizations, (2) the number of diplomatic embassies, (3) the number of conjoint treaties (outside the realm of human rights), and (4) the degree of participation in world trade. The aforementioned data sources also include information on these indicators. (For an example of an analysis utilizing these variables, *see* Snyder and Kick 1979.)

Throughout these analyses, we will also characterize countries by their levels of economic development, type of political regime, and dominant religious tradition. Measures of industrialization, urbanization, and political structure may be found in Banks (1986). Indicators of religious tradition may be found in Barrett (1982). Our proposed analyses, here, employ the standard methods of time series analysis, explaining changes in our dependent variables in terms of prior values of an array of independent variables (Gujarati 1988).

Dynamic Analyses of Rates of Policy Adoption by Specific Countries

A main focus of our research involves looking at the impact of variables describing the institutionalization of rights in international organizations and world conferences on rates of adoption of rights policies by individual countries. We contend that increases in the number of rights affirming organizations, conventions, and conferences will lead to (1) increases in the rates of national adoption, (2) increases in the effect of linkage to the world system on rates of national adoption, and (3) decreases over time in the impact of such national-level characteristics as political, social, and economic development.

Our approach here is to conduct event history analyses of the rates of national adoption of particular rights variables (Tuma and Hannan 1984). Event history models will enable us to identify a country's "hazard," or likelihood, of adopting a particular policy at a particular point in time ($h[t]$) as a function (g) of a vector of independent variables (x) describing both that country and its ties to world society, and a function (q) of time (t) and of characteristics of world rights institutionalization at particular points in time. Thus,

1. $h(t) = g(x)q(t)$, or
2. $\log h = \log g(x) + \log q(t)$, where
3. $\log g(x) = \beta_0 + \beta_1 X_{1(t)} + \beta_2 X_{2(t)} + \ldots$, where particular variables (X_1, and so on) are properties of the country and its relations to world society.

If we are considering the analysis of national adoptions of women's rights policies, for instance, we would look at the impact of such variables as economic development and the expansion of the service sector, which may enhance the position and importance of women, and at the impact of the presence of women in political office and the number of women's political organizations, which may indicate their power. These are properties of the country itself, at any time point. But we are also interested in the effect of a country's involvement in the world system, which we suppose increases its hazard of adopting policies institutionalized as preferable in that system. Therefore, we would employ measures of (1) national involvement in such international organizations as those of the United Nations system; (2) density of diplomatic ties with other countries; and (3) measures of national ties to international bodies, especially those espousing women's rights or, more broadly, human rights.

In equation 2 above, $\log q(t)$ has various functional forms (e.g., Gompertz models may be especially appropriate; *see* Tuma and Hannan 1984). Or, one may utilize partially parametric methods to estimate the functional form. In our situation, a good many properties of time period are of great substantive interest, and would be explicitly incorporated in the analyses. That is, variables indicative of high world institutionalization in a given rights area in a particular period may generally increase national adoption rates. Such variables include (1) the proportion of countries in the world that have already adopted the particular rights policy by a particular time period; (2) the proportion of dominant or hegemonic countries that have done so; (3) the extent to which international organizational structures support the particular rights; (4) the extent to which professionalized or scientized measures of the rights in question (e.g., the status of women on particular dimensions) are promulgated in international publications in a particular period; (5) the rate of recent national adoptions of relevant policies (which may produce a special institutional pressure on further potential adopters).

More refined models that incorporate the effects of historical time periods will be more useful since we argue that the impact of particular national properties is itself dependent on time period (and the level of world institutionalization that characterizes particular time periods). Thus, we argue above that the impact on rights adoptions of measures of national development declines under conditions of high world rights institutionalization—which can generate pressures that influence a variety of countries. Earlier research, for example, demonstrated that the effect of national mass educational enrollment level on subsequent enrollment rate growth declined after World War II, a period in which world pressure for educational expansion had a very high impact on various countries regardless of their initial educational levels (Meyer, Ramirez, and Soysal 1992). As another example, event history analyses showed that the impact of national characteristics on the initial rate of adoption of a mass educational system declined sharply after World War II (Meyer et al. 1992). Other examples of event history analyses in our work include our study of changes in political party system (Thomas and Meyer 1980) and more recently our analysis of the extension of the franchise to women (Ramirez et al. 1992).

CONCLUSION

We propose quantitative cross-national studies of the expansion of citizenship principles and the impact of the globalization of civil, political, and social rights on the rules and policies adopted by nation-states over time. We focus on citizenship and human rights in general and on their articulation for women more particularly. Our basic argument is that global standardization has produced a context in which the rapid development of these rights and the policies elaborating them is increasingly *unrelated* to variations in national characteristics and increasingly *related* to a global normative culture which fosters the adoption of such rights. The global elaboration of these rights intensifies this world political culture and gradually leads to isomorphism among nation-states in their formal organization of citizenship principles often proclaimed as universal human rights.

These cross-national studies will evaluate empirically the implications of both global institutionalization and societal-level explanations. The results will permit researchers to assess the relative effects of transnational and national factors on the adoption of citizenship principles and human rights norms over time. Moreover, the findings will encourage more theoretically focused case studies of human rights policy formation processes. The worldwide institutionalization of human rights regimes will probably have mostly symbolic short-term effects at the country level. However, the global process may generate more positive long-term effects within countries in the following ways: (1) the norms become available and then part of the stock-in-trade of national political and bureaucratic elites; (2) national-level professions develop around these norms, making it a professional group interest to pursue them; and (3) both bureaucrats and professionals have world-level standards and organizations to refer to and to reinforce criticism of local conditions. These processes are better understood at the national level (cf. Edelman 1992); our study is a theoretical and research effort at the global level. The dynamics of citizenship development involve nation-states and individuals, but these are embedded in the broader world of standards of progress, equality, and justice. These standards are pervasive, elaborated in widespread social science and legal theories, and articulated in international organizations and in national legal systems and policies. The degree of transnational consensus achieved is often underestimated in a literature that focuses on the gaps between principles and practices and between formal structuration and behavioral violations. Within this literature an enormous amount of bad faith or instrumental formalism is attributed to a broad spectrum of nation-states. This assessment is sometimes accurate, but theoretically inadequate.

Within the global institutionalization perspective, what is striking is the triumph of world models within which progress-oriented nation-states and rights-bearing citizens and persons are clearly privileged. It is precisely this triumph that facilitates the identification of gaps, the enumeration of violations, and the development of organizations and experts which affirm the standards worldwide. Alternative models, justifying racism, sexism, absolute parental control over children, or absolute state control over the population, have faded from the world scene. Thus, extensive linkages with the broader world in the contemporary era lead to the activation of the favored citizenship principles and human rights scripts. This process of identity enactment is often at odds with local circumstances; the outcome is an array of rather obvious gaps and violations. Instead of coping with these inconsistencies by embracing some alternative model, nation-states are more likely to commission investigations or studies of this abusive situation or that failure to comply with a citizenship principle. Since this process frequently reveals further inconsistencies, thereby further stigmatizing the nation-state, it will not do to dismiss this process as a mere exercise in legitimation. Only by fully recognizing the authority and influence of the triumphant world models can one begin to address the issues this research agenda seeks to tackle.

REFERENCES

Abbott, Andrew, and Stanley de Viney. 1989. "Sequences of Welfare Adoption." Paper presented at the annual meetings of the American Sociological Association.

Anderson, Benedict. 1991. *Imagined Communities: Reflections on the Origins and Spread of Nationalism*. London: Verso.

Ashley, Richard. 1987. "State Formation and International Anarchy: Beyond the Domestic Analogy in the Study of Global Collaboration." In H. Alker and R. Ashley, eds., *Anarchy, Power, and Community: Understanding International Collaboration.*

Banks, A.S., ed. 1986. *Political Handbook of the World.* Binghamton, NY: CSA.

Barr, Kenneth. 1979. "Long Waves: A Selected Annotated Bibliography." *Review* 2(4): 675–718.

Barrett, David. 1982. *World Christian Encyclopedia.* Nairobi: Oxford University Press.

Berkovitch, Nitza. 1994. "From Motherhood to Citizenship: The Worldwide Incorporation of Women into the Public Sphere in the Twentieth Century." Dissertation, Department of Sociology, Stanford University.

Blaustein, Albert P., and G.H. Franz. 1971. *Constitutions of the Countries of the World.* Dobbs Ferry, NY: Oceana Publications.

Boli, John. 1989. *New Citizenship for a New Society: The Institutional Origins of Mass Schooling in Sweden.* Oxford: Pergamon Books.

Boli, John. 1981. "Human Rights or State Expansion? Cross-National Definitions of Constitutional Rights, 1870–1970." Pp. 173–93 in Ved P. Nanda, James Scarritt, and George W. Shepherd, eds., *Global Human Rights.* Boulder, CO: Westview.

Bollen, Kenneth. 1986. "Political Rights and Political Liberties in Nations: An Evaluation of Human Rights Measures, 1950 to 1984." *Human Rights Quarterly* 8: 567–591.

Bollen, Kenneth. 1980. "Issues in the Comparative Measurement of Political Democracy." *American Sociological Review* 45:370–390.

Boulding, Elsie. 1976. *Handbook of International Data on Women.* New York: Sage.

Bradley, Karen, and Francisco O. Ramirez. 1996. "World Polity and Gender Parity: Women's Share of Higher Education, 1965–1985." *Research in Sociology of Education and Socialization.*

Bull, Hedley, and Aaron Watson, eds. 1984. *The Expansion of International Society.* Oxford: Oxford University Press.

Collier, David, and R. Messick. 1975. "Prerequisites versus Diffusion: Testing Alternative Explanations of Social Security Adoption." *American Political Science Review* 69:1299–1315.

Columbia Human Rights Law Review. 1981. Special Issue on the Rights of the Child.

Cook, R.J., and B.M. Dickens. 1979. "Abortion Laws in Commonwealth Countries." *International Digest of Health Legislation* 30:395–502. Geneva: World Health Organization.

Dareste, F.R. with P. Dareste. 1891, 1910, 1928–34. *Les Constitutions Modernes.* Paris: Callamel.

Diamond, Larry, Juan Linz, and Martin Seymour Lipset. 1988. *Democracy in Developing Countries.* Boulder, CO: L. Rienner.

DiMaggio, Paul and Walter Powell. 1983. 'The Iron Cage Revisited: Institutional Isomorphism and Collective Rationality in Organizational Fields." *American Sociological Review* 48:147–160.

Donnelly, Jack. 1986. "International Human Rights: A Regime Analysis." *International Organizations* 40(3).

Duchacek, Ivo. 1973. *Rights and Liberties in the World Today.* Santa Barbara, CA: ABC-Clio.

The Economist Newspaper Limited. 1982. *World Business Cycles.* London.

Edelman, Lauren B. 1992. "Legal Ambiguity and Symbolic Structures: Organizational Mediation of Civil Rights Law." *American Journal of Sociology* 97:1531–1576.

Erstling, Jay A. 1977. *The Right to Organize: A Survey of Laws and Regulations.* Geneva: International Labour Organization.

Featherstone, Mike. 1990. *Global Culture.* Newbury Park, CA: Sage.

Flora, Peter, and Arnold Heidenheimer, eds. 1981. *The Development of Welfare States in Europe and America*. New Brunswick, NJ: Transaction Books.

Forsythe, David P. 1991. *The Internationalization of Human Rights*. Lexington, MA: Lexington Books.

Giddens, Anthony. 1984. *The Constitution of Society*. Berkeley: University of California Press.

Giddens, Anthony. 1987. *The Nation-State and Violence*. Berkeley: University of California Press.

Graveson, R., and F. Crane. 1957. *A Century of Family Law, 1857–1957*. New York: Sweet and Maxwell.

Gujarati, Damodar N. 1988. *Basic Econometrics*. New York: McGraw-Hill.

Halberstam, M., and E. F. Defeis. 1987. *Women's Legal Rights*. Dobbs Ferry, NY: Transnational.

Hannan, Michael, and John Freeman. 1989. *Organizational Ecology*. Cambridge: Harvard University Press.

Hooper, Jon. 1988. Human Rights or Citizenship Rites: The Quest for Definition in National Constitutions, 1870–1970. Dissertation, Department of Sociology, Stanford University.

Jackson, Robert, and Carl Rosberg. 1982. "Why Africa's Weak States Persist: Empirical and Juridical Statehood." *World Politics* 35:1–24.

Kate, Alan. 1986. *The Legal Traditions and Systems: An International Handbook*. New York: Greenwood.

Katzenstein, Mary. 1984. "Feminism and the Meaning of the Vote." *Signs* 10:4–26.

Katzenstein, M. F., and C. M. Mueller. 1987. *The Women's Movements of the United States and Western Europe*. Philadelphia: Temple University.

Krasner, Stephen, ed. 1983. *International Regimes*. Ithaca, NY: Cornell University Press.

Langley, Winston. 1991. *Women's Rights in International Documents*. Jefferson, NC: McFarland.

Lapham, Robert, and W. Parker Mauldin. 1985. "Contraceptive Prevalence: The Influence of Organized Family Planning Programs." *Studies in Family Planning* 3:117–30.

Mackie, Thomas. 1991. *The International Almanac of Electoral History*. Washington, DC: Congressional Quarterly.

MacKinnon, Catherine. 1983. "Feminism, Marxism, Method, and the Feminist Jurisprudence." *Signs* 8:635–658.

Mann, Michael. 1987. "Ruling Class Strategies and Citizenship." *Sociology* 21:339–354.

Marshall, T.H. 1964. *Class, Citizenship, and Social Development*. Garden City, NY: Doubleday.

McEneaney, Betsy, and Francisco O. Ramirez. 1996. "Enactment of Liberalized Abortion Laws in 120 Nations." Paper presented at the annual meetings of the American Sociological Association, New York.

McNeely, Connie L. 1995. *Constructing the Nation-State: International Organization and Prescriptive Action*. Westport, CT: Greenwood.

Meyer, John, John Boli, George Thomas, and Francisco O. Ramirez. 1996a. "World Society and the Construction of Actors." Paper presented at the Institute for International Studies Workshop, Focus on Sovereignty and Governance, Stanford University.

Meyer, John, John Boli, Francisco O. Ramirez, and George Thomas. 1996b. "Theories of Culture: Institutional versus Actor-Centered Arguments: The Case of World Society." Paper presented at the annual meetings of the American Sociological Association, Washington, DC, 1995. Precis published in *Sociology of Culture Section Newsletter*, Vol. 10 (Spring/Summer).

Meyer, John. 1980. "The World Polity and the Authority of the Nation-State." In A.J. Bergesen, ed., *Studies of the Modern World System*. New York: Academic Press.

Meyer, John, Francisco O. Ramirez, Richard Rubinson, and John Boli-Bennett. 1977. "The World Educational Revolution, 1950–1970." *Sociology of Education* 50: 242–258.

Meyer, John, and Brian Rowan. 1977. "Institutionalized Organizations: Formal Structure as Myth and Ceremony." *American Journal of Sociology* 83:340–363.

Meyer, John, and W. Richard Scott. 1983. *Organizations and Environments*. Newbury Park, CA: Sage.

Meyer, John, Francisco O. Ramirez, and Yasemin Soysal. 1992. "World Expansion of Mass Education, 1870–1980. *Sociology of Education* (April).

Meyer, John, David Kamens, and Aaron Benavot. 1992. *School Knowledge for the Masses: World Models and National Curricula in the Twentieth Century*. Philadelphia: Falmer Press.

Modelski, George, and W.R. Thompson. 1987. "Testing Cobweb Models of the Log Cycle of World Leadership." In G. Modelski, ed., *Exploring Long Cycles*. Boulder, CO: Lynne Rienner.

Nanda, Ved, James Scarritt, and George Shepherd, eds. 1981. *Global Human Rights*. Boulder, CO: Westview.

Newland, Kathleen. 1975. *Women in Politics: A Global Review*. Washington, DC: Worldwatch Paper 3.

O'Connor, Sorca. 1988. "Women's Labor Force Participation and Preschool Enrollment: A Cross National Perspective, 1965–1980." *Sociology of Education* 61: 15–28.

Orloff, Ann. 1993. "Gender and The Social Rights of Citizenship: The Comparative Analysis of Social Policies and Gender Relations." *American Sociological Review* 58: 303–328.

Orloff, Ann, and Theda Skocpol. 1984. "Why Not Equal Protection? Explaining the Politics of Public Social Spending in Britain, 1900–1911 and the United States, 1880–1920." *American Sociological Review* 49:726–750.

Parsons, Talcott. 1966. *Societies: Evolutionary and Comparative Perspectives*. Englewood Cliffs, NJ: Prentice-Hall.

Peaslee, Amos J. 1965–70, 1956, and 1950. *Constitutions of Nations*. The Hague, The Netherlands: Martinus Nijhoff.

Powell, Walter W., and Paul J. DiMaggio. 1991. *The New Institutionalism in Organizational Analysis*. Chicago: University of Chicago Press.

Ramirez, Francisco O. 1981. "Statism, Equality, and Housewifery: A Cross-National Analysis." *Pacific Sociological Review* 24:179–195.

Ramirez, Francisco O. 1987. "Global Changes, World Myths, and the Demise of Cultural Gender: Implications for the USA." Pp. 257–274 in Terry Boswell and Albert Bergesen, eds., *America's Changing Role in the World System*. New York: Praeger.

Ramirez, Francisco O. 1996. "The Political Incorporation of Women: Transformations in Gendered Identity." Paper presented at the Workshop in Institutional Analysis, Department of Sociology, Tucson, Arizona.

Ramirez, Francisco O. 1998. "The Nation-State, Citizenship, and Educational Change: Institutionalization and Globalization." Pp. 47–62 in W.K. Cummings and N.F. McGinn, eds., *International Handbook of Education and Development: Preparing Schools, Students, and Nations for the 21st Century*. New York: Elsevier.

Ramirez, Francisco O., and Jane Weiss. 1979. "The Political Incorporation of Women." Pp. 238–252 in John Meyer and Michael Hannan, eds., *National Development and the World System*. Chicago: University of Chicago Press.

Ramirez, Francisco O., and John Boli. 1987. "The Political Construction of Mass Schooling: European Origins and Worldwide Institutionalization." *Sociology of Education* 60:2–17.

Ramirez, Francisco O., and Yun-Kyung Cha. 1990. "Citizenship and Gender: Western Educational Developments in Comparative Perspective." *Research in Sociology of Education and Socialization* 9:153–173.

Ramirez, Francisco O., and Marc Ventresca. 1992. "Institutionalizing Mass Schooling: Ideological and Organizational Isomorphism in the Modern World." Pp. 47–60 in Bruce Fuller and Richard Rubinson, eds., *The Political Construction of Education: School Expansion, The State, and Economic Change*. New York: Praeger.

Ramirez, Francisco O., Yasemin Soysal, and Suzanne Shanahan. 1992. "Women's Acquisition of the Franchise: An Event History Analysis." Paper presented at the annual meetings of the American Sociological Association, Pittsburgh.

Reanda, Laura. 1984. "Human Rights and Women's Rights: The United Nations Approach." *Human Rights Quarterly* 3:11–31.

Robertson, Roland. 1992. *Globalization*. Newbury Park, CA: Sage.

Ruggie, John Gerard. 1987. "Human Rights and the Future International Community." *Daedalus* 112:93–110.

Shreir, Sally, ed. 1988. *Women's Movements of the World: An International Directory and Reference Guide*.

Simmel, George. 1955. *Conflict and the Group of Web Affiliations*. Translated by Kurt Wolff and Reinhard Bendix. Glencoe, IL: The Free Press.

Sivard, Ruth. 1985. *Women: A World Survey*. Washington, DC: World Priorities.

Small, Melvin, and J. David Singer. 1973. "The Diplomatic Importance of States, 1816–1970: An Extension and Refinement of the Indicator." *World Politics* 25: 577–599.

Snyder, David, and Edward Kick. 1979. "Structural Position in the World System and Economic Growth, 1955–1970: A Multiple Network Analysis of Transnational Interactions." *American Journal of Sociology* 84(5):1096–126.

Sommers, Margaret. 1993. "Citizenship and the Place of the Public Sphere: Law, Community, and Political Culture in the Transition to Democracy." *American Sociological Review* 58:587–620.

Soysal, Yasemin. 1994. *Limits of Citizenship: Migrants and Postnational Membership*. Chicago: University of Chicago Press.

Stepan, John, ed. 1979. *Survey of Laws on Fertility Control*. New York: United Nations Fund for Population Activities.

Strang, David, and Patricia Chang. 1993. "The International Labor Organization and the Welfare State: Institutional Effects on National Welfare Spending, 1960–80." *International Organization* 47: 235–262.

Thomas, George, John Meyer, Francisco O. Ramirez, and John Boli. 1987. *Institutional Structure: Constituting State, Society, and the Individual*. Newbury Park, CA: Sage.

Thomas, George, and Pat Lauderdale. 1988. "State Authority and National Welfare Programs in the World System Context." *Sociological Forum* 383–399.

Thomas, George, and John Meyer. 1980 "Regime Changes and State Power in an Intensifying World-State-System." Pp. 139–158 in Albert Bergesen, ed., *Studies of the Modern World-System*. New York: Academic Press.

Tilly, Charles. 1975. *The Formation of National States in Western Europe*. Princeton, NJ: Princeton University Press.

Tuma, Nancy, and Michael Hannan. 1984. *Social Dynamics: Models and Methods*. New York: Academic Press.

Turner, Bryan. 1990. "Outline of a Theory of Citizenship." *Sociology* 28:379–395.

United Nations. 1946–92. *Yearbook on Human Rights*. New York: UN.

United Nations. 1988. *Human Rights: A Compilation of International Instruments*. New York: UN.

United Nations. 1989. *Compendium of Statistics and Indicators on the Situation of Women*. New York: UN.

United Nations. 1992. *Abortion Policies: A Global Review*. New York: UN.

United Nations Education, Scientific, and Cultural Organization. 1955, 1958, 1961, 1966, 1971. *World Survey of Education*. New York: UNESCO.

United Nations Fund for Population Activities. 1979. *Survey of Laws on Fertility Control*. New York: UNFPA.

Zucker, Lynn. 1983. "Organizations as Institutions." In *Research in the Sociology of Organizations*. Greenwich, CT: JAI Press.

4 WOMEN'S ALTERNATIVE PATH TO CITIZENSHIP

AN EXAMINATION OF GLOBAL EMPLOYMENT POLICY

Nitza Berkovitch

Rights proliferate, penetrate to new domains, and acquire new meanings. New groups arise that are considered to be entitled to different kinds of rights (e.g., women, children, disabled, animals). At the same time, new types of rights emerge (e.g., cultural rights, ecological rights) and new domains of social life are formulated as appropriate for regulation via rights granted by the state (e.g., the domestic sphere, the environment) (*see* Falk 1994; Meyer et al. 1987; Steenbergen 1994; Turner 1994).

Accordingly, old rights are being reshaped, their meaning changed and reformulated. Thus, for example, some "protective" labor laws for women, once conceived as a major social achievement, are now presented as being discriminatory and, as such, unjust. The configuration of granting rights is changing as well. Whereas in some of the older European states the pattern of granting rights followed Marhall's historical pattern, newly emerging states usually grant political rights and civil rights at the same time, usually immediately after independence. This is true also for women's rights. For example, whereas in older nation-states women usually received political rights much later than men, in the new ones the two events have taken place at the same time (Ramirez et al. 1994).

What most researchers fail to consider is that the above processes take place on a world level. Most countries experience these changes around roughly the same historical periods, regardless of their age and other national characteristics (e.g., Boli 1987). Emphasizing internal processes and structures as accounting for the spread of citizenship overlooks the increasing similarities among nation-states in regard to historical timing of granting specific types of rights to specific social groups.

Indeed, in each nation-state, the process may take a different form and be governed by different dynamics, depending on the specific historical, political, and social conditions. However, all of these processes constitute a world transformation that has to be accounted as such. Highlighting the global nature of the process in which rights emerge, are transformed, and have diffused in many countries around the globe, points to forces that operate outside the boundaries of individual nation-states and that cannot be reduced to factors which originate at the national level. In this conceptualization, the wider context in which countries operate is given theoretical primacy. Following institutionalist theory, conceptualizing nation-states as subunits within a world polity underscores the world nature of these processes (Meyer 1980; Ramirez 1987).

As Turner (1990) points out in his critique, Marshall's (1950; 1973) theory of citizenship rights did not contain an explicit theory of the state. This lack of theorization implies that the state operates in a way that is free from any constraints, and especially from those of an international capitalist system. However, the world system is not only an economic structure, it is also a cultural and political one. Within this theoretical framework, the wider context is conceptualized as a cultural and political world system—a world polity—that constitutes a wider system of cultural constraints and rules. And these rules determine, to a large degree, the possibilities and alternatives that shape nation-states' action: "[T]he world institutional order is an accounting structure or an ontology that comprises a set of taken-for-granted rules and conventions that constitute the institutional environment for international discourse and nation-state development" (Thomas et al. 1987:3–40; *also see* various articles in that volume).

One principal nation-state activity that has been shaped and modified by this institutional environment is that of granting different types of rights and citizenship to various groups. Therefore, world changes in the patterns, domains, and meanings of rights can be accounted for by an exploration of changes in global discourse. This global discourse—the production of various sorts of texts as well as multiplicity of organizational activities—is being produced by the main carriers of world culture—global actors (Meyer 1994). Moreover, a variety of international organizations, especially those that proliferated after the Second World War, constitute an integral part of the world polity and produce and reproduce international organizational fields in every conceivable domain (Barrett 1995; Boli and Thomas forthcoming; Finnemore 1993; McNeely 1993; Strang and Chang 1993). Thus, the purpose of the present chapter in particular is to explore the ways in which global organizations have transformed, from mid-19th century until 1985, the meanings attached to one type of rights—economic rights—to one group of people—women.

Gender, Citizenship, and the Public/Private Split

The notion of citizenship and theories of rights have been criticized as not adequate to explain women's position. The main argument is that the private/public dichotomy—a major social and ideological organizing principle—is missing from the analysis. The distinction between the "private" and the "public" is central for understanding the ways in which the notion of citizenship has emerged and for understanding its gendered nature. The ideological differentiation that assigns women to "reign" over the private and makes the public the exclusive domain of men also privileges the latter over the former. At the same time, rights and citizenship are concepts that apply to patterns of and entitlement to participation in the public sphere, and supposedly bear no relevance for rules that organize the private sphere. However, feminist scholarship has brought an understanding that focuses on highlighting the different meanings and relevance that citizenship and rights, as conceptualized by "liberal" thinkers and practiced by nation-states, have for men and women. This intellectual project of "gendering" rights explores the ways in which the public/private split, being interwoven within the concept of rights, operates to mask women's subordination into the private and women's blocked access to the public (Arnaud and Kingdom 1990; Kingdom 1990; Lloyd 1984; Okin 1989; Pateman 1988, 1989; Vogel 1994).

However, not enough attention has been made to the changing gendered nature itself of the public/private. Following Nicholson (1986), I argue that the public/private gendered dichotomy needs to be investigated within a historical perspective since its territoriality, meaning, and, consequently, its implication for women's citizenship has changed over time. Here, I explore the ways in which global discourse grants, justifies, and shapes women's access to a particularly definitive domain of the public sphere—paid employment—in order to understand women's changing economic citizenship. Exploring the discursive and nondiscursive practices of global actors unmasks the path women's citizenship has traveled. Early on, such practices were shaped by conceptions that highlighted their gendered nature, whereas, later on, recognition of their explicit association to the private sphere and domestic functions and roles diminished. Yet, men's rights to employment was not considered to be affected by their relations to the private sphere. Thus, focusing on the world transformation of conceptions and legislation of employment reveals that women have traveled an alternative path to citizenship.

Women and Employment Law

Employment legislation was essentially the first to acknowledge women's participation in the public sphere. It is the domain in which the state was mobilized to regulate women's participation patterns in public activities. During the 19th century, in almost all European countries, the state produced a wide variety of measures that had relevance to women's patterns of employment. This was also due to the fact that around that period the state started to intervene and to regulate labor relations in general. Indeed, legislation that concerned women's' employment in several countries served as a decisive turning point that signaled and legitimized state's intervention in labor relations (Skalar 1993). In other domains, such as politics and education, women's participation was either unregulated by state law or banned altogether. Note that suffrage was generally granted to women much later (Ramirez et al. 1994). Thus, investigation of labor laws is a useful starting point to examine the process of state incorporation of women in the public sphere as a world phenomenon.

Employment policy regarding women was also one of the first women's issues to become an *international* concern. Suffrage, though a major issue for women's organizations, was dealt with and acted upon by official global forces only at the post–World War II period. Also, the first negotiation among heads of states at the turn of the century to pass international labor laws concerned protective measures that applied to women only, which continues to occupy world polity attention today. But the ways in which women's employment was discussed, conceptualized, and enacted have changed dramatically. Investigating these changes highlights the ways in which global conceptions of women's roles and identities in the public sphere has transformed during the last century.

In what follows, I discuss global discourse, as produced by global actors in particular—that is, world organizations—regarding women's employment for over a century. I divide this period into three stages based on transformations in world polity structure and culture: (1) from the mid-19th century to the First World War; (2) the inter-war era; and (3) the post–Second World War era. First, I discuss initial attempts at international cooperation which took place in the earlier period, to set international labor standards regarding labor conditions in general and women's in particular. Next, I investigate the ways in which the protective measures advocated at the turn of the century were elaborated and expanded by the International Labor Organization in the inter-war period. Then, I show the transformation of global policies that have helped to reshape women's participation in paid employment with the rise of the rights discourse that took place at the post–World War II period. Each stage has involved a process of changing the gendered nature of the public and the private, and women's relations to each.

The 1850s to World War I

During the second half of the 19th century, nation-states started to discuss regulating labor conditions and to pass labor laws, all of which were in the form of "protecting" women's employment. They included mainly prohibition of employment immediately after childbirth, of night work, and of work underground and in hazardous occupations. Some countries gave women time off with the explicit intention that they could perform their "duties" at home. Before the First World War, more than 20 countries had established some form of protective laws. In addition to the European countries, New Zealand, Australia, and Japan did that as well (Anderson and Zinsser 1988; Blanpain 1977–1990).

Not accidentally, around the same time various efforts were made to homogenize the various national labor laws. These attempts were part of a larger project that included individuals, social movements, and nation-states, all aiming to establish links across national boundaries to solve world social problems. One of the major issues promoted by these transnational reform movements was the need to improve working conditions in general, and women's and children's in particular, in the various counties. However, the means to obtain this goal—the setting of international labor standards—was rather controversial, with arguments that contradicted the notion of state sovereignty. Yet, engendering no debate was the notion that if such standards were to be accepted, "protecting the working woman" should be the main issue to be included. Indeed, one striking feature of the long efforts was that this idea was included in all of the proposals that were brought up and negotiated at that time.

The idea of homogenizing labor laws across national boundaries was first brought up by individuals. For example, following an attempt made by Robert Owen two decades earlier in 1818, Blanqui published a book pointing to the long hours and "starvation wages" in which women and children were employed (*see* Follows 1951). In 1847 an Alsatian manufacturer made specific reference to prohibition of employment at night of men under 18 and *all* women as part of a reform in labor laws suggested in a petition sent to several European governments, urging them to take steps to enact an international law for improving labor conditions (Johnston 1924; Shotwell 1934). The cause was later joined by social movements and finally by state officials, all trying to get governments to cooperate on labor issues and to take some action. During the 1860s and 1870s, an interest in "international factory legislation" spread to Germany, France, Austria, Belgium, and Switzerland among political economists, Christian social reformers, intellectual socialists, social philosophers, and some politicians.

An overview of the various proposals shows clearly that women and children laborers were the groups that were widely considered as urgently in need of legal protection (Follows 1951). The socialist movement took up this campaign as well, and already in their First International meeting in Geneva in 1866, a resolution on the prohibition of night work for women was adopted. A demand that governments take steps to bring about international labor legislation was also expressed (Johnston 1924; Price 1945; for an opposing view, *see* Follows 1951). A more elaborate platform of restrictive measures was adopted in the Second International meeting, including, among other things, shorter workdays, prohibition of night work, prohibition of employment in hazardous occupations, prohibition of employment immediately before and after childbirth, and introduction of female inspectors in all industries that employ women (Sowerwine 1982). Because of the formation of socialist and labor parties all over Europe during the last two decades of the 19th century, organized labor was perceived to be a real threat to the existing system, and heads of states, in fear of massive agitation, started to comply with some of the demands.[1]

In the meantime, the German emperor invited 14 other Western European countries to attend a meeting in Berlin on the same matter.[2] It is interesting to note that the emperor also asked and received the endorsement of Pope Leo XII for the idea and aims of the conference (Johnston 1924). In that meeting, a series of resolutions was adopted, among them, the complete exclusion of women from mine work, as well as a series of measures on employment of children.

In the late 1890s, a Swiss proposal for a preparatory conference to discuss regulation of Sunday work and employment of women and children was circulated. Eventually, a technical conference of experts was held in Berne in 1905, attended by most European countries. At this conference, the delegates adopted a draft convention on the prohibition of night work for women (alternatively referred to as the introduction of 11-hour night's rest). Note that the basic ideas that underlined the agreement were not disputed; the discussions focused mainly on details. In the diplomatic conference that took place a year later, the agreement concerning night employment of women was ratified by all 14 states represented in the conference (and also by Japan, which was not represented but signed the agreement), taking precedence over other issues that had been discussed (Shotwell 1934).[3]

In the next stage, another international technical conference took place in 1913, drafting conventions regarding prohibition of employment of minors at night and establishing a maximum day of 10 hours for the employment of women and minors. Again, these two took precedence in a long list of issues. Although the outbreak of the war prevented their submission to a diplomatic conference scheduled for 1914, they were adopted after the war with the establishment of the International Labor Organization (ILO) in 1919.

A wide array of topics had been suggested on earlier occasions while discussing international legislation: regulating child labor, prohibiting Sunday work, shortening length of the workday for all workers, instituting relief measures in case of inability to work, improving safety conditions, and so forth. Out of this selection only night work of women and some safety regulations were incorporated into international agreement. Note that it was usually the case that women were considered together with children in reference to employment, although, in this case, the discussion was on regulation of women's employment alone.

The different groups that were involved in the formation of protective legislation for women had different motivations, and there is a variety of interpretations ranging from conspiracy to benevolence as to what drove the promotion and adoption of these (Boxer and Quataert 1987; Koven and Michel 1993). Thus, for instance, social reforms aimed at "improving" working conditions of the "weaker" groups have often been considered part of a conspiracy of male workers facing increasing competition to restrict women's employment (e.g., Kessler-Harris 1982). Another type of explanation viewed those regulations as one important component of a pronatalist population policy, in that it attempted to reduce infant mortality and to protect potential mothers' health (Franzoi 1987). It is important to note that some of the feminist organizations in England and in the United States objected to this kind of regulation for the fear that greater legal "protection" for women would make it more difficult for them to find employment. However, this view had no voice in the official world, and almost no resistance to protective legislation was brought at the international level.

All these interpretations shared the same underlying assumption; namely, that women constitute a different type of worker, and therefore, that their employment status could be determined on different terms than those of other workers, that is, men. Women's "maternal functions" and familial roles were defined as being in contradiction with their employment activities. Since the former was privileged over the latter, the state was encouraged to intervene in the form of specific legislation to make women's patterns of participation, that is, their "productive" activity, compatible with their reproductive roles. While acknowledging women's role as active participants in paid employment, the laws also highlighted their peculiar position in the public sphere.

The horrors of the war and fears of a possible class war, as in the Bolshevik revolution in Russia, set the agenda for both the League of Nations and the International Labor Organization (ILO), founded immediately after World War I. The ILO was assigned the mission to secure "world peace" via the promotion of "social justice." Improving working conditions of labor in the various countries was considered to be a major means for that purpose, and setting international labor standards was an integral part of the scheme. Thus, in order to overcome fears of international competition and to blunt social unrest, the ILO was invested with the authority to homogenize labor laws around the globe, all in the name of promoting "social justice" (Johnston 1924; Luard 1977).

"Social progress," with regard to women workers, was interpreted by the ILO as improving "the lot of working womanhood" by protecting them from the hazards and harshness that were involved in existing working conditions. Women's familial roles and maternal functions were the ones to be maintained and protected. In that sense, the creation of the ILO did not mark a departure from the prewar era. On the contrary, the establishment of a world organization with a broad mandate to instruct nation-states to modify their national legislation to be consistent with world models actually meant a broader legitimacy and wider endorsement of this model of women's roles and incorporation into the public sphere.

Note that in that period, when the ILO dealt with "rights" it meant the rights of organized labor, that is, the freedom of association and rights of collective bargaining. This right, granted to labor as a functional status group, was consistent with the corporatist nature of the organization: the ILO has a tripartite governance structure comprised of representatives of employers, workers, and governments of each member state. Some women's movements demanded individual rights—economic rights equal to men's—but those were not recognized by the ILO and were not incorporated into its activities (Berkovitch forthcoming; Miller 1994). "Rights" were not interpreted as equalizing the status of one group to another, and certainly "women" were not constructed as a category that *was* or *should* be equivalent to the category of male workers. It was a gendered category whose access to paid employment was and should be shaped by its functions in domestic spheres, that is, by its maternal roles.

Though equal pay was mentioned in the 1919 ILO charter, no resolutions on that matter were adopted until the late 1930s. All lobbying efforts made by international women's organizations, to take more concrete action in regards to "women's rights," failed. This is not to say that the ILO did not concern itself with "women's issues." The reverse holds true. Women's issues were on its agenda since its inception, but in the form of "women's protection." Indeed, the ILO expanded, broadened, and institutionalized working women's protection on many fronts. During all the inter-war years, it adopted a series of measures that included restrictions on employment in certain types of jobs (e.g., in the mines), at certain hours (at night), and at certain periods of women's life cycle (before and after childbirth).

Already in 1919, during the first conference of the ILO, the issues of women's employment at night and women's employment before and after childbirth were discussed, resulting in the adoption of related international conventions.[4] These issues were the only aspects of women's employment that the ILO would focus on, to be joined later by similar measures such as prohibition on women working in hazardous occupations. Maternity provisions and prohibition of certain types of work, their expansion or relaxation, were the only women's issues to be discussed and to produce international agreements. For example, although the prohibition specified by the 1906 Berne Convention, mentioned above, exempted small factories, "since the committee's point of view that night work for women is undesirable . . . this prohibition should be as far as possible universal" (League of Nations 1919:102). Consequently, the new conventions applied to all employers, regardless of size and number of employees. Thus, the view of women as "domestic creatures" was further institutionalized through the action taken by official world bodies. All measures taken to regulate women's employment were considered in light of their domestic roles and maternal functions. For example, the length of women's confinement before and after childbirth was to be determined, to a large degree, by the care for the health of the child. The exclusion of women from work that involves hazardous materials was related to their maternal roles and reproductive functions. The prohibition of night work was done for "placing women under better physiological conditions and also in better moral conditions, so that not only will she be a good worker but also a good mother" (League of Nations 1919:103).

It is important to note that this conception of working women was shared also by some international women's organizations, especially those associated with trade union movements. The First International Congress of Working Women, organized in 1919 by the Women's Trade Union League of America Federation, and attended by delegates from seventeen countries, demanded the "prohibition of the employment of women only in the trades which cannot be made healthy for women as potential mothers" (Waggaman 1919).

The economic crisis of the 1930s emphasized, even more strongly than before, the peculiar position of women as workers in the public sphere. As competition with men in the labor market became more acute, women's marital status became defined as an indicator of whether she was entitled to the "right to work." However, men's marital status was never considered to be relevant to his employment status. All over Europe, during the 1930s the employment of married women "was under attack." As reported by the ILO Yearbook for the years 1930 to 1937, wherever there was a "fall of demand for labor," a "campaign against double earning" was launched. However, whereas the term "attack on double earning" may seem gender neutral, the actual measures were very much gender specific. Many countries adopted measures that aimed at restricting or forbidding altogether the employment of married women and, at the same time, to cut their unemployment benefits. For example, as reported in Germany (ILO 1933:149–150),

A whole series of measures were adopted to divert women from economic activities in order to make more room for men, or to limit female employment as far as possible to work traditionally performed by women. . . . The employment of women in domestic work was promoted by inducing private households to employ more female domestic servants. With this end in view, domestic workers were excluded from unemployment insurance and a reduction was made in the rate of their contribution to invalid insurance.

Nowhere was there a distinction between married and unmarried men in respect to protection of jobs. There were no restrictions on employment of single men to protect the jobs of women who were the sole providers for their dependents. The "attack on double earning" was actually an offensive against the right to employment of married women alone. Various Catholic organizations joined the campaign against working mothers, and formed the "back to home" movement. They advocated "indirect measures that would make it unnecessary for the mother to go out to earn (higher family wages, family allowances, etc.) or would act as an inducement for her to devote herself to the home of her own free will" (ILO 1933:151. *See also* Anderson and Zinsser 1988).

However, an unexpected development was brought about by the economic depression. The notion that men and women should be paid equally for the same work began to be voiced by official and nonofficial world organizations. Within the ILO, it was framed within an instrumental context as a means to protect men's wages that were claimed to be affected by the competition with "low-paid women workers" (ILO 1931). As a consequence, equal pay and minimum wages for women were discussed as two alternative solutions for the problem of protecting male workers from the existence of a low-paid class of workers. Very few countries, however, passed equal pay measures in that period. Some adopted laws of minimum wages for women only. Other countries, such as in five Australian states, preferred another solution: a decision of the 1933 Court of Arbitration fixed the basic wage for women at 52 percent of that of men (Open Door International 1935). But the overwhelming majority preferred either administrative or legal measures that restricted the employment of married women altogether. It was only with the improvement of the economic situation that the objection to the employment of married women lessened and nation-states began to remove some of the restrictions and even to adopt measures that intended to support the extension of women's employment (ILO 1936–37).

Within the women's movements, the principle of equality in employment was framed within a wider context of equality and rights. This principle, however, was not the first priority within the movement as a whole (Berkovitch forthcoming). As in the previous period, socialist women and those connected to the trade union movement emphasized improving the working conditions of women over equality with men. But others, such as the International Council of Women and the International Suffrage Women's Association, put forward the notion of equality in all domains, including employment. Although this debate was clear already in 1919 during the Paris Conference that provided for the establishment of the ILO, and some delegates of women's organizations appeared before the Commission on International Labor Legislation advocating the principles of equality of opportunity and equal pay, [5] the majority emphasized the need of protection (Whittick 1979). Indeed, in the late 1920s, the idea to get the League of Nations to adopt an Equal Rights Treaty appeared and divided the women's movement (Miller 1994). However, the economic crisis gave impetus to the call for equality within the women's movement, and other women's organizations joined the campaign. They tried to get the ILO to adopt and promote the idea of the right to work as a fundamental and inalienable human right, also for women, married or unmarried (ILO 1933). That was done in a clear opposition to a proposal submitted in 1935 to the International Labor Conference by the Christian Associations of Young Workers, which recommended limiting women's work as a remedy for unemployment. Women's organizations, in turn, petitioned the Conference "to afford equal protection for the occupational interests of working men and women alike" (ILO

1935–36:188–89). Thus, the economic crisis intensified the call for equal employment rights within the women's movement, which was later endorsed by international governmental organizations as well.

In 1936, for the first time, the principle of equality between men and women in employment was pronounced by an international governmental agency, the Latin American Section of the ILO (1936). One year later, the International Labor Conference adopted a resolution stating that "it is for the best interests of society that women should enjoy full political, civil, and economic rights." However, the same resolution reiterated the importance of protective measures as a safeguard against "economic exploitation, including the safeguard of motherhood" (ILO 1937:146). In 1939, a similar resolution proclaimed the role of the ILO as not only protecting "our working womanhood" but also raising her position" (ILO 1939:95). It did not say that women's position in general should be equal to men's, but it does acknowledge again the principle of equal pay—all that, still without doubting the benefit of "protective" legislation for working women.

Post–World War II

With the end of World War II, the discourse that had shaped "women" and "women's issues" changed dramatically. To put it briefly, it appeared that conceptions of women's "natural" attachment to the family diminished and, with that, their distinctive character as such began to erode, at least to a certain extent. The old grounds for women's rights were dismissed. In the new ideology of "rights" and "equality" that invaded most major world institutions of the postwar era, "women" were transformed from a distinct category that required protection to a category of individuals that needed to be incorporated into all domains of public sphere. The 18th-century language of "natural rights" that served men to gain equality was revived under the notion of "human rights," enabling additional groups, women among them, to claim entitlement to equal protection and equal rights from their respective governments.

Putting women's rights on the agenda and assigning nation-states the task of making their respective women citizens into full members, must be considered in the wider context of processes that have taken place in the post–Second World War era: the changing nature of the world polity and the emergence of human rights on the international agenda. After the Second World War the world polity expanded dramatically. New governmental organizations were established—chief among them the United Nations (UN) and its associated agencies with a comprehensive mandate and a universal membership. There was also an outburst of nongovernmental organizations in every conceivable field (Boli and Thomas 1993), and the cooperation between official and the nonofficial organizations was enhanced. These activities resulted in a more coherent and rationalized world polity, with authority to regulate many more domains and with the organizational infrastructure to carry out the regulations.

The second relevant contemporary feature is that human rights emerged as a concern for the international community. Previously, states avoided granting the international community any responsibility for the rights of individuals with regard to a state's treatment of its own citizens (Armstrong 1982; Donnelly 1986).[6] As put succinctly by Farer (1988:93), "until the Second World War, most legal scholars and governments affirmed the general proposition, albeit not in so many words, that international law did not impede the natural right of each equal sovereign to be monstrous to his or her subjects." However, in response to the atrocities committed during the Second World War, the jurisdiction of the new international bodies was elaborated to supervise the ways in which nation-states treat their respective citizens. The UN and other official bodies adopted various human rights documents and created several bodies that were commissioned to monitor the implementation of the documents (Armstrong 1982; Donnelly 1986; Gibson 1991; Szego-Bokor 1978). In addition, the concern over maltreatment of persons in all parts of the world mobilized thousands of individuals from all over the world; a multiplicity of nongovernmental organizations played an active role in the emerging field of global human rights (Thoolen and Verstappen 1986).

That was the context in which the discourse about women's rights in general and women's economic rights in particular was shaped and transformed in the post–Second World War era. During that period, three primary changes took place. (1) The principle of "equality in employment" emerged and was widely endorsed. (2) The most accepted labor laws for women, protective legislation, declined. (3) The meaning of maternity protection changed, and was expanded and transformed into "parental leave." All three reflected and enhanced the new world model of women's participation in the public sphere: women's incorporation into employment should be compared and equalized to that of men (equal pay) and not be affected by their familial functions (i.e., the decline of protective legislation) that had been de-gendered (parental leave). Major world organizations, old and new, took the lead in this campaign, once promoted by women's organizations alone, encouraging nation-states to incorporate it in their national legislation. Already toward the end of the war, the shift in the ILO's position regarding women's employment was proclaimed. Though still framed within an instrumental context (in order to prevent competition among workers), a major document that outlined the employment policy for the postwar era recommended "that the guiding principle for the redistribution of war workers in the peacetime economy should be carried out on the principle of sex equality." (ILO 1944:95)

Yet, women's employment was still regarded differently than men's, with the principal line being that women should seek and should enjoy the right to employment only if necessary, and wise policy should eliminate this necessity.

> Many women who took up war work under pressures of circumstances or out of patriotism will wish to return to family life when the war is over. This tendency will be reinforced if full employment can be achieved, since the women in the household can then count on a family income large enough to make their earnings unnecessary. (ILO 1944: 96)

When the war ended and, in the decades to follow, family wages— that is, men's wages—were rarely mentioned in reference to women's right to employment and to equal returns. Men's economic rights became the reference point to which women should be elevated and, since men's marital status was not considered relevant to their employment status, neither should be women's. Both the ILO and the UN started to act in this direction. "The right of individuals to work without regard to sex and marital status" was incorporated in the first postwar ILO resolutions dealing with women's employment (ILO 1947a:591–603). Within the UN system, the Commission on the Status of Women,[7] already in its second session, discussed the issue of equal pay and, consequently, the Economic and Social Council adopted a resolution stating that discrimination "is not compatible with the dignity of woman" and that women shall benefit on the same basis "as men in regard to employment and remuneration" (UN 1947/48:604). This resolution was the result of an initiative taken by the women's section of the World Federation of Trade Unions, supported by four other women's international organizations.[8] It became clear that equality in employment, once hotly debated within the women's movement, ceased to be an internally contested issue. All parts were mobilized to this campaign (Berkovitch forthcoming).

In the years to come, major international documents that were adopted, and organizational activities that took place within the ILO and the UN, incorporated and enacted the principle of economic rights for women, imposing demands on nation-states to take action to ensure equal pay. This principle appeared in major UN documents (e.g., The Universal Declaration of Human Rights, article 23), and resolutions (e.g., UN 1947/ 48:604), as well as in measures proposed by technical experts (e.g., ILO 1946, 1949) and by state delegates and experts (ILO 1947b:74).

In this world campaign, "social progress" now is equated not only with improving working conditions and regulating employment relations, but with promoting the "rights of women" as well. Economic rights and the right to equal pay have been framed within a larger context of fundamental rights. Labor discrimination has been defined as a violation of the "dignity of woman." In the debates that arose around the various resolutions, it was only on technical ground that objections were raised with any support, focusing on difficulties involving implementation. No world forum of the postwar era would reject the principle of equality or object to the notion of women's rights.

With this changing world conception of both women's rights and the authority of global actors, the stage was set for formulating an international convention regarding women's economic rights. In 1951 the International Labor Conference adopted the Equal Remuneration Convention. It was the first time that an authoritative world organization adopted a document that focused exclusively on women's rights, conceptualizing it within the framework of equality and justice. Moreover, this document was in the form of a multilateral treaty that stated the intention that nation-states would take positive action in that direction. Thus, women's economic rights were the first women's issues to be put within the framework of "rights" and to be promoted by an international official body.

Whereas there was still some hesitation among member states, for fear that the principle of equal pay might lead to disadvantage in the world economy, this position was later challenged and wholly replaced by the idea that equality is a *prerequisite* to full economic development planned rationally and implemented bureaucratically. Under this logic, discrimination, and not egalitarian policy, would be defined as the costly strategy: "discrimination is not only morally unjust but also economically indefensible" (ILO 1958:404). The following years witnessed a proliferation of activities around women's employment, all framed in the context of the Convention. New studies and the collection of data were carried out in the name of "freedom and dignity" as well as "economic security" and "equal opportunities with men."

In 1958, the ILO adopted the Employment (Discrimination) Convention. Whereas the earlier Equal Remuneration Convention was concerned with eliminating sex distinctions with regard to pay only, this convention referred to all aspects of employment (promotion, vocational training, access to employment and to particular occupations, and terms and conditions of employment) and to discrimination based on various social criteria (race, color, sex, religion, political opinion, national extraction, or social origin), in addition to that of sex. On that occasion, in addition to supportive arguments regarding economic efficiency, a strong attack on discrimination was voiced: "unless we deal with it [discrimination] as we deal with murder, robbery, or any other crime, that is by punishing it, all our high-flown pronouncements exalting equality of opportunity or treatment are but as sounding brass and tinkling cymbal" (ILO 1958:407). A clear indicator of the legitimacy of the principle of equality expressed in these two conventions is the fact that they each received one of the highest rates of ratification of all ILO conventions. By 1985, both were ratified by more than 100 countries.[9]

PROTECTIVE LEGISLATION: "FALLING FROM GRACE"

As noted earlier, protective labor laws singled out women as workers whose patterns of and rights to employment are affected by the primordial/cultural functions attributed to women as a group. With the increasing emphasis on equality and on employment as a fundamental right, this type of protective legislation came under attack. It was posed as a contradiction to the request for equal opportunities for women in the labor market.

In the era after the First World War, only the Scandinavian countries rejected the notion of special legislation for women and adopted protective legislation based on the type of work and not the gender of the workers. It was not until the 1950 Asian Regional Conference of the ILO in Ceylon that the first doubts in an official international forum were expressed. However, besides occasional reference to the issue in the years that followed, little was done or said about the matter.

Things did start to change in 1975, the year that was proclaimed by the United Nations as the International Women's Year, and more so during the decade that followed—the Decade of Women. It was then that intense activity gave a major boost to the topic and brought it back to the agenda. The ILO, the major advocate of protection of women (and children) since its inception, changed its position radically and major efforts have been devoted to the revision and modification of its policy.

Thus, in the mid-1970s, all discussions relating to protective legislation began to be shaped by the discourse of equality between men and women. This discourse took away the ground for claims that women should be treated differently because of roles that are external to the labor market. In that spirit, the ILO, like most other international bodies in 1975, adopted a series of resolutions (e.g., Resolution Concerning Equal Status and Equal Opportunity for Women and Men in Occupation and Employment), drafted declarations, and initiated related studies (ILO 1977), all expressing the goal of equality and rights. In general, those documents cast doubt on protective legislation and expressed the need to rethink and to modify gender-based legislation. For example, the central document that was adopted during the UN's International Women's Year, the 1975 Declaration On Equality of Opportunity and Treatment for Women Workers, dismissed any notion of unique needs that women, qua women, might have. Other major documents, such as the 1979 UN Convention of Elimination of All Forms of Discrimination and those adopted in the 1985 Women's World Conference (Nairobi Forward Looking: Strategies for the Advancement of Women, 1985), discussed protective legislation explicitly in relation to all workers and not to women alone. This process of rethinking and revising gender-based legislation was not confined to the UN and the ILO; other international bodies, such as the European Economic Council, went through the same process as well (Docksey 1987; Vallance and Davies 1986).

Maternity Provisions: Transformation and Expansion

Whereas protective measures began to lose credence from the 1970s on, maternity provisions continued to expand. There has been a world trend in the globalization and expansion of maternity provisions in all international documents and national legislation. In this process, such provisions have been adopted by more countries, as well as broadened in scope and application where they already existed. Within the context of "equality," the meaning and purpose of this kind of policy has been transformed. Maternity protection was expanded through its reconceptualization as a necessary prerequisite for the implementation of the principle of equal treatment, and not for the well-being of newborns or for "the protection of motherhood." Though it is important to note that some still voiced the argument that these provisions are a necessity so that women would be able to fulfill their main responsibilities to their families, they became an absolute minority.

In the early 1950s, two international conventions and a recommendation concerning maternity protection were adopted by the International Labor Conference. The Maternity Convention from 1919 was replaced by an expanded and broader version, the 1952 Maternity Protection Convention, accompanied by a recommendation that provided for even wider benefits and protection. In addition, the 1952 Social Security Act (Minimum Standards), that dealt with maternity protection and benefits as part of a wider range of issues, was adopted (ILO 1952).

The transformation of the meaning attached to maternity provisions is manifested in the debates around the 1952 Maternity Convention. First, there was a great deal of consensus regarding the need to revise and expand the old provisions. At that point, the issue of "safeguarding . . . the future by protecting the physical health of the future citizen and workers" was still mentioned, but it was accompanied by the new aim of "basic and scientific principles of social justice" as the main motivation for the Convention (ILO 1952:340). Later, the former argument would disappear almost completely and the latter would prevail.

The provisions intended to facilitate the reentry of mothers to paid employment and to guarantee their ability to exercise what was defined as a basic right, the right to work: "protection of maternity is a logical consequence and a prerequisite of woman's right to work and to receive equal pay." The main arguments against the 1952 Convention were technical and concerned with whether it provided the best means to protect working mothers against discrimination. The context that framed the debate "social justice" and "national growth"—replaced the framework of "protection of mothers and children" that dominated the scene in previous years.

In the 1960s the changes that started to appear a decade earlier became more evident. These changes were expressed explicitly in a series of texts that marked a clear departure from previous conceptions (*see* ILO 1964:820–22). First, it was suggested that the Conference adopt a Recommendation on Women with Family Responsibilities to encourage governments to establish policies and services that would "enable women with family responsibilities who wish or have to work away from their homes to do so without being exposed to any discrimination" (ILO 1964:457). This recommendation was supplemented by four resolutions in which the emphasis was not only on "providing the services and facilities for the care of children," but on meeting "the needs and preferences of the women concerned . . . so that their possibilities of employment and promotion would not be hampered," and in facilitating "entry and re-entry into employment after an absence due to family responsibilities." [10]

In the mid-1960s, the common domestic division of labor began to be discussed as possibly detrimental to women's employment rights and, as such, became a concern for global actors. It was recognized, for the first time, that men have, in addition to their public roles, some family responsibilities; the home is not the exclusive domain of the woman: "We must get rid of the traditional view that women only are responsible for the personal care of the family, whereas men only are responsible for the economy of the family" (ILO 1965:386). Accordingly, in 1970, the UN Commission on the Status of Women initiated studies regarding "the need for an educational campaign to provide guidance on the sharing of responsibilities within the family" (UN 1970).

From then on, in principle, "working mothers" disappeared almost completely and, instead, the labor market became populated with "working parents."[11] The 1972 ILO resolution called for a coherent program of activities designed to promote equality with particular reference, among other things, to provide for facilities to enable *working parents* to meet their family responsibilities. This trend culminated in 1981 with the drafting of the Convention on Workers with Family Responsibilities. One of the most relevant characteristics of this convention is its gender-neutral language. It expresses the need to introduce measures in response to the specific needs of those workers who have family responsibilities and to equalize their position with those who do not have such responsibilities. The most novel measure to be introduced was parental leave: either parent should have the possibility of obtaining leave of absence for the purpose of taking care of children or another member of the immediate family. Whereas in the early 1970s it was an unknown phenomenon, by 1990 over 20 countries (all European) had established parental leave (and in most cases, with the same provisions and scope as maternal leave).

In the late 1960s, "development" emerged as a new issue on the world agenda, becoming prominent during the 1970s (Chabbott forthcoming). The intersection of "human rights" discourse and that of "development" reinforced the de-gendering process discussed above (Berkovitch 1995). Within the development framework, all workers are conceptualized as valuable resources; the economy cannot spare any worker. Therefore, all provisions must be taken so that family and maternity care will not prevent those who now "constitute a reservoir of untapped brain and hand power" to be added to the "skill and talent banks of the world" (ILO 1964:470).

The same idea was expressed in a variety of major documents of the late 1970s and 1980s. For example, the 1979 Convention on Elimination of Discrimination Against Women and the World Plan of Action adopted in the 1985 Women's World Conference (Nairobi Forward Looking Strategies) encouraged measures to provide for parental leave and advocated the principle of shared domestic responsibilities. In 1984 the European Parliament passed a resolution to adopt a Directive on Parental Leave (Vallance and Davies 1986), and the European Commission proposed a Directive on Parental Leave and Leave for Family Reasons, characterizing the sharing of family and occupational responsibilities as a *sine qua non* for the attainment of effective equality of opportunity in the labor market, to be promoted in particular by the provision of parental leave and child care facilities (Docksey

1987). The proposed directive, however, was vetoed over many years by the government of the United Kingdom. On the other hand, the idea reappeared in the Social Charter of 1989 as a recommendation on child care policy (Meehan 1993).

Thus, the main emphasis shifted to enable women to exercise their right as citizens to employment and to contribute to "the well-being of society" and for "greater national income." It was not their outside work that should not threaten their familial roles but rather their familial roles that should not hamper their equal access to employment and its benefits. In short, their opportunities in the public sphere should not depend on their position in the private one.

Concluding Comments

What are the rules that constitute women as active economic citizens? On what terms should women participate in paid employment? Are these terms and rules different than those for men? The answer to the latter is "yes." Women's route to citizenship has traveled a path that was different than men's; it has traveled along, in between, and across the line that divides our social world into the public and the private domains.

Investigation of global discourse produced by global actors highlights the changing construction of the rules that organize paid employment and women's rights to participate in it. Principles governing women's rights and access to the labor market have changed dramatically during the period under investigation. This transformation has taken place via the changing relation between women's attachment to the private sphere and their participation in the public sphere. Early on, the former shaped the latter; women's familial functions were thought of as being in jeopardy when they assumed public roles, and, therefore, women needed state protection to allow them to fulfill their assigned domestic roles. Thus, women's gender marked and shaped their access to paid employment. Later, women's public roles were conceived as having priority over the former. The assumptions that underlie more recent policies and legislation is that women's association with the domestic sphere should bear no relevance to their public participation. In that sense, women are constituted as "workers," similar to men, at least in principle. Thus, focusing on the transformation of women's citizenship and rights to participate in the public sphere, reveals the gendered nature of these concepts.

These changes have major consequences on national legislation in respect to state policy in regard to women's employment. It is mostly these activities, carried by global organizations, that are responsible to a large degree for the fact that most states have embodied the principle of equality in employment in their national legislation (Berkovitch 1994). Sixty-six percent of all countries have adopted such legislation that specifically refers to women's equality in employment. Moreover, the overwhelming majority (approximately 90 percent) has done so from 1960 on, with the intensification of world-level campaign and initiatives on the matter. In addition, many countries have revised (and continue to do so) their protective legislation, those laws that put restrictions on employment of women alone. In some cases, the restrictions have been relaxed, and in others, abolished altogether. Thus, exploration of world-level production of social constructs such as "women's rights" is an essential project for understanding the proliferation of citizenship rights and principles of equality and equity worldwide.

NOTES

1. Heads of states thought of improved working conditions as a factor that leads to diminishing productivity. Therefore, getting all industrialized naions to adopt such laws would keep international competition fair (see exchange of letters in Shotwell 1934, vol. 1, appendix I).

2. The following countries attended: Austria-Hungary, Belgium, Denmark, Great Britain, France, Germany, Holland, Italy, Luxembourg, Norway, Spain, Switzerland, and Sweden.

3. The only other convention that was adopted concerned the manufacturing, sale, and importation of matches containing white phosphorus, and was ratified by only seven of the countries.

4. 1919 Convention Concerning the Employment of Women before and After Childbirth (no. 3) and 1919 Convention Concerning Employment of Women during the Night (no. 4).

5. It was made possible after the long and repeated lobbying efforts on part of women's organizations. See Riegelman and Winslow 1990.

6. The one exception is the international movement for the abolition of slavery.

7. The Commission was established in 1946, first as a Sub-Commission of the Human Rights Commission. Later it became a full-status commission, one of the six such functional commissions of the Economic and Social Council (Reanda 1992).

8. The Co-Operative Women's Guild, Women's International Democratic Federation, The Liaison Committee of Women international organizations, and the Women's International League for Peace and Freedom.

9. Only eight ILO conventions (out of 157) have ever gained such high endorsement. The majority of conventions were ratified by about 40 countries (ILO 1984)

10. The four resolutions were: Women Workers in a Changing World; Economic and Social Advancement of Women in Developing Countries; Part-Time Employment; and Maternity Protection.

11. For example, see text of the 1972 Resolution Concerning Women Workers (International Labour Organization 1972). See also the Declaration on the Elimination of Discrimination against Women adopted in 1967 by the General Assembly of the UN.

REFERENCES

Anderson, Bonnie S., and Judith P. Zinsser. 1988. *History of Their Own.* Vol. II. New York: Harper and Row.

Armstrong, David. 1982. *The Rise of the International Organization: A Short History.* New York: St. Martin's Press.

Arnaud, A. J., and E. Kingdom. 1990. *Women's Rights and the Rights of Man.* Aberdeen: Aberdeen University Press.

Barrett, Deborah A. 1995. "Reproducing Persons as a Global Concern: The Making of an Institution." Dissertation, Stanford University.

Berkovitch, Nitza. Forthcoming. "The Emergence and Transformation of the International Women's Movement." In *World Polity Formation Since 1875: World Culture and International Non-Governmental Organizations,* edited by John Boli and George Thomas. Stanford: Stanford University Press.

Berkovitch, Nitza. 1994. "From Motherhood to Citizenship: The Worldwide Incorporation of Women into the Public Sphere in the Twentieth Century." Dissertation, Stanford University.

Berkovitch, Nitza. 1995. "Women and Development: Emergence of a Global Agenda." Paper presented at the Social Science History Association Meetings, Chicago.

Blanpain, Roger. 1977–1990. *International Encyclopedia of Labour and Industrial Relations.* Deventer: Klumer.

Boli, John, and George M. Thomas. Forthcoming. *World Polity Formation Since 1875: World Culture and International Non-Governmental Organizations.* Stanford: Stanford University Press.

Boli, John, and George M. Thomas. 1993. "The World Polity under Construction: A Century of International Non-Governmental Organization." Paper presented at the American Sociological Meetings, Miami.

Boli, John. 1987. "Human Rights or State Expansion? Cross-National Definitions of Constitutional Rights, 1870–1970." Pp. 133–149 in *Institutional Structure: Constituting State, Society, and the Individual,* edited by George Thomas, John W. Meyer, Francisco Ramirez, and John Boli. Newbury Park, CA: Sage.

Boxer, Marylin J., and Jean H. Quataert, eds. 1987. *Connecting Spheres: Women in the Western World, 1500 to the Present.* New York: Oxford University Press.

Chabbott, Collette. Forthcoming. "Defining Development: The Making of the International Development Field, 1945–1990."

Dietz, Mary G. 1987. "Context Is All: Feminism and Theories of Citizenship." *Daedalus* 116(4):1–24.

Docksey, Christopher. 1987. "The European Community and the Promotion of Equality." Pp. 1–23 in *Women, Employment, and European Equality Law,* edited by Christopher McCrudden. London: Eclipse.

Donnelly, Jack. 1986. "International Human Rights: A Regime Analysis." *International Organization* 40(3):599–642.

Falk, Richard. 1994. "The Making of Global Citizenship." Pp. 127–140 in *The Condition of Citizenship,* edited by Bart Van Steenbergen. Newbury Park, CA: Sage.

Farer, Tom J. 1988. "The UN and Human Rights: More than a Whimper, Less than a Roar." Pp. 95–138 in *United Nations, Divided World: The UN's Role in International Relations,* edited by Adam Roberts and Benedict Kingsbury. Oxford: Clarendon Press.

Finnemore, Martha. 1993. "International Organizations as Teachers of Norms: UNESCO and Science Policy." *International Organization* 47(4):565–598.

Follows, John W. 1951. *Antecedents of the International Labour Organization.* Oxford: Clarendon Press.

Franzoi, Barbara. 1987. "'. . . With the Wolf Always at the Door . . .': Women's Work in Domestic Industry in Britain and Germany." Pp. 146–155 in *Connecting Spheres: Women in the Western World, 1500 to the Present,* edited by Marilyn J. Boxer and Jean H. Quataert. New York: Oxford University Press.

Gibson, John. 1991. *International Organizations, Constitutional Law, and Human Rights.* New York: Praeger.

International Labour Organization. 1931, 1933, 1935–36, 1936, 1936–37, 1937, 1939. *Yearbook*. Geneva: International Labour Office.

International Labour Organization. 1944. *The Organization of Employment in the Transition from War to Peace*. Report III. International Labour Conference. 26th Session. Montreal: International Labour Office.

International Labour Organization. 1946. *Official Bulletin* 29(7). Geneva: International Labour Organization

International Labour Organization. 1947a. International Labour Conference. 30th session, *Record of Proceedings*.

International Labour Organization. 1947b. *Official Bulletin* 30(1). Geneva: International Labour Organization.

International Labour Organization. 1949. *Official Bulletin* 32(5). Geneva: International Labour Organization.

International Labour Organization. 1950. *Equal Remuneration for Men and Women Workers for Work of Equal Value*. Report V(1), International Labour Conference. 33rd session. Geneva: International Labour Office.

International Labour Organization. 1951. International Labour Conference. 34th session, *Record of Proceedings*. Geneva: International Labour Office.

International Labour Organization. 1952. International Labour Conference. 35th session, *Record of Proceedings*. Geneva: International Labour Office.

International Labour Organization. 1958. International Labour Conference. 42nd session, *Record of Proceedings*. Geneva: International Labour Office.

International Labour Organization. 1964. International Labour Conference. 48th session, *Record of Proceedings*. Geneva: International Labour Office.

International Labour Organization. 1965. International Labour Conference. 49th session, *Record of Proceedings*. Geneva: International Labour Office.

International Labour Organization. 1972. *Official Bulletin* 55(1). Geneva: International Labour office.

International Labour Organization. 1977. *Women at Work* (2). Geneva: International Labour Office.

International Labour Organization. 1984. International Labour Conference. 70th session, Report of the Director General. Geneva: International Labour Office.

Johnston, G.A. 1924. *International Social Progress: The Work of the International Labour Organization of the League of Nations*. London: George Allen & Unwin.

Kessler-Harris, Alice. 1982. *Out to Work*. Oxford: Oxford University Press.

Kingdom, Elizabeth. 1990. "Gendering Rights." Pp. 99–103 in *Women's Rights and the Rights of Man*. Aberdeen: Aberdeen University Press.

Koven, Seth, and Sonya Michel, eds. 1993. *Mothers of a New World: Maternalist Politics and the Origins of Welfare States*. New York: Routledge and Kegan Paul.

League of Nations. 1919. International Labour Conference. First Session, *Record of Proceedings*. Washington, DC: International Labour Office.

Lloyd, Genevieve. 1984. *The Man of Reason: 'Male' and 'Female' in Western Philosophy*. London: Methuen.

Luard, Evan. 1977. *International Agencies: The Emerging Framework of Interdependence*. Dobbs Ferry, NY: Oceana.

Marshall, T. H. 1950. *Citizenship and Social Class*. Cambridge: Cambridge University Press.

Marshall, T. H. 1973. *Class, Citizenship, and Social Development*. New York: Doubleday.

McNeely, Connie L. 1993. "The Determination of Statehood in the United Nations, 1945–1985." *Research in Political Sociology* 6:1–38.

Meehan, E. 1993. *Citizenship and the European Community*. London: Sage.

Meyer, John W. 1980. "The World Polity and the Authority of the Nation State." Pp.

109–137, in *Studies of the Modern World System*, edited by Albert J. Bergesen. New York: Academic Press.

Meyer, John W. 1987. "World Polity and the Authority of the Nation-State." Pp. 41–70 in *Institutional Structure: Constituting State, Society, and the Individual*, edited by G. Thomas, J. W. Meyer, F. Ramirez, and J. Boli. Newbury Park, CA: Sage.

Meyer, John W. 1994. "Rationalized Environments." Pp. 28–54 in *Institutional Environments and Organizations*, edited by W.R. Scott and J. W. Meyer. Thousand Oaks, CA: Sage.

Meyer, John W., Francisco Ramirez, Henry Walker, Nancy Langton, and Sorca O'Connor. 1987. "The State and the Institutionalization of the Relations Between Women and Children." In *Feminism, Children and the New Families*, edited by S. Dornbusch and M. Strober. New York: Guilford Press.

Miller, Carol. 1994. "'Geneva—the Key to Equality.'" *Women's History Review* 3(2):219–245.

Nicholson, Linda. 1984. "Feminist Theory: The Private and the Public." Pp. 221–230 in *Beyond Domination: New Perspectives on Women and Philosophy*, edited by Carol Gould. New Brunswick, NJ: Rowman and Allanheld.

Nicholson, Linda. J. 1986. *Gender and History: The Limits of Social Theory in the Age of the Family*. New York: Columbia University Press.

Okin, Susan M. 1989. *Justice, Gender, and the Family*. New York: Basic Books.

Olsen, Frances. 1984. "Statutory Rape: A Feminist Critique of Rights Analysis." *Texas Law Review* 63: 387.

Open Door International. 1935. *Proceedings of the 4th Conference*, Copenhagen.

Pateman, Carole. 1988. *The Sexual Contract*. Stanford: Stanford University Press.

Pateman, Carole. 1989. *The Disorder of Women*. Stanford: Stanford University Press.

Price, John. 1945. *The International Labour Movement*. London: Oxford University Press.

Ramirez, Francisco O. 1987. "Institutional Analysis." Pp. 316–328 in *Institutional Structure: Constituting State, Society, and the Individual*, edited by George Thomas, John. W. Meyer, Francisco Ramirez and John. Boli. Newbury Park, CA: Sage.

Ramirez, Francisco O., Yasemin Soysal, and Suzanne E. Shanahan. 1994. *The Changing Logic of Political Citizenship: Cross National Acquisition of Women's Suffrage Rights 1890–1990*. Paper presented at the annual meetings of American Sociological Association.

Reanda, Laura. 1992. "The Commission on the Status of Women." Pp. 265–303 in *The United Nations and Human Rights: Critical Appraisal*, edited by Philip Alston. Oxford: Clarendon Press.

Riegelman Lubin, Carol, and Anne Winslow. 1990. *Social Justice for Women: The International Labor Organization and Women*. Durham and London: Duke University Press

Rose, Nikolas. 1987. "Beyond the Public/Private Division: Law, Power and the Family." *Journal of Law and Society* 14(1):61–76.

Shotwell, James. 1934. *The Origin of the International Labor Organization*. New York: Columbia University Press.

Skalar, Kathryn K. 1993. "The Historical Foundations of Women's Power in the Creation of the American Welfare State." Pp. 43–93 in *Mothers of a New World: Maternalist Politics and the Origins of Welfare States, 1830–1930*, edited by Seth Koven and Sonya Michel. New York: Routledge and Kegan Paul.

Sowerwine, Charles. 1982. *Sisters or Citizens? Women and Socialism in France since 1876*. Cambridge: Cambridge University Press.

Steenbergen, Bart van. 1994. "Towards a Global Ecological Citizen." Pp. 141–152 in *The Condition of Citizenship*, edited by Bart Van Steenbergen. Newbury Park, CA: Sage.

Strang, David, and Patricia M. Y. Chang. 1993. "The International Labour Organization and the Welfare State: Institutional Effects on National Welfare Spending, 1960–1980." *International Organization* 47(2):235–263.

Szego-Bokor, Hanna. 1978. *The Role of the United Nations in International Legislation.* Amsterdam: North Holland.

Thomas, George M., John W. Meyer, Francisco O. Ramirez, and John Boli. 1987. *Institutional Structure: Constituting State, Society, and the Individual.* Newbury Park, CA: Sage.

Thomas, George M., and Pat Lauderdale. 1987. "World Polity Sources of National Welfare and Land Reform." Pp. 198–214 in *Institutional Structure: Constituting State, Society, and the Individual,* edited by G. Thomas, J. W. Meyer, F. Ramirez, and J. Boli. Newbury Park, CA: Sage.

Thoolen, Hans, and Berth Verstappen. 1986. *Human Rights Mission: A Study of Fact Finding Practice of Non-Governmental Organizations.* Boston: Martinus Nijhoff.

Thornton, Margaret. 1991. "The Public/Private Dichotomy: Gendered and Discriminatory." *Journal of Law and Society* 18(4):448–463.

Turner, Bryan S. 1994. "Post Modern Culture/Modern Citizens." Pp. 153–168 in *The Condition of Citizenship,* edited by Bart Van Steenbergen. Newbury Park, CA: Sage.

Turner, Bryan S. 1990. "Outline of a Theory of Citizenship." *Sociology* 24:189–127.

United Nations. 1947/48. *United Nations Yearbook.* New York: Columbia University with the United Nations.

United Nations. 1970. *United Nations Yearbook.* New York: Columbia University with the United Nations.

Vallance, Elizabeth, and Elizabeth Davies. 1986. *Women of Europe: Women MEPs and Equality Policy.* Cambridge: Cambridge University Press.

Vogel, Ursula. 1994. "Marriage and the Boundaries of Citizenship." Pp. 76–89 in *The Condition of Citizenship,* edited by Bart Van Steenbergen. Newbury Park, CA: Sage.

Waggaman, Mary T. 1919. "First International Congress of Working Women, Washington, DC." *Monthly Labor Review* 9(6):280–298.

Whittick, Arnold. 1979. *Woman into Citizen.* Santa Barbara, CA: ABC-Clio.

5 CITIZENSHIP IN THE CURRICULUM

THE GLOBALIZATION OF CIVICS EDUCATION IN ANGLOPHONE AFRICA, 1955–1995

Mary Rauner

In the modern world of nation-states, citizenship defines who is and who is not a member in a society and who receives the rights and obligations associated with membership. Historically, the status of citizenship in the modern state was confined to men who participated in the deliberation and exercise of power. Over time, citizenship has expanded, both in scope (including civil, political, and social rights) and in membership (including populations such as nonproperty-owning men, women, and children) (Marshall 1964; Ramirez 1989). Today, citizenship extends across societies (Barbalet 1988) and even transcends the limits of national borders (Soysal 1994).

A major way that lessons in citizenship are transmitted is through the formal education system and much sociological theory emphasizes this process (Dreeben 1974; Inkeles and Smith 1974; Parsons 1959). Civics education, in particular, is the discipline that most directly embodies what children need to know to be active participants in their society. While there is general consensus that the main goal of civics education is to prepare people for active citizenship, the actual content of civics education is subject to debate. This analysis emphasizes the content of civics education because it reflects what a country's political and educational leaders consider valuable to teach their future citizens.

From a functionalist perspective, the content of civics education material is a reflection of national issues and characteristics such as the year of independence or the type of polity. For example, a country with a good human rights record is more likely to include lessons on human rights than a country with a bad human rights record. Institutionalist theory provides an alternative approach, maintaining that the content of education material is strongly influenced by a model of education which is less reflective of any one polity and more derivative of a theorized polity or cultural framework which is developed and legitimated on a worldwide level (McNeely 1995; Meyer 1987; Ramirez and Boli 1987; Soysal 1994).

I continue in this institutionalist tradition by exploring, through the study of civics education material, the incorporation of the concepts of citizenship and globalism into what institutionalists call "global culture." Within the broad rubric of civics education, I focus on the coverage and elaboration of the concepts of citizenship and human rights and the trend toward regionalization and globalization. Specifically, I analyze civics education material in Anglophone African countries from the post–World War II era until 1995. Anglophone Africa, consisting of countries with similar colonial legacies, is a regional example of what I argue is a global trend.

Theoretical Background

I assert that by 1955, a worldwide model of society was developed. Over the next 40 years, the worldwide model of society became increasingly well-defined and moved from a national model of society to a postnational model of society, which transcends the boundaries of the nation-state (Soysal 1994). Based on various national and transnational characteristics, certain societies historically conform to either the national or postnational model of society. However, over time, I expect to find a worldwide trend toward the postnational model. I suggest that this shift was facilitated by international institutional carriers which influence a country's vision of society (Berger, Berger, and Kellner 1974). As a postnational model of society emerges over time, national educational policy-makers are influenced by this model, which eventually gets reflected in civics education material. Therefore, if the postnational model of society emphasizes global citizenship and human rights, civics education material will also emphasize these concepts.

An extensive institutionalist literature focuses specifically on explaining national-level educational change as driven by a worldwide educational model (Ramirez and Meyer 1992). In these studies, it is argued that the development and institutionalization of mass education itself is a distinctive global project (Meyer, Kamens, and Benavot 1992). Some studies document the global trends of the national-level development and expansion of compulsory education (Ramirez and Meyer 1992), standardized educational grade sequencing (Benavot and Riddle 1988), and the expansion of women's share of higher education (Bradley and Ramirez in press). Another study shows the worldwide decline of specialized vocational education (Benavot 1983). Focusing specifically on curriculum, recent institutionalist studies found considerable and increasing homogeneity in general curricular outlines throughout the world (Meyer et al. 1992; Wong 1991). This analysis complements research on the increasing homogeneity of a standardized curriculum by exploring the globalization of the actual content of civics material throughout Anglophone Africa.

Drawing on the work of Soysal (1994), I briefly describe the national and postnational models of society along three dimensions: time of domination in the world model; territorial limitations; and source of legitimation.

In the national model of society, a country looks inward and is concerned with national development and the strengthening of itself as an independent nation-state. This model was the dominant model of society after the completion of World War II, when countries began to restore their economies and reclaim their national identities. This was a prominent agenda item for any country, and was especially so for African countries as they became independent from their former colonizers. The postnational model of society became dominant in more recent years, fostered by an increased global interdependence and a more rapid and efficient transference of information through sources such as international organizations.

The national model is nation-state bounded, connecting the individual with the state. In this model, a country has jurisdiction over people within its borders (Soysal 1994). In the currently dominant postnational model, the status of citizenship is less restricted, making it possible, for example, to have legal citizenship in more than one state or to be a citizen in one country while receiving rights and privileges in another.

In the national model of society, the nation is the source of legitimation, meaning that the discourse surrounding national-level decisions emphasizes acting in the best interest of the nation and its citizens. Decisions made within a country that adheres to a postnational model are legitimate if the discussions surrounding them focus on benefitting people in general, in addition to citizens of a particular nation-state.

MODELS OF CIVICS EDUCATION

As illustrated in Table 5–1, civics education in societies which conform to the national model of society is likely to solely emphasize internal civics issues (for example, what it means to be a citizen of Kenya), and the lessons would be very patriotic in nature (for example, an emphasis on the meaning behind various national symbols such as the national flag, anthem, and seal). This national model of society emphasizes the history, structure, and functions of the government and elements of civic pride such as unique country characteristics. The concept of citizenship in this model emphasizes national membership in a specific country, and human rights refers to the rights and obligations that come with being a citizen of that particular nation.

Table 5–1. Civics Education in National and Postnational Models of Society

	National Model of Society	Postnational Model of Society
General Nature of Civics Lessons	Patriotic (national seal, anthem, flag)	Focus on the region / the world
	Internal (history, structure, and function of local and national government)	Focus on regional and international organizations (nationalism remains)
Citizenship	Citizen of a nation	Citizen of a region and the world (citizen of a nation remains)
Human Rights	Rights and obligations are based on national-level definitions of membership	Human rights and obligations are based on regional and global-level definitions of membership (national-level definitions remain)
	Nature of rights and obligations are based on national level issues	Nature of rights and obligations are based on regional and global-level issues (national-level issues remain)

Within this model there is no "imagined community" beyond the nation-state (Anderson 1983).

In countries that adhere to a postnational model of society, civics education material would begin to emphasize extra-national perspectives, while maintaining some elements of the national model. In addition to being a citizen of a particular society, individuals in the postnational model are "granted" citizenship status based on their status as human beings. Civics material would begin to include historically excluded groups, such as women, children, ethnic minorities, and immigrants in their discussion of citizens, because the notion of citizenship would be linked not only to national membership but also to the notion of transnational personhood. The nature of the rights and obligations granted to these citizens would be based on regional or global issues, such as protecting the world's environment and demanding human rights for people throughout the world, regardless of national origin. I also expect to find a stronger emphasis on regional and global-level political structures in the postnational model, such as an explanation of the structure and functions of the Organization of African Unity (OAU) and the United Nations (UN). These structures are irrelevant in a world made up exclusively of territorially bounded nation-states and their citizens. In a changing world which emphasizes the increasingly transnational status of the person, this structure acquires greater relevance.

Civics Education Research

A vast and theoretically diverse literature exists on the relationship between general or civics education and civic attitudes, values, and actions. Much of this work attempts to explain the connection between education and civics-related outcomes through school-based socialization processes (Dahl 1992; Ikelov 1991; Inkeles and Smith 1974; Lipset 1959; McMahan and Leaphart 1993; Torney-Purta and Schwille 1986).

There is also a substantial literature devoted to prescriptions of what should be included in civics education curriculum. Basic goals considered important include (1) developing an understanding of and a value for democratic principles; (2) understanding citizen rights and responsibilities; (3) developing individual political efficacy; (4) understanding of symbolism in democracy; and (5) developing an awareness of alternative views and the recognition of their validity (ASESP 1994; Banks 1990; CCE 1994; Gandal and Finn 1995). A major change in the most recent generation of civics curriculum is the movement toward a focus on global citizenship and global responsibility, including the understanding of the international system and the knowledge of the implications of the universal declaration of human rights (Reardon 1994).

Other research explores how and why curricular changes occur (Apple and Christian-Smith 1991; Goodson 1988); however, some of these studies focus less on the relationship between societal and worldwide influences, and more on the ways in which countries, specifically those which are "less-developed," are influenced by more powerful countries.

Studies that document historical or even current content of civics education are scarce. What does exist is country-specific (ASESP 1993a) or regional (Merryfield and Muyanda-Mutebi 1991; Reimers 1994) in scope. These studies, while informative, are restricted to a single time-period, and issues of curricular change and stability over time can not be adequately addressed without a longitudinal approach. This research project is both longitudinal and cross-national, covering the period from 1955–1995 and including countries in Anglophone Africa.

Much of the related literature discusses the direction of influence as moving from the center (powerful, "developed" countries) to the periphery (less-powerful and "less-developed" countries) (Altbach 1991). During colonial times, curricula were imported directly from the colonizing country (Altbach 1987; Farrell and Heyneman 1988). In more recent years, the influence may be less direct, but it is still strong. Although curriculum may be developed internally, limited resources may require the ministries of education to choose from existing material in other countries, to modify material from other countries to fit local conditions, or to publish material in existing publishing houses, usually located outside the country (Altbach and Kelly 1988). Even when a country has the resources to develop and publish its own material, the "international knowledge network" ensures the continuation of external influence (Altbach 1987). Sources of influence through this "network" include educational development projects, educational research, and the work of international consultants, often funded by influential international organizations such as the World Bank and the United Nations. Furthermore, because many top-level educational decision makers were educated in Western schools, it is likely that they maintain links with these knowledge bases through colleagues in other countries, attendance at international conferences, and access to scholarly journals (Altbach 1991). Institutionalist approaches also stress external influences. From a broader structural framework, they argue that global models of the nation-state have developed and influenced national-level decision making about the content and form of schooling (Frank, Schofer, and Torres 1994; Meyer et al. 1992).

Thus, I expect that the content of civics curriculum will be affected by the worldwide transition from a national model of society toward a postnational model of society. Specifically, I expect that the concepts of citizenship and human rights will take on an increasingly global focus. This leads to a basic hypothesis with more specific postulates regarding civics education in Anglophone African countries: From 1955–1995, there was a movement in Anglophone Africa toward a postnational model of society in civics education. Evidence of the postnational model is more likely to be found in civics education material from the more recent period (1985–1995).

(a)   The concept of citizenship during the more recent time period is more likely to include traditionally excluded groups such as women, children, immigrants, and ethnic minorities. Citizenship will begin to be based on the concept of global citizenship in addition to the old model of national citizenship.

(b)   Civics education material in the more recent time period is more likely to emphasize regional and global issues and organizations than in the earlier time period.

(c)   From 1985–1995, civics education material is more likely to describe rights and obligations as granted to individuals based in part on their status as human beings than solely as citizens of a particular nation. The nature of rights and obligations is based on regional or global issues in addition to national level issues.

This post–World War II era is the beginning point for this research because it is a time of dramatic global change. A new world order was established and many colonized countries, mainly in Africa, became independent and subsequently more connected to and influenced by the international community. The years following the Second World War were also a time of educational revolution, when educational enrollments sharply increased (Meyer et al. 1992) and educational systems became the most legitimate source of cultural capital throughout the world. In addition, the organizational structure and ideological arms of education systems began to look strikingly similar the world over (Ramirez forthcoming). This period also marked a dramatic improvement in channels of communication and transportation, which fostered the transmission of these changes.

Data Description and Methodology

Civics education material for a total of 14 Anglophone African countries were obtained at the library of the African Social and Environmental Studies Programme (ASESP) in Kenya.[1] Several criteria determined the collection of this civics education material. For each country where data were available, at least one document was gathered from each of two time periods

(1955–1965 and 1985–1995). In selecting specific types of material for analyses, priority was given to (1) student textbooks (preferably more than 20 pages in length, as shorter documents may indicate supplementary material and not a principle text), followed by (2) student workbooks, (3) textbooks (teacher's versions), (4) syllabi, (5) curricula, and (6) curricular frameworks.

Not all countries teach a discipline specifically called "civics," so to gather only "civics" material would limit considerably the number of cases for analysis. Instead, all material which covered the issues of human rights and citizenship were collected. Priority was given to material that fell under the disciplinary categories of (1) civics, (2) social studies, (3) politics (preferably with a civics-oriented subtitle such as "the citizen and society"), (4) government, (5) history, and (6) general studies. Civics education content is most likely to be found under one or more of these categories. To measure the emphasis on and the content of the concepts of citizenship, human rights, and regional/global issues over time, I examine the following: (a) the tables of content in textbooks; (b) the major and minor headings in syllabi and curricula; (c) the objectives in textbooks; and (d) the general objectives or specific grade level objectives in syllabi or curricula.

Material was collected for grades equivalent to the 10th grade in the United States education system. This level is targeted because it is during this stage of the educational process that students' comprehension levels are higher and the issues highlighted in this study are likely to be covered in most depth (Oppenheim and Torney 1974; Torney-Purta 1992). Of the 14 countries included in this study, I analyze eight constant cases (Ghana, Kenya, Malawi, Nigeria, Sierra Leone, Swaziland, Tanzania, and Uganda) for the analysis of the table of contents and four constant cases (Kenya, Malawi, Nigeria, and Tanzania) for the analysis of the civics education objectives.

The table of contents and the objectives of the material are analyzed in two ways. The first set of analyses includes the material from all Anglophone African countries for which I have data, and the second set of analyses includes only the constant cases, cases with data from both time periods. This longitudinal analysis of Anglophone African civics education material takes two forms. The first measures the change in emphasis on the concepts of citizenship, human rights, and global and regional issues. The second measures the ways in which these issues are discussed.

For both of these sets of analyses, I calculate the percentage of emphasis on the following concepts—citizenship, human rights, and regional/global issues—for both time periods. Two percentages (measures of topical emphasis) are calculated for each set of analyses: (a) the percent of countries that refer to each issue, for example the percent of countries that refer to human rights;[2] and (b) the emphasis of each issue relative to all key issues covered in the material, for example, the percent of all issues covered that address human rights.[3]

To complement the analysis which measures the level of emphasis placed on specific concepts in civics educational material, an analysis of the context within which these various issues are discussed is also undertaken. This analysis measures the ways in which the specific topics of citizenship, human rights and global/regional issues are covered in educational material.

FINDINGS

Findings from the analysis of civics material from Anglophone African countries offer insights into change over time in civics education in one part of the world (*see* Tables 5–2 and 5–3). For each major theme (regional and global issues, citizenship, and rights and responsibilities), I discuss the changes both in the extent to which each theme is emphasized and in the ways in which these themes are discussed. I then review the institutional carriers which I argue helped foster these changes.

Regional/Global Issues

The most dramatic change of topical emphasis was the increase in regional and global issues. In the analysis of both the tables of contents and the objectives, regional and global issues were emphasized considerably more in the more recent time period (1985–1995) than in the first time period (1955–1965). These findings are consistent with the expectation that there would be an increase in emphasis on regional and global issues and organizations.

In terms of context, regional issues in the earlier time period consisted mainly of the geography of bordering nations. In the more recent years, the emphasis on regional geography increases and the discussion becomes more elaborated, including issues of the history, culture, people, and civilization of the region, as well as the relationship between the country and the region in which it is located. There is also more discussion of regional organizations, such as the Organization of African Unity (OAU), in the more recent time period.

The emphasis on global issues in Anglophone African educational material also increased dramatically over the time period covered in this analysis. Early on, global issues were limited to a discussion of the geography of the world and of the organizational structure and functions of the United Nations (UN). In more current education material, there is a more elaborate discussion of the UN, and coverage of other international organizations such as the World Bank begin to be included. There is also an increase in discussion of global-level issues such as population and the environment, as well as the international systems of justice, banking, agriculture, communication, and transportation.

CITIZENSHIP

In the analysis of the constant cases (eight for the tables of contents and four for the objectives), the emphasis placed on citizenship remained the same or increased slightly from 1955–1995. In the evaluation of material from all Anglophone African countries in the analysis, the emphasis on citizenship remained the same or decreased slightly over time. These findings suggest that the emphasis on citizenship has not changed much over time and run contrary to the expected increase in emphasis on citizenship. However, a more contextual analysis sheds light on what initially appears to be a static topic and suggests some qualitative changes in the nature of citizenship.

In the earlier materials, there were no explicit definitions about who is included in the citizenry; for example, "a citizen is a person who lives in a certain country" (Nyasulu and Potter 1966), or "all citizens have rights and duties" (Meienberg 1966). In more recent years, more refined definitions of citizens are included. In one text, an entire section was devoted to explaining that there are two ways of becoming a citizen, by birth and by registration (Murapa and Sithole 1986).

As expected, there was an increase over time in the inclusion of women, ethnic minorities and other traditionally excluded groups in the citizenry. In one text from the current time period, students are identified as "citizens of their school" (Lucan 1969), as opposed to the earlier version in which students are considered part of a future adult citizenry. Girls and women also begin to be explicitly included in the citizenry, as well as people with various socioeconomic levels, languages, and religious beliefs (Murapa and Sithole 1986). In one case, the emphasis on equality and inclusion is especially visible in the description of gaining citizenship by birth. The book explains that citizenship by birth only follows the father but not the mother. It then proceeds to explain that this law is discriminatory toward women. This illustrates a movement away from privileging the nation-state (the law), toward privileging a more universalistic assumption (that men and women should be granted equal treatment).

Rights and Responsibilities

The results of the evaluation of the emphasis on rights and responsibilities were varied. In the analysis of the tables of contents, the emphasis remained the same or increased, while the emphasis in the analysis of the objectives decreased slightly over time. Again, it is the contextual analysis which provides the most helpful understanding of the longitudinal changes.

In the earlier time period (1955–1965), the types of human rights and responsibilities had a more national flavor. Examples include the rights to public services (laws, government, administration) and social services (education, health, water, housing, and food) and the obligations to vote, uphold the law, pay taxes, and be loyal to one's country. In the more recent time period, more regional and global oriented rights and obligations begin to be added to the national ones. In these more recent materials, there are more frequent references to human rights as being "universal" and an increase in the discussion of the UN's Declaration of Human Rights. There is also an increased focus on rights and responsibilities that are distinctly "transnational," such as the universal right to "leave any country including his (sic) own and return to his country" and the right to live in peace, as well as transnational responsibilities such as preserving the global environment (Clarken and O'Mara 1987). Thus, while the earlier civics education material reflected a vision of an exclusively national citizenship, the more recent focus resonates with the emergent global emphasis on peace and the environment.

In the more recent time period, a discussion also emerges about extending rights and obligations to children as "citizens of their school" with the rights to shelter, education, protection, and friendship and the obligations to respect teachers, behave well, and pay attention to lessons. Children are also considered "citizens of their community," which brings the rights to use its facilities, share its activities, get protection, and make friends, and the obligations to be respectful to elders, be cooperative, and show consideration for others (Lucan 1969).

The basis upon which rights and obligations are extended to individuals also changes over time. In the earlier time period, the discussion about granting rights and obligations to citizens was based on their status as national citizens. In the more recent time period (1985–1995), the discussion of national-level citizenship remains, but there is some discussion of rights being granted not just to citizens, but to all people, based on their status as human beings. For example, one sentence in the statement of objectives from a Kenyan textbook states that Kenyans should be alerted to their "rights, duties and responsibilities not only as Kenyans, but as *citizens of Africa and the world*" (Singh 1988, emphasis added). Falling under the broader category of citizenship, discussions of national symbols such as the flag and the national anthem are emphasized in both the earlier time period as well as in the more recent time period. World, regional, and subnational notions of citizenship are added to but do not replace national citizenship ideas.

Table 5–2. Results from Anglophone African Civics Education Data: Tables of Contents

| | Constant Cases: Both Time Periods Ghana, Kenya, Malawi, Nigeria, Sierra Leone, Swaziland, Tanzania, Uganda (N=8) | | | | Total Cases | | | |
| | Percent of countries that refer to each concept | | Emphasis of each issue relative to all issues covered | | Percent of countries that refer to each concept | | Emphasis of each issue relative to all issues covered | |
	Time 1	Time 2	Time 1	Time 2	Time 1	Time 2	Time 1	Time 2
Regional (Africa)	44%	89%	10%	31%	44%	91%	10%	25%
Global/International Perspective	56%	100%	11%	34%	56%	98%	14%	36%
Citizenship	33%	38%	15%	18%	33%	29%	15%	10%
Rights/Responsibilities	33%	44%	16%	18%	33%	41%	16%	16%

Table 5–3. Results from Anglophone African Civics Education Data: Objectives

	Constant Cases: Both Time Periods Kenya, Malawi, Nigeria, Tanzania (N=4)				Total Cases			
	Percent of countries that refer to each concept		Emphasis of each issue relative to all issues covered		Percent of countries that refer to each concept		Emphasis of each issue relative to all issues covered	
	Time 1	Time 2	Time 1	Time 2	Time 1	Time 2	Time 1	Time 2
Regional (Africa)	20%	75%	50%	60%	29%	80%	50%	68%
Global/International Perspective	40%	100%	15%	27%	57%	83%	15%	25%
Citizenship	60%	60%	12%	12%	57%	50%	13%	12%
Rights/Responsibilities	40%	40%	18%	14%	43%	33%	17%	15%

Institutional carriers, such as international organizations, serve as transmitting agencies for modern consciousness (Berger et al. 1974). In the case of Anglophone African civics education, these organizations are national (the British Ministry of Overseas Development and the United States Agency for International Development—USAID), regional (the African Social and Environmental Studies Programme—ASESP), and international (the United Nations Educational, Scientific, and Cultural Organization—UNESCO). I suggest that information is transmitted through these organizations to other countries in the form of international conferences. When countries are participants in conferences or members of these organizations, the likelihood increases that their version of civics education will mirror that of the current world model. I expect, then, that as Anglophone African countries become increasingly linked to international organizations which articulate the postnational model of society, their civics education material will increasingly reflect this discourse.

Conferences specifically addressing Anglophone African civics education are few in number, but date back to 1968. The discourse surrounding civics education at these conferences changed over time from a national model to a postnational model of civics education. Earlier conferences focused on the child's relationship to its society (ASESP 1993b), while more recent conferences focus on more global issues, such as democracy, human rights, and world peace (NCSS 1994).

The first conference on civics education in Anglophone Africa was held in Mombasa, Kenya in 1968. This conference was developed out of a resolution from an earlier conference held in Oxford on curriculum development for Africa. The motivation behind an exclusive civics focus was that educational infrastructural and access issues had been addressed at previous conferences, whereas education for citizenship development was neglected. It was attended by African educators and representatives from educational organizations and donor agencies from the United States, Britain, and Denmark. The conference focused on articulating a need for a new approach to the teaching of social studies in African primary schools and the objectives of social science teaching. Discussion of the actual content of social studies was very "national" in orientation, with the goal of preparing citizens who are "informed, reflective, concerned, and who participate in shaping a better future for their society and for themselves" (ASESP 1993b).

The African Social and Environmental Studies Program (ASESP) was established as an organizational outcome of the conference. Its original mandate was to facilitate and promote the creation and implementation of social studies education curricula. Since its inception in 1968, the ASESP has organized conferences, consulted with ministries of education on civics education, and written reports and curricular frameworks for countries throughout Africa. The ASESP claims that its approach has now been largely adopted by all its member countries (NCSS 1994), illustrating its role as a major institutional carrier for information on civics education throughout Anglophone Africa. Over time, it has focused increasingly on issues reflecting a postnational model of civics education, currently describing the purpose of social studies as "helping young people to develop the ability to make informed and reasoned decisions for the public good as citizens of a culturally varied, democratic society in an increasingly interdependent world" (NCSS 1994).

Almost 25 years after the Mombasa conference, a United States organization, the National Council for the Social Studies (NCSS), held its Third International Social Studies Conference in Africa (Nairobi, Kenya). In a dramatic change from the earlier conference mentioned here, the areas of concern in Nairobi centered on more global oriented issues, such as (1) promotion and managing the growth of democracy; (2) human rights, peace, and good governance during the 1990s and beyond; (3) environmental education for sustainable development; and (4) educational policies, programs, and practices for the 1990s and beyond (NCSS 1994). One attendee commented that the conference challenged all in attendance to "question what all of us as global citizens can do together to improve our world" (Isele 1994). The change in discourse surrounding these two conferences is reflective of the changes that took place at the global level—from a national model to a postnational model of the nation-state and civics education.

SUMMARY

The findings presented here are consistent with the main hypothesis that there is a movement, in Anglophone Africa, toward a postnational model of society in civics education. This is evidenced in the increase in emphasis of both regional and global issues as well as a change in the nature of the discussion toward a more universal conception of citizenship and human rights. Future research along these lines will include a global analysis of civics education material, with the expectation that civics curriculum throughout the world will reflect worldwide changes from a national model of society to a postnational model of society.

NOTES

1. Anglophone African countries for which data are included in this analysis are Botswana, the Gambia, Ghana, Kenya, Lesotho, Malawi, Namibia, Nigeria, Sierra Leone, Swaziland, Tanzania, Uganda, Zambia, and Zimbabwe.

2. The percentage of countries that refer to each issue is calculated by dividing the number of countries with references to a concept by the total number of countries.

3. The second analysis, the emphasis of each issue relative to all key issues covered in the material, is calculated by dividing the number of references to one issue by the total number of references to all key issues.

REFERENCES

Altbach, Philip G. 1987. "Textbooks in Comparative Context." Pp. 159–175 in *Educational Technology: Its Creation, Development and Cross-Cultural Transference,* edited by R. Murray Thomas and Victor N. Kobayashi. Oxford: Pergamon.

Altbach, Philip G. 1991. "Textbooks: The International Dimension." Pp. 242–258 in *The Politics of the Textbook,* edited by Michael W. Apple and Linda K. Christian-Smith. New York: Routledge.

Altbach, Philip G., and Gail P. Kelly. 1988. "Textbooks and the Third World: An Overview." Pp. 3–17 in *Textbooks in the Third World,* edited by Philip G. Altbach and Gail P. Kelly. New York: Garland.

Anderson, Benedict. 1983. *Imagined Communities: Reflections on the Origin and Spread of Nationalism.* London: Verso.

Apple, Michael W., and Linda K. Christian-Smith. 1991. "The Politics of the Textbook." Pp. 1–21 in *The Politics of the Textbook,* edited by Michael W. Apple and Linda K. Christian-Smith. New York: Routledge.

ASESP (African Social and Environmental Studies Program). 1993a. "A Baseline Survey of Social Studies Curricula, Teaching, Learning and Assessment in Primary Schools and Teachers Colleges in Kenya and Uganda." ASESP.

ASESP (African Social and Environmental Studies Program). 1993b. "The Re-Birth of Social Studies in Africa: ASESP Silver Jubilee of the Report of a Conference on African Educators, EDC and Credo on Social Studies—Conference in Mombasas, Kenya, 1968." ASESP.

ASESP (African Social and Environmental Studies Program). 1994. "ASESP Social Studies Curriculum and Teaching Resource Book for Africa." ASESP.

Banks, J.A. 1990. "Citizenship Education for a Pluralistic Democratic Society." *Social Studies* 81:210–214.

Barbalet, J.M. 1988. *Citizenship: Rights Struggle and Class Inequality.* Milton Keynes: Open University Press.

Benavot, Aaron. 1983. "The Rise and Decline of Vocational Education." *Sociology of Education.*

Benavot, Aaron, and Phyllis Riddle. 1988. "The Expansion of Primary Education, 1987–1940: Trends and Issues." *Sociology of Education* 61: 181–210.

Berger, P.L., B. Berger, and H. Kellner. 1974. *The Homeless Mind: Modernization and Consciousness.* New York: Vintage.

Bradley, Karen, and Francisco O. Ramirez (in press). "World Polity and Gender Parity: Women's Share of Higher Education, 1965–1985." *Research in Sociology of Education and Socialization.*

Center for Civics Education (CCE). 1994. *National Standards for Civics and Government.* Calabasas, CA: Center for Civics Education.

Clarken, Rodney H., and Felix R. O'Mara. 1987. "Social Studies in Botswana." In *Botswana Educational Research Association.* Gabarone.

Dahl, R. 1992. "The Problem of Civic Competence." *Journal of American Democracy* 3:45–59.

Dreeben, Robert. 1974. "On What is Learned in School." In *Power and Ideology in Education,* edited by J. Karabel and A.H. Halsey. New York: Oxford University Press.

Farrell, Joseph P., and Stephen P. Heyneman. 1988. "Textbook in Developing Countries: Economic and Pedagogical Choices." Pp. 19–44 in *Textbooks in the Third World: Policy, Content, and Context*, edited by Philip G. Altbach and Gail P. Kelly. New York: Garland.

Frank, John D., Evan Schofer, and John C. Torres. 1994. "Rethinking History: Change in University Curriculum, 1910–1990." *Sociology of Education* 67:2312–2342.

Gandal, Matt, and Chester Finn. 1995. "Teaching Democracy." *Freedom Papers.*

Goodson, Ivor F. 1988. "The Making of Curriculum." Pp. 184–196 in *The Making of Curriculum: Collected Essays*, edited by Ivor F. Goodson. London: The Falmer Press.

Ikelov, Orit. 1991. "Political Socialization and Schooling Effects Among Israeli Adolescents." *Comparative Education Review* 35:430–446.

Inkeles, A., and D.A. Smith. 1974. *Becoming Modern*. Cambridge: Harvard University Press.

Isele. 1994. "Africa's Cry for the Social Studies." *Social Education* 58:378.

Lipset, S.M. 1959. "Some Social Requisites of Democracy: Economic Development and Political Legitimacy." *American Political Science Review* 53:69–105.

Lucan, Talabi Aisie. 1969. *Civics for Sierra Leone*. New York: Longman.

Marshall, T.H. 1964. "The Development of Citizenship to the End of the Nineteenth Century." Pp. 71–122 in *Class, Citizenship, and Social Development*, edited by T.H. Marshall. Garden City: Doubleday.

McMahan, Walter, and Stephanie Leaphart. 1993. "Democratization and Human Rights: Human Resource Development's Direct and Indirect Effects." AID, Washington, DC, LAC Bureau, EHRTS Project.

McNeely, Connie L. 1995. *Constructing the Nation-State: International Organization and Prescriptive Action*. Westport, CT: Greenwood.

Meienberg, Hildebrand. 1966. *Tanzanian Citizen: A Civics Textbook*. Eastern Africa: Oxford University Press.

Merryfield, Merry M., and Peter Muyanda-Mutebi. 1991. "Research on Social Studies in Africa." Chapter 53 in *Handbook on Social Studies Teaching and Learning*, edited by James P Shaver. New York: Macmillan Publishing Company.

Meyer, John W. 1987. "The World Polity and the Authority of the Nation State." Pp. 41–70 in *Institutional Structure: Constituting State, Society, and the Individual*, edited by George M. Thomas, John W. Meyer, Francisco O. Ramirez, and John Boli. Newbury Park, CA: Sage.

Meyer, John W., David H. Kamens, and Aaron Benavot. 1992. *School Knowledge for the Masses: World Models and National Primary Curricular Categories in the Twentieth Century*. Washington, DC: The Falmer Press.

Murapa, R., and M. Sithole. 1986. "Junior Secondary Civics for Zimbabweans." Harare: Longman Zimbabwe.

NCSS. 1994. "The Third International Social Studies Conference." In *Social Studies Education: Challenges and Opportunities in a World of Rapid Change*. Nairobi, Kenya.

Nyasulu, A.M., and D. Potter. 1966. *Civics for Malawi*. Limbe: Longman of Malawi.

Oppenheim, A.N., and Judith Torney. 1974. *The Measurement of Children's Civic Attitudes in Different Nations*. Stockholm: Alquist and Wiskell International.

Parsons, Talcott. 1959. "The School Class as a Social System: Some of its Functions in American Society." Pp. 434–456 in *Education, Economy and Society*, edited by K. and J. Floud Halsey. New York: Free Press of Glencoe.

Ramirez, Francisco O. 1989. "Reconstituting Children: Extension of Personhood and Citizenship." Pp. 143–165 in *Age Structuring in Comparative Perspective*, edited by David Kertzer and K. Schaie. Hillsdale, NJ: Erlbaum.

Ramirez, Francisco O. Forthcoming. "Mass Schooling." In *Sociology and Education: An Encyclopedia*, edited by Sadovnik Levinson and Cookson.

Ramirez, Francisco O., and John Boli. 1987. "The Political Contruction of Mass

Schooling: European Origins and Worldwide Institutionalization." *Sociology of Education* 60:2–17.

Ramirez, Francisco O., and John W. Meyer. 1992. "Educational Globalization: The Effects of World Models on National Educational Systems. A Proposal to the Spencer Foundation." Stanford University.

Reardon, Betty A. 1994. "Human Rights and Values Education: Using the International Standards." *Social Education* 58:427–429.

Reimers, Eleanora Villegas. 1994. "Civic Education in the School Systems of Latin America and the Caribbean." USAID/ LAC (Bureau for Latin America and the Caribbean).

Singh, Malkiat. 1988. *History and Civics*. Nairobi: SOMA Group, Ltd.

Soysal, Yasemin Nuhoglu. 1994. *Limits of Citizenship: Migrants and Postnational Membership in Europe*. Chicago: University of Chicago Press.

Torney-Purta, Judith. 1992. "Cognitive Representations of the Political System in Adolescents: The Continuum from Pre-Novice to Expert." *New Directions for Child Development* 56:11–25.

Torney-Purta, Judith, and J. Schwille. 1986. "Civic Values Learned in School: Policy and Practice in Industrialized Countries." *Comparative Education Review* 30:30–49.

Wong, S.Y. 1991. "The Evolution in Social Science Instruction (1900–1986): A Cross-National Study." *Sociology of Education* 64:33–47.

6 STATE AND CITIZENSHIP UNDER TRANSFORMATION IN WESTERN EUROPE

Lars Bo Kaspersen

Discussions of the development and change of citizenship in Western Europe most often focus on economic, social, and/or domestic political issues (e.g., Barbalet 1988; Hindess 1987; Marshall 1950; Meehan 1993; Turner 1986, 1993). However, this chapter takes us beyond these discussions and attaches importance to the military and security dimension of the state in order to understand the modern concept of citizenship. The problem of defense has historically been one of the most fundamental concerns and functions of the state, and the importance of this aspect in the development of citizenship is too often not given enough attention in the theoretical literature on citizenship.

One of my basic theses is that the development of modern citizenship, the liberal-representative democracy, and the nation-state must be seen in close connection with the changes in the defense structure of the states in Europe in the period from the mid-18th century to the mid-19th century. On the Continent, the introduction of conscription was one of the most important conditions for the development of the modern egalitarian version of citizenship, with equal rights and obligations for all citizens—a concept of citizenship that at the same time defines identification and affiliation of the citizen to a specific state.

By presenting the state and the problem of defense as a primary structural condition of the rise of the nation-state and citizenship, we are obviously led also to discuss the importance of the new defense structure in Europe introduced after World War II, centered around the North Atlantic Treaty Organization (NATO). It provides a lens through which to examine the current process of transformation of the nation-state and citizenship.

My second main thesis is the claim that there is a close connection between the foundation of NATO and the development of the European Community (EC) and subsequent European Union (EU). I want to stress that, from the outset, the European Community was seen more as a security policy project and not merely an economical one. Consequently, I analyze the implications of NATO and, later, the European Community—now the European Union—for the traditional notion of citizenship affiliated with the nation-state.

In this chapter, I analyze the development and transformation of citizenship in Western Europe (primarily the northwest European EU members) from the emergence of the modern nation-state until today. In particular, my analysis concentrates on the period from the end of World War II until the ratification of the Maastricht Treaty and the establishment of the EU—a period in which the traditional nation-state and the associated concept of citizenship have undergone some fundamental changes. After some theoretical considerations and an exposition of the main concepts, I discuss the development of citizenship, with an emphasis on the importance of conscription. Subsequently, I delineate specific aspects of that development that have implications for the transformation of state and citizenship in postwar Western Europe, discussing the importance of a changed defense structure with NATO as the pivot and the emergence of EC/EU. Finally, I show the impact of these changes on citizenship in Western European nation-states and discuss the development of rights and obligations in the context of the EU.

SOME THEORETICAL REFLECTIONS

Different theoretical perspectives throw different lights on the problems of state and citizenship. For example, the development of citizenship can be seen as a result of the mutual struggle between classes or individuals for more rights and privileges. Another perspective conceives the state as autonomous and, thus, depicts the struggle of rights and obligations as a power struggle between the state and the people. A third perspective can incorporate the importance of the external relations of state and civil society. A fourth way of approaching the problem is to focus on issues of identity and nationality, drawing upon social psychology and cultural studies.

While incorporating different theories can be fruitful, I adopt a theoretical perspective that precludes a whole range of important issues regarding citizenship. To focus on one facet of a problem can be very useful as certain types of often disregarded relations and dimensions are brought to light. In the same way as a binocular enables you to see a very sharp but narrow and limited aspect of the horizon, specific theoretical concepts enable you to focus on one single aspect of the problem for analytical purposes.

My point is to focus on the importance of the state and its defense structure in order to explain the rise and development of citizenship. To take as a point of departure a conception of the state with an emphasis on defense is very different from most theories of citizenship, which are often embedded in social theories stressing economic relations—in other words, a civil society perspective. Thus, citizenship becomes a question of the struggle of individuals, groups, and/or classes for rights and consequently more freedom (Giddens 1982; Held 1989a; Marshall 1950; Turner 1986). In these theories, citizenship and social class are seen as two mutually conditioned concepts, just as the unequal distribution of g⁻⁻ds and the development of rights are seen as two sides of the same story. Class struggle or the struggle of individuals for rights is treated as the most important dynamic in explaining the development of citizenship.

That kind of theoretical perspective indeed throws light on some important aspects of the concept of citizenship and raises central questions concerning status, inequality, and social integration. A class angle, however, is also problematic because it ignores the fundamental importance of the state as a sovereign entity issuing and guaranteeing citizen rights and obligations. The state has its own interests independent of class interests, and the state attempts to maneuver internal and external demands in an attempt to achieve its own goals and to maintain status as a free and independent state in the state system.[1] A theoretical perspective that stresses the state and its own interests as a point of departure for understanding citizenship points to dimensions of the concept of citizenship that are omitted or undeveloped in most theories based upon a civil society perspective.

STATE AND SOVEREIGNTY

Most analyses of the development of citizenship are grounded in Marxist or liberal theories. These theories see the state as a means for either the class, a social movement, or the single individual to pursue its own ends; the state is seen as a means to obtain rights and privileges. Here, however, I reverse this theoretical perspective and regard citizenship from the point of view of the state. Citizenship is here defined as part of the praxis of the state, with praxis defined as a subject organizing its means towards an end.[2] In this view, the estate, class, or citizen becomes a means for the state to obtain its ultimate goal of maintaining sovereignty and continuous recognition as a state subject in the interstate system.[3]

To the extent that the state appears as an element in traditional analyses of citizenship, it is often seen as a continuation of the class struggle (Marxism) or a reflection of the interest of the people (liberal theories). In liberalism, society and state are seen as a fusion of individuals, and in Marxism as a social formation consisting of classes. In both traditions, the state is conceived as a political center of power and an administrative apparatus directly deduced from society. The state functions as a necessary superstructure to maintain social order. Mann (1988:1–2) summarizes the critique of these state theories in the following way:

> Nowadays there is no need to belabor the point that most general theories of the state have been false because they have been reductionist. They have reduced the state to the pre-existing structures of civil society. This is obviously true of the Marxist, the liberal and the functionalist traditions of state theory, each of which has seen the state predominantly as a place, an arena, in which the struggles of classes, interest groups and individuals are expressed and institutionalized, and—in functionalist versions—in which a General Will (or, to use modern terms, core values or normative consensus) is expressed and implemented. Though such theories disagree about many things, they are united in denying significant autonomous power to the state.

Society and state are conceived as a *fusion* of the internal composite parts of society. The state only appears as a necessary means for the individuals or the ruling class to ensure and protect their conditions of existence (e.g., property rights and freedom of trade). Consequently, these theories put little emphasis on the praxis of the state in which the state interacts with other states and, subsidiary to civil society, is struggling to maintain and develop its own conditions of existence. However, it is the very agency of the state internally and externally that creates the state. The state is not merely generated "from within" by individuals; it produces and reproduces itself in its own praxis. In other words, the state is an entity constituted in a double relation of recognition. It is partly constituted in its relation to other states and partly in relation to the civil society, with the relation of recognition to other states important in this context.

My conceptualization of the state in this way is inspired by the works of Michael Mann (1986; 1993), Anthony Giddens (1985), Anders Boserup (1986), Charles Tilly (1992), Carl von Clausewitz (1976), and Carl Schmitt (1976; 1985). Whereas Giddens and, especially, Boserup, with inspiration from Clausewitz, contribute to an understanding of the state as praxis, Mann provides the basis for an understanding of the state as an arena with institutional and functional dimensions. For my purposes here, I essentially disregard the institutional aspects and turn more to the functional aspects of the state. A state has several functions, among others, the maintenance of internal order, the maintenance of infrastructure, economic redistribution, and defending the domain against external enemies—and, as mentioned above, I focus here on the function of defense.

Clausewitz (1976) and Boserup (1986) argue that the problem of defense must be seen as a mutual struggle of recognition—as a life and death struggle, as a matter of existence based on conceptions of the state as independent, sovereign, and subject to recognition by other states in the interstate system. In the last instance, the struggle of recognition is indeed political, but the means can be military, economical, or ideological.

Conceptualizing the state in this way has consequences for the concept of sovereignty. In both Marxism and liberalism, sovereignty is regarded as a relationship between the state and the individuals/classes within the borders of the state. The individuals are born with sovereignty which, subsequently, is handed over to the state. However, when the state is constituted in a relation of recognition by other states, sovereignty from the outset is a relationship between the state and other states. "To maintain sovereignty is not a matter of rule over a domain of sovereignty and 'to intervene' but a question of preventing others from doing it" (Boserup 1986:929).

The next step is to examine the relationship of sovereignty and legitimation between the state and civil society, or the "internal aspects of sovereignty" (Held 1989b:215). So far, political theory has primarily concentrated on this relationship in an attempt to develop the most just and democratic form of government. Yet, the internal problem of sovereignty must be seen in connection with the external defense of sovereignty. The most fundamental changes in the form of government and constitution can rarely be seen as a result of an internal struggle of sovereignty; the extent and depth of such changes are widely determined by external conditions. The internal struggle of sovereignty plays an important role in shaping citizenship, and analysis of that relationship gives a deeper knowledge of the actual content of citizenship. However, the internal problem of sovereignty only plays a secondary role in my analysis. When this chapter primarily aims to point to aspects contributing to a change of the very structural condition of the state and thus citizenship, it emphasizes changes in the external relations of the state.

The struggle of recognition forces states into a competition that can be fatal if they do not participate. If the neighboring states decide to use military means, it is crucial that a state possess sufficient defense capabilities to sustain sovereignty and, thereby, its existence as an independent state.[4] Consequently, the struggle has several significant implications for the state and for the civil society as well. The state has to create sufficient resources that can be mobilized if need be. These resources are "made" in the civil society and, consequently, the struggle of state recognition is reflected in the structure of the civil society. In order to create an ability and capacity to defend itself, the state has to participate in the development of a strong and well-working civil society. Citizenship is a means by which the state strengthens its resources for the external struggle.

The Political, the War, and the State of Exception

My theoretical framework of the exogenously constituted configuration of the state implies that the extent and character of the struggle of recognition between the states becomes more salient than posited in other theories. The German legal and political theorist Carl Schmitt (1976, 1985) takes this point, specifying that the struggle of recognition is a political relation that exists partly between states and partly between persons, groups, or movements in civil society within the state territory. Schmitt argues that the "differentia specifica" of the political is a friend-foe relation. In a discussion of Schmitt's work, Hirst (1990:109) points out that

> . . . the political exists when differences reach the point where groups are placed in a relation of enmity, where each comes to perceive the other as an irreconcilable enemy to be struggled against and if possible defeated. Such relations are political and possess an existential logic that overrides the motives which may have brought groups to this pass.

Schmitt (1976) approves the Hegelian idea that the very struggle between two entities constitutes this relationship and their two identities respectively, arguing that the concept of state presupposes the concept of the political. The state is constituted in a political struggle including military struggle which, in a Clausewitzean sense, is the means of politics. The political struggle gives rise to the political order within the states. Politics becomes, in this context, a struggle between states in which a social and political order is imposed and developed within the state borders. After imposing a social order, the state can use the civil society to pursue its own ends in the struggle of recognition. This point clearly has implications for the citizenship. From the point of view of the nation-state, the principle of conscription and later rights are the most fundamental and necessary part of the social and political order because the development of citizenship can ensure support and legitimation from specific groups, classes, organizations, and individuals. This makes it possible to pursue political ends outside the state—in other words, civil society contains the means of the state to achieve recognition in the state system.

Contrary to the predominant conceptions in liberal democratic theory, it is not the law that constitutes the political order. Schmitt (1985) sees very clearly that, in the last instance, the legal order and the constitution of a specific state rest on something outside the legal order itself. This "outside" is exactly the political. Politics and the struggle of recognition of states are prior to the law, and law is constituted in the "state of exception" (Schmitt 1985).

A specific constitution and legal order can only survive if there is permanent pressure on the specific state from the other states in the state system. If this pressure changes (i.e., if the struggle of recognition changes character), it can lead to an alteration of the social order and consequently, constitutional reforms. (Examples can be found in the constitutional reforms in Prussia after the defeat by Napoleon at the battle of Jena in 1806, or Yeltsin's reforms and new constitution after the collapse of the Soviet Union.) In other words, the importance of politics and the state is crucial in the analysis of the development of citizenship in Western Europe.

Citizenship

Citizenship, in particular, can be seen as the result of two types of praxis. The first type of praxis concerns the state. The appearance of rights and obligations is the result of the praxis of the state that mediates between, on the one hand, the relations to other states and, on the other hand, the relations to citizens, associations, parties, and social movements in civil society. The state uses citizenship as means to create a domestic social order, putting it in a strong position in the external struggle. The state produces and reproduces itself in this praxis. Citizenship is used as a means.

Individuals, organizations, and social movements also contribute to the development of citizenship when they, in their praxis, constantly attempt to produce and reproduce their own conditions of existence that claim rights and membership in a specific state. In the following analysis, I emphasize the praxis of the state, but it is also important to make it clear that both types of praxis are always present. Therefore, my understanding of citizenship does not imply that the development of rights and obligations is only a top-down process with the people as passive spectators.

Citizenship should be divided into *formal* and *substantial* parts (Brubaker 1989, 1992). The formal part defines the membership of the state of a given legal subject. Consequently, the formal side of citizenship determines who is "inside" and who is "outside." The substantial part concerns different types of rights and obligations. While the modern concept of citizenship emerging with the French Revolution and Napoleon comprises many obligations, most important, however, are the obligations to pay taxes and to do military service. Rights themselves have been characterized as civil, political, and social (cf. Marshall 1950). The civil element consists of rights that are necessary for individual freedom; civil rights are personal liberty, freedom of speech, thought, faith, equality before the law, ownership, and so forth. Political rights include the right to participate in the exercise of political power, eligibility, and the franchise. Social rights are defined as a right to a minimum of economic and social welfare with the possibility to live a life in agreement with the norms predominating in a specific society.

Marshall (1950), in his analysis of England, argued that the development of civil rights became a necessary platform for the emergence of political rights. In a similar way, the working class used political rights as a means to obtain social and economic rights. This development can be seen in Continental Europe although with some variations. Marshall ignored, however, the importance of conscription for the development of rights.[5]

The Development of the State, Sovereignty, and Citizenship in Western Europe

The development of the rights and obligations that we today associate with nation-state citizenship came about through a long and a very heterogeneous process in the Western European states, originating in the collapse of the feudal structure of society. The Westphalian Peace heralded a dramatic change in the European state system, marking the final collapse of the medieval state system. The medieval period was characterized by a large number of principalities and city states in which sovereignty could not be located at one level. This was further strengthened by the dominant role of the church.

Feudalism, with its "parcellized sovereignty" (Anderson 1974), was replaced by the territorial state, whose sovereignty was increasingly concentrated in one place: in the hand of the sovereign, referring to either a monarch (Hobbes 1992) or parliament (Locke 1989). Territorial states became sovereign, demarcated entities that constituted the basic unit in the international state system, formally independent and recognizing each other.

Gradually, the state became territorially demarcated in relation to other states and internally centralized, and civil society emerged. This state was able to universalize its jurisdiction and its fiscal legislation over a specific territory recognized by other states (Mann 1986). At the same time the state aimed at achieving monopoly of violence, with total monopoly first occurring after the French Revolution—in the era of the nation-state.

The development of the centralized territorial state also implies very different changes in the area of rights. In general, it can be said that this period was characterized by alterations in the relationship between the sovereign and the individuals of civil society. In the feudal period there was no direct relationship between the prince/king/emperor on the one side and the majority of the people on the other. Existing rights and privileges were tied to estates and guilds and not to persons. During the 18th century these conditions changed dramatically as the notion of natural law developed and became important in most European countries. This happened simultaneously with the removal of the power monopoly of the nobility. The mediating link between the peasant and state disappeared. Not until after the initiation of the nation-state was a direct relationship between state/monarch and peasant established based upon conscription and citizen rights.

The feudal order and the power of nobility were undermined by the demand for a new defense structure raised by the king and the state. During the 18th century, the defense structure in Western Europe changed, with mercenary troops supplemented and supplanted by an increasing number of conscripted soldiers. In the beginning, the nobility controlled the process of levying troops, but the monarch gradually began to levy troops directly without using the nobility. The monarch's increasing control of the military through the right to levy troops was supplemented by control over taxation, and central power was further strengthened by these elements. Taxation and troop levying were used as a means to transform estate privileges (Elias 1982; Tilly 1992). Estates were replaced by "the individual" who slowly appeared and became important for state power.[6] State power then was increasingly dependent on the individual, who became a resource both as a taxpayer and a soldier. However, "proper" citizens rights and personal citizenship had not yet appeared. In other words, the concept of citizenship before the emergence of the nation-state had a fundamentally different character than personal citizenship. In that period, citizenship as a concept was in a sense misleading, as rights or, more precisely, privileges did not follow the person, but the estate.

Citizenship in the modern egalitarian version, with equal rights and obligations for all citizens which at the same time define the affiliation of the citizen to a specific state with a territory, is closely associated with the rise of the modern nation-state in Western Europe. This development commenced at the end of the 18th century, when France was forced to reorganize the structure of society because of a weakening in its relations to its neighbors. The domain of sovereignty was under pressure, especially from the growing British sea power (Giddens 1985; Kennedy 1988; Mann 1993; Tilly 1992). The defeat in North America and the discontent of the rising bourgeoisie which carried the biggest burden in terms of taxes (the nobility was widely exempt from taxpaying during absolutism) led to the French

Revolution. Different circumstances weakened France, but the defense structure based upon mercenaries seemed more and more inefficient. Moreover, mercenaries were a big tax burden on the bourgeoisie, giving them even more arguments for introducing parliamentary democracy. It gave them the opportunity to decide how to distribute the fiscal burden.

After Napoleon's seizure of power, the decisive restructuration transforming France into the leading great power in Europe took place. Napoleon introduced reforms creating an army of citizen soldiers with high morale and spirit, soldiers who were no longer fighting for money and mammon, but for the Mother Country—for the Nation—for the Tricolor—for France! The foundation for the citizen (or more precisely, the national citizen) was laid with the combination of new political and civil rights stemming from the declaration of the Revolution and the new form of conscription. Napoleon's army challenged the power balance in Europe and, in that way, forced other states to introduce similar reforms if they wanted to be able to defend their sovereign domains in the future.

With the introduction of general conscription in 1793 in France, the foundation for modern democracy and the modern citizen was created. This conscription reform started a whole range of processes whereby some of the consequences were intended and others unintended. The creation of a "People" or a "Nation" with patriotism and revolutionary fanaticism made up a mass army. This caused several changes both in France's relationship with the other European states and in France's internal construction. The superiority of the mass army forced external opponents to make similar reforms that partly strengthened the national elements in the state concerned, and partly gave the state power "access to a total mobilization of the resources of the nation in the form of manpower, money and material" (Jespersen 1991:259). Furthermore, conscription caused a massive claim for corresponding rights. It brought the People—which meant the bourgeoisie—to power. Despite the fact that the state succeeded in suspending many reforms after the periods of war, it was only a short respite. The development and the consolidation of parliamentary democracy and the modern citizen could not be prevented in the long run. The state was not capable of binding the peasant without conferring some rights. Consequently, the peasant became a *national* citizen endowed with rights as well as obligations. Because conscription was the pivot in the very development of citizenship, not surprisingly it was only men who achieved complete status as a subject or citizen; women received no share of political rights (Højrup 1995; Jespersen 1991; Tilly 1992).

The legal theoretical basis of the development of these egalitarian citizen rights and obligations was still "natural law," but legislation became closely linked to the nation-state (Tamm 1991) based upon the principles of contractual law (i.e., rights and obligations going together). National legislation began to contribute to a strengthening of the nation-state and its domain of power.

In many countries in Western Europe the bourgeois democracy, capitalism, and "national" consciousness were developed in a mutually conditioned interaction with fundamental changes in the external relations of the state. This complexity of transformation processes merged into a kind of "nation-building process," in which the nation and the national become a dominant ideology.[7] State and nation merged together and, for the first time in history, created a unity.[8] Consequently, the nation-state and citizenship developed as a tandem couple pivoted upon the problem of defense.

The very content of the concept of citizenship was altered and extended several times right up to the present. First, civil and political rights (the franchise, the right to speak, freedom of the press, freedom to travel, etc.) appeared; they were the logical condition for the state to break down the old systems of privileges during absolutism. Moreover, these rights were necessary for the development of capitalism, and therefore established a logical connection between individual citizens and the growing market, whereby the citizen obtained the right to function in the economic system. When a citizen wants to produce, buy, or sell to a market, he must be recognized by the state as a subject of law (Andreasen 1989). The French Revolution, with the subsequent bourgeois-democratic constitution, symbolized the ratification of civil and political rights.

Social and economic rights with unemployment benefits, minimum wages, pensions, and sickness benefits came later with the European working-class movement. These rights first became a part of the citizenship in the 20th century; the years of reconstruction after the two world wars were very important for the development of these rights.

In sum, it can be said that the development of the nation-state in Western Europe was a process in which the state increasingly controlled the domain of sovereignty. The external threat to sovereignty from the end of the 17th century and the beginning of the 18th century signaled not only the start of a new defense structure, but also of a transformation of civil society. Above all, it was reforms of the army, with conscription as the most important aspect, that led to a development and complexity of civil, political, and social rights. Through rights and obligations, the state regulated, controlled, and intervened in civil society and the day-to-day life of the people. Citizens had become a vital resource to the state. (Indeed, the construction of an education system, health system, and other welfare arrangements can partly be seen as an attempt of the state to strengthen its resources.)[9]

The Nation-State and National Citizenship under Transformation?

By the end of the 18th century, changes in the defense structure—with conscription as a central dimension—had become a contributory factor to the development of modern citizenship. Consequently, following the logic of that development, we might examine the consequences of the new defense structure introduced after World War II, primarily based on NATO, for contemporary Western European nation-states and, especially, for links to citizenship.[10]

Given this context I emphasize two important institutional and structural conditions that directly or indirectly question the sovereignty of the classic nation-state—with sovereignty defined as the capability to defend one's own domain—and, consequently, citizenship. First I discuss the importance of NATO in terms of nation-state sovereignty and in relation to the formation of the European Community. Second, I focus on the European process of integration, the European Union, and its consequences for citizen rights.

"Blocism" and Imaginary War

World War II was, as Schmitt (1976) put it, a "state of exception," establishing a new social order in the state system and within the states. Indeed, the war continued as a "virtual" war (Boserup 1986) or an "imaginary" war (Kaldor 1990) in a bipolar state system with two blocs confronting each other. Europe lost its hegemonic position and power in the international system, with the United States and Soviet Union becoming the dominant hegemonic powers in the two blocs. The United States and Western Europe organized as a defense "bloc" through NATO (1947), while the Soviet Union and Eastern Europe created the Warsaw Pact (1955).

The "Cold War" period from 1947 to 1989 was an "imaginary war" in which both blocs rearmed and prepared for war, or more precisely, they prepared in order to avoid total war. It was generally conceded that total war was impossible to wage since both sides possessed nuclear weapons. However, at the subnuclear level, the two blocs were directly and indirectly involved in strategic wars in the Third World, most notably in Vietnam and Afghanistan.

A consequence of this imaginary war was continuous peace (or, more correctly, a pause) between the states within the two alliances. Strong fear of the external enemy had a "positive" effect on strong tensions that traditionally dominated the relationship among the states within the blocs. All states gathered their resources and strength towards the external enemy, the opposing bloc. Moreover, the creation of NATO in 1947 also led to strong, internal pacification in Western Europe (Giddens 1985; Kaldor 1990), which at the same time provided a solution to internal defense problems. This created a completely new and unaccustomed situation in Europe.

NATO and European Integration

For more than 150 years, the most serious security problem in Europe had been the German-French relationship, with immense tensions leading to several wars. Consequently, in the postwar years, a major item on the European agenda was improvement of the relationship between Germany and France. The main problem was how to tie these two states to each other in order to prevent a new war. However, the rise of "blocism" (Kaldor 1990) and NATO effectively removed the internal defense problem in Western Europe. The principal enemy was then the Eastern Bloc and no longer other Western European states. Accordingly, with no defense problem between the states within Western Europe, the demand for a defense against each other was reduced. NATO, dominated by the United States (US), became the central foundation of defense for Western Europe. Although NATO consists of de jure independent sovereign states, the treaty had unintended consequences for internal defense in the member states (Mann 1993).

> NATO and the Warsaw Pact were quite different from the nineteenth-century alliances, or from the wartime alliances of the twentieth century, in that they were rigid and institutionalized. In practice, through strategies, integrated command systems, the supply of equipment, joint exercises, etc., if not in theory, there were no really independent European armed forces within the blocs. Individual European countries retained their sovereignty, in the sense of administrative power over their citizens and their mutual recognition of each other, without the need for national military power. (Kaldor 1990:24)

With the principal enemy an external entity and defense transferred to NATO, there was no need to sustain separate national production machinery: When states no longer have a mutual defense problem, the process of economic integration has no natural end point (Boserup 1989). Thus, the changed defense structure based upon NATO constituted part of the closer cooperation in Western Europe that later paved the way for the formation of the European Economic Community (EEC 1957), European Free Trade Association (EFTA 1959), and the European Union (EU 1993).

Citizenship in Western Europe

The foundation of citizenship changed after the end of the Second World War. The connection between nationality (natio/etnos) and the allotment of rights and obligations (demos) was challenged as a result of massive immigration from the former colonies to the colonial powers (e.g., England and France), and intensified by waves of guestworkers in the 1960s and refugees in the 1980s. In this light, formal aspects of citizenship (i.e., who is included in the state and who is excluded from the state) are brought into question (e.g., Brubaker 1989; Hammar 1986, 1990).

Here, however, I look to the implications of NATO and, later, the EEC for the understanding of the substantial aspects of citizenship. Previously unchallenged connections between obligations and rights embedded in the nation-state began to crumble. In principle, most citizenship obligations remain within the framework of the nation-state while, since 1945, different types of rights have become embedded both in the nation-state and in different international organizations (e.g., the United Nations, the Council of Europe, and the EC). Thus, I concentrate on the significance of NATO and the European Community for understanding the substantial aspects of citizenship, that is, the kinds of obligations and rights that follow from citizenship status.

Obligations and Citizenship in Contemporary Western Europe

Conscription was the pivotal feature affecting the continental Western European nation-state and citizenship.[11] It was introduced partly due to defense problems and partly because state budgets could not bear the expenses of standing armies of mercenaries. In order to compensate for the introduction of conscription, the state first had to introduce civil and political rights for the peasants and later to all men. Allotment of these rights were the basis for a stronger loyalty and patriotism than money could buy from mercenaries. The patriotic, conscripted soldiers in principle defended themselves and their life conditions by fighting for the nation-state. In their capacity as citizens with rights and obligations, they constituted the social contract and the state. Thus, conscription implied that the citizen, by actively defending his home country, at the same time demonstrated his national and democratic loyalty. Consequently, the loyal, conscripted soldier formed the basic strength in the defense of the nation-state. This strength increased with the allotment of rights to the citizens (e.g., private property, freedom of trade, the franchise, etc.).

The rise of the modern form of conscription in most countries became the precondition for the development of the egalitarian citizenship, and this close connection continued after the war. In fact, in many countries, the fear of a new war led to a strengthening of conscription. Even England introduced conscription for the first time in peacetime (Morgan 1990). Later, "offshore" countries like the United States and England abolished conscription—not least because of their geopolitical position as "islands"—and it was replaced by professional forces. Continental Europe, however, has maintained the principle of conscription although the practice and concept have undergone some changes (Bjerg 1991; Shaw 1991).[12] In general, conscription is still a citizenship obligation (although principally only for men), but its importance for the nation itself has declined. If this obligation previously could be characterized as the inner essence of citizenship in terms of both military and ideological importance, it is primarily only of symbolic and ideological importance today. This is especially true for the states in northwestern Europe.

The reduced importance of conscription as an obligation of citizenship is mainly due to two circumstances. First, it concerns the emergence of the new defense structure after World War II. The traditional, patriotic, national army is no longer important in the same way when the defense is embedded in a NATO construction (in which the US carries the biggest burden). Second, technological developments have also pushed towards replacement of manpower by technology that can be operated more easily and better by a professional army. Accordingly, most states have a defense structure supplemented with professional forces.

These two aspects have contributed to reducing the importance of conscription for citizenship in the postwar period. This tendency has continued after the revolutions in Eastern Europe and the Soviet Union and the beginning of demilitarization. In several places, the number of soldiers in the conscript-based army has been reduced and, as in France, some proposals to abolish conscription altogether have been introduced (Shaw 1991).

Although a reconciliation of citizenship and conscription is a possibility in a future Europe, it is hardly a likely outcome. The present world (dis)order relies on other forms of military operations than can be accomplished by traditional forces based upon conscripted soldiers. The picture of the external "enemy" is blurred and, despite the uncertainty in Russia and other parts of the world, more and more military operations seem to take place under the wings of international organizations such as NATO or the United Nations in conflict areas like the former Yugoslavia, Rwanda, and

Somalia. The new thinking is that these missions might better be carried out by professional and international trained forces.

It is also difficult to see how citizenship and conscription could be united within the framework of the European Union. Citizenship has so far been seen as a strategy of integration from the point of view of the European Union, and most likely it will be used as such in the future. It is hardly likely, however, that the strategy of citizenship will include a proposal for a common European conscription. It will only increase the popular resistance against the EU project. Moreover, a defense based upon a mass army of conscripted soldiers would hardly be the most usable army in relation to the conflicts the European states might confront in the next decade.

The defense of the modern Western European state is no longer based only upon national mass armies. Consequently, the citizen has lost importance as the primary defense resource of the state. Conscription in the postwar period, especially in the last 20 to 30 years, has had a primarily symbolic meaning for citizenship; tax liability seems to be the most important obligation of the citizen towards the state today.

The significance of war for the Western European countries has diminished—at least in relation to each other—and defense is no longer the primary function of the state. Consequently, the importance of tax liability is changing too. Besides financing public administration, infrastructure, and the education system, taxes are now primarily used as a means of distribution or, in other words, as an instrument of social policy.

Indeed, tax liability is a sensitive and contested political issue. Most citizens probably approve or accept this obligation in general, but several economical and political struggles are fought about the amounts and forms of taxes. Similar to conscription, tax liability is still a nation-state issue. The increasing European integration has not (yet?) caused these obligations to be moved to the transnational or regional level. The EU has at most had an indirect influence on tax policy in the member states. There are adjustments to other European tax systems, but these have not been caused by direct legal claims or impositions from the EU. They have been caused by pressures from the market after creating the single market (Clemmesen and Hoffman 1993).

Today, we can see the Western European Union (WEU) and the Economic and Monetary Union (EMU) as two aspects of the process of integration that attempt to handle these matters.[13] However, despite these current changes it must be stressed that both obligations that constituted the core of the traditional citizenship are still embedded within the framework of the nation-state. Conscription, however, exists in a reduced version and tax liability has taken on a redefined role.

Today a citizen in an EU country has rights and obligations that are conferred from and guaranteed by the individual member states. Within several areas, however, many of the rights traditionally determined by the nation-state are now an EU matter. Besides rights codified in the European Convention of Human Rights, several citizen rights have developed in the EU context.

First, note that the EU does not have a written constitution, although several writers see one developing (Mancini 1989). However, all kinds of rights constituting the contours of a possible EU citizenship are embedded in the different treaties or created by the European Court of Justice (ECJ). So far, the EU has developed civil, political, and social rights for its members. The civil and political rights are primarily codified in the treaties, while the social rights can be found in the Social Charter and, more importantly, are developed by administrative praxis and by decisions made by the ECJ. The amount of rights figuring in the treaties, in the decisions from the ECJ, and in the other organizational legislation (regulations and directives) are enormous.

For example, the EU has a "democratic deficit" with limited possibilities for people in Europe to control the power of the EU. In other words, the scope of civil and political rights is very limited. The Maastricht Treaty (The Treaty on European Union, 1992) has been seen as an attempt to reverse this situation by strengthening the role of the European parliament and, therefore, the citizens' possibility to control the power of the Commission and the Council. The treaty has also extended other rights. It has enabled EU citizens living in another EU country to vote and be elected to the European Parliament in their country of residence. Also, local elections (municipal and county level) are now open to other EU citizens. Furthermore, there is now an Ombudsman to whom all citizens can apply if they find their rights denied in any member state. An EU citizen has the right to seek diplomatic protection in an embassy of another EU country or in a third country in which his/her own country has no representation. An EU citizen also has the right of free movement and residence within the territory of the member states. However, this right is limited according to the fulfillment of one basic condition: proof of financial independence and independence in terms of social security. In addition, it should be mentioned that these political and civil rights are limited to citizens holding nationality in a member state. "The main condition to be recognized as a citizen of the Union is to be first a citizen of one of the member States, that is, a national of one of these member states" (Martinello 1993:7).

Social and economic rights have also been extended, especially after the Maastricht Treaty. However, these can be traced back to 1958 when the Treaty of Rome provided the basis of regulations about social security for migrant workers. In addition, in the 1970s and 1980s the EC dealt with worker participation and equality among the sexes in the workplace (Meehan 1993).

An extended set of rights has been issued at the EU level. For example, the ECJ has insisted that social protection is a fundamental right. Already in the 1960s, the Court stated that there must be "no discrimination when exercising the right of freedom of movement."[14] Moreover, concerning social security and social assistance for the self-employed and migrant workers and their families, the ECJ has stressed the importance of freedom of movement and nondiscrimination based on nationality. The ECJ has "repeatedly upheld the inviolability of rights in matters of social security" (Meehan 1993:87–88).[15]

Also, women's rights have been addressed in EU regulations and directives. Meehan (1993) points, for example, to issues of equal pay; equal pay for equal work is required by the Treaty of Rome. This point has been further developed to encompass equal treatment in general regarding terms and conditions of employment, such as in recruitment, promotion, and training.

From these brief illustrations, it should be clear that citizenship rights can be found at the international and regional EU level. Rights are no longer determined by one authority only, but both through the EU and the nation-state. It is important to stress, however, that access to EU rights requires membership—that is, citizenship—in a member state. Although a range of rights exists, they are limited in important ways. The citizens in the EU have been given rights that make them into traveling citizens, working citizens, and consuming citizens, but they are still not recognized as political citizens (Neunreither 1995:2–3).

Note also that EU regulations and directives are binding, but if rights codified in a regulation or directive are violated by the member states, the EU has few possibilities of sanctions. The Maastricht Treaty does make some provisions for sanctions: "If the Court of Justice finds that the Member State concerned has not complied with its judgment it may impose a lump sum or penalty payment on it."[16] The EU means of sanction are few; even with them, the member states still have the monopoly on the means of sanctions internally.

TOWARDS A CONCLUSION

After the Second World War, a new social order and defense structure developed in Europe. In Western Europe this order resulted in the foundation of NATO and later the EU. The new defense structure has not reduced the formal sovereignty of the Western European states as such, but their defense ability is now determined largely by NATO. Although the monopoly of the means of violence has not disappeared from the nation-state level, one consequence of the presence of nuclear weapons and NATO has been a strong dependence on NATO and the United States. Another consequence of NATO and the shift in defense is a closer and increasing interdependence and integration in Western Europe.

This displacement of one of the most important functions of the state has also influenced conscription, which in its origin was a means to the development of the nation-state, an integral part of nation-building. When defense became a NATO issue, the significance of conscription was reduced. The existence of the state in postwar Europe is no longer based on the ability of defense. Other functions, previously overshadowed by the problem of defense and military activities, now have become more important for the state. The primary purposes of the state have become maintenance of internal social order, development of the internal infrastructure, and economic redistribution.

This point has consequences for the other central citizen obligation, tax liability. Taxes no longer primarily function as a resource for military defense. Basically, taxes have now become a means of economic distribution. The reorganization of the functions of the state from military to internal purposes contributes to strengthening the welfare initiative—a process that already started in the inter-war period. With the United States carrying the main burden of the defense budget, the Western European countries can operate with minimal defense expenditures and, thereby, form and sustain the economic basis for a welfare state that is unique in human history.

The absence of the threat of war has transformed domestic politics. It is no longer necessary to mobilize for common national efforts and, consequently, the importance of national politics in that vein has declined. Traditional class and party politics no longer stand alone. More and more, politics has moved to other levels and has taken other forms. Social movements have become more and more dominant in the political landscape in the last 30 years, placing practical and moral issues, such as environmental problems, animal rights, and abortion, on the agenda (Hirst and Thompson 1995).

Keep in mind that NATO, the "solution" to the internal defense problem, and the greater interdependence between the states have made possible a dramatic European process of integration, but it is a process that has not (yet?) taken the shape of a supranational authority. Citizens in Europe today tend to only feel very little affiliation to the EU. One reason for this is probably the fact that they have only few associated rights and obligations. They do not see themselves as being a part of a European project in the same way as occurred during the emergence and consolidation of the nation-state. With the end of the Cold War, it seems even more difficult to get wide, popular support for a European "superstate." Many Europeans have difficulties finding an advantage to a completely integrated Europe.

This is a different situation than existed with the 19th century European nation-state in which concepts of nation, people, state, and sovereignty formed a unity. The majority of the people could see an advantage to supporting the state, because partly they obtained protection and rights that provided the means to survive and make a living (the right to property, freedom of trade, etc.). It would be difficult for today's European project to go through a similar development. There is no center—no "powercontainer" (Giddens 1985)—in Europe from which the necessary power can be generated. Furthermore, there is no "Other" outside Europe that can be used to generate a European identity. A new state only arises from necessity. This necessity could be an external ideological, economical, or military competitor. Europe can never by itself find its own identity or create its own borders. As argued by Schmitt (1985) and Hegel (1991), an entity can never generate itself from "within." Identity and a line of demarcation can only be created relative to an "outside"—by an "other." Only if the "other" is defined as a military or survival threat will it result in abolition of the monopoly of the means of violence, the monopoly of finance, and the monetary system of the nation-state. These monopolies might then be transferred to the European level.

However, even if Europe and Europeans do define themselves as an operational "whole" in relation to an "other," then war offers no real solution to such a struggle of recognition. The nuclear bomb and the industrialized war has made war as a means of politics obsolete or unfeasible. The struggle of recognition taking place today between states or alliances with nuclear weapons is carried on through primarily economic means. However, the form that this struggle will take in the future is impossible to predict, and this is exactly the reason that we find ourselves standing at a historical crossroads.

So far, no "other" exists in relation to the EU in the way discussed here and, consequently, the citizen has no need to identify with the EU. Contrary to traditional nation-building processes wherein the endeavors of the state and the citizens simultaneously led to the development of rights and obligations, in the EU citizenship is mainly implemented from "above." When the majority among the EU citizens cannot see themselves as participants in a common project, they will never create pressure from below in a struggle for citizenship rights (Schmitter 1995). Consequently, only the actors finding their own advantage in an integrated Europe will struggle for privileges and rights. So far, it is mainly trade and industry that have gained most privileges from this situation (Schmitter 1995). Similarities can be found in the period before the emergence of the nation-state where towns, the rising bourgeoisie, and other groups fought for and obtained their privileges. Rights in the EU have so far mainly appeared as particular privileges allotted to special groups. The problems of integration are, therefore, intensified since the majority cannot see the possibilities and advantages in the European project for the citizen.

NOTES

1. Here the state is often spoken of as if it is a single person. Obviously, the state cannot be equalized to a single person. The modern state is a complex and very differentiated organization with a variety of institutions and functions. For some purposes, however, it can be reasonable to speak about the state as an independent, autonomous entity because it brings to light some of the ends a state pursues independently of state form, type of governance, and so forth. In other words, it reveals the logical connection between these ends and the means taken up by the state. A reference to a state as an actor can seem allegorical, but we must bear in mind that, here, state must be understood as a state with different agencies that, therefore, are loci of decisions with actions. The character of these state agencies varies over time and from place to place. For example, it can be a monarch, government, parliament, a specific part of the administration, or a dictator. The common feature is that all are actors within the locus of decisions and actions, where actions, to a certain extent, are consequences of actors' decisions (Hindess 1986, 1987).

2. Praxis is a very contested concept in philosophy and social sciences. Here I exclusively use a concept derived from Hegel (*see* D'Hondt 1970; Højrup 1995).

3. When the state seeks to maintain sovereignty it is not a given end. It is an objective that the state since the 16th and 17th centuries formulated as a result of the discourse of balance of power that became increasingly dominant in Europe. The aim of the state was not as such a function of the state's location in the state system, but rather through the deployment of specific discursive means to formulate this aim.

4. N.B., this is not another attempt to take so-called "realist" theories from international relations and bring them into sociology. Although it is contested if there is a set of elements defining 'realism' (and 'neorealism'), it has often been argued that the state is the central unit in an anarchical system of states (for 'realists' and 'neorealists' positions, see Carr 1939; Morgenthau 1947; Waltz 1979; Wight 1977). A realist position assumes that a state is a fusion of individuals and, since human beings are power-seeking entities, states inevitably produce war. I reject these basic tenets. I have argued elsewhere that a state is only partly constituted from its internal parts (Kaspersen 1993). Moreover, states do not make wars but the *relationship* between states can under certain circumstances result in war. The *relationship* between states creates cooperation and conflicts since each state in order to become a state needs to be recognized by other states. My theoretical perspective does not rest upon ascribing properties to individual states, such as being evil or greedy for power. Furthermore, unlike the "realists," I conceptualize the state and the state system as ever-changing entities that take different forms in different historical periods. For my purposes here, I merely claim that in the nation-state era from the 18th century and onwards the state became a significant entity in an international state system.

5. This is probably because he lived in an "off-shore" country with a strong sea power where conscription was of minor importance. *Also see* note 7.

6. The appearance of the individual in European history is brilliantly analysed by Foucault (1975), Hegel (1991), and Elias (1978, 1982).

7. Herder and Fichte in Germany, Grundtvig in Denmark, Rule Britannia, Land of Hope and Glory, God save the Queen in Britain, and so forth.

8. The total unity and congruence between territory, a set of functional tasks and identity has only rarely been found. The few exceptions are Ireland, Denmark and roughly Sweden and Greece. The state, however, where the people share a linguistic, religious, and symbolic identity has been the ideal for many states (Schmitter 1995; Tilly 1992).

9. Note that a close relationship between conscription and citizenship cannot be found in Great Britain. Britain deviated from the continental path to the nation-state and citizenship. A main reason is the geopolitical position of Britain. As an "island" and strong seapower, it always managed to defend itself without a large army. Continental powers like France, Prussia/Germany, Austria, and Russia always lived in direct confrontation with each other. This permanent threat from a neighboring country was a main reason for the development of large armies and, as a consequence, also a strong centralized state apparatus. In other words, it was not necessary in the same way for Britain to keep an army in peace time. Conscription only became "necessary" during wars and it was in World War I that Britain first conscripted soldiers (Levi 1993). That war was also significant in the introduction of rights. For example, political rights were allotted to women who proved necessary to the state by replacing men in the factories during the war; some social rights emerged also (Marwick 1968, 1974). The same pattern was repeated after World War II when many social rights were introduced (Marwick 1968; Shaw 1987).

10. Obviously, there is a whole range of issues in addition to defense that might influence a potential transformation of the nation-state and citizenship. Among other things that might be mentioned are the problem of globalization as a consequence of the increasing interdependence, international organizations, and multinational corporations. These dimensions, however, are outside the frame and problematic of this chapter. (For important discussions on these matters *see*, e.g., Cable 1995; Hirst & Thompson 1992, 1994a, 1994b, 1995a, 1995b, 1996.)

11. This is not entirely correct in the British case, *see* note 7. Consequently, my analysis focuses on the continental states.

12. For example, today it is possible to do nonmilitary forms of national service.

13. The Western European Union is a defense and security alliance between Belgium, France, Greece, Holland, Italy, Luxembourg, Portugal, Spain, the United Kingdom, and Germany. After the Maastricht Treaty it has become an integral part of the development of the EU. The Economic and Monetary Union is one of the main elements of the Maastrict Treaty (1992). The purpose is to create an institutional structure in order to coordinate the economic and fiscal policies among the member states in the EU.

14. 4/66 Labots v. Raad van Arveid.

15. 149/82 Robards v. Insurance Officer.

16. Article 171, 2.

REFERENCES

Anderson, Perry. 1974. *Lineages of the Absolutist State*. London: Verso.

Andreasen, P.H. 1989. "Ændret Militærstrategi bag Demokrati-Reformer" (New Military Strategy Behind the Democratic Reforms). *Information* September 14th.

Barbalet, J.M. 1988. *Citizenship*. Milton Keynes: Open University Press.

Bjerg, Hans Chr. 1991. *"Til Fædrelandets Forsvar"* (To the Defense of the Fatherland). Copenhagen: Værnepligtstyrelsen.

Boserup, Anders. 1986. "Staten, Samfundet, og Krigen hos Clausewitz" (State, Society, and War in Clausewitz). Pp. 911–930 in C. von Clausewitz, *Om Krig* (On War), vol. 3, edited by Niels Berg. Copenhagen: Rhodos.

Boserup, Anders. 1989. Preface in *Lønkapital Under Folkestyre*, by T. Højrup. Copenhagen: Rosinante.

Boserup, A. 1990. "Krieg, Staat, und Frieden. Eine Weiterfürung der Gedanken von Clausewitz." Pp. 244–263 in *Die Zukunft des Friedens in Europa: Politische und Militarische Voraussetzungen*, edited by Carl Friederich von Weizäcker. Munich/Vienna: Carl Hanser Verlag.

Brubaker, W.R., ed. 1989. *Immigration and the Politics of Citizenship in Western Europe and North America*. Lanham: University Press of America.

Brubaker, W.R. 1992. *Citizenship and Nationhood in France and Germany*. Cambridge, MA: Harvard University Press.

Cable, V. 1995. "The Diminished Nation-State: A Study in the Loss of Economic Power." *Dædalos* 124(2):23–51.

Carr, E.H. 1939. *The Twenty Years Crisis 1919–1939: An Introduction to the Study of International Relations*. London: Macmillan.

Clausewitz, Carl von. 1976. *On War*. Princeton, NJ: Princeton University Press.

Clemmesen, Frans, and Henrik Hoffman. 1992. "Skattesystemet uden Grænser" (The Tax System without Borders). *GRUS* 38.

Council of the European Communities/Commission of the European Communities. 1992. *Treaty on European Union*. Luxembourg: Office for Official Publications of the European Communities.

Det nye EF: Traktaten om Den Europæiske Union (The New EC: Treaty on the European Union). 1992. Copenhagen: Centralorganisationen af Metalarbejdere i Danmark, Industriens Arbejdsgivere og den Danske Europabevægelse.

D'Hondt, Jacques. 1970. "Téléologie et Praxis dans la 'Logique' de Hegel." In *Hegel et la Pensée Moderne*, edited by J. Hyppolite. Paris.

Elias, Norbert. 1978. *The History of Manners* (The Civilizing Process, vol. 1). Oxford: Blackwell.

Elias, Norbert. 1982. *Power and Civility* (The Civilizing Process, vol. 2). Oxford: Blackwell.

Foucault, Michel. 1975. *Discipline and Punish*. London: Allen Lane.

Giddens, Anthony. 1982. *Profiles and Critiques in Social Theory*. London: Macmillan.

Giddens, Anthony. 1985. *Nation-State and Violence*. Cambridge: Polity Press.

Hammar, Tomas. 1986. "Citizenship: Membership of a Nation and of a State." *International Migration* 4:735–747.

Hammar, Tomas. 1990. *Democracy and the Nation State*. Aldershot: Avebury.

Hegel, G.W.F. 1991 [1821]. *The Philosophy of Right*. Cambridge: Cambridge University Press.

Held, David. 1989a. "Citizenship and Autonomy." Pp. 162–184 in *Social Theory of Modern Societies*, edited by D. Held & J.B. Thompson. Cambridge: Cambridge University Press.

Held, David. 1989b. *Political Theory and the Modern State*. Stanford: Stanford University Press.

Hindess, Barry. 1986. "Actors and Social Relations." Pp. 113–126 in *Sociological Theory in Transition*, edited by M.L. Wardell & S. Turner. London: Allen & Unwin.

Hindess, Barry. 1987. *Politics and Class Analysis*. Oxford: Basil Blackwell.

Hintze, Otto. 1975. *The Historical Essays of Otto Hintze*, edited by F. Gilbert. New York: Oxford University Press.

Hirst, Paul. 1990. *Representative Democracy and Its Limits*. Cambridge: Polity Press.

Hirst, P., and G. Thompson. 1992. "The Problem of 'Globalisation': International Economic Relations, National Economic Relations, National Economic Management and the Formation of Trading Blocs." *Economy & Society* 21(4):357–396.

Hirst, P., and G. Thompson. 1994. "Globalisation, Foreign Direct Investment and International Economic Governance." *Organisation* 1(2):277–303.

Hirst, P., and G. Thompson. 1995. "Globalisation and the Future of the Nation-State." *Economy & Society* 24(3):408–442.

Hirst, P., and G. Thompson. 1995b. "The Myth of Globalisation." *Prospect.*

Hirst, P., and G. Thompson. 1996. *Globalisation in Question.* Cambridge: Polity Press.

Hobbes, Thomas. 1992 [1651]. *Leviathan.* Cambridge: Cambridge University Press.

Højrup, Thomas. 1995. *Staat, Kultur, Gesellschaft: Zur Entwicklung der Lebensformanalyse.* Marburg: Arbeitskreis Volkskunde und Kulturwissenschaften.

Jespersen, Knud. 1991. *Stat og Nation* (State and Nation). Vol. 4 in the series Det Europæiske Hus (The European House), edited by Søren Mørch. Copenhagen: Gyldendal.

Kaldor, Mary. 1990. *The Imaginary War.* Oxford: Basil Blackwell.

Kaspersen, L.B. 1993. "The Concept of State and Society in Sociology: A Critique of the Fusion Theory in Sociology." Paper presented at the Social Science History Association Annual Convention, Baltimore, MD.

Kennedy, Paul. 1988. *The Rise and Fall and Great Powers.* London: Fontana.

Levi, Margaret. 1993. "The Institution of Conscription." Paper presented at the Social Science History Association Annual Meeting, Baltimore, MD.

Locke, John. 1989. *Two Treaties of Government.* London: J. M. Dent & Son.

Mancini, G. Federico. 1989. "The Making of a Constitution for Europe." *Common Market Law Review* 26:595–614.

Mann, Michael. 1986. *The Sources of Social Power.* Cambridge: Cambridge University Press.

Mann, Michael, ed. 1990. *The Rise and Decline of the Nation State.* Oxford: Basil Blackwell.

Mann, Michael. 1988. *States, War and Capitalism.* Oxford: Blackwell.

Mann, Michael. 1993. "Nation-States in Europe and Other Continents: Diversifying, Developing, Not Dying." *Dædalus,* Summer.

Marshall, T.H. 1950. *Citizenship and Social Class.* Cambridge: Pluto Press.

Martinello, Marco. 1993. "European Citizenship, European Identity, and Migrants: Towards the Postnational?" Paper presented at the ECPR Joint Sessions of Workshops, Leiden.

Marwick, A. 1968. *Britain in the Century of Total War.* Harmondsworth: Penguin.

Marwick, A. 1974. *War and Social Change in the Twentieth Century.* London: Macmillan.

Meehan, Elisabeth. 1993. *Citizenship and the European Community.* London: Sage.

Morgan, Kenneth. 1990. *The Peoples Peace: British History 1945–1990.* Oxford: University of Oxford Press.

Morgenthau, H. 1947. *Politics Among Nations: The Struggle for Power and Peace.* New York: Knopf.

Neunreither, K.H. 1995. "Citizens and the Exercise of Power in the European Union: Towards a New Social Contract?" Pp. 1–18 in *A Citizens' Europe,* edited by Allan Rosas and Esko Antola. London: Sage.

Ruggie, John G. 1993. "Territoriality and Beyond: Problematizing Modernity in International Relations." *International Organization* 47(1).

Schmitt, Carl. 1976. *The Concept of the Political.* New Brunswick, NJ: Rutgers University Press.

Schmitt, Carl. 1985. *Political Theology.* Cambridge, MA: MIT Press.

Schmitter, Phillip. 1995. "If the Nation-State Were to Wither Away in Europe, What Might Replace It?" Stanford University: Unpublished Manuscript.

Shaw, Martin. 1987. "The Rise and Fall of the Military-Democratic State: Britain 1940–85." Pp. 143–158 in *The Sociology of War and Peace*, edited by C. Creighton & M. Shaw. London: Macmillan.

Shaw, Martin. 1991. *The Post-Military Society*. Philadelphia: Temple University Press.

Tamm, Ditlev. 1991. *Retshistorie* (Legal History). Copenhagen: Jurist og Økonom-forbundets Forlag.

Tilly, Charles. 1992. *Coercion, Capital, and European States*. Oxford: Blackwell.

Turner, Brian S. 1986. *Citizenship and Capitalism*. London: Allen & Unwin.

Waltz, Kenneth. 1979. *Theory of International Relations*. New York: Random House.

Wight, Martin. 1977. *Systems of States*. Leicester: Leicester University Press.

7 Rights, Relationality, and Membership

Rethinking the Making and Meaning of Citizenship*

Margaret R. Somers

Attention to the meaning and making of citizenship rights has been glaringly absent from recent sociolegal research agendas for far too long. Thirty years have passed since Reinhard Bendix's *Nation-Building and Citizenship,* and over 40 since T. H. Marshall first published his masterful series of lectures, *Citizenship and Social Class* (Bendix 1977; Marshall 1950). Happily this is beginning to change with the recent contributions of, among others, Jeffrey Alexander (1992:289), Rogers Brubaker (1992), Anthony Giddens (1982, 1987), Michael Mann (1987:339), Charles Tilly (1990a,b), Bryan Turner (1986), and Alan Wolfe (1989). Now we truly have cause for scholarly celebration with the republication in a new edition of the T. H. Marshall volume (1992).[1] Hardly could this be more timely. Rarely have Marshall's driving themes—the politics of citizenship, rights, and social change—more dramatically been yoked together than in the revolutions and upheavals of recent years. Across Europe and Asia, societies constructed and reconstructed on a framework of national state control and putative economic redistribution have collapsed or have been fundamentally challenged by the dynamic momentum of an extraordinary source of power—the mobilizing force of popular claims to citizenship rights and identities. The world-historical impact of these events is obvious. The implications for sociological reflection should also be both large and urgent: Just what is this power we call citizenship and how and why is such an identity constructed as a dynamic force in history?

The exigency of this question makes it important to consider why until very recently sociological discussion of citizenship has been so relatively scant. Among Western intellectuals the reasons for this silence are not hard to identify. The persistence (currently the increase) of Western social inequalities in the face of celebrated liberal freedoms seems only to highlight the structural shallowness of that which we most commonly associate with citizenship—formal civil rights and a limited concern for individual liberties. The discourse of citizenship has similarly been suspect by its association with liberalism's apparent focus on individual rather than social rights. It is thus not surprising that sociologists have concentrated on the politics of class, social inequalities, and state power, with research into the development of economic institutions and movements for social and economic change dominating inquiry.

But there is a sociological message in the political charge recently ignited around the world: People are empowered by an "identity politics"; social change has been made by those whose sense of who they *are* has been violated fundamentally; and it increasingly appears that the identity of one's self as a "rights bearing" person is perhaps the most inviolable, and the most empowering.[2]

And there are other elements of this message. Despite the similarities of the Eastern European movements, for example, the recent mobilizations—from Prague to Latvia—have nonetheless unfolded in the context of local political cultures, that which the activists call "civil society." Indeed, what is most notable about these rights claims is their political specificity: the politics of citizenship discourse requires them to be called "natural," but in practice they have been consistently justified by membership in historically constructed political communities and cultures. People have argued their rights claims to be held by virtue of political membership in public spheres and civil societies that are not comprised of the sovereign individual, the market, or the state. It is a social and political realm foreign to most social science research.[3]

The implications of this seem striking: The politics of citizenship must be rethought. Citizenship is a "contested truth"—its meaning politically and historically constructed. We need to explore the conditions for the making of citizenship claims as well as why it is that the context of participatory claims has been in the pluralities of local civil societies rather than through markets or directed primarily at national state institutions. And, above all, we need to look at the ways that political issues of participatory and civil rights have been integral to—rather than exclusive of— those of market and class inequalities. The themes of civil society and the public sphere suggest realms where economic, legal, and political conceptions of justice converge to influence the formation of rights.

T. H. Marshall wrote in a very different time from ours, and it may seem a far stretch to link recent political upheavals to a work that was intended to explain Western European development, and Britain in particular, in the 1950s—then in its glory days of expanding market controls and state welfare institutions. Marshall's focus, however, on the perduring historical and structural tensions between social class inequalities on the one hand, and the formal equalities of citizenship on the other, is no less relevant today. And although it would be tempting to use Marshall's historical study of the West as a foil for a structural comparison with the East, this essay will not attempt to take on such a challenge; rather it will explore Marshall's work on the same ground that he did.

The reasons for this are straightforward: Like virtually all ambitious works of historical sociology based on the English case, Marshall always intended his work to be a general theory of citizenship. And so it has been treated. Yet it is precisely because Marshall's is a general theory of citizenship that recent approaches to the topic still take it to be the standard against which all discussion should be measured (e.g. Barbalet 1989; Turner 1986). And like most general theories that have become standard discourse, to the extent that it has been challenged, these challenges have accepted Marshall's argument as appropriate for the English case but then go on to suggest revisions for the new case or cases being studied. To the extent that Marshall is once again being appropriated for comparisons with the East, this will happen again. But this approach to classical texts misses the point: True homage to Marshall requires reconsidering his thesis in the context of its original empirical grounds—the formation, course, and consequences of citizenship in English history. Only then can we freshly evaluate his contribution.

The first part of this essay will discuss the most troubling aspects of Marshall's argument and will formulate five thematic counterpoints of contention. The second section offers a counter-argument to Marshall's historical analysis by focusing anew on the conditions for the development of early citizenship rights.[4] And the third section will present a more closely grounded example of an alternative view to the making and meaning of citizenship in one type of local political culture.

T. H. Marshall and Citizenship: Point Counterpoint

Marshall's classic *Citizenship and Social Class* is an explanation for the successive growth of citizenship rights in the context of the development, course, and consequences of the capitalist mode of production. Marshall's pathbreaking achievement was to expand and redefine citizenship away from solely a narrow concept of formal individual liberties to one that also embraced social and economic rights. His definition is three-dimensional, including civil, political, and social rights.[5] Civil rights are those we associate with formal individual liberties—habeas corpus, the right of association, the right to sell one's labor on a free market, and the right to justice—the courts of law without which no right would be politically meaningful. Political liberties are participatory rights—the right to vote, to elect representatives, and so on. Social rights are what he calls the "consumer" rights of the modern welfare state. This bundle of rights attaches to persons through what Marshall calls the "status" of citizenship.

It is the relationship between the rights endowed by citizenship status premised on equality on the one side and the fundamental inequalities inherent in the social class system on the other that most interests Marshall. The two sides represent, in his words, "warring principles"—those of status equality and right against contract inequality and markets. Developing a theory to account for the origins and consequences of these warring tensions in modern society forms the heart of his work.

In Marshall's explanation the engine of modern citizenship resides in the forces and conflicts of capitalism. A nascent capitalist demand for free individuals available for labor markets along with bourgeois gentry needs for mobile property get the motor going and lead to the achievement of civil rights. Once set in motion, the drive is kept going through successive popular mobilization by the subsequent contradictions between capitalist social forces and the exclusions and inequalities of the class system. Eventually, all three citizenship rights are sequentially instituted through socioeconomic change and class formation. This initial premise leads his historical periodization to coincide with epochs of class formation.

In the first stage of the 18th century the triumph of the gentry in the Glorious Revolution ushered in civil citizenship; political citizenship was a product of the 19th-century ascendancy of the middle class; while social citizenship came in the 20th century with the power of the working class and the institutionalization of the welfare state. For Marshall each phase of citizenship is not organically contained in the preceding one. He allows for separate developmental stories for each component. He also dismisses a teleology of rights which derive ultimately from individual property rights. But although the rights are not logically derived in this way, he nonetheless insists that the emergence proceeded in necessary stages, each right a product of the developmental logic of capitalism and its processes of class formation. In this context, the meaning of the growth of citizenship is fundamentally Marshall's story of the enlargement of individual rights to greater degrees of autonomy and equality.

Marshall's definition of citizenship as embracing three spheres has yet to be surpassed. The strength of his classifications lies in what they reveal about the political nature of social life and the recognition that both social and political rights can only be explained by attention to that. And indeed one must endorse Marshall's inclusive three-dimensional view of citizenship. His emphasis on the institutionalization of rights as a necessary component of their realization is another contribution. But his greatest contribution perhaps is his originality and clarity in posing what has now become a common problematic among political sociologists—the inherent tension between capitalism and democracy or, in his formulation, between market inequality and the principle of equality. Marshall's intellectual inheritance from R. H. Tawney and other social democrats, as well as his own moral impulses, allow him to powerfully articulate the unexpected consequences of the unification within a single society of these contrary tendencies—the inequalities consequent to legal freedoms in law and markets on the one hand and those toward the equalizing goals of social welfare and democratic education on the other.[6]

FIVE POINTS OF CONTENTION

There are, nonetheless, serious problems with Marshall's account of the growth of citizenship, the meaning he ascribes to it, and its relationship to capitalist development. To be sure, his primary interest was in building a theory that could make sense of its paradoxical consequences for 20th-century social and economic relations. But Marshall's theory of contemporary society is not structurally static; its powerful analysis of the tensions between citizenship and society, as well as among the different dimensions of rights, depends entirely on the historicity of their emergence. To fully consider his theory, there is no choice but to seriously address its historical foundations.

An institutional and narrative approach suggests alternative formulations to five of his explanatory themes—the causal dynamic, the historical agency, the timing, the spatial distribution, and the meaning of citizenship. In brief: (1) Where Marshall sees the causal motor of self-propelling capitalist social forces at work in the development of citizenship, a more nuanced analytic perspective would focus on a shifting configuration of political, legal, community, and economic institutions at work in the development of a series of national laws and institutions that only contingently could be transformed into specific political cultures of citizenship rights. (2) Where Marshall sees the agents of citizenship to be social classes, it was as members of contesting institutions rather than as such social categories as class that cross-cutting social groups became the protagonists in the drama of rights formation.[7] (3) Where Marshall sees modern citizenship rights "proper" emerging only with the demise of traditional feudal society and the rise of modern capitalist society, the explanation and the causal path of our *modern* citizenship cannot be severed from the legal institutional arrangements of the medieval epoch long before the development of a capitalist society. Moreover, there was an uncertain contingency in the enlargement and expansion of rights that cannot be reduced to any macro-processes of feudalism's demise, capitalism's rise, or societal modernization in general. (4) Where Marshall sees a national uniform extension of rights as a key indicator of modern citizenship, the rights of citizenship were notably more localized and unevenly spatially distributed; there was, moreover, an uneven capacity for and consequences of exercising those rights. (5) And where Marshall sees citizenship as the gradual enlargement of individual rights to wider spheres of society through the equality of status, my analysis defines citizenship rights as a hybrid set of relationships that at once embodies institutional membership and social attachments, as well as the capacity for the autonomous individual exercising of those rights (Somers 1986).

Structural Dynamic and Institutional Analysis

Marshall's analysis of political developments is firmly anchored in the ideal-typical social entities of feudalism and capitalism. The motor of his sequential process of citizenship formation operates in the needs and inevitable social contradictions of the capitalist mode of production. Modern *national* citizenship rights as we know them were nonexistent before capitalism. Any initial impulses toward, or even early expressions of, "premodern" rights were thoroughly impeded by the antimarket ascriptiveness of feudal society. Only the equality of contract necessary to and promoted by capitalist markets enabled their initial takeoff. The expansion of citizenship was in turn driven by capitalism's ensuing conflicting principles—legal equality and social inequality. Marshall then gives his evolutionary theory a social democratic twist; rather than moving from status to contract, he moves from status to contract and status.

An institutional and narrative approach is distinguished from Marshall's in that the processes of citizenship formation are not seen to be anchored in holistic ideal-typical social categories—such as those of feudalism and capitalism. Institutional and narrative analysis uses a relational, rather than a categorical, approach to analyzing social arrangements. *Society* is the term that usually performs the work of characterizing the "social system" in sociolegal analysis. When we speak of understanding social action, for example, we speak of locating the actors in their *societal* context.

But "society" as a concept is rooted in a falsely totalizing and naturalistic way of thinking about the world. For most practicing social science research, a society is a social *entity*. As an entity, it has a core essence—an essential set of social springs at the heart of the mechanism. This essential core is in turn reflected in broader covarying societal institutions that the system comprises. Thus, when sociologists speak of feudalism, for example, we mean at once "feudal society" as a whole, a particular set of "feudal class relations" at the core of this society, a "feudal economy," and a concomitant set of "feudal institutions" such as *feudal* political units and *feudal* peasant communities. Most significantly for social and historical research, each institution within a society must *covary with each other*. Thus in "feudal societies," the state by definition must be a feudal state whose feudal character covaries with all other feudal institutions; feudal workers must all be unfree and extra-economically exploited peasants. And in "industrial society," a "modern industrial/capitalist" state must be detached from civil society and the industrial economy, and industrial workers must be individual and free. To be sure, the synchrony is not always perfect. In periods of transition from one society to another, there is a "lag effect," and remnants of the old order persist against the pressures of the new. But despite these qualifications, the systemic metaphor assumes that the parts of society covary along with the whole as a corporate entity.

For both empirical and epistemological reasons, an institutional/ relational/narrative approach rejects categorical—sometimes called ideal-typical—units of analysis. Empirically, there is simply too much contrary evidence to allow one any longer to believe in a holistic medieval (ca. 1100–1500) societal entity defined by a governing set of feudal relations. Susan Reynolds (1994), for example, has convincingly shown us that the construction of the feudal societal entity as a unit of analysis was almost entirely an intellectual construct of 17th- and 18th-century legal scholars and Scottish philosophers, rather than the result of contemporary sources. Once this conceptual lens of "feudalism" was consolidated into the heart of 18th- and 19th-century social and economic analysis (e.g., Smith, Fergusson, Ricardo, Marx, Weber), our reading of contemporary sources was filtered through this totalizing naturalistic vision.[8] Epistemologically, the ideal-type category of "feudalism"—while always surrounded by qualifications as to its purposefully "abstract" and "nonempirical" use as a heuristic—all too inevitably slides from "idealized heuristic concept" to *description* to *explanatory* construct. From there, it is a short, but inexorable, distance to that of defining as anomalous, irrational, unintelligible, or simply filtering out any structural characteristics or social activities that do not fit the conceptual bundle of "feudalism" now reified into paradigmatic status.[9]

I thus concur with Charles Tilly, Harrison White, and Michael Mann who each agree in his own way that "it may seem an odd position for a sociologist to adopt; but if I could, I would abolish the concept of 'society' altogether" (Mann 1986:2; Tilly 1984; White 1990). To make variable and contingent forms of social action and political arrangements intelligible and coherent, these systemic categorical typologies must be broken apart and their parts disaggregated and reassembled on the basis of relational institutional clusters. For a social order is neither a naturalistic system nor a plurality of individuals, but rather an indeterminate configuration of cultural and institutional relationships. If we want to be able to capture the contingency and complexity of social life, we need a way of thinking that can substitute relational metaphors for totalizing ones.

Institutional and narrative analysis makes this possible. The approach presupposes that institutional relationships and relational networks consistently "outrun" social categories. Institutions are defined as organizational and symbolic practices that operate within networks of (breakable) rules, (fixed and unfixed) structural ties, (often-contested) public narratives, binding (and unbound) relationships that are embedded in time and space (Friedland and Alford 1991:232; Jepperson 1991:143; March and Olsen 1984:734; Meyer and Rowan 1991:41; Polanyi 1957; Polanyi et al. 1957:243).[10] The approach conceptually disaggregates categorical entities and reconfigures them as institutional clusters through which people, power, and organizations are contingently connected and positioned. Instead of "society," I thus use the term *relational setting* (Somers 1986; Somers 1992: 591). A relational setting is a patterned matrix of institutional relationships among cultural, economic, social, and political practices. It invokes spatial and geometric network metaphors rather than systemic ones (Mann 1984; Moore 1978; Smith 1966). The most significant aspect of a relational setting is that there is no governing entity according to which the whole setting can be categorized; it can only be characterized by deciphering its spatial and network patterns and temporal processes. As such, it is a relational matrix, similar to a social network.

One of the most important characteristics of a relational setting is that it has a history (MacIntyre 1981) and thus must be explored over time and space. Temporally, a relational setting is traced over time not by looking for the indicators of social development but by empirically examining if and when the interaction among the institutions of the setting appears to have produced a decisively different outcome from what was indicated in previous examinations. Social change, from this perspective, is viewed not as the evolution or revolution of one societal type to another, but by shifting relationships among the institutional arrangements and cultural practices that comprise one or more social settings.

From this perspective, it becomes plausible to explore the variable ways in which citizenship formation develops within relational settings of contested but patterned relations among people and institutions. It makes it possible to see that citizenship identities and practices developed in analytic autonomy from the bundle of attributes associated a priori with the categories of feudalism and capitalism. From an institutional and relational perspective, rather than in the transition to capitalism or in the "birth of class society," the conditions for the possibility of citizenship rights can be located in the 12th–14th century legal revolution of medieval England that produced both national and local public (participatory) spheres as well as a national political culture based on the *idealized master narrative* of English legal and constitutional rights.

The English crown in the 12th century created the institutional outlines of a *national public sphere* by conjoining a revolutionary new territorial-wide public law (common law) with the public (nonfeudal) local governing bodies of the realm. It did so by appropriating from below and extending throughout the land the political and legal public conventions of the medieval cities and (to a lesser extent) those of the public villages. Excluded from the incorporation into royal common law were the private manorial courts. As a result, the national public sphere took on qualities and conventions of urban and nonfeudal public civil society "writ large." As in medieval and early modern urban cultures, seemingly opposing institutions converged in England's national public sphere. Remedies of procedural justice (civil citizenship) promising the public liberty of the rule of law coexisted with both substantive national regulatory and redistributive statutes (potential forms of social citizenship) as well as institutions which promised—or demanded—community participation (potential forms of political citizenship) in the administration of law. As in the municipalities, however, the actual impact of these institutions of potential citizenship rights was not uniform. Precisely because they were embedded in public spheres, the practical meaning of these laws on people's lives depended almost wholly on the varying degrees of power that different local bodies were able to exert in the processes of appropriating political benefits or resisting political tribulation.

My use of the term *public sphere* can be both related to and distinguished from the use of the term made famous by Jürgen Habermas (1989).

Habermas's most important contribution was to provide a conceptual means of differentiating between state and economy and public participatory arenas that *mediate,* rather than belong to, either the state or the market. In this respect, the concept of the public sphere provides a means of addressing the way in which England's legal arena and infrastructure depended for its very workings on the compulsory participation of the local and county population. At the same time, we are reminded that this public sphere of participatory law was not of—and thus could not be fully controlled by—either the state or the market. Indeed, it is a sphere where the public associates to both influence and defend against otherwise unmediated national states and markets. I do not, however, accept or incorporate the following aspects of Habermas's conceptualization: (1) that public spheres resulted historically in the 18th century from long-term socioeconomic transformation in Western European trade and commerce; (2) that, as a *normative ideal,* the term can refer only to the class-specific arena of *bourgeois* rational discourse; (3) that identities are formed a priori to participation in the public sphere; (4) that the public sphere can be analytically or historically understood while maintaining the exclusionary gender practices built into Habermas's own normative ideal. My use of the public sphere makes it a contested *participatory* site in which actors, in their overlapping identities as legal subjects, national citizens, economic actors, and family and community members, engage as a public body in negotiations and contestations over public matters and national law. In my use, the public sphere is a "structured setting" which may or may not—depending on distributions of power, participatory and associational capacities, and popular political cultures—be transformed into a more democratic arena of popular participation and cultural contestation.[11]

While the struggles over rights were deeply embroiled with the inequalities—indeed the violence—of capitalism, these struggles and their institutional concomitants were consistently mediated through constitutional and juridical channels. Indeed, as an institutional force in the historical landscape, the culture of contingent rights played a constitutive (rather than a dependent) role in shaping the patterns and timing and character of both feudal and capitalist relations as they changed and developed over the centuries. The history of struggles over citizenship becomes less intelligible in the absence of a full picture of these cultural and institutional foundations.

By appropriating and extending throughout the land the political culture of the city, English state building institutionalized a working definition of liberty and rights linked to public law, local participation and, above all, public membership. Beginning in the 17th century these ideas had to compete with a newly developed idea of liberty based solely on individual rights to property produced from autonomous labor. These Lockean ideas of natural rights have dominated the social histories of citizenship and democratization, including Marshall's. But not only did the former public conception and practices of rights prove remarkably robust in their competition with Locke's ideas; arguably, they were more significant in shaping modern popular conceptions of and claims to citizenship.

Agency

The actors in Marshall's account of citizenship are social classes whose categorical attributes and interests in effect thrust them into the historical arena. In his thesis the dynamism behind these struggles, however, lies less in the class actors than in the contradictory principles between the inequalities of class under capitalism and the formal equality of status under citizenship.

In contrast, the actors in my account are members of particular communities, groups, and networks of institutional actors in different sectors of the public sphere.[12] At different times and places, and for different reasons, these membership groups formed alliances or antagonisms with other groups. Some of the contending and coalescing groups included peasant families in pastoral regions of England, monarchical state builders, baronial challengers to the crown, merchant middlemen engaged in the rural putting-out industry, small-fry constables engaged in enforcing the law in local villages, and the artisans and journeymen of guilds. Depending on circumstances and resources, national membership rules were successfully converted into rights, blocked or neglected in the course of these alliances and contestations.

The explicit reasons motivating particular alignments at particular times included economic reasons, as well as religious, familial, political, moral, military, and so on. Usually there was a combination of reasons. But regardless of the particularities of any given coalition or conflict, the issues were fought out over competing conceptions of membership rules. Because labor relations, for example, were embedded in legal policies applicable to all members of the national state, struggles over labor conditions became struggles over the appropriation of law and the conversion of these potentially tyrannical labor regulations into positively defined rights.

In these contestations, legal, cultural, and economic institutions and practices were both the resources and the outcomes of these alliances and antagonisms. It would be difficult, if not impossible, to know which came first in any causal sequence. Examples of some of the institutions and cultural resources involved included the legal right to remedy against the "over mighty," guaranteed trial by jury drawn from one's neighborhood, the administration of justice and governance through local juridical bodies, the discourse of the universality of law, the doctrine of the "king's two bodies," and the existence of statutory regulations mandating that minimum and maximum wages be locally administered.

Perhaps most important, the outcomes of these struggles were less attached to their agency in class or status groups but in the political and legal dynamics that unfolded in local sites of contestation—local public spheres. Only occasionally were the agents' intentions or interests translated directly into the sought-after results; more commonly, the struggles over rights and their institutional expression led in directions wholly unanticipated. This was especially true in the frequent popular appropriations of the promises of universal justice.

Periodization

Marshall's sequential timing of citizenship—from civil, to political, to social—is a direct outgrowth of his initial anchoring of the process in capitalism and its class agents. This initial premise leads his historical periodization to coincide with epochs of class formation—since each right is a product of the developmental conflicts of capitalism and its stages of class formation. Indeed, so strongly does he formulate the functionality of stages of rights for capitalist periodization that he understates the obvious lexically ordered tendency for the development of one type of right to provide leverage in the claim for the next.[13] It follows from this that Marshall's is an amended form of political mode modernization theory: Modern citizenship can only be truly identified with the decline of traditional feudal society (status) and the rise of a modern capitalist one (contract). Although his amendment of modernity (contract plus status) is a major contribution, like all versions of modernization, a fundamental discontinuity must be located in the transition between the two. This is why Marshall acknowledges the presence of "traditional" limited types of feudal rights but argues that a qualitative break occurred between these and the early emergence of modern rights in the 18th century. It also forces him to limit the presence of political rights to the 19th century, and social rights to the 20th.

By contrast, there was a contingent and uneven process to the institutionalization of citizenship rights which does not correspond to a periodization of the transition from feudalism to capitalism—despite the obvious historical interactions between economic processes and citizenship practices. Indeed, virtually all English communities claimed, exercised, benefited, and suffered from both the expansion and the contraction of all three types of citizenship rights long before the triumph of their "proper" capitalist cause. In certain settings, all three dimensions of citizenship existed and were exercised in institutional and practical terms *before* anything resembling the capitalist mode of production arrived in the English countryside. At times, one or more of these rights became faint through repeal or desuetude, while at other times, they were central players in the historical drama. Rather than offering a qualitative break from this period, causal explanation for the particular character of modern citizenship rights must begin— although, of course, not end—from these medieval legal institutional beginnings. No longer can precapitalist legal rights be dismissed as "prehistory" only to be replaced by the new players on the social stage that emerge in the epochs of capitalist markets. To be sure, new players do emerge, and emerge to be significant causal factors in the development of citizenship. But they neither replace, displace, nullify, nor even reinvent the institutional configuration that preceded them. Rather, the impact of these new forces of modernity is largely influenced by the *outcome of their convergence* with previously existing legal institutions and practices.

The Problem of Place: Scope and Scale

Marshall views modern citizenship rights as society-wide and universal in scope since they develop concomitantly with holistic societal transformations. The scale of citizenship, the classes who carried the changes out, the breadth of the economic changes, and ultimately the institutionalization of the rights themselves were universal rather than local. In taking such a view, Marshall follows his disciplinary training in the social sciences with its neglect of spatial distinctions and cultural differences within single notions of holistic societies.

By contrast, the paradox of England's national public sphere is that a formal territorial-wide body of law produced highly localized and multiple practices of rights and enforcement procedures. The conversion of laws to rights was local and contingent in effect and was always adapted to the particular settings where the laws were implemented. This was a direct result of the peculiar nature of England's national legal infrastructure. Its hybrid conjoining into the structure of rule of national, county, and local spheres of power, community, and law created a point of juncture at the sites of local governance. These in turn served as local public spheres. As I will show below, whether these public spheres were to become sites of popular participation varied radically depending on the setting and the local political relationships. Not surprisingly, the struggles for and over rights were also highly local and unevenly distributed over the social and geographical landscape.[14]

For Marshall, the essence of a right is precisely that it is possessed by an autonomous individual. In Marshall's tradition of philosophical liberalism, the status of citizenship is by definition a social *category;* the rights it confers can only be carried by individuals abstracted from their actual relational settings.[15] That Marshall identifies serious conflicts between individual freedoms and the distributive measures necessary for greater social equality does not affect this ontological premise of the rights-bearing individual.

A right is a legal claim brought to bear on a state. When viewed through an institutional lens, those laws that became the source of citizenship rights did not fit into either end of the dichotomy between individual and communitarian conceptions of rights, or negative and positive liberties.[16] In the development of English citizenship, rights developed in *relational* terms (an outcome of what I will call "autonomy in membership" and "liberty in embeddedness"). It was the relationality of rights that provided the means for exercising autonomy and independence.[17] Citizenship rights were indeed rights that supported a high degree of independence; at the same time they were predicated on the attachments and the constraints of membership within a particular group—from family, to village, to trade union, to local civil society, and public sphere. As will be evident in my discussion below, even the achievement of the civil right to liberty presupposed the achievement of a prior right to membership as well as the maintenance of social attachments. Indeed, the history of rights sadly reveals their diminishment with the attenuation of social attachments, while the attenuation of memberships also reveals the concomitant loss of individual empowerment and independence.[18]

This historical view changes the meaning of citizenship. Rather than being a category of social status, the rights of citizenship comprise a bundle of enforceable claims that are variably and contingently appropriated by members of small civil societies and differentiated legal cultures—albeit within a territorially defined nation-state. But a right, like all forms of moral and legal power, is not logically attached to any one social category or persons; rather, rights are free-floating cultural and institutional resources that must be appropriated and in turn given meaning only in the practical context of power and social relations. In this sense, for example, the legal discourse of common law is one of the most powerful of *abstract* rights—who actually benefits from it depends on the distribution of power among those groups seeking to justify their claim. According to that discourse, a citizenship right, like all rights, is not a "thing"; it is a social practice.[19]

The above five points of contention are all elaborated in my alternative account of citizenship formation, an account propelled by a set of questions and observations. The first concerns periodization: For Marshall the three dimensions of citizenship were historically sequential; they may not have been derivative, but their successive phasing was historically necessary and followed a developmental modernizing continuum. But if his schema makes sense, how are we to explain the loss in the early 19th century of long-standing social citizenship rights such as apprenticeship regulations? (Mantoux 1955; Polanyi 1957; Prothero 1979; Rule 1982, 1986; Thompson 1971:77)

After all, social citizenship is supposed to emerge only in the 20th century. And why was there a *decrease* in political citizenship after a notable period of democratic expansion in the 17th (Hirst 1975; O'Gorman 1992:135; Plumb 1969:90; Pocock 1985)? Why did England have 500 years of poor laws which incontrovertibly sedimented into 20th-century social rights? And why were minimum wage regulations first passed in 1604—three centuries before Marshall's social citizenship—only to be repealed in 1814 (Minchinton 1972)?[20] We know, of course, that Marshall knew all this historical evidence; indeed, he discusses the poor laws at length. But it is precisely the value of a critical legal social science to take the same empirical data and use it to reconfigure an alternative interpretation—in this case, one that does not a priori bifurcate citizenship between traditional and modern manifestations.

The same sorts of questions of periodization are applicable for reflecting on the agency involved in citizenship formation. Marshall's explanation raises one of the most perplexing of questions when viewed in the context of the following observation: Rather than there being a radical rupture from "traditional society" to "modernity" when viewed over the very long term, a remarkable degree of continuity in rights claims can be identified before and after the transition from "feudalism" to "capitalism." The long-term evidence is striking: From as early as the 14th century, certain groups of peasant and later rural-industrial communities from the pastoral regions of England claimed rights of and expectations of the law in language and in actions remarkably similar to those of their 19th-century progeny in the industrial northern regions of England (where historians have generally identified the beginnings of popular rights claims with the onset of Chartism— the first mass working-class movement for the franchise).[21] From the 14th through the 16th to the 19th centuries, these laboring families also linked the independence and cohesion of their communities to the participatory rights and distributive ideals of English citizenship long before the "proper" capitalist cause. Continuity, of course, is a relative concept—not an empirical fact. In this case, my claim for continuity is made *relative* to the universal presupposition among scholars of a radical rupture in popular behavior between a preindustrial or traditional society and industrial modern society (depending, of course, on what point in time that curtain of "modernity" is lifted). It is in this context of an unquestioned notion of transformation consequent to the transformation of societal categories from preindustrial to industrial—and not from the obvious point that continuities were inflected by concomitant transformations—that a certain degree of substantive continuity in popular political culture is especially notable.[22]

The crucial point is that these popular forms of collective action were highly local and regionally specific. No less striking than a notable degree of substantive continuity in popular political culture over the centuries is the evidence of persistent *spatial* and *regional* specificity in popular rights claims and attitudes toward the law.[23] It was only "the people" from the pastoral, later rural-industrial, and eventually (by the 19th century) industrial villages who, from the 14th century on, demonstrated explicitly positive expectations of their public political, social, and civil rights.[24] Rural-industrial communities appear almost "guild-like" and artisanal in their political cultures and expectations of citizenship rights.[25] There is less evidence for any such positive expectations toward the law among those laboring peoples located in the arable regions and comprised primarily of large commercial agricultural labor or, at an earlier time, of unfree villeins.[26] While still unfree villeins, these peasants had possessed a degree of customary rights that held relatively firmly in their manorial courts. Some peasants were even able to use these rights to gain copyhold status and eventually access to common law.[27] But for the vast majority, it appears that the contrast was notable: Far from believing that they had "rights," the poor among the arable regions experienced the institutions of law and justice as oppressive, indeed tyrannical. Localism and variation rather than universality clearly marked the development of citizenship rights.

Any theory of the historical development of rights claims would have to be able to account for these surprising problems of time and space.[28] These are therefore the questions that organize my counterexplanation to Marshall's.

Citizenship Formation: An Outline of an Alternative Account

The first national entity in England to institutionalize the rules that led contingently to citizenship rights and obligations was the medieval public sphere. An alternative account must trace the making of England's public sphere and its differential impact on the locales in which citizenship rights were developed and contested in medieval and early modern England.[29] It is a history of coalitions and contentions, alliances and antagonisms, which played out in a shifting configuration of institutional relationships. The premise of my alternative account is that the development and the precise character of modern citizenship is as much a direct outcome of these medieval institutional and cultural foundations as it is an outcome of the intervening forces of capitalist revolutions and class formation in the 17th and 18th centuries. It was the *nexus* between the sequential institutional path of citizenship formation and the structural overlay of marketization that was decisive.

The Making of a Legal Revolution

The history of the formation of a national public sphere must begin in 11th and 12th-century England before the presence of a unified territorial-wide state. Decentralization was the hallmark of this so-called feudal society, and it is generally characterized as a single feudal culture of "parcellized sovereignties" comprised of mighty fiefdoms with the crown being one among many feudal landlords. This ideal-typical characterization of medieval society doggedly persists despite its empirical weaknesses, as Susan Reynolds (1994) has recently reminded us. More in line with an institutional and relational approach to the medieval world, I will map the landscape roughly into four different political and legal cultures.

The first of these (and the most commonly associated with "feudalism") was made up of the rich arable regions of England dominated by large manors and their lords and administered through manor courts *(hall moots)*. These private spheres of power (which varied tremendously in size and resources) most closely fit the stereotype of the feudal social order—a hierarchical chain of relationships connecting lords, vassals, and a large population of servile unfree peasant laborers *(villeins)*. In this system of vertical ties, each link played a part in the story of citizenship formation. The most powerful of the manorial lords formed the core of the baronical competition to the crown (leading to the Magna Carta in 1215), which both responded to and catalyzed monarchical state building. It was the relationship of the vassals to their lords, however, that is most significant for our story.[30] Although subordinated in a chain of command and obligation, these obligational chains by their nature concomitantly endowed vassals with significant rights (what I call "relational rights") which gave them a great deal of autonomy. As we will see below, these relational rights come to play an exemplary role in the development of concepts of rights among broader segments of the population. At the bottom of the chain of relations were the unfree villein peasants (Ault 1972; Burrow 1974:255; Gatrell 1982:23; Gray 1963; Homans 1962; Pollock and Maitland 1968; Somers 1986; Vinogradoff 1908, 1923; Webb and Webb 1963).

The second sphere, and probably the least familiar, was made up of the scattered areas of pastoral, woodland, and relatively nonarable lands. These pastoral regions were populated primarily by small free-holding peasant villagers who farmed and lived in scattered villages and hamlets. In contrast to our prevailing images of feudal society, these nonopen field regions had few great manors; often there was no single resident dominating manor. Governance took place through local public courts—some ancient country and "hundred" courts—which were formally under the jurisdiction of royal sheriffs. In comparison with manorial villeins, these free villagers had considerable legal and social freedoms by virtue of their embeddedness in public jurisdictions. Their land and rights, nonetheless, were under the constant threat of encroachment by powerful manorial lords outside their immediate environs. Before these free peasants were corralled into an "alliance" between "the people and the (public) law," the primary system of defense against such encroachment was the strict system of horizontal rights and obligations embedded in their inheritance practices and community relationships, as well as in their local courts and councils. These legal and cultural practices came to serve the villagers well in their later struggles to appropriate formal membership laws into actual local citizenship rights (Dodgshon 1978:81; Hallam 1981; Homans 1962, 1969:29; Power 1942; Thirsk 1967, 1961:70).

The third sphere—a kind of hybrid—was comprised of towns, municipalities, and urban boroughs. On the one hand, towns and boroughs were usually located in land controlled by manorial lords. In this setting, urban tenants had the same obligations to the lord as did servile peasant labor; they were answerable to the lords in the manor court and forced to labor regularly on their lands. At the same time, their mercantile activities required a great degree of social coordination, and to this end numerous self-governing institutions outside the manor courts developed over time. The first of these was the merchant guild. Its members looked with envy at the rights of vassals, noting that the autonomy endowed by these rights was directly contingent on particularly defined relationships with the lords.[31]

Finally, the fourth sphere was that of the monarchy. In comparison with the rest of Europe, the post-conquest English monarchy was extremely centralized and bureaucratized.[32] Nonetheless, the crown was hemmed in ultimately by its relentless and urgent need to fill the coffers of war and the power of manorial lords and urban merchants to resist providing the financial support for monarchical military ambitions on the other.[33] The antagonisms between the crown and the barons was exacerbated by royal frustration over both its limited access to baronial resources and its difficulty in controlling the violence of the warring countryside and the political demands of rebelling barons. Even merchant wealth was beyond monarchical reach; indeed, there was good reason to believe that mercantile political loyalties and wealth would follow the lead of the barons' revolts (Anderson 1974; Bagehot 1965; Corrigan and Sayer 1985; Pollock and Maitland 1968; Sayer 1992:1382; Strayer 1970).

The crown, the towns, and the pastoral bodies had nothing in common except an overwhelming mutual antagonism to the manorial spheres of private power. Mercantile antagonism reflected the demands of these urban dwellers for the same degree of autonomy from feudal lords as was possessed by manorial vassals. And in this desire for municipal juridical independence, merchants and urban artisans were united. Merchants, moreover, were indeed inspired by baronial revolts; if their wealth was so much in demand, they saw no reason why they should not expect in return a share in wider political power (Ardant 1975:164). Finally, pastoral peasant antagonism reflected the constant attempts on the part of manorial lords to "manorialize" their freeholding farms, rob them of their free legal status, and ultimately to subject them to the condition of relative rightlessness characteristic of those peasants ultimately answerable only to the "will of the lord" in the manor courts.

How did the English crown overcome the political and jurisdictional competition from private manorial and baronial power? In the 12th through 14th centuries, the English crown carried out a legal revolution by deploying Norman administrative institutions and centralizing principles of Roman law, ancient juridical customs of the realm, selected parts of the canon law, and a host of other free-floating resources. What made it revolutionary was both the fact of a crown being able to achieve such precocious territorial-wide unification at this time and the method used to accomplish it—a monarchical strategy to forge institutional links with those prefeudal public juridical units and administrative centers that remained intact throughout the period of wide privatization through manorialism. At the same time, through a widely expanded elaboration of royal legal rules and regulations, especially the king's peace, the English crown formally encircled all the local governing bodies of the realm—public and private—by creating powerful territorial-wide public legal institutions that functioned over and above private feudal power. These included the Royal Courts and traveling Assizes as well as royal administrative appointees drawn from the local population.

The result was an early (relative to the rest of Europe) national state that incorporated a majority of juridical and administrative units into a single entity but *without dismantling the original, local bodies.*

This new legal administrative sphere was thus at heart an institutional matrix of complex connections. It can be pictured as a social map that was transformed from a multiplicity of separate (usually warring) entities to a mapping of multiplex linkages among, and encirclement by, a wide network of public institutions. Most crudely put, over many years and many conflicts the monarchy had managed to carve out a structural institutional "alliance" between "the people" and the "law."[34] The alliance took the institutional shape of a configuration of linkages among the crown, urban merchants, and nonmanorial governing bodies—a geometric matrix of networks and linkages in continual relational tension and movement among and between the connecting nodes. Rather than setting up an alternative political apparatus entirely outside its baronial competitors as in the French case, the English crown thus built a national legal sphere by incorporating into a single formal entity the preexisting public legal and governing bodies, their political institutions and practices. These local conventions and rules, and those from the mercantile cities in particular such as guild and mercantile law, were in turn nationalized by the state through new centralized institutions. Local laws *writ large* were then in turn reapplied to the localities through local administrators who were nonetheless ultimately accountable to the national state.

Susan Reynolds's *Kingdoms and Communities in Western Europe, 900–1300,* argues that all early medieval European realms defined themselves as communities and that kingdoms constituted themselves out of such overlapping communities (1984). This is certainly true at the level of self-definition as rulers sought to "naturalize" their territorial consolidation through ideologies of community and population homogeneity.[35] But the mechanisms and impact of structural consolidation can be more precisely analyzed when viewed on a continuum between the making of a national "community" through incorporation and compulsory participation from the preexisting local bodies, as in the English case, and the making of a national "community" through the direct imposition of state administrators onto preexisting competing units. Tilly presents a two-dimensional typology which he uses to differentiate different states' paths of growth. The two axes of the typology are extent of concentration of capital and extent of concentration of coercion. From this schema, Tilly defines three trajectories: the coercion intensive path, the capitalized coercion path, and the capital-intensive path (Tilly 1990a:130). England, when compared to France, her main military rival, looks far more like the dualistic structure of worlds within world consolidation. When viewed from either of these continuums, an appropriate question to ask would be whether the more "legitimate" strategy of English state building became a post hoc ideology that internationalized itself.[36]

I have of course presented a hypostatized and abstract picture of a dramatic historical process driven by momentous conflicts and power relations. This is not the place, however, to spell out in a large canvas that drama of struggle and state building and the making of the national legal sphere. Suffice it to say here that this is the institutional foundation of the English national state. It is this configurational institution to which members of previously separate local bodies first came to belong as national members. And it was this legal sphere that first imposed the rules and legal obligations of national membership.

Early English Citizenship and a Political Culture of Rights

England's national legal sphere was thus constructed through the conjoining and interdependence of local bodies, institutions, practices, and doctrines within a central organizing body. This was a public realm built on mandatory *community inclusion, and participatory law and governance.* The consequence of this historical process was the creation of a hybrid political culture which was both new and old, national and local, and which embodied all the principles and power relations of the different local cultural spheres. What was new was membership in a national body to which subjects were both answerable and by which they were endowed with certain rights. These rights were only meaningful in the context of their linkage to membership in the national sphere and access to its legal system over and above that of private power. What was old, however, was just as important. The linkages were not between the crown and individuals but between public national institutions and local village ones—local juries, the constabulary, local assizes, and so on. The possible benefits and likely sanctions of national membership such as "protective labour regulations" were utterly contingent on membership in these local institutions, making individuals and families also answerable and responsive to local practices and sanctions, to the old duties and rights attached to local membership.

As a mutually constituted realm, neither the national nor the local had power without the other. Alone, local bodies could not protect themselves from manorial power and, eventually, market exploitation; the crown in turn depended on this newly expanded power base. To borrow a term from a scholar of urban life, this hybrid-like configuration was comprised of "worlds within worlds," or what I will call "membership within membership" (Rappaport 1989). "Self-governance at the king's command" was the paradoxical contemporary expression of this political culture constructed on relational tensions and mutual interdependencies among groups and institutions. The resulting political culture was also a hybrid embodying all these principles. And the three dimensions of citizenship that emerged were direct outgrowths of this hybrid political culture created of worlds within worlds.

Civil Citizenship

The first dimension (although not necessarily chronologically) was the right and the obligation to public justice—the origins of civil citizenship. With the formal consolidation of a national legal sphere, the spread, accessibility, institutionalization, and the discourse of public law began to compete with private manorial jurisdiction in shaping English political culture. Its explicit promise was first of all adjudication and peace keeping. But its competitive edge came from its promise to remedy the local wrongs of mighty feudal lords—a remedy of right that could counter through law the unequal position of rightlessness of the weak when confronted with the local power of private justice. Even though we are speaking of a period when king's remedies only went to certain wrongs, and when manorial courts still had broad jurisdiction, the discursive ideal of common law was its claims to universality. As a universal discourse, common law created surprisingly universal expectations. These expectations in turn became resources for popular mobilizations to lay claim to the universal ideals of the rule of law. The frequency of struggles for its realization underlines just how uneven was its application in practice.

Based not on enacted laws or policies but on the principle of law as a set of public rules to resolve conflict and ensure equal protection to all, principles of civil right established the basis of liberty to be "freedom from . . . ," that is, freedom from the overbearing power of private feudal power by the protection of the public law. Linked in the 17th century to the theory of natural rights and property rights in labor and the individual, procedural civil justice gave rise to the animating myths of the "free-loom Englishman" and England's much touted "rule of law" as it made universality before the law and the right to rebel against a tyrannical monarch (allegedly called into existence solely to protect the individual's rights) central to its organizing principles. Yet in their origins, these principles of right and property were not connected to the formulation of property as individual ownership in the juridical language of civil law and Locke, but to property as political membership—the contrast being between rights invested in things and rights invested in political relationships (Pocock 1985:51; Tuck 1979;

Tully 1980).[37] The king's writ, for example, did not determine in advance how property disputes should be resolved but rather ordered the dispute to be moved into the public courts, thus giving certain classes of people—to be sure, not all—the right to be heard in courts of public justice, not the a priori determination of the content of that justice. Once in the royal courts, however, it was the Assize of Clarendon which determined the procedure. Enacted by the crown in the 12th century, the Assize worked in such a way that membership rather than property "ownership" determined political and legal rights. The Assize declared that freeholders were no longer subject to absolute political power by private lords in disputes over their land, even when the freeholder did not "own" the land. If the community supported the freeholder's claim, the freeholder was now given the right to public justice in the king's courts. Because they came from a freeholding heritage, rural-industrial families in particular carried a legacy that rooted economic survival in public membership.

One of the more interesting twists on civil citizenship lies in the non-common law practice of *equity*. When in the 14th century the Chancery first began to take up the business of justice, it offered itself as an alternative means of receiving justice to the lengthy and expensive procedures of the common law courts. In the Chancery no pleading was necessary by lawyers, no jury had to be convened—although expert witnesses were to be brought; and the initiation of the proceeding was a result of a petition from below. The key to this new swifter form of justice by which the "less mighty" could be protected against the "over mighty" was that by reaching directly to the king's courts, equity bypassed powerful county influence. As a procedure, equity was so popular that the conciliar courts were inundated with petitions for its use and it became the basis of procedure and judgment in the Privy Council, the Star Chamber, and the Court of Requests (Baker 1983; Elton 1982; Fischer and Lundgreen 1975:456; Maitland 1979).[38]

The substance of equity, however, was broader than mere procedural simplicity. In essence it was a concept of justice in which particular *circumstances,* considerations of hardship and mercy, and the putatively highminded conscience of the king—rather than abstract procedural principles—were factored into the passing of judgments. St. Germain was the most notable 16th-century theorist of equity (Hansen 1970:157):

> Equity is righteousness that considers all the particular circumstances of the deed, which is also tempered with the sweetness of mercy. . . . And the wise man says: be not overmuch righteous, for the extreme righteousness is extreme wrong. . . . And therefore to follow the words

of the law were in some case both against justice and the common-wealth: wherefore in some cases it is good and even necessary to leave words of the law and to follow that reason and justice require. And to that intent equity is ordained.

Used in the "poor man's courts" where the costs of presentment were not prohibitive, equity appealed to the poor because it claimed, in principle at least, to focus on the relationship between circumstances and justice. It was meant to be a law that was appropriate and adaptable to changing circumstances. As such, it directly competed with common law procedures which were so strictly tied to the letter of the law that the "spirit of necessity" was lost. St. Germain stated the purpose of the Court of Chancery (Hansen 1970:157):

And the Court of the Chancery is called of the common people the court of conscience, because the chancellor is not strained by rigour or form of words of law to judge but *ex aequo* and *bono* according to conscience.

Rather than the law in its pristine logic, equity ruled as just the principles of "natural justice, common sense, and common fairness"—principles that were applied by the state's conciliar courts to the task of redressing injustices inflicted on the poor by the unequal power of the "over mighty." The discretionary conscience of the king was to be the basis of such redress; and as long as such conscience was frequently mobilized, the centralized power of the crown could increase. By meeting the needs of those who felt lack of justice at the hands of the rigidities of common law procedures, and by providing redress where other forums of law had failed to adapt to changing circumstances (Elton 1982:152), the courts of equity forged direct links between the people and the institutions of the state while simultaneously carrying on the process of monarchical centralization through the law. It was these procedural burdens of common law less than its substantive failures that propelled the growth of equity in the royal courts until the time of the English civil war in the 17th century.[39]

If the king's conscience came to be a boon to the poor, the king's body—that is, his actual corporeal person—was of less importance. In English legal practice there was an English version of the Roman doctrine of the "king's two bodies" (Hansen 1970; Kantorowitz 1957). The doctrine specified that every person in the realm, including the king, was subject to the law—even if the king was himself the maker of laws. The king, in his person, for all the pomp attached to his physical being, was thus in principle subservient to the law even as *the kingship*—his office—was above it. The crown appropriated the principle of the invincibility of *office* to support the entrenchment of centralized administrative techniques and the power of the conciliar courts. By doing so, English monarchs created the conditions for the expectations of moral obligation and justice from the crown *without necessarily attaching and enduring allegiance to the particular person of the king himself.*

A remarkable mythology of the rule of law was the consequence of the Anglicanization of the doctrine of the king's duality. From oppressive legal proceedings to the most heinous impositions of tyranny by the state, the failing of the law itself was not blamed but rather corrupt individuals, ministers, particular events, and even kings who were abusing the rule of law. Only the English were so obsessed by the conviction of universality of law that they claimed it was within the bounds of law to commit revolution and detach a king's head. To Milton are attributed fits of "legal antinomianism" in his cries for the utter legality of regicide (Harding 1966; Nenner 1980). The king's two bodies was essential doctrine for both parliamentarians and the conservative agents of the Restoration (Nenner 1980).

> Nothing more slackens the reins of government, and the stability of peace, which is upheld by the reverent awe and respect which the people and subjects give to the Magistrate, than when by injustice and unworthiness, they bring their persons and authority under contempt and dislike; but that they seem not as Gods but Idols, which have eares but heare not, eyes but see not, mouths but *speak not true judgement. Against such Magistrates, people are prone to think it, not only just, but meritorious to rebel.* (Ganden 1980:47)

The doctrine was also at the heart of the law's promise of universality. That the king in his person, for all the pomp attached to his physical being, was allegedly a servant of the law created the conditions for popular expectations of moral obligation and justice from the royal law without attaching an enduring allegiance to the particular person of any one monarch. Universality was at the very core of English common law; king and pauper alike were equally subject to the law. There was no ambiguity about this; the term "magistrate" was applied equally to local political authorities so that in public narrative the power, duties, and accountability of Westminster were allegedly analogous to those of local authorities, and expectations of both were one and the same. If no authority was above the law, it followed naturally that if any acted as if they were, they were subject to legal removal by the injured parties. What was the definition of a governor and legislator? Even a Newcastle Whig answered in 1774 by declaring them as but "trustees to the public" so that any such magistrates who abuse the laws by making "laws more favourable to themselves than to him [the public]," or if they "execute the laws more favourable to one than to another, or stretch them to an oppressive purpose to serve their own ends—they *should be displaced, from the prince to the parish officer; and others chosen in their stead*" (Brewer 1980:133). The dissociation of the rule of law from the *rulers* of law gave eminent rationality—a thoroughly "modern" concept—to an expectation of justice.[40]

POLITICAL CITIZENSHIP [41]

The second aspect of the political culture of rights, and the oldest of all, was compulsory participation in local governance, administration, and law—the origins of political citizenship. As described above, the public sphere integrated into participatory roles of local courts and villagers, and the crown drew new lines of loyalty throughout the territory. It would be easy to dismiss any democratic outcomes in this structure of participation. But for two reasons this would be a mistake. First, English governance was channeled through its legal system. The local courts served as political arenas and institutions. Second, it was precisely in legal institutions that local participation was not limited to county elites but spread deeply into the communities.[42] The vastly smaller number of English salaried officials, in contrast to the Continental system, was made up by the heavy use of laymen.[43] Joseph Strayer points out that by the 13th century England's royal government was "involving almost the entire free population of the country in the work of the law courts (1970:41).[44] These popular institutions included juries; bodies of "expert witnesses" drawn from the communities requisite to almost all legal and administrative procedures; petitions; proclamations from the central government; village courts; the method of appointment of the constable; the commands to participate in, and the obligation to raise, hue and cry; and to a limited extent, the participatory capacities exercised in the 16th and 17th centuries by a surprisingly large number of small artisans and freeholders, electors and nonelectors alike.[45]

Political citizenship was thus built on a Janus-faced contingency: The power of the centralized machinery—despite its coercive mechanisms, its prerogative courts, its county agents, its threatening letters, and its allures of patronage—had always to contend with the participatory power of local populations.[46] This counter-pressure, moreover, was grounded in and expressed through more than customary practices or social pressures. Popular participation in local and national governance was institutionally incorporated by local popular juridical institutions into the heart of the English bureaucratic apparatus.

A number of paradoxical outcomes developed from this. As a system of state-centered participatory rule—or self-governance at the king's command—the structure of rule could be neither fully state controlled nor fully decentralized. The result was a system of reciprocal enhancement of power between the center and the local branches of the state as the strength of each depended on and in turn fostered the strength of the other. This in turn produced a politicized and negotiable chain of command in the English structure of rule; it was forced to operate through a contingent balance of coercion, negotiation, and multiple points of bargaining among all the bodies in its chain of command. The state could not rule unconditionally but rather was forced to bargain with, exhort, and be vulnerable to local politics and popular practices. "Ruling," observes 17th-century historian Cynthia Herrup, "was a repeated exercise in compromise, co-operation, co-optation and resistance" (1983). As a consequence of participatory rights and duties, there was no a priori monopoly of power, and the actual implementation of rights hinged on negotiation and political bargaining.

SOCIAL CITIZENSHIP

The third aspect of citizenship was the regulation of economic life— the origins of Marshall's social citizenship. The most important of these was the body of industrial and welfare policies devoted not to eliminating but to regulating markets—from labor to grain. With the 1349 and 1351 Ordinance and Statute of Laborers, a body of national laws regulating labor relations was first introduced to cover the entire realm. These were continually reintroduced and adjusted through the famous 1563 Elizabethan Statute of Artificers regulating wages and apprenticeship practices, through the neglected 1604 statute instituting *minimum* wage regulations in the rural-industrial regions, until their final repeal in 1813 and 1814.[47] Even more well known, of course, are the Poor Laws—versions of which date to the late 13th century—which included "unemployment benefits" and the recognition of structural unemployment. Many other welfare policies could be included, from the assizes of bread to regulation of working hours.

But why should these laws—usually described as modes of social control and class power—fall under the category of citizenship rights? To understand that, it must be noted that the most significant feature of English welfare and industrial policies was that they were implemented through the normal channels and processes of government and law. The public courts doubled as labor tribunals; local justices and constables served as the administrative personnel; and juries, petitions, legal arbitrations, and national courts were all part of the administrative labor process (Davies 1956; Dobson 1980; Putnam 1906, 1908; Tawney 1972). The consequences were tremendous: Labor relations operated within the structure of public law, and struggles over labor relations were converted into contestations between employers, workers, and political authorities over whether these laws would be tyrannies or rights.

In the context of political citizenship, this in turn had momentous consequences: Labor relations were negotiated through a legal system built on multiple points of participatory access. By forging a direct link into the villages through JPs, constables, juries, and village courts, and by delegating to local authorities the task of administering labor regulations, the crown had in one swoop made vulnerable to local power all the essential aspects of labor relations—labor supply, labor costs, and the cost of provisioning. Politics, not markets, would determine labor relations. Neither municipal guild regulations, nor magnate or gentry landlords, nor merchant capitalist employers would have a legal claim to an *unmediated* administrative or economic relationship to labor as the public sphere subjected all forms of the private labor contract (whether the private party was a commercial landlord or merchant capital), agricultural and industrial labor alike, to public legal jurisdiction. That all forms of the labor contract were now subject to public participatory legal mediation arguably had more impact on the abolition of feudal villeinage (serfdom) and the continued assertion of the right to freedom from private manorial and/or merchant capitalist power than did the "transition from feudalism to capitalism" or other forms of class power and demographic change.

Two Legal Cultures

What were the consequences of the politicizing of the labor contract within a public structure of rule whose chief features were its malleability, indeterminacy, and participatory accessibility? Because the English state was built on a participatory basis, exactly how labor relations were resolved in practice depended on the nature of the different local bodies and regions in which the law was actually exercised. *A single public body of membership rules generated, in practical terms, intensely local legal and political cultures.* The structure of rule in general and the character of labor relations in particular took different shape depending on who had the power to participate.

In the agrarian regions, the power to participate was eventually monopolized by large landholding gentry who used the civic liberty of the public law to free themselves from private magnates and assert themselves through the new-found power of public judicial institutions. Within their spheres of unfreedom, however, villeins did have certain customary rights in the manor courts.[48] Some of the luckier peasant families were able over the course of a couple of centuries largely to escape from villeinage into the much more advantageous position of copyholders. Once ensconced in copyhold, they managed to win a wider range of rights for themselves by means first of equity jurisdiction and eventually the common law.[49] Their freedom flowed in the same direction as in the nonmanorial regions, and the closer they were able to move toward public law, the better off they were. The majority of lesser peasants remained relatively rightless, however, the burden of their obligations shifting from the manorial lord to the gentry landlord as they were gradually transformed into agrarian landless laborers by the 17th century. Laboring peasants in these regions with little or no autonomous power were unable to take advantage of public participatory rights and, despite the legal freedom granted by public law, were subordinated anew through the legal process.

In pastoral/rural-industrial regions, by contrast, the absence of powerful social and political elites, the longer history of legal freedom, and the presence of more solidaristic popular communities meant that civic liberties and public participatory law promoted more favorable outcomes to the laboring population. As active participants in the processes of governance, they were able on occasion to prevent private sources of power—both gentry and merchant capitalists—from exploiting to complete advantage the public institutions of law while they were simultaneously able to demand and appropriate the law to strengthen their own independence.[50]

The local contextualizing of legal processes thus generated different patterns of justice and rights in different types of English regions.[51] There were historically persistent patterns of difference in the structure of early labor markets, in the degree of popular participation in political and legal institutions, in the character of corporate village institutions, and in conceptions of justice and rights. Neither class nor status divisions can account for these differences since those in similar class situations maintained different degrees of power across regions. Instead, these cultural patterns were part of the interaction between England's participatory legal institutions and the presence of contrasting regional political cultures. Popular empowerment varied in the degree to which local populations were able to appropriate the law into a "judicial citizenship."

The significance of the political contingency, plasticity, and multiple points of participatory access in the structure of the public sphere was that it made the institutions of citizenship not the a priori domain of any one class or group but rather a "multiple-use" structure—potentially available to be appropriated by those who had the capacity to appropriate public institutions. No one person, authority, institution, or class was simply free a priori to impose and realize its interests; each was rather forced to negotiate and bargain within the structural constraints and, to be sure, with certain positional structural advantages, of the participatory public sphere. The fluency of the law and the administrative chain of command and the centrality of popular institutions and local governmental offices converged to made it possible under different conditions for different parties to grab hold of legal mechanisms and turn them to their own advantage. A culture of localism and participatory practices made the meaning of citizenship highly contested and variable depending on distribution of power to exercise rights.

I now take a deeper look at one of those legal cultures within the public sphere: the medieval municipalities and their guilds.

The Political Cultures of Towns and Guilds: The Relationality of Rights

Images of medieval cities and guilds are more constructed and exploited in theories than analyzed in their historical practices. The effort here will be to ignore the "ideology of normative past" that infuses the historiography and social theory of urban life and to instead focus on what has been neglected—a focus on the forms of urban life and analysis of the intersection of cultural and institutional life.[52] One reason for doing this is that medieval urban life provides an exemplary pattern of a political culture of citizenship rights both in formation and in action. It illustrates how struggles among local governing bodies and between spheres of power transformed into varieties of institutional relationships—relationships marked by ongoing tensions. These dynamic patterns become embodied and expressed within a political culture and are themselves sources of historical change.

A second reason for looking closer at the medieval towns concerns their special impact on the development of England's public sphere. Principles of substantive justice and mercantilist policies for regulating economic life were common to all European state-building strategies. But the manner in which England established territorial-wide political control over economic life was unique—both in its relationship to the urban policies and in its impact on the national political culture. By the 14th century English cities and towns can be characterized by their "autonomy in membership" or "liberty in embeddedness." This meant that their legal self-governance and characteristically medieval economic autarky was wholly contingent on institutional ties of political reciprocity with the crown and the public sphere at large. In its struggles for expanded national wealth (again, for the wages of war), the English crown was able to take advantage of this less than absolute autonomy of the medieval cities. On the Continent early absolutist regimes were unable to counter the complete autonomy of the urban burghers and guilds and thus had to "invent" anew their regulative institutions. Only in England was the crown able to appropriate from below and extend throughout the land the political and legal conventions of the medieval cities. From the mid-14th century through the 17th-century Stuart regime, English monarchs and state builders engaged in a steady process of forcing open fiercely insulated town policies and instituting throughout the country at large the same vast system of regulative and redistributive laws that had previously been limited to urban, guild, and even canon law. Continental monarchs, by contrast, were left with only national regulative control over commodity markets and foreign trade.

These statutes and conventions were a key feature in shaping the development of the English political culture of citizenship—especially in the crucial realm of social rights. In contrast to continental Europe where the culture of the guilds was restricted to urban settings, England's public sphere blended the political and legal cultures of town and country labor.[53] Since urban culture and law was thus so central to the public sphere as a whole, we must look more closely to understand the foundations of the national political culture.

Liberty in Embeddedness: The City and the Crown

In popular lore, medieval cities are most renowned for having been a refuge for personal liberty in an age of arbitrary feudal power and insecurity (Black 1984:39, 42; Bloch 1961; Harding 1980:427, 442; Smith 1963). "A year and a day" was the customary amount of "city-air" an escaped villein needed to gain freedom. But this was not the kind of freedom Pirenne and others identified as the origins of capitalist individualism.[54] Indeed Pirenne and Weber and even Marx to a degree all believed the motor of modern capitalist growth—whether conceived in Pirenne's terms as freemarket individualism, or Weber's as the site of rational domination and legitimacy—lay in the mercantile activities of the medieval cities. Pirenne in particular has been hugely influential in locating in the towns the origins of cultural individualism. But capitalist breakthroughs did not originate primarily from the cities; nor was the secret to its success unregulated mercantile activity. Our interest in the freedoms of the city must take us to a rival and relatively unrecognized concept of liberty—both economic and personal.[55]

The "liberty" of the towns had both a corporate and a personal meaning. But it was from the corporate that individual liberty derived.[56] The hallmark of the English town—and London is of course the most outstanding case—was its liberty in membership and its autonomy in embeddedness. I use the terms to characterize the fact that the very triumph of the English urban commune and its strength of self-governance was contingent on its embeddedness within the political framework of the realm. This is in marked contrast to the autonomy of Italian communes (e.g., the Lombards) the autonomy of which was independent from any wider sphere.[57] This wider national power was in turn sustained by what was also unusual in comparative terms—the inclusion, rather than the locking out, of urban groups in the wider political sphere. How did this autonomy in embeddedness develop?

The story of the political culture of urban rights begins with the initial subordination of towns to fiefdoms or royal *desmesnes* described above. The struggle for municipal independence takes shape in the 12th century. In a case of discursive appropriation, urban dwellers found a cultural and institutional resource in the language of rights in play between feudal lords and their vassals.[58] This was a language that invested rights in the inviolability of relationships, responsibilities, and above all membership. This discourse, however, could not be inexorably attached to the social foundations of vassallage; with political effort, merchants and artisans appropriated and transformed the specificity of these rights to a potentially similar relationship between themselves and the crown.

The language of rights in reciprocity was a considerable cultural resource for a political struggle. In the late 12th and early 13th centuries the English crown was in desperate need of merchant wealth, and had numerous occasions to feel the threatening implications of merchants in alliance with baronial political rebellions. English towns thus began the process of wresting juridical and political power from feudal magnates through winning grants of self-governance from the crown. These charters of liberties, as they were called, endowed local autonomy under ultimate royal law. In return they paid royal taxes and bought royal farms. The first great victory was the establishment in 1191 of the London commune—"subject to the king's pleasure" (Williams 1963:2). Londoners founded their commune on a sworn association of citizens with its own juridical personality which existed within a reciprocal relationality with the crown.

Corporate membership in the national public sphere was thus the prerequisite for urban liberties. Communal independence was achieved not through city-state status but by reshifting institutional alignments from those of subordination within private spheres of manorial power, to those of partial autonomy within the sphere of public power. The rights that were gained were the rights of citizens—to rule and be ruled. The cultural and institutional foundations of Marshall's civil, political, and social citizenship rights took shape within this pattern of autonomy in membership.

This triumph of quasi-autonomy was nonetheless precarious; continual struggles to maintain juridical and legal independence, now with the crown, characterized the whole 13th century. But by the 14th century, autonomy in membership developed to the point where not only were merchants included in Parliament, an extremely unusual development in comparative terms, but artisan powers and juridical autonomy were locally and nationally enlarged and buttressed. The strength of the reciprocity is revealed in the *granting* of liberties by the English crown. Neither French territorial lords nor urban burghers needed monarchical grants; they simply took their power. Instead of consolidating tensions within a single public sphere, the French monarchy was forced for centuries to coexist in direct competition with these separate spheres of power.

Guild, Citizenship, and the Public Sphere

This account must now move from the "macro" relationship of town and crown, to the "micro" level of individual and guild. The process of individual freedom followed a similar course to that of the communal. Just as communal liberty developed through institutional and membership realignments, so the freedoms and the rights of the urban individual were also contingent on membership—both locally and within the multiple ties and relationships of the larger public sphere.

In the 12th and 13th centuries, artisanal labor was proliferating. In the early days of municipal independence, artisans of lesser wealth, primarily craftspeople, found themselves defenseless against the new town authorities (often comprised of urban dynasties) who were not interested in giving the commoners the same powers as themselves. The mode by which artisanal rights were gained within the town parallels the struggle of the commune as a whole within the fiefdom: Total autonomy was traded for partial practical autonomy through the formation of crafts guilds based on strict rules and regulations of membership.[59] Before exploring the culture of guild membership, it is important first to understand its struggle for existence.

Economic regulation is the first thing we associate with the power of guilds.[60] But alone economic regulations were weak. The challenge and the necessity if guilds were indeed to provide a base for artisanal freedom was for them to become legally constituted bodies, not just informal solidaristic groups. Just as only through membership would an individual gain her own power of autonomy and freedom from greater power, only through constitutional inclusion would artisans as a group gain the power of autonomy and self-governance. This didn't come easily.

The essential step by which individuals found their own local freedom in membership in strictly regulated guilds occurred through a direct "alliance" between guild and crown. In a process of struggle lasting almost a half-century, guilds battled local elites of merchants and authorities to win not only official recognition by, but notable power within, both local and national governance. The triumph occurred in 1319 by Royal Charter under King Edward II. Article 7 was crucial: all "inhabitants to be admitted [into the freedom] shall be of some mistery"; anyone seeking to obtain the freedom who did not belong to a guild "shall then only be admitted with full assent of the commonality assembled" (Rappaport 1989:31). In translation, that meant that to become a citizen, one had to enter into or "possess" the "freedom" of the town or city. Yet entry to the freedom and thus to citizenship *could only be achieved through membership in a guild* (a "mistery").

This remarkable feat was institutionalized in the 1319 charter which became popularly known as the Magna Carta of the London commonality. It represented, according to G. A. Williams, the "highest peak of achievement that a popular movement ever attained in medieval London" (1963:282). That achievement forged a mighty bond between guild membership and citizenship—a bond accomplished through what Rappaport calls "a collaboration of crown, city and companies" (1989: 49). Although not created by the crown, guilds were nonetheless required to be registered with the state, which in turn endowed charters of local self- governance. The charters confirmed the ancient privileges of citizenship, and during the two centuries after Edward II granted his famous charter, more than one hundred London guilds were incorporated as livery companies, each with similar provisions and ordinances.

Despite the considerable restrictions and obligations of guild membership by the 16th century, the overwhelming majority of Londoners elected to assume them to gain rights of the freedom. From 1531 through the 1550s the average number of artisans admitted each year into 12 companies (two-fifths of all men admitted in 1551–53) rose by 69 percent. This was more than three times the increase in the city's population; by the mid-16th century, approximately three-quarters of London's men were free. Remarkably, nine-tenths of all London citizens had entered the freedom through obtaining apprenticeship and guild membership.[61] One half of all men were citizens in Norwich and York, while in Coventry four out of five male householders were free by the early 16th century (Dobson 1973:15; Palliser 1983:220). Part of the explanation for this may have been that "foreigners" were not expelled from the towns but coopted into the regulations of membership. London apprenticeship fees, moreover, were significantly reduced in the Acts of 1531 and 1536. Nonetheless, that charters combined the right to self-rule and the guarantee that citizenship alone endowed the right to practice one's craft was certainly the overwhelming reason.

State building and local membership were mutual partners in the enlargement of citizenship rights. The strength of guild law, to the extent that it was structurally allied with the muscle of public law, can be underlined with an example of failed autonomy. As guilds became more hierarchicalized in the 15th and 16th centuries, the journeymen engaged in numerous attempts to establish journeymen's and yeomen's guilds that were autonomous from their masters. This act of counter-sovereignty was a threat to the crown and to Parliament of an entirely different order. Through the establishment of what was to be a long chain of "anti-combination" laws, journeymen's guilds were legally forbidden. Outside of membership in the public sphere, the freedom they sought had no chance of survival.

The Property of Membership: The Culture of the Guild

But what exactly did it mean to be in a guild? The answer to that question lies in the institution of apprenticeship.[62] The strictest guild regulation was that more was required for a skilled artisan to ply the trade than mere knowledge of a craft. To practice the "arte and mistery" of a craft required membership. Only members of a guild could legally practice their craft in a town, but only an apprenticeship earned guild membership. Seven years was the standard apprenticeship time required to acquire the adequate skills and hence the right of entry to a guild. At the end of the service, the craftsperson (now a journeyman) was taken through a public ceremony in which he or she swore by oath to follow the guild's rules and obligations.[63] With that oath the artisan was entitled to the mutual benefits of membership, which included guaranteed citizenship, livelihood, employment, mutual aid, religious life, social organizations—indeed an entire cradle-to-grave culture.

But the meaning of an apprenticeship was not primarily one of a temporary period of training. Paradoxically, it was not "over" at the end of seven years. Like an academic credential, the apprenticeship now became the artisan's permanent property—*permanent as long as practiced within the regulative confines of the guild*. This last point is the essential one. Even though the property of apprenticeship reflected the journeyman's specific skill and investment of time, this was not mobile property that attached to the individual craftsperson.[64] Far more significantly, the achievement of a successful apprenticeship was the achievement of a guaranteed place in a deep culture of attachments—along with all the rights and obligations consequent to those attachments.

The property of skill acquired during an apprenticeship was in fact a social membership. The medieval word for skill is "mistery" (as in the "art and mistery of weaving"), indicating that knowledge of a craft was viewed as a specialized secret.[65] Used in this way, skill could be seen as an individual attribute—a form of "human capital"—that no one could take away from the owner. But mistery had another meaning and use that prevailed over the first—it was also the medieval word for the craft guild itself, the social body, the fellowship, the corporate and instituted group (Oxford English Dictionary 1933; Brentano 1963).[66] Unlike the word "skill," which is singular and individual, mistery was simultaneously individual and corporate. To possess the mistery was to simultaneously "possess" knowledge and membership.

But for both aspects of the concept, skill was a social mistery, not a technical one. It was thus a form of cultural capital rather than human capital as we now understand it. An unskilled worker was not unskilled because he or she was untrained. Indeed, through a wide array of illegal practices, many unskilled workers in fact were technically trained. The definition of "unskilled" was to be without an apprenticeship. And without an apprenticeship one was excluded from a mistery, beyond the bounds and the bonds of relationality, and thus excluded from the rights of membership. The attachments of membership, not training or ability alone, conferred legality and the property of skill.[67]

Citizenship Rights in Action

The rubric of citizenship entailed civil, political, and social rights. The chief expression of civil liberty was in the guaranteed access to public law, the right to defend by law, the capacity to sue and to plead in court under an impartial judge, and the security against arbitrary violence that civil law promised. Citizens could only be prosecuted in the courts of the city for city offenses, and no citizen could sue another or be forced to plead in civil courts outside the walls of the city.[68] The promise of the universality of law—of course, more recognized in the breach—served as a form of empowerment against numerous sources of the over mighty ("we cannot be equal with those more powerful").

At times by choice, at others by compulsion, political rights were the most active dimension of citizenship. The right and necessity to local self-rule mediated the relationship between crown and individual artisan. Only citizenship permitted political participation. Since membership in a guild was the prerequisite for admission into the freedom, guilds effectively determined who exercised full political rights. (These included the right to participate in public ceremonial processions and "mistery plays" which affirmed the political identity of membership [Adams-Phythian 1976:106].)

Local governance was institutionalized through the courts. As a public lawmaking body, guild leaders served public legal functions such as council member, alderman, jury members, and constables (Berman 1983:391). Guilds, moreover, had their own courts. Both town and guild courts were institutions of governance and administration, as well as of formal juridical procedure. In addition, they served as forums for public discussion and resolution of the disputes of public life and labor (economic conflicts, unfair labor, etc.). Participation in the administration of law, and often with more power than municipal governments, made guilds what Rappaport calls the "courts of daily life" (1989:29). Local governance was permanently shaped by the political culture of the guild.

The third set of rights to which all citizens were entitled came under the category of the right to social justice. Social justice, by law and by guild, was defined as the right to livelihood, to a fair wage, to available employment, to poverty benefits, mutual aid, burial rites, tramping privileges, and many more.[69] Possession of the freedom was again the prerequisite for these rights to justice, and by controlling entry to citizenship, the guild's corporate power of membership became the means to social justice. That rights were defined as monopoly and restriction seemed not a contradiction. As I have tried to show, this was a political culture that embedded freedom in regulation and membership; the regulation of livelihood was the job of the freedom (Rappaport 1989:45). In the 14th century, the ancient right of citizenship was reconfirmed: Only citizens could sell in towns, and only freemen could legally practice their crafts. Justice, regulation, and the freedom coexisted in this unfamiliar political culture.

The culture of the guild was thus constructed on attachment and membership. The body of rights and obligations stemmed from the strength and upkeep of those relationships. But guilds neither promised nor offered the traditional world of Gemeinschaft. The purpose of the property of membership was precisely to provide the foundations for artisanal independence and personal liberties.[70] The prominent emphasis among artisans on independence and autonomy suggests the importance of distinguishing the moral from the institutional conception of rights. The right to the freedom of practicing one's skill, as well as that of citizenship, achieved the goal of individual empowerment. But this empowerment only had viability when rooted in the institutional foundations of attachments and membership. Only the posses-sion of membership allowed for individual empowerment and the meaningful exercise of rights.

The property of skill and relationality thus turned out to be the key to the city. A multiple matrix of linkages had been established: To become a citizen, one had to enter into or possess the freedom. Yet entry to the free-dom, and thus to citizenship, could only be achieved through the channel of guild membership and apprenticeship. Making the guild the source of public and private empowerment was no mean accomplishment; according to Unwin, it gave the crafts a major hold on the constitution and provided the basis for virtually all the political achievements that were to follow (1963:70).

Creating a public sphere as in part the city writ large did not auto-matically confer these citizenship rights on all people, or to the same effect. But among "the people," inclusions and exclusions (including gender exclu-sion) were less based on class divisions or land ownership than on the po-litical contingencies of membership—indeed on the possibilities of member-ship—in the different sorts of social bodies in which English law actually operated.

Conclusion

This institutional, narrative, and relational approach to citizenship formation has several general implications. The first concerns the role of the state: The long neglect of the state in sociolegal analyses has finally been corrected.[71] In this process, however, too little attention has been paid to the ways in which the development of institutionalized legal and political power—both in promise and in structure—was a possible source of popular empowerment and a po-tential resource against both private power and the coercive aspects of the state itself—indeed a central aspect of identity formation.[72] Power under the law was plural, porous, and contingently embedded in local arenas and sites of contestation, rather than unitary, absolute, and wielded only from above. The plasticity of legal and economic power suggests why different patterns of rights claims could develop in different local bodies. Shifting analysis away from the "role of the state" to the character of the public sphere brings attention to the impact of competing private and public spheres of power over and above traditional class divisions. A malleable and contested legal power was at the core of Anglo citizenship formation and the development of a political cul-ture of rights in relationality.

A second point addresses the recent sociolegal moves to abandon the determinacy of economic relations and instead to concentrate principally on culture, discourse, and ideology. These revisions have been invaluable. Para-doxically, however, they have often had the unintended consequence of re-inforcing by neglect the "economism" of social history. Stressing culture or even politics as separate spheres leaves intact the fiction that markets are self-regulating, autonomous systems. It locates labor and property and ma-terial life on one side of a binary opposition and cultural and political con-cerns on the other. But livelihood is too important to leave to the economists. The challenge to what Polanyi called the "economistic fallacy" must be two-fold: It must not only reject the notion that the state (or culture or religion) is driven by the logic of the economy.[73] More fundamentally, it must chal-lenge the idea that there exists a "logic" of the economy that is not itself politically and culturally constructed.[74] Indeed, even the conceptual unity of something called "capitalism" must be questioned.[75] Without both revisions, the special status of the economy is often reinforced by the use of such terms as "extra-economic," "noneconomic," or the "relative autonomy of the state"—all of which underline the economy as the baseline of social pro-cesses.[76]

These concerns bear directly on the difficulty of decoupling the study of citizenship from its saturation in the intellectual legacy of 19th-century classical social theory of modernity and turning instead to medieval institu-tional foundations.[77] A two-fisted criticism usually lies in wait for those who attempt to do so. The first is the accusation of nostalgia; the second is the accusation of teleology. Both criticisms reflect the enduring power of that very same classical social theory's "master narrative" of modernity. Both suggest that for social scientists, medieval history is little known but much appropriated for normative purposes in its "feudalism" garb.

The concern that a focus on medieval institutions is nostalgic rather than analytic clearly reflects two related problems. The first is the extraor-dinary degree to which the presupposition of the progressive nature of capi-talism remains embedded in scholarship across the ideological spectrum. The deep-seated suspicion of "reactionary romanticism" is shared by liberal and Marxist social scientists alike. The second problem is the perseverance of a holistic conception of society.[78] It has proved almost impossible to give up the idea of society—a social science concept that depends on the notion of a singular societal core essence with synchronic covariation among the parts. A careful institutional analysis, however, entails rejecting that the notions of either a "traditional" or a "modern" society bear any resemblance to his-torically grounded concepts that can actually explain anything empirical. This rejection is in turn an attempt to present an analysis of institutional relationships rather than societal types. Medieval guilds, for example, had institutional aspects both seemingly "traditional," and seemingly "modern."[79]

The worry about teleology reflects another overwhelming issue: the tenacity of our paradigmatic sociolegal *knowledge* culture to define a priori what is even to be considered rational scholarship in the first place, as well as what sorts of ideas are even admissible to being considered candidates for truth or falsehood.[80] At the heart of our sociolegal knowledge culture is a master narrative about the making of modern society and its legal institutions. Central to this master narrative is the foundational claim for a massive rupture in history that took place at some time known as the "transition from feudalism to capitalism" (or, alternatively, during the "Industrial Revolution"). Since it is this very sociolegal knowledge culture that has melded abstract categories such as "society" with this master narrative of discontinuity and the progressive nature of capitalism, we should hardly be surprised to find ourselves declaring as "teleology"—or "neo-Whiggism"— any argument that purports to find the analytic roots of the modern world not in the break from, but embedded within, the institutional practices of the medieval legal and public sphere. Surprised, no; but we should, nonetheless, be skeptical of our habitual intellectual collusion with the very categories of incoherent knowledge that have long made so many legal practices incoherent.[81]

The alternative approach to citizenship and rights formation presented here does not by any means suggest that there were not incomparable contrasts between 14th-century and, say, 16th-century England—let alone between 14th-, 19th-, and 20th-century England. There were. Nor does it suggest that new powerful and influential institutional players (e.g., markets in land, labor, and capital) did not emerge to contest, collude with, and transform preexisting social and legal practices. There did. But these and many, many other similar arguments are the reigning theoretical protagonists we find in virtually every extant account of the historical development of rights, citizenship, and democracy. Given the unexpected turns of contemporary history, it is worth asking ourselves whether we want to continue to exclude—even from consideration—challenges from *outside* the accepted terms of sociolegal debate about modernity.

My long-term comparative research, however, surely suggests the hubris and recklessness of the historical sociologist. To be sure; but it nonetheless also makes possible a decisive break with axiomatic connections between economic and "societal" transformation on the one side and legal practices and political cultures on the other. Citizenship can no longer be viewed as a product of progressive stages of socioeconomic development or of the transition from feudalism to capitalism. Indeed, the analysis is meant to call into question the master concepts of our sociolegal knowledge culture—classical notions of political and societal modernization, as well as the primacy of socioeconomic categories—highlighting instead the centrality of ambiguous relationships of legal power, contingent institutions of popular empowerment, and contested cultures of rights.

The analysis presented here also builds on recent methodological challenges increasingly being launched by historical sociologists concerning the causal dynamic of the sociolegal master narrative. Prevailing approaches have used the "variables approach" in which time and space are epistemologically absent, and in which each moment in a single process is defined as a different case; hence the compatibility of this methodology with the master narrative of rupture and discontinuity. New approaches to causality, by contrast, insist on a form of narrative causality that incorporates ideas about "path dependency," historical sedimentation, histoire evenementuelle, and above all, the constitutive role in historical explanation of temporality, sequence, and contingency.[82] From this perspective, embedded institutional practices do not simply disappear or become "lag effects" with the onset of different modes of production or capitalist markets. A causal narrativity allows us to view modern citizenship and rights formation as one conjunctural moment in a long historical process of contestation and continuity between and among different historical forces. These processes are "gathered up," as it were, indeed "sedimented," into the core of our modern institutions and practices. We could not sever these institutions from their causal narratives even if we wanted to. To find institutional roots of modern citizenship before the birth of capitalism is not to suggest that things either had to turn out the way they did (which is the meaning of teleology) or that there were not fundamental structural changes. It is rather to argue that the method of causal narrativity enjoins us to search as far as necessary to find the conditions of possibility of modern citizenship rights. This is narrative causality, as well as institutional and relational analysis—not teleology. If that search for causal contingencies takes me to the 12th through 14th centuries—so be it.

NOTES

*This chapter previously appeared in *Law and Social Inquiry,* 19, 1 (1994): 63–112. Reprinted by permission of the University of Chicago Press.
1. With a lengthy introduction by Tom Bottomore.
2. On "identity-politics," *see* Calhoun (1991:51); Somers and Gibson (forthcoming); Cohen and Arato (1992); Cohen (1985:663); Touraine (1985:749); Aronowitz (1992).

3. Wolfe (1989) documents the exclusion of civil society from social science research. *See also* Cohen and Arato (1992); Calhoun (1992:1; 1993:267); Alexander (1991, 1992); Alexander and Smith (1993:151).

4. This is of course not the place to elaborate a full-scale historical sociology of citizenship but rather to raise serious questions about Marshall's causal argument in the context of his "pre-citizenship" epoch. For a broader analytic deconstruction of Marshall focusing more on "modern" citizenship, *see* Somers (1993a:587).

5. Marshall also has an orphan category of "industrial rights, which he defines as an aggregate of civil liberties relevant to the industrial sphere of labor.

6. Marx of course was the first to pose this problem. More recently it was addressed by Wolfe (1979) and by O'Connor (1973). Polanyi (1957) has still the most compelling but underrecognized elaboration of the problem.

7. The critique of social categories as analytic focus is a major part of institutional analysis. The theoretical treatise on this is White (1990).

8. *See* Somers (1986:ch. 2) for a discussion of the need to disaggregate our conceptual vocabulary for "feudal society."

9. A paradigm is more than a theory; it is an entire "problematic" or "knowledge culture" which defines what questions, concepts, and hypotheses are even admissable for discussion in the first place, and what is even to be a candidate to be considered as empirically true or false. *See* Kuhn (1962); Hacking (1982); Somers (1996); Reynolds (1984) discusses the process of "filtering-out."

10. Especially useful is Friedland and Alford's (1991:243) definition of an institution as "simultaneously material and ideal, systems of signs and symbols, rational and transrational . . . supraorganizational patterns of human activity by which individuals and organizations produce and reproduce their material subsistence and organize time and space. . . . They are also symbolic systems, ways of ordering reality, and thereby rendering experience of time and space meaningful."

11. My conception shares much with others' critiques of Habermas's term, especially on the inseparability of the family from a constitutive role in the public world, e.g., Fraser (1989) and on the centrality of conflict and negotiation among a wider notion of publics than in Habermas's bourgeois ideal, specifically including popular and working-class publics, e.g., Eley (1992); Calhoun (1992).

12. The word community is a loaded term. It is used here as an analytic variable and not as a term referring to the notion of *Gemeinschaft*. *See* Calhoun (1990: 105); Chatterjee (1990:119); White (1990).

13. Rick Lempert suggested this useful point to me.

14. The epistemological implications of recent work in historical geography have been little noted by sociologists. Exceptions include Tilly (1984); Mann (1984:ch.1). On the importance of historical geography and social theory more generally, *see* Entrikin (1991) and Agnew and Duncan (1989).

15. On the epistemological significance of relationships over categories *see* White (1990); White, Boorman and Breiger (1976a:730, 1976b:1265). For an application in historical sociology, *see* Bearman (1993).

16. Indeed so dichotomous is this false distinction that most communitarians do not even accept the concept of rights as ontologically consistent with their view of the self. For critiques of the view that rights-claims and community membership identities are fundamentally opposed, *see* especially Walzer (1982); Sewell (1987); Minow (1987:1860); Hall and Held (1989:16). For two especially valuable overviews of the rights debate, *see* Hartog (1987:1013) and Tushnet (1989:403).

17. *See* Minow (1987) for a similar definition of rights to the one I am using here.

18. Mann (1984:14–16) addresses the ontological implications of these issues in his distinction between a "societal" versus a "social being."

19. *See* Hartog (1987) for a similar conception of the contested character of American constitutional rights.

20. There are similar problems of periodization in the more elaborate comparative schema of Rimlinger (1971); *see also* Briggs (1967:25).

21. For examples in the 18th century, *see* Rule (1981); Dobson (1980); Snell (1985); Porter (1982). For the 17th century *see* Wrightson (1982); Snell (1985); Underdown (1985). For the 16th century, *see* Sharp (1982). For the 15th and 14th centuries, *see* Tawney (1972:37); Webber (1983); Dobson (1983); Aston (1987); Hilton (1973, 1976).

22. Part of the problem with advocating continuity is that it invokes fears of either Whiggishness or conservative Burkeanism, the latter most recently illustrated in the work of J. D. C. Clark. It should be clear, however, in the course of this essay that stressing continuity over rupture is not a political choice but an analytic one that derives from an institutionalist conceptual framework—hardly one associated with either Whigs or Burkeans.

23. For a sampling of regional differences *see* Charlesworth (1983); Gregory (1982); Sharp (1982); Poos (1983:27); Bohstedt (1983).

24. Although the phenomena of widespread rural industrialization in the 17th and 18th centuries has long been noted among certain economic historians, the new and more theoretically informed notion of proto-industry is a recent development. *See* Tilly (1983:123); Kreidte et al. (1982); Braun (1966, 1978:289).

25. On artisanal politics from the 14th to the 19th centuries, *see* especially Leeson (1980); Dobson (1980); Rule (1981); Prothero (1979). For comparisons with French artisans, *see* especially Sonenscher (1985, 1987a, 1987b); Sewell (1986:45).

26. *See* Somers (1986) for full discussion of these differences.

27. *See* Ault (1972); Gray (1963); Yeazell (1987:46,132).

28. Rick Lempert has pointed out correctly that these questions can be sensibly posed as a sociology of knowledge question: Why do we ignore certain rights and not others in our theories of modern citizenship? The answer, in part, is that theories of citizenship are embedded within a prevailing sociolegal knowledge culture (similar to Kuhn's paradigm) constituted by a master narrative about modern law and institutions which largely defines in advance what is to count as a modern right in the first place. The importance of this sociolegal knowledge culture is taken up in the conclusion at greater length. *See also* Somers (1996).

29. For additional recent reformulations, *see* Tilly (1990a,b); Brubaker (1992).

30. Reynolds (1994) brings a formidable challenge to our traditional use of vassalage to describe a central mechanism of the European medieval world.

31. On guilds and towns, *see* Thrupp (1963:230); Brentano (1963:xlic); Abrams and Wrigley (1977); Wrigley (1987); Reynolds (1977); Corfield (1976:214); Black (1984); Rappaport (1989, 1988); Nussdorfer (1988); Bossenga (1988); Nightengale (1989:3); Attreed (1992:205).

32. The capacity for its "precociousness" in centralized administrative methods has been made legendary through the remarkable findings of the Domesday Books.

33. No one has done more for us to come to appreciate the centrality of war to state formation than Charles Tilly (especially 1990a).

34. For various historical approaches to the concept of "the people," *see* Hill (1981:100); Rogers (1987); Williams (1976); Prothero (1979:59).

35. Tilly (1990a:106, 115) deals with the necessities of national homogenization.

36. This interesting question was raised by an anonymous referee of the journal *Law and Social Inquiry*.

37. An extremely interesting recent discussion is Shapiro (1995). *See also* Reynolds' (1994) discussion of property; and Somers (1996).

38. All were under the control of the King's Privy Council and served as alternative educational arenas to the common law courts for statesmen and civil servants.

39. For examples of equity in copyholding *see* Gray (1963).

40. Noticeably absent from my argument is discussion of the king's peace or

the criminal law—arguably the dimensions of royal law that most ordinary people were confronted with daily. There is a wealth of literature and debate on the social history of the criminal law (*see*, e.g., the vast debate surrounding Hay [1975] and Thompson [1975]). Less attention has been paid these other aspects of law that I argue were so central to the formation of citizenship identities.

41. The next few paragraphs draw from Somers (1993a).

42. In France, by contrast, the community was excluded. *See* Lenman and Parker (1980:11).

43. Whereas the French state sold and controlled over 12,000 judiciary jobs throughout the land churning out a massive army of central bureaucrats who tried (but failed) to swallow up local community practices, in England in the 16th century there were only 15 Royal judges; *see* Lenman and Parker (1980).

44. *See also* Pollock and Maitland (1968:79, 136); Holdsworth (1914); Plucknett (1956).

45. *See* especially Green and Cockburn (1988); O'Gorman (1992:135); Herrup (1983:169, 1987).

46. This approach dovetails with the recent scholarship of Herrup (1987); Beattie (1986); Brewer and Styles (1980); Herrup (1985:102).

47. *See* Minchinton (1972).

48. The classic text on customary rights of peasants in the manorial courts is still George Homans (1960).

49. *See* Ault (1972); Gray (1963); Yeazell (1987).

50. Examples of laborers acting upon and expressing their notion of citizenship rights are numerous. One example comes from Essex in 1686 when woolen workers mobilized fellow workers using the forceful notion that a regulated labor market was a right; those who abused that right were not "free traders" but "law breakers"; and the collective freedom of English citizens was tied to these rights. A similar conviction was expressed in a pamphlet published in 1768: "It cannot be said to be the liberty of a citizen, or of one who lives under the protection of any community; it is rather the liberty of a savage" (Thompson 1971). Early in the 18th century Parliament received many petitions from workers in the wool producing districts demanding enforcement of apprenticeship law since, as one petition summarized the state of affairs, "great numbers of persons of all trades have intruded into the petitioners' trade so that they cannot get a livelihood" (Lipson 1943:288). For additional discussion of communities pressing for and acting upon notions of citizenship rights, *see* Bohstedt (1983) and Charlesworth (1983); Williams (1984:56).

51. The import of the "law in context" was originally developed in the early 20th-century American school of Legal Realism; *see* Kalman (1987). More recently, the contextual focus has been taken up by anthropologists; *see* Geertz (1983:167) and Moore (1978).

52. The phrase comes from Perez Zagorin.

53. Weber (1958) argues this from a vast comparative perspective.

54. Nor was the city the only place; *see* Somers (1986).

55. The liberal versus communitarian polarization can be seen as more of a philosophical prejudice than a historical one.

56. On the process of transition from corporate to individual liberty, *see* Harding (1980:442).

57. On Italian cities, *see* Martines (1979). *See also* the work of Miller (unpublished ms.) who has written on the historical conditions in which Machiavelli formulated his political theories.

58. I am grateful to Larry Miller for his suggestions on this aspect of feudal "inspiration" for the expansion of rights to the urban sphere.

59. The merchant guild preceded the crafts guild, but the latter (composed of masters and journeymen) became far more important.

60. *See* note 21.

61. Sources on guild membership and citizenship include Reynolds (1977:chs. 5, 6, 8); Rappaport (1989:53); Thrupp (1963); Black (1984); Berman (1983:359).

62. On apprenticeship, *see* especially Lipson (1943:ch.8).

63. For the surprisingly impressive number of women in guilds, *see* Smith (1963); Leeson (1980:27); on oaths and obligations, *see* Prothero (1979: 37); Thrupp (1963:184, 232); Hibbert (1963:157, 210); Leeson (1980).

64. Tramping, one of the most important forms of labor migration, was contained within social membership networks; *see* Leeson (1980).

65. In ancient Greece, the craftsmen were, like priests and doctors, believed to possess some secret power.

66. For various references to "mystery," "mistery," "misterium," "misterium artis," or "mestera misteria, from ministerium," as the collective body of the craft guild (rather than the skill itself) *see* Hibbert (1963:210); Berman (1983:391); Reynolds (1977:165); Black (1984:14); Leeson (1980:26).

67. On illegal shops as unapprenticed ones, *see* Lipson (1943).

68. On the legal rights of individuals, *see* Jewell (1972:53); Weber (1958:91); Berman (1983:360, 381, 386, 396, 401); Stephenson (1933:143); Black (1984:34, 38, 40); Rappaport (1989:35).

69. On social justice as mutual aid, economic regulations and monopoly, *see* Unwin (1904); Black (1984: ch.2); Berman (1983:391); Hibbert (1963:159, 202, 206).

70. For the strongest evidence on this point, *see* Black (1984); *see also* the numerous guild documents collected in Smith (1963).

71. *See* e.g., Evans et al. (1985).

72. Social historians have been far more attentive to this. *See* Thompson (1971); Brewer and Styles (1980). For discussion on these and other approaches to the law, *see* Stone (1981a:189); Green and Cockburn (1988).

73. *See* especially Polanyi (1977).

74. *See* Hirschman (1986, 1984:89); Polanyi (1957a); Granovetter (1985:481); Block (1989); Swedberg (1987:1); Somers (1991a, 1991b); Block and Somers (1984); Bell (1981:46); Sahlins (1976); McCloskey (1985); Sewell (1980:10); Zelizar (1988:614).

75. *See* Somers (1989:18, 1992, 1996); Sabel (1988:30). Although relatively neglected by social theorists, Bell (1974) made a version of this epistemological argument years ago in his formulation of the differentiation of spheres between culture, politics, and economy.

76. Brenner (1989) and Anderson (1974) use these terms.

77. On the foundational role of 19th-century social thought, *see* especially Tilly (1984).

78. Tilly (1984) addresses the reasons for this perseverance, as does Mann (1986:ch.1).

79. Were its ritual practices of solidaristic inclusion and exclusion through the property and rituals of apprenticeship, for example, more or less modern, or more or less traditional, than, say, the rituals, rites, and certificates involved in a graduate reining toward the Ph.D.?

80. For a discussion of knowledge cultures *see* Somers (1996).

81. For an especially congenial argument to the one presented here, *see* Gordon (1984, 1996).

82. *See* especially, Sewell (1996); Abell (1987:567); Abbott (1992:428); Aminzade (1992:456); Quadagno and Knapp (1992:481); Somers (1993b); Stark (1992:17).

REFERENCES

Abbott, Andrew. 1992. "From Causes to Events: Notes on Narrative Positivism." *Sociological Methods and Research* 20:428-455.

Abell, Peter. 1987. "Rational Equitarian Democracy, Minimax Class and the Future of Capitalist Society: A Sketch towards a Theory." *Sociology* 21:567-590.

Abrams, Philip, and E. A. Wrigley, eds. 1977. "Towns in Societies: Essays in Economic History and Historical Sociology." Cambridge: Cambridge University Press.

Adams-Phythian, C. 1976. "Ceremony and the Citizen: The Communal Year at Coventry 1450–1550." *In The Early Modern Town*, edited by P. Clark. London: Longman.

Agnew, John A., and James Duncan. 1989. *The Power of Place: Bringing Together Geographical and Sociological Imaginations.* Boston: Unwin Hyman.

Alexander, Jeffrey C. 1991. "Bringing Democracy Back In: Universalistic Solidarity and the Civil Sphere." In *Intellectuals and Politics: Social Theory in a Changing World*, edited by C. Lamont. Newbury Park, CA: Sage.

Alexander, Jeffrey C. 1992. "Citizen and Enemy as Symbolic Classification: On the Polarizing Discourse of Civil Society." In *Cultivating Differences: Symbolic Boundaries and the Making of Inequality*, edited by M. Lamont and M. Fournier. Chicago: University of Chicago Press.

Alexander, Jeffrey C., and Paul Smith. 1993. "The Discourse of American Civil Society: A New Proposal for Cultural Studies." *Theory and Society* 22:151–207.

Aminzade, Ronald. 1992. "Historical Sociology and Time." *Sociological Methods and Research* 20:456–480.

Anderson, P. 1974. *Lineages of the Absolutist State.* London: New Left Books.

Ardant, Gabriel. 1975. "Financial Policy and Economic Infrastructure of Modern States and Nations." In *The Formation of National States in Western Europe*, edited by Charles Tilly. Princeton: Princeton University Press.

Aronowitz, Stanley. 1992. *The Politics of Identity Class, Culture, Social Movements.* New York: Routledge, Chapman and Hall.

Aston, T. H., ed. 1987. *Landlords, Peasant, and Politics in Medieval England.* Cambridge: Cambridge University Press.

Attreed, L. 1992. "Arbitration and the Growth of Urban Liberties in Late Medieval England." *Journal of British Studies* 31:205–235.

Ault, W. O. 1972. *Open Field Farming in Medieval England: A Study of Village By-Laws.* London: George Allen and Unwin.

Bagehot, W. 1965. *The English Constitution,* edited by R. Crossman. London: Fontana.

Baker, Journal H. 1983. *An Introduction to English Legal History.* London: Butterworths.

Barbalet, J.H. 1989. *Citizenship.* Minneapolis: University of Minnesota Press.

Bearman, Peter. 1993. *Relations into Rhetorics.* New Brunswick, NJ: Rutgers University Press.

Beattie, John. 1986. *Crime and the Courts in England: 1660–1800.* Princeton, NJ: Princeton University Press.

Bell, D. 1981. "Models and Reality in Economic Discourse." In *The Crisis in Economic Theory,* edited by D. Bell and I. Kristol. New York: Basic Books.

Bell, D. 1974. *Cultural Contradictions of Capitalism.* New York: Basic Books.

Bendix, Reinhard. 1977. *Nation-Building and Citizenship.* Berkeley: University of California Press.

Berman, Harold J. 1983. *Law and Revolution:The Formation of the Western Legal Tradition.* Cambridge, MA: Harvard University Press.

Black, Anthony. 1984. *Guilds and Civil Society in European Political Thought from the Twelfth Century to the Present.* London: Methuen.

Bloch, M. 1961. *Feudal Society.* Chicago: University of Chicago Press.

Block, F. 1989. *Post-Industrial Possibilities: A Critique of Economic Discourse.* Berkeley: University of California Press.

Block, F., and M.R. Somers. 1984. "Beyond the Economic Fallacy: The Holistic Social Science of Karl Polanyi." In *Vision and Method in Historical Sociology,* edited by T. Skocpol. Cambridge: Cambridge University Press.

Bohstedt, John. 1983. *Riots and Community Politics.* Cambridge: Harvard University Press.

Bossenga, Gail. 1988. "Regulating the Local Economy: Guilds and the Town Council in Eighteenth-Century Lille." Presented at the Social Science History Association, Chicago.

Braun, Rudolf. 1978. "Early Industrialization and Demographic Change in the Canton of Zurich." In *Historical Studies of Changing Fertility,* edited by Charles Tilly. Princeton: Princeton University Press.

Braun, Rudolf. 1966. "The Impact of Cottage Industry on an Agricultural Population." In *The Rise of Capitalism,* edited by David Landes. New York: Macmillan.

Brenner, R. 1989. "Capitalism, Aristocracy and the English Revolution." Davis Center Paper, Fall.

Brentano, Lujo. 1963. "On the History and Development of Guilds and the Origin of Trade-Unions." In *English Gilds,* edited by Toulmin Smith. London: Oxford University Press.

Brewer, John. 1980. "The Wilkesites and the Law 1763–74. A Study of Radical Notions of Governance." In *An Ungovernable People?,* edited by John Brewer and John Styles. New Brunswick: Rutgers University Press.

Brewer, John, and John Styles, eds. 1980. *An Ungovernable People?* New Brunswick, NJ: Rutgers University Press.

Briggs, Asa. 1967. "The Welfare State in Historical Perspective." In *The Welfare State,* edited by C. I. Shotland. New York: Harper and Row.

Brubaker, Rogers. 1992. *Citizenship and Nationhood.* Cambridge: Harvard University Press.

Burrow, J. W. 1974. "'The Village Community' and the Uses of History in Late Nineteenth-Century England." In *Historical Perspectives: Studies in English Thought and Society,* edited by N. McKendrick. London. Europe.

Calhoun, Craig. 1990. "Community: Toward a Variable Conceptualization for Comparative Research." *Social History* 5:104–107.

Calhoun, Craig. 1991. "The Problem of Identity in Collective Action." In *Macro-Micro Linkages in Sociology,* edited by Joan Huber. Beverly Hills, CA: Sage.

Calhoun, Craig. 1992. "Introduction: Habermas and the Public Sphere." In *Habermas and the Public Sphere,* edited by C. Calhoun. Cambridge: MIT Press.

Calhoun, Craig. 1993. "Civil and Public Sphere." *Public Culture* 5:267–280.

Charlesworth, Andrew. 1983. *An Atlas of Rural Regional Protest.* London: Croom Helm.

Chatterjee, Partha. 1990. "A Response to Taylor's 'Mode of Civil Society.'" *Public Culture* 3:95–119.

Cohen, Jean. 1985. "Strategy or Identity: New Theoretical Paradigms and Contemporary Social Movements." *Social Research* 1985:663–716.

Cohen, Jean, and Andrew Arato. 1992. *Civil Society and Political Theory.* Cambridge: MIT Press.

Corfield, P. 1976. "Urban Development in England and Wales in the Sixteenth and Seventeenth Centuries." In *Trade, Governments and Economy in Pre-Industrial England,* edited by D. C. Coleman and H. H. Johns. London: Weidenfeld.

Corrigan P., and D. Sayer. 1985. *The Great Arch: English State Formation as Cultural Revolution.* Oxford: Blackwell.

Davies, Margaret. 1956. *The Enforcement of English Apprenticeship, 1563–1642: A Study in English Mercantilism.* Cambridge: Harvard University Press.

Dobson, C. R. 1980. *Masters and Journeymen.* London: Croom Helm.

Dobson, R. B. 1973. "Admissions to the Freedom of the City of York in the Later Middle Ages." *Economic History Review* 26:1–22.

Dobson, R. B. 1983. *The Peasants Revolt.* London: Macmillan.

Dodgshon, R. A. 1978. "The Early Middle Ages, 1066–1350." In *An Historical Ge-*

ography of England and Wales, edited by R. A. Dodgshon and R. Butlin. London: Academic Press.

Eley, Geoff. 1992. "Nations, Publics, and Political Cultures: Placing Habermas in the Nineteenth Century." In *Habermas and the Public Sphere,* edited by C. Calhoun. Cambridge: MIT Press.

Elton, G. R. 1982. *The Tudor Constitution Documents and Commentary.* Cambridge: Cambridge University Press.

Entrikin, Nicholas. 1991. *The Betweenness of Place: Towards a Geography of Modernity.* Baltimore: Johns Hopkins Press.

Evans, Peter D., Dietrich Rueschemayer, and Theda Skocpol. 1985. *Bringing the State Back In.* Cambridge: Cambridge University Press.

Fischer, W., and P. Lundgreen. 1975. "Financial Policy and Economic Infrastructure of Modern States and Nations." In *The Formation of National States in Western Europe,* edited by Charles Tilly. Princeton, NJ: Princeton University Press.

Fraser, Nancy. 1989. *Unruly Practices.* Minneapolis: University of Minnesota Press.

Friedland, R., and R. Alford. 1991. "Bringing Society Back in: Symbols, Practices, and Institutional Contradictions." In *The New Institutionalism in Organizational Analysis,* edited by W.W. Powell and P.J. DiMaggio. Chicago: Chicago University Press.

Ganden, John. 1980. "A Sermon Preached before the Judges at Chemeford," cited in John Walter, "The Essex Grain Rioters." In *An Ungovernable People?,* edited by John Brewer and John Styles. New Brunswick, NJ: Rutgers University.

Gatrell, P. 1982. "Studies in Medieval English Society in a Russian Context." *Past and Present* 96:22–50.

Geertz, Clifford. 1983. "Local Knowledge: Fact and Law in Comparative Perspective." In *Local Knowledge.* New York: Basic Books.

Giddens, Anthony. 1982. *Profiles and Critiques in Social Theory.* London: Macmillan.

Giddens, Anthony. 1987. *Nation-State and Violence,* vol. 2. Berkeley: University of California Press.

Gordon, R. W. 1984. "Critical Legal Histories." *Stanford Law Review* 36.

Gordon, R. W. 1996. "The Past as Authority and as Social Critic: Stabilizing and Destabilizing Functions of History in Legal Argument." In *The Historic Turn in the Human Sciences,* edited by Terrence J. McDonald. Ann Arbor: University of Michigan Press

Granovetter, M. 1985. "Economic Action and Social Structure: The Problem of Embeddedness." *American Journal Sociology* 91:481–510.

Gray, Charles M. 1963. *Copyhold, Equity, and the Common Law.* Cambridge: Harvard University Press.

Green, Thomas A. 1955. *Verdict According to Conscience.* Chicago: University of Chicago Press.

Green, Thomas A., and J. S. Cockburn, eds. 1988. *Twelve Good Men and True: The Criminal Trial Jury in England, 1200–1800.* Princeton, NJ: Princeton University Press.

Gregory, Derek. 1982. *Regional Transformation and Industrial Revolution.* Minneapolis: University of Minnesota Press.

Habermas, Jürgen 1989. *The Structural Transformation of the Public Sphere.* Cambridge: MIT Press.

Hacking, Ian. 1982. "Language, Truth and Reason." In *Rationality and Relativism,* edited by S. Lukes and M. Hollis. Cambridge: MIT Press.

Hall, S., and D. Held. 1989. "Left and Rights." *Marxism Today* 33.

Hallam, H.E. 1981. *Rural England, 1066–1348.* Brighton: Harvester Press.

Hansen, Donald. 1970. *From Kingdom to Commonwealth: The Development of Civic Consciousness in English Political Thought.* Cambridge: Harvard University Press.

Harding, Alan. 1966. *A Social History of English Law.* Gloucester: Peter Smith.

Harding, Alan. 1980. "Political Liberty in the Middle Ages." *Speculum* 55:423–443.

Hartog, Hendrik. 1987. "The Constitution of Aspiration and the 'Rights that Belong to Us All.'" *Journal of American History* 74:1013–1034.

Hay, Douglas, ed. 1975. *Albion's Fatal Tree: Crime and Society in Eighteenth-Century England.* New York: Pantheon Books.

Herrup, Cynthia. 1983. "The Counties and the Country: Some Thoughts on Seventeenth-Century Historiography." *Social History* 8:169–181.

Herrup, Cynthia. 1985. "Law and Morality in Seventeenth-Century England." *Past and Present* 106:102–123.

Herrup, Cynthia 1987. *The Common Peace.* Cambridge: Cambridge University Press.

Hibbert, A. B. 1963. "The Economic Policies of Towns." In *The Cambridge Economic History of Europe: Economic Organization and Policies in the Middle Ages,* vol. 3, edited by M. M. Postan.

Hill, C. 1981. "Parliament and People in Seventeenth-Century England." *Past and Present* 92:100–124.

Hilton, R. H., ed. 1976. *Peasants, Knights, and Heretics.* Cambridge: Cambridge University Press.

Hilton, R. H. 1973. *Bond Men Made Free.* London: Methuen.

Hirschman, A. 1984. "Against Parsimony." *American Economic Papers and Proceedings* 89.

Hirschman, A. 1986. *Rival Views of Market Society and Other Recent Essays.* New York: Viking.

Hirst, Derek. 1975. *The Representation of the People? Voters and Voting under the Early Stuarts.* Cambridge: Cambridge University Press.

Holdsworth, William S. 1914. *A History of English Law.* London: Methuen.

Homans, George. 1960 [1940]. *English Villagers of the Thirteenth Century.* New York: Norton.

Homans, George. 1962. *Sentiments and Activities.* Glencoe: Free Press.

Homans, George. 1969. "The Explanation of English Regional Differences." *Past and Present* 42:18–34.

Jepperson, R. 1991. "Institutions, Institutional Effects, and Institutionalism." In *The New Institutionalism in Organizational Analysis,* edited by W. W. Powell and P. J. DiMaggio. Chicago: University of Chicago Press.

Jewell, Helen. 1972. *English Local Administration in the Middle Ages.* New York: Barnes and Noble.

Kalman, Laura. 1987. *Legal Realism at Yale.* New Haven, CT: Yale University Press.

Kantorowitz, E. 1957. *The King's Two Bodies: A Study in Medieval Political Theology.* Princeton: Princeton University Press.

Kreidte, P., H. Medick, and J. Schlumbohm. 1982. *Industrialization before Industrialization.* Cambridge: Cambridge University Press.

Kuhn, Thomas. 1962. *The Structure of Scientific Revolutions.* Chicago: University of Chicago Press.

Leeson, R. A. 1980. *Travelling Brothers.* London: Granada.

Lenman, Bruce and Geoffrey Parker. 1980. "The State, the Community, and the Criminal Law in Early Modern Europe." In *Crime and the Law,* edited by V. A. C. Gatrell. London: Europa.

Lipson, E. 1920. *Economic History of England: The Middle Ages.* Vol. 1, ch. 8. London: A. and C. Black.

Lipson, E. 1943. *An Introduction to the Economic History of England.* London: A. and C. Black.

MacIntyre, A. 1981. *After Virtue: A Study in Moral Theory.* Notre Dame: University of Notre Dame Press.

Maitland, Frederick. 1979 [1908]. *The Constitutional History of England.* Cambridge: Cambridge University Press.

Mann, Michael. 1984. *The Sources of Social Power.* New York: Cambridge University Press.

Mann, Michael. 1987. "Ruling Class Strategies and Citizenship." *Sociology* 21:339–354.

Mann, Michael. 1986. *The Sources of Social Power.* New York: Cambridge University Press.

Mantoux, P. 1955 [1928]. *The Industrial Revolution in the Eighteenth Century.* New York: Harper and Row.

March, J., and J. Olsen. 1984. "The New Institutionalism: Organizational Factors in Political Life." *American Political Science Review* 78:734–749.

Marshall, T. H. 1950. *Citizenship and Social Class and Other Essays.* Cambridge: Cambridge University Press.

Marshall, T. H. 1992. *Citizenship and Social Class,* with an introduction by Tom Bottomore. Concord: Pluto.

Martines, Lauro. 1979. *Power and Imagination: City-States in Renaissance Italy.* New York: Knopf.

McCloskey, Donald N. 1985. *The Rhetoric of Economics.* Madison: University of Wisconsin Press.

McDonald, Terrence J. 1996. *The Historic Turn in the Human Sciences.* Ann Arbor: University of Michigan Press.

Mendels, Franklin. 1972. Proto-Industrialization: The First Phase of the Industrialization Process." *Journal of Economic History* 32:241–261.

Meyer, J., and B. Rowan. 1991. "Institutionalized Organizations: Formal Structure as Myth and Ceremony." In *The New Institutionalism in Organizational Analysis,* edited by W. W. Powell and P. J. DiMaggio. Chicago: University of Chicago Press.

Miller, Larry. "Machiavelli's Politics." Unpublished ms.

Minchinton, W. E. 1972. *Wage Regulation in Pre-Industrial England.* New York: Barnes and Noble.

Minow, Martha. 1987. "Interpreting Rights: An Essay for Robert Cover." New Haven, CT: *Yale Law Review 1860.* (96)

Moore, S. F. 1978. *Law as Process.* London: Routledge and Kegan Paul.

Nenner, Howard. 1980. *By Colour of Law: Legal Culture and Constitutional Politics in England, 1660–1689.* Chicago: University of Chicago Press.

Nightengale, Pamela. 1989. "Capitalists, Crafts and Constitutional Change in Late Fourteenth-Century London." *Past and Present* 124:124–335.

Nussdorfer, Laurie. 1988. "Urban Politics and the Guilds in Early Modern Europe: Guilds and Government in Baroque Rome." Presented at the Social Science History Association, Chicago.

O'Connor, James. 1973. *Fiscal Crisis of the State.* New York: St. Martin's.

O'Gorman, F. 1992. "Campaign Ritual and Ceremonies: The Social Meaning of Elections in England, 1780–1860." *Past and Present* 135:79–116.

Palliser, D. M. 1983. *The Age of Elizabeth: England under the Later Tudors, 1547–1603.* London: Longman.

Plucknett, T. 1956. *A Concise History of the Common Law.* Boston: Little, Brown.

Plumb, J. 1969. "The Growth of the Electorate in England from 1600–1715." *Past and Present* 45:91–116.

Pocock, G. A. 1985. *Virtue, Commerce, and History.* Cambridge: Cambridge University Press.

Polanyi, Karl. 1957 [1944]. *The Great Transformation.* Boston: Beacon Press.

Polanyi, Karl. 1977. *The Livelihood of Man.* New York: Academic Press.

Polanyi, Karl, C. Arensberg, and H. Pearson, eds. 1957. *Trade and Market in the Early Empires.* New York: Free Press.

Pollock, F., and F. Maitland. 1968. *The History of the English Law before the Time of Edward I.* Cambridge: Cambridge University Press.

Poos, Larry. 1983. "The Social Context of the Statute of Labourers' Enforcement." *Law and History Review* 27:27–52.

Porter, Roy. 1982. *English Society in the Eighteenth Century.* Harmondsworth: Penguin Press.

Power, E. 1942. *The Wool Trade in English Medieval History.* Oxford: Oxford University Press.

Prothero, Iowerth. 1979. *Artisans and Politics in Early Nineteenth-Century London: John Gast and His Times.* Baton Rouge: Louisiana University Press.

Putnam, Bertha. 1908. *The Enforcement of the Statutes of Labourers during the First Decade after the Black Death, 1349–1359.* New York: Columbia University Press.

Putnam, Bertha. 1906. Justices of Labour in the 14th Century." *The English Historical Review* 21:517–538.

Quadagno, Jill, and S. Knapp. 1992. "Have Historical Sociologists Forsaken Theory? Thoughts on the History/Theory Relationship." *Sociological Methods and Research* 20:481–507.

Ranciere, Jacques. 1986. "The Myth of the Artisan." In *Work in France: Representations, Meaning, Organization, and Practice,* edited by Steven Kaplan and Cynthia Koepp. Ithaca, NY: Cornell University Press.

Rappaport, Steve. 1988. "The Extent and Foundations of Companies' Powers in Sixteenth-Century London." Presented at the Social Science History Association Meetings, Chicago.

Rappaport, Steve. 1989. *Worlds within Worlds: Structures of Life in Sixteenth Century London.* Cambridge: Cambridge University Press.

Reynolds, Susan. 1977. *An Introduction to the History of English Medieval Town.* Oxford: Oxford University Press.

Reynolds, Susan. 1984. *Kingdoms and Communities in Western Europe, 900–1300.* Oxford: Oxford University Press.

Reynolds, Susan. 1994. *Fiefs and Vassals.* Oxford: Oxford University Press

Rich, E.E., and Edward Miller. 1941. *The Cambridge Economic History of Europe.* Cambridge: Cambridge University Press.

Rimlinger, Gaston. 1971. *Welfare Policy and Industrialization in Europe, America and Russia.* New York: Wiley.

Rogers, D. T. 1987. *Contested Truths: Keywords in American Politics Since Independence.* New York: Basic Books.

Rule, J. 1981. *The Experience of Labour in Eighteenth-Century Industry.* London: Croom Helm.

Rule, J. 1986. *The Labouring Classes in Early Industrial England 1750–1850.* London: Longman.

Sabel, C. 1988. "Protoindustry and the Problem of Capitalism as a Concept: Response to Jean H. Quataert." *International Labor & Working-Class History* 33:30–37.

Sahlins, M. 1976. *Culture and Practical Reason.* Chicago: University of Chicago Press.

Sayer, Derek. 1992. "A Notable Administration: English State Formation and the Rise of Capitalism." *American Journal of Sociology* 97:1382–1415.

Scott, Joan W. 1988. "Work Identities for Men and Women: The Politics of Work and Family in the Parisian Garment Trades in 1848." In *Gender and the Politics of History.* New York: Columbia University Press.

Sewell, Jr., William H. 1980. *Work and Revolution in France: The Language of Labor from the Old Regime to 1848.* Cambridge: Cambridge University Press.

Sewell, Jr., William H. 1986. "Artisans, Factory Workers and the Formation of the French Working Class, 1789–1848." In *Working-Class Formation: A Comparative Study of France, Germany and the United States,* edited by Ira Katznelson and Aristide Zolberg. Princeton: Princeton University Press.

Sewell, Jr., William H. 1987. "Le citoyen/la citoyenne: Activity, Passivity, and the Revolutionary Concept of Citizenship." In *The Political Culture of the French Revolution*, vol. 2: *The French Revolution and the Creation of Modern Political Culture*, edited by Colin Lucas. Oxford: Pergamon Press.

Sewell, Jr., William H. 1996. "Three Temporalities: Toward a Sociology of the Event." In *The Historic Turn in the Human Sciences*, edited by Terrence J. McDonald. Ann Arbor: University of Michigan Press.

Shapiro, Ian. 1995. "Resources, Capacities and Ownership: The Workmanship Ideal and Distributive Justice." In *Early Modern Conceptions of Property*, edited by John Brewer and S. Staves. New York: Routledge.

Sharp, Buchanan. 1982. *In Contempt of All Authority: Rural Artisans and Riot in the West of England, 1586–1660.* Berkeley: University of California Press.

Smith, Lucy Toulmin. 1963. "Introduction." In *English Gilds*, edited by Joshua Smith Toulmin. London: Oxford University Press.

Smith, M. G. 1966. "A Structural Approach to Comparative Politics." In *Varieties of Political Theory*, edited by D. Easton. Englewood Cliffs, NJ: Prentice-Hall.

Snell, K. D. M. 1985. *Annals of the Labouring Poor: Social Change in Agrarian England 1660–1900.* Cambridge: Cambridge University Press.

Somers, M.R. 1986. "The People and the Law: Narrative Identity and the Place of the Public Sphere in the Formation of English Working Class Politics, 1300–1850, a Comparative Analysis." Dissertation. Harvard University, Cambridge, Massachusetts.

Somers, M.R. 1989. "Workers of the World, Compare!" *Contemporary Sociology* 18:325–329.

Somers, Margaret R. 1991a. "Karl Polanyi's Intellectual Legacy." In *The Life and Work of Karl Polanyi*, edited by Karl Polanyi-Levitt. Montreal: Black Rose Books.

Somers, M.R. 1991b. "The Political Culture Concept: The Empirical Power of Conceptual Transformation." Presented at the American Sociological Association Meetings.

Somers, M.R. 1992. "Narrativity, Narrative Identity, and Social Action: Rethinking English Working-Class Formation." *Social Science History* 16:591–630.

Somers, M.R. 1993a. "Citizenship and the Place of the Public Sphere: Law, Community, and Political Culture in the Transition to Democracy." *American Sociological Review* 58:587–620.

Somers, M.R. 1993b. "We're No Angels: History and Science, Networks and Narratives in Sociological Analysis." Unpublished manuscript.

Somers, M.R. 1995. "Misteries of Property: Relationality, Families, and Community in the Making of Political Rights." In *Early Modern Conceptions of Property*, edited by John Brewer and S. Staves. Berkeley: University of California Press.

Somers, M.R. 1996. "Where Is Social Theory after the Historic Turn? Knowledge Cultures, Narrativity, and Historical Epistemologies." In *The Historic Turn in the Human Sciences*, edited by Terrence J. McDonald. Ann Arbor: University of Michigan Press.

Somers, M.R., and Gloria Gibson. Forthcoming. "Reclaiming the Epistemological 'Other': Narrative and the Social Constitution of Identity." In *From Persons to Nations: The Social Constitution of Identity*, edited by Craig Calhoun. Oxford: Blackwell.

Sonenscher, Michael. 1985. "The Sans-Culottes of the Year II: Rethinking the Language of Labour in Revolutionary France." *Social History* 9:1087–1108.

Sonenscher, Michael. 1987a. "Journeymen: The Courts and the French Trades, 1781–1791." *Past and Present* 114:77–109.

Sonenscher, Michael. 1987b. "Mythical Work: Workshop Production and the Compagnonnages of Eighteenth-Century France." In *The Historical Meanings of Work*, edited by P. Joyce. Cambridge: Cambridge University Press.

Stark, David. 1992. "Path Dependence and Privatization Strategies in East Central Europe." *Eastern European Politics and Societies* 6:17–54.

Stephenson, Carl. 1933. *Borough and Town: A Study of Urban Origins in England.* Cambridge, MA: Harvard University Press.

Stone, Lawrence. 1981. *The Past and the Present.* Boston: Routledge and Kegan Paul.

Strayer, Joseph. 1970. *On the Medieval Origins of the Modern State.* Princeton: Princeton University Press.

Swedberg, Richard. 1987. "Economic Sociology." *Current Sociology* 35:1–221.

Tawney, R. H. 1972. "The Assessment of Wages in England by the Justices of the Peace." In *Wage Regulation in Pre-Industrial England,* edited by W. E. Minchinton. New York: Barnes and Noble.

Thirsk, Joan. 1961. "Industries in the Countryside." In *Essays in the Economic and Social History of Tudor and Stuart England,* edited by F.J. Fisher. Cambridge: Cambridge University Press.

Thirsk, Joan. 1967. "The Farming Regions of England." In *The Agrarian History of England and Wales,* edited by Joan Thirsk. Cambridge: Cambridge University Press.

Thompson, E.P. 1971. "The Moral Economy of the English Crowd." *Past and Present* 50:76–136.

Thompson, E.P. 1975. *Whigs and Hunters: The Origin of the Black Act.* New York: Pantheon.

Thrupp, Sylvia. 1963. "The Guilds." In *The Cambridge Economic History of Europe: Economic Organization and Policies in the Middle Ages,* edited by M. M. Postan, E. E. Rich, and E. Miller. Cambridge: Cambridge University Press.

Tilly, Charles. 1983. "Flows of Capital and Forms of Industry in Europe, 1500–1900." *Theory and Society* 12:123–142.

Tilly, Charles. 1984. *Big Structures, Large Processes, Huge Comparisons.* New York: Russell Sage Foundation.

Tilly, Charles. 1990a. *Coercion, Capital, and European States, A.D. 990–1990.* New York: Basil.

Tilly, Charles. 1990b. "Where Do Rights Come from?" New School for Social Research, Working Paper No. 98.

Tilly, Charles. 1992. *Citizenship and Social Theory.* Beverly-Hills: Sage.

Touraine, Alain. 1985. "An Introduction to the Study of Social Movements." *Social Research* 52:749–787.

Tuck, Richard. 1979. *Natural Rights Theories: Their Origin and Development.* Oxford: Oxford University Press.

Tully, James. 1980. *A Discourse on Property: John Locke and his Adversaries.* Cambridge: Cambridge University Press.

Turner, Bryan S. 1986. *Citizenship and Capitalism.* London: Allen and Unwin.

Tushnet, Mark. 1989. "Rights: An Essay in Informal Political Theory." *Politics and Society* 17:403–451.

Underdown, David. 1985. *Revel, Riot and Rebellion: Popular Politics and Culture in England 1603–1660.* New York: Oxford University Press.

Unwin, A. 1904. *Industrial Organization in the Sixteenth and Seventeenth Centuries.* Oxford: Oxford University Press.

Unwin, G. 1963 [1908]. *The Gilds and Companies of London.* London: Methuen.

Vinogradoff, Paul. 1908. *English Society in the Eleventh Century: Essays in Medieval History.* New York: Russell and Russell.

Vinogradoff, Paul. 1923. *Villianage in England: Essays in English Medieval History.* New York: Russell and Russell.

Walter, John. 1980. "The Essex Grain Rioters." In *An Ungovernable People?* edited by John Brewer and John Styles. New Brunswick, NJ: Rutgers University Press.

Walzer, M. 1982. *Spheres of Justice.* New York: Basic Books.

Webb, Sidney, and Beatrice Webb. 1963. *The Manor and the Borough.* Hamden: Archon Books.

Webber, R. 1983. *The Peasants' Revolt.* Lavenham and Suffolk: Terrence Dalton.

Weber, Max. 1958. *The City*. Translated and edited by D. Martindale and G. Newsmith. New York: Free Press.

White, Harrison. 1990. *Identity and Control*. Princeton: Princeton University Press.

White, Harrison C., A. Boorman, and R. Breiger. 1976a. "Social Structure from Multiple Networks I." *American Journal of Sociology* 81:730–780.

White, Harrison C., A. Boorman, and R. Breiger. 1976b. "Social Structure from Multiple Networks II." *American Journal of Sociology* 81:1384–1446.

Williams, Dale. 1984. "Morals, Markets, and the English Crowd in 1766." *Past and Present* 104:56–73.

Williams, G. A. 1963. *Medieval London From Commune to Capital*. London: Athlone Press.

Williams, Raymond. 1976. *Keywords: A Vocabulary of Culture and Society*. Oxford: Oxford University Press.

Wolfe, Alan. 1979. *Limits of Legitimacy*. New York: Free Press.

Wolfe, Alan. 1989. *Whose Keeper?* Berkeley: University of California Press.

Wrightson, K. 1982. *English Society, 1580–1680*. London: Hutchinson.

Wrigley, E. A. 1987. *People, Cities and Wealth*. Oxford: Blackwell.

Yeazell, Steven. 1987. *From Medieval Group Litigation to the Modern Class Action*. New Haven, CT: Yale University Press.

Zelizar, Viviana. 1988. "Beyond the Polemics of the Market: Establishing a Theoretical Agenda and Empirical Agenda." *Sociological Forum* 3:614–634.

8 THE CLASSIFICATORY LOGICS OF STATE WELFARE SYSTEMS

TOWARDS A FORMAL ANALYSIS

John W. Mohr

In the process of conferring the rights of citizenship, modern nation states constitute their citizens as subjects within a variety of discursive registers. The English sociologist T.H. Marshall was one of the first commentators to point out that this process included the construction of citizens as the bearers of social rights. In Marshall's schema, social rights embraced a broad range of demands, "from the right to a modicum of economic welfare and security to the right to share to the full in the social heritage and to live the life of a civilized being according to the standards prevailing in the society" (1964:72). In effect, Marshall argued, to be a citizen of a modern state was to possess the right to demand a certain style of life and to be able to petition the state to insure for its provision.

In practice, however, social rights do not exist apart from the bureaucracies which implement them. Thus, as Yeheskel Hasenfeld and his colleagues have argued, in order to gain access to their social rights, individuals are compelled to enter into "bureaucratic encounters" wherein they are subjected to the classificatory logics of whichever agencies are charged with the task of evaluating and processing their claims (Hasenfeld, Rafferty, and Zald 1987). In this encounter, an interpretation is invoked and imposed, a set of meanings are brought to bear, and the individual petitioner is located within a system of discourse. Generally speaking, these discourse systems consist of predefined repertoires of social identities, organized as a role structure (Mohr 1994). The number, character, and relative standing of these identities tend to be somewhat stable (though they are regularly being contested). Three types of classificatory projects—regarding claims, needs, and solutions—provide the foundations for a set of mutually constitutive fields of meaning within which these identities are differentiated one from another. Simply put, to claim the rights of citizenship is—in this regard—to enter into a relationship wherein one's subjectivity is specified according to a pre-existing menu of identities possessing the right to make certain types of claims, having diagnosable needs, and for whom recognizable solutions embodied within established organizational repertoires of action are deemed to be appropriate.

This implies that the relationships which link citizens and welfare states consist, in essence, of systems of meanings which serve to govern practices and to frame the nature of claimants' needs and rights. In making this assertion I am echoing the position recently advanced by a number of scholars, many of them working from the feminist tradition, who have drawn attention to the crucial role that discourse systems play in the construction and implementation of social welfare institutions. Nancy Fraser, for example, in her analysis of the gendered character of American social policies, has argued that welfare programs are, "among other things, institutionalized patterns of interpretation." Fraser emphasizes in particular the ways in which "welfare practices construct women and women's needs according to certain specific—and in principle, contestable—interpretations, even as they lend those interpretations an aura of facticity that discourages contestation" (1989:146).

Of course the interpretive dimension of welfare practices has always been an important part of the way that scholars have understood the history of welfare institutions. Historians almost invariably emphasize the ways in which the contestation over meanings—distinctions between the worthy and the unworthy poor, for example—are fundamental to how poverty institutions are constructed. This was also a basic tenet of the older institutional theories of the welfare state. It was certainly a fundamental dimension of Karl Polanyi's (1957) account of how the Speenhamland system came to be replaced by the English Poor Law of 1834. And yet, more recent research on the comparative study of welfare states, especially those studies which emphasize the use of quantitative methodologies, have tended to more or less ignore these types of meaning systems or to accept the distinctions more or less at face value.

Two different types of problems occur as a result. On the one hand, as Fraser's work suggests, by not sufficiently attending to the discursive dimension of social policies, analysts run the risk of misconstruing the nature of social welfare practices. For example, feminist research has drawn our attention to the extraordinarily complex ways in which identities are differentiated, eligibilities are given alternative moral weightings, needs are socially constructed and benefit programs can be intrusive, coercive, or controlling as well as respectful, enabling, or liberating. By calling for a more thoroughly interpretative analysis, Fraser points to the importance of developing a kind of "thick description" of how social rights are constructed, imposed, and experienced. Without such an analysis we are seriously constrained in our ability to understand and, thus, to compare the social policies enacted at different times and places.

More than this, by slighting the discursive element of social welfare institutions we jeopardize our ability to understand the causal mechanisms that bring them into being. Without attending to the complex ways in which social policies are constructed as contested systems of meanings, analysts tend to fall into the trap of oversimplifying the internal dynamics of the institutional field, and of presuming that the significant causal mechanisms are largely exogenous to that field. In this chapter I argue that the discursive (or ideological) side of welfare states is just as important as the practical (or structural) side. I also argue that formal methods of analysis can be an appropriate means of studying these systems of meanings. I begin with a brief analysis of the way that most comparative research on the welfare state has tended to approach these matters and a summary of how feminist work has adopted a different stance. This is followed by a short discussion of the nature of the classificatory logics of social welfare institutions in which I highlight the qualities which make them excellent candidates for formal analysis. I conclude the paper with an example of how formal methodologies can be employed to analyze these types of meaning systems. I do this by looking at how gender differences were encoded into the discourse used to describe the clientele of social welfare organizations operating in New York City during the Progressive Era.

Meanings, Methods, and Frameworks in The Study of Welfare States

The research literature on the nature of welfare states is enormous. There are any number of ways of dividing up this scholarly terrain. We could, for example, distinguish work according to its level of analysis. Thus, there are society-level studies which tend to focus on power dynamics within the class structure or the political economy of society as a whole (Esping-Anderson 1990), state-level analyses which emphasize the size, character, capacities, and degree of "fit" of state organizations within the broader political economy (Skocpol 1992), agency-level investigations that focus on the internal logic of the bureaucracies charged with implementing specific policies (Mashaw 1983), and "street-level" studies which describe the cognitive limitations, resource scarcities, and administrative contradictions of the bureaucrats who actually interact with and respond to the claims of citizens and clients (Lipsky 1980).

Most scholarly reviews of this literature, on the other hand, tend to emphasize the divisions which exist between the various theoretical stances that purport to explain comparative and historical variations in the size and character of welfare state provisions.[1] Such an approach tends to identify distinctions such as those which separate "logic of industrialism" theories (Wilensky 1975), neo-Marxist theories (O'Connor 1973), state capacity theories (Skocpol and Ikenberry 1983), and power resource theories (Esping-Anderson and Korpi 1984) from one another. This type of taxonomy has also tended to be especially visible within the comparative research literature itself, since much of the published work over the course of the last two decades has explicitly adopted a theory testing approach. Thus, to cite just a few examples, Walter Korpi (1989) tests the efficacy of industrialization, neo-Marxist, popular protest, state autonomy, and power resource theories as predictors of the social provision of health care benefits. Charles Ragin (1994) compares the "logic of industrialism" perspective against state autonomy (or "state-centered") and power resource (or "political class struggle") theories in a project designed to explain national variations in types of pension programs. Numerous other examples could be cited, including many very different choices of theory combinations to be tested. Thus, for example, Larry Griffin, Joel Devine, and Michael Wallace (1983) compare and contrast the efficacy of various types of neo-Marxist theories— "economic structuralism," "class struggle," and "political business cycle" approaches—in order to predict changes in overall relief expenditures and social insurance payments in the United States during the postwar era.

As important as these various theoretical distinctions are, it is also useful to notice how much these perspectives have in common. Indeed, it might be argued that the similarities outweigh the differences. In order to highlight this fact I divide the welfare state literature along a different fissure. In what follows I will focus on the differences between this larger group (which I'm calling the formal comparativists) and the community of scholars who work from within a feminist framework.[2] The most obvious difference between these two groups is that the feminists, more or less by definition, tend to privilege the role of gender. Without discounting the importance of that primary distinction, I am going to focus instead on some of the ways in which I think attention to questions of gender has led feminist scholars to approach the study of social welfare institutions differently. It seems to me that there are three crucial distinctions.

First is the overarching research design. The general goal of the formal comparativists is to explain the nature of the welfare systems which particular countries exhibit at specific moments in time. Variations in the level of provision of social benefits, what Marshall referred to as the social rights of citizenship, constitute the dependent variable in this model. Independent variables are any features of the society which are hypothesized to explain this variation.[3] Theoretical disputes among the formal comparativists are tied to differences in the choice of preferred independent variables. Thus the "logic of industrialism" perspective of Harold Wilensky (1975) highlights the importance of economic and technological development as the root cause for the growth of welfare states;[4] state autonomy theorists such as Theda Skocpol (Skocpol and Ikenberry 1983) emphasize the character and capacities of state institutions, as well as the expertise and vested interests of state bureaucrats, and so on. The main point is that formal comparativists use some feature of the broader social organization of society to explain the nature of welfare states.

In contrast, feminist scholars are far more likely to emphasize the mutually constitutive character of this relationship. While they are clearly interested in understanding how patriarchal relationships in society have led to the construction of certain types of social welfare arrangements, they are just as likely to emphasize the ways in which social policies promote the patriarchal character of the broader society (Abramovitz 1988; Gordon 1990a,b; Wilson 1977). Thus, in contrast to the overwhelming tendency of the formal comparativists to treat social policies as a secondary or derivative social phenomena, feminists are just as inclined to privilege these policies as central determinants of how systems of power and domination are perpetuated in society as a whole.

The second salient characteristic of the formal comparativists' project is its *materialist* orientation. Concrete, measurable, demonstrable features of the demography, the economy, the polity or the political economy are presumed to be the primary causal factors. In the earliest examples of this type of research (Wilensky and Lebeaux 1965), specific measures of economic production, levels of technological development, the degree of professionalization and the nature of social stratification were used as markers for the overall level of industrialization. In more recent work, attention has shifted away from teleological theories of societal development towards far more nuanced theories of political economy and political conflict. Thus, for example, power resources theorists such as Walter Korpi (1989) focus on the relative strength of different social classes within the economy and the polity. This shift from universalistic theories (modernization, industrialization, democratization) towards power base theories has clearly been an important improvement. However, the materialist orientation has remained more or less intact. Classes and class interests (or state structures and the interests of state agents) are treated as objective social forces which push for and against the development of social rights. Here the classificatory logic of social welfare institutions are treated in much the same way that Durkheim and Mauss (1963) studied classification systems in traditional societies—as ideological reflections of the more objective, material structures of social organization.

Feminist scholarship, on the other hand, begins from the perspective that what matters is not the objective social quality of sex, but the cultural system of meanings embodied in gender relations. This means that they tend to be far more in tune with the way in which cultural meaning systems shape and condition the types of social distinctions that come to be treated as objective. When feminist scholars look at the welfare state they are predisposed to seeing how institutionalized systems of interpretation shape the ways in which women are treated by social welfare policies. And they have been quick to point out that the sorts of social categories that make up the foundations of most welfare systems—especially gendered categories such as "widow," "mother," "unwed mother," and the like—are symbolic constructs which contain within them ideologically coded assumptions about gender roles, the construct of the "family wage," the separation of public from private spheres as well as many morally charged cultural prejudices. A good example is the way in which a culturally defined sexual double standard has come to inform the way that single mothers in the United States (in their roles as "beneficiaries" of the federal AFDC program) are held to a type of moral policing which is not imposed on beneficiaries of typically masculine relief programs. Thus, feminists are far more likely to see the root cause of social policies as deriving from institutionalized systems of cultural meanings embedded in the broader society.

The third significant difference between these two paradigms is the amount of attention which is paid to interpreting the character of social welfare institutions. The defining feature of the formal comparativists' approach is the relative simplicity with which social welfare systems have tended to be conceptualized. Initially, variation among welfare states was measured by overall expenditures in social programs (scaled as proportion of GNP).[5] The larger the percentage of expenditures on social programs, the closer a country was presumed to have come to Marshall's ideal of social citizenship. Aside from the obvious measurement problems associated with determining just what should be included as a social expenditure, this approach tends to empty all of the meaning out of welfare institutions. Programs are either big or they are small. Differences in types of programs are not considered, nor are the ideas, the ideologies, or the force of rhetoric that accompanies and very powerfully shapes the experience of claiming one's social rights.

Formal comparativists have not been insensitive to this problem. On the contrary, there has been a steady improvement over time in the degree of subtlety with which welfare institutions have been transformed into dependent variables. The first important development was the shift towards a far more sophisticated attempt to measure the types of social welfare provisions that states provided. Thus, rather than measuring overall levels of expenditures, researchers began trying to explain the occurrence of certain classes of welfare programs or categories of social provisions (e.g., Alber 1981; Coughlin and Armour 1983). This in itself was a significant advance because it meant that it was possible to assess the kinds of demands that citizens could make against the state. However this, too, was a relatively crude way of assessing the character of social rights because it left open the question of how claimants were constructed and differentiated by welfare states.

More recently, formal comparativists have begun to include measures of the kinds of eligibility criteria that citizens can use in making claims against the state. Gøsta Esping-Anderson (1990), for example, identifies three different types of claims—those grounded in claims of citizenship alone, those established on the basis of contributory inputs, and those which derive from claims based on levels of need.[6] By combining measures of the types of claims and the types of services provided, Esping-Anderson has been able to develop a far more nuanced measure of the character of social rights that exist in given societies at specific moments of time. He identifies clusters of societies as examples of specific welfare state "regime-types." In doing so, he has moved the formal analysis of welfare institutions closer to a set of measures of welfare states that captures the nuanced variations in the character of social rights and thus, closer to an understanding of the ways in which systems of meanings matter.

And yet, even Esping-Anderson's model of welfare regimes is a long way from the sort of "thick description" that Nancy Fraser and other feminist scholars have sought to provide. For example, although Esping-Anderson has emphasized the significance of how claims making is organized within regime-types, the meaning of these various types of claims is not explored in any detail. Rather the claims have a static, analytically predetermined character. This is because Esping-Anderson *derives* his taxonomy of claim types from his conceptual model of the role that social policies play within the broader political economy. Thus, his taxonomy of claims is vulnerable to the criticism of feminist scholars who have complained that it is grounded upon an implicit model of an ideal-typical citizen conceived as a male wage-earner (Orloff 1993). In short, even where mainstream scholars have moved to employ more sophisticated models of the character of social policies, they have still remained quite distant from the types of "close readings" that are necessary to achieve the sort of interpretative analysis that feminist scholars have called for.

Various scholars (especially from the feminist side of the aisle) have begun to push for a rapprochement between these two research approaches by showing how the consequences of feminist analyses have concrete implications for the ways in which welfare regimes are conceptualized and measured (Bussemaker and van Kersbergen 1994; Daly 1994; Hobson 1994; Orloff 1993). While these are important insights, they represent only one type of potential reconciliation—one which tends to privilege the conceptual framework and, ultimately, the broader methodological assumptions of the formal comparativists. My goal is to propose a rather different kind of rapprochement. Rather than suggesting ways in which the insights of feminist readings of welfare practices ought to inform more conventional measurements of welfare regimes, I am going to turn this around and suggest some ways in which the tools of formal analysis can be used to inform feminist readings of the meanings that are implicitly embedded within welfare states. While this shift may appear to give primacy to the statistical methodologies of the formal comparativists, ultimately I believe such an endeavor ends up privileging the conceptual framework and thus, the broader interpretive project which feminist scholars have championed.

TOWARDS A FORMAL ANALYSIS OF CLASSIFICATORY LOGICS

As I suggested earlier, the primary unit of analysis for an interpretive study of social welfare institutions is the social identity. Examples could include "single mothers with dependent children," "government pensioners," "disabled blind persons," and so forth. These identities are arrayed within a system of meaningful differences that may be usefully summarized as a set of discourse roles (Mohr 1994). Three classificatory projects are especially important for differentiating identities from one another.

First, as the formal comparativists originally noted, social welfare institutions vary in terms of the types of solutions that they provide to beneficiaries. Typically these include the following sorts of state activities: the provision of unemployment insurance, means tested and non-means tested income maintenance programs, housing allowances, sick benefits, old age pensions, parental leave benefits, child care services, and so forth. It should be clear that none of these practices exist independently of some categorical subject (identity) which is the object of these actions. Thus, to speak of unemployment insurance is to speak simultaneously of the "unemployed." To refer to old age pensions is to implicitly invoke the category of the "aged."

Second, as Esping-Anderson and Walter Korpi have demonstrated, identities are also meaningfully differentiated in terms of the types of claims that they are empowered to make upon the state. Esping-Anderson distinguished between claims grounded in citizenship, contributory payments, and need. We could add various other types and subtypes to this list such as the claims that derive from different categories of contributions—payment into a social insurance system as opposed to a pension earned for service to the state. And, again, as feminist scholars have been quick to emphasize, there are categories of claims which tend to be gendered; the claims which women may make by virtue of being dependent upon a husband is an example.

Third, as Nancy Fraser has explained, there is a system of differences founded upon the types of needs that specific identities are presumed to confront. Thus, to cite an example that Fraser employs, there is currently a lively debate being waged in American policy circles about the needs of poor women who receive federal welfare (AFDC) funds. Conservative critics such as Charles Murray (1984) maintain that what these women really *need* is to be released from the "bondage" of welfare, and be left to fend for themselves in the market economy. Liberals counter that what these women really *need* is a more generous and encompassing system of welfare programs such as daycare for their children, job training programs that can provide them with genuinely useful skills, and job opportunities that will pay them a livable wage. Here, the operant social identity is the impoverished female head of a household that is lacking a traditional male "breadwinner." The presumptive needs of women in this category are being debated by policy experts who seek to prescribe one or another programmatic solution on the basis of their interpretation of what these women need. Fraser (1989:162) argues that with the rise of welfare states, "needs talk" has come to be "institutionalized as a major vocabulary of political discourse" and that it coexists "with talk about rights and interests at the very center of political life."[7]

I have suggested that each of these exist as classificatory projects. This means that, in general, social welfare agencies are likely to recognize a relatively small subset of empirically occurring distinctions and that they are likely to be embedded in a coherent and systematic structure of relationships (Starr 1992). At the same time, however, it is important to point out that the meanings that are associated with these three classificatory domains are by no means exhausted by the classification systems themselves. On the contrary, each domain is itself embedded within a complex, ever-changing, and (probably) fiercely contested system of discourse. To fully understand a given classificatory structure it would be necessary to turn to examine the institutional field which is responsible for producing the discursive system. Such an analysis would demand an investigation of the relevant players within the field, the system of power that defines the likelihood of gaining success within the field, and the ways in which the players are arrayed with respect to that system of power (Bourdieu and Wacquant 1992).[8] Note, by the way, that according to Bourdieu, no analysis of an institutional field can be conducted without attending to the system of cultural meanings (the field specific capital) which characterizes the field. This is one reason why the inattention on the part of formal comparativists to the systems of meanings that operate in social welfare institutions is likely to lead to an impoverished account of the system of politics and power which operates there. This also suggests another reason why an interpretive study of the classificatory logics of social welfare institutions is an essential task.

Thus, by reminding us of the role of interpretation and meanings in the constitution of citizens as the bearers of social rights, feminist scholars have performed an enormous service. But shifting our attention to the ways in which meanings are embedded within the classificatory logics of social welfare states does not imply that we must surrender the goal of developing a formal analysis of the character of welfare states. It is certainly true that meanings are often quite ephemeral and, consequently, not always amenable to formal analysis. Much of the time these more symbolic elements of social life can only be reached by a kind of subjective intuitionism that is sometimes referred to as interpretative (or *verstehen*) analysis. The failure of feminists (or others) to make use of formal methods of analysis for addressing these sorts of interpretative issues reflects a long-standing tradition in sociology. With the notable exception and rather special case of public opinion research, sociologists have generally been slow to apply formal methodologies to the study of the symbolic domains of social life. Ideas, symbols, and meanings have tended to be seen as more ephemeral, less concrete, and not appropriate for formal, quantitative analysis.

It is also true, however, that certain types of social meanings are easier to study with formal methods than are others. Classification systems are distinctive precisely because their function is to mark off boundaries within cultural systems and to do so in a relatively unambiguous way. Thus, the meanings that they convey are generally relatively *shallow*. This is not to say that specific classifications may not contain enormously rich, complex, and polysemic associations. However, in order for a classification system to operate effectively it must also be able to convey the relevant cultural distinctions in a succinct and efficient manner. Thus, as a first principle, classifications tend to be constructed of shallow meanings, which is to say that they can often be reduced to a small number of relatively simple distinctions without losing their effectiveness as classificatory devices (Rosch 1978).

They are also notably stable in the sense that, by nature, they tend to be shared by a communicative group or a community. To operate in such a context, classification systems, like linguistic systems, have a tendency to evolve at a rather slow pace. Other things being equal, the greater volatility there is to a classification system, the less likely it is to endure as a functional system of shared distinctions.

Finally, classificatory distinctions are built from sets of differences that tend to be internally referential to the classification system itself. It thus becomes a relatively simple matter to "interpret" classifications so long as one is willing to restrict oneself to the system of differences that are explicitly embedded within the internal logic of that system. Put another way, categories take on meaning largely with reference to other categories within the same classificatory order. This makes them especially susceptible to formal analysis.

All of this explains why it is that anthropologists have always been drawn to the study of classification systems as a way of trying to *crack the code* of other cultures (D'Andrade 1995). As I've just noted, classifications have the distinct advantage of being relatively simple systems of meaning to work upon. But they also have another important advantage, which is that they are often located at a functionally important site within a given institutional system. That is, their relative simplicity as a system of meaning makes them not only easier to crack, but also easier to use. They are in Mary Douglas' (1986) words, "good to think with." Thus classificatory systems often provide the organizing gestalt or skeletal infrastructure upon which extraordinarily complex systems of meaning and action are established. All of this makes them ideal candidates for empirical observation and formal analysis.

What is true for anthropologists studying distant cultures is no less true for scholars interested in understanding the institutional dynamics of welfare states. My argument is that we can and should make use of these properties of classification systems as a way of gaining a better understanding of the discursive or ideological side of social welfare institutions, and that we ought to employ formal methodologies to do so. There are several advantages to such an approach.

On the one hand, the use of formal methods allows us to compare and contrast cases with one another (both across time and across societies) and to do so in ways that are replicable by other scholars. Formal methods also allow us the opportunity to test hypotheses about the way that meanings are organized within welfare states and to assess the impact of those sets of meanings both as independent and dependent variables within some causal theory. And finally, formal methods can sometimes be employed as a way of seeing institutional phenomena from a different perspective, making possible the identification of variations, trends, and developments that would not have otherwise been observable (Franzosi and Mohr 1997). As a way of grounding this discussion in a more concrete basis I turn now to an example of how meanings can be extracted from the study of social welfare classification systems.

GENDER CLASSIFICATIONS IN NEW YORK CITY DURING THE PROGRESSIVE ERA

The issue I take up here has to do with the problem of how classificatory systems carry meanings which reflect an underlying system of discourse. Specifically, I will examine how gendered assumptions are embedded within the classificatory practices used to describe the needs of clients treated by social welfare organizations. Here again I turn to the ideas of feminist scholars, who have suggested that the American welfare state is gendered in a very distinctive way. They suggest that welfare practices are clearly divided into a "two-channel" or "two-tiered" system of relief. This general idea is described by Nancy Fraser. She explains that there are two different types of welfare programs in the United States (1989:149):

> One set of programs is oriented to individuals and tied to participation in the paid work force—for example, unemployment insurance and Social Security. This set of programs is designed to supplement and compensate for the primary market in paid labor power. A second set of programs is oriented to households and tied to combined household income—for example, AFDC, food stamps, and Medicaid. This set of programs is designed to compensate for what are considered to be family failures, in particular the absence of a male breadwinner.

Fraser argues that there are many differences between these two types of welfare programs. The former sort tend to individualize recipients. Claims are linked to contributory payments and recipients are conceived as having the legitimate right to make a nonstigmatized claim against the system. These programs are usually geared toward supplementing participation in the primary labor market and, ideal-typically, the recipients tend to be male.

In contrast, recipients of the second set of programs are, in Fraser's (1989:150) words, "not individualized but familialized." They are intended to "serve what are considered to be defective families, overwhelmingly families without a male breadwinner." The ideal-typical recipient is a female who makes "her claim for benefits on the basis of her status as an unpaid domestic worker, a homemaker, and mother, not as a paid worker based in the labor market." In this second tier, recipients are constituted as 'clients' who must petition the state for 'public charity.' To be eligible they have to meet requisite levels of 'neediness' and be willing to submit themselves to various forms of surveillance, behavioral supervision, and scrutiny of their character and moral standards.

While Fraser's description pertains to the conditions of the contemporary welfare state, Bárbara Nelson (1990) has suggested that the origins of this system stretch back to the Progressive Era when the foundations of modern American welfare institutions were first being established. There is some controversy over the question of precisely when and in what respect the gendered character of the American welfare state was developed. Elsewhere, Krista Paulsen and I have traced the contours of these arguments in some detail and tried to pin down the precise periods during which various kinds of gendered assumptions were encoded into the American social welfare system (Mohr and Paulsen 1996). In this chapter, however, I will focus on the way in which classifications that were employed by social welfare organizations operating in New York City can be used to gauge and interpret the discourse regarding the needs of social welfare clients that was prevalent in the American welfare system during the Progressive Era.

Specifically I will ask whether relief practices were "gendered" during the Progressive Era in the same sorts of ways that Fraser has described the contemporary American welfare state. Were women more likely than men to be "familialized" during these years? Were their needs more likely to be linked to the demands of a domestic household? Were they more likely to be interpreted as being in need of moral supervision? We can also ask about men's relationship to the social welfare system. Here we would want to know whether men's needs were construed as being tied to their participation in the labor force.

Data and Measures

To answer these questions I employ information about how various social welfare organizations in New York City classified the people who made use of their services. Because the great majority of social welfare services were provided by nonfederal organizations during these years, I have included in this analysis every organization in the city of New York (public and private) that was listed in the New York City Charity Directories at four points in time—1888, 1897, 1907, and 1917. These Directories were intended to serve as comprehensive practical guidebooks for practitioners in the field. They listed every organization that was deemed to be relevant to the task of 'relief work' along with detailed descriptions of what services these organizations provided and what restrictions existed as to the kinds of applicants that would be accepted. I recorded all information published in the Directories regarding the categories of people that were provided with services by each organization. Each description of a class of persons treated or provided with services was treated as a separate observation for the purposes of this analysis. There were a total of 12,927 coded identities in the database from these four years. A verbatim record of each identity description was entered into the database. In some cases, the identity term consisted of a particular noun that was used to designate the class of individuals referred to. These included terms such as: "paupers," "orphans," "widows," "tramps," "ex-prisoners," "idiots," and "lunatics." In most cases, however, a single noun term was inadequate to accurately designate the class of individuals referred to, and some more complex string of nouns and adjectives were employed in the Directory listing to specify the intended social category.

These more complex identity terms included the following sorts of designations: "needy stage-dancers," "unmarried women pregnant for the first time," "destitute Protestant female children of the better class suffering from incurable diseases who are without means or friends able to support them," and "all soldiers of any of the late wars who are unable from wounds received in the line of duty to earn a living by labor." Excluding basic prepositions, articles, and 'to-be' verbs, the mean number of words in these identity terms ranges between about 3.4 and 3.8 for the four years, though some identities consist of as many as 25 (nonexcluded) words.[9]

For the purposes of this analysis I selected the subsample of identities that were clearly gendered. Any identity that satisfied the criteria for either "male" or "female" (as specified by the text strings identified in Table 8–1) were included in this analysis. I then looked to see how these identities were classified. Because I was interested in the question of how meanings were encoded in the discourse regarding needs, I coded each identity according to whether or not it was associated with any of eight different categories of need.[10] These included any reference to the individual being impoverished (POOR), in ill health (SICK), disabled in some manner (DISABLED), having needs that were associated with being a parent (DOMESTIC), being defined according to their moral needs (MORAL), being in need

TABLE 8–1. Text Recognition Strings for Needs Classifications

MALE: boy; brother; gentleman; male; man; men; father; husband; son; widower.

FEMALE: daughter; female; gentlewoman; girl; lady; mother; sister; wife; woman; widows.

DISABLED: blind; blinded; cripple; crippled; deaf; deaf-mute; deafness; debilitated; defective sight; defective; defects; deformed; deformity; disabled; epilepsy; epileptic; paralytic; physical development has been arrested; physical development has been impaired; physical development has been retarded; semi-paralytic; stammerer; stammering; unable from disease contracted in the line of duty; unable from wounds received in the line of duty; unable to gain a livelihood.

DOMESTIC: about to be confined; child-bed; childbirth; during confinement; father; from the maternity hospitals; lying-in; maternity; mother; nursing mother; parent; pregnant; with a baby; with children; with their infants.

HOMELESS: evicted from their homes; evicted; eviction; excluded from their homes; homeless; rounder; tramp; unhomed; vagrancy; vagrant; wanderers; wandering; who have no home; without homes.

INTEMPERATE: addict; addicted; addiction; alcohol addiction; alcohol cases; alcohol habit; alcoholic habitues; alcoholic; delinquent; dissolute habits; dissolute; drug addiction; drug addicts; drug habits; drunk; drunkards; drunkenness; habit trouble; inebriate; inebriety; intemperance; intemperate; intoxication; minor misdemeanants; morphine habit; narcotic habit; opium cases; opium habit.

MORAL: able and willing to work; ambitious; anxious to make the most of themselves; anxious to reform; bad character; moral character; degraded; deserving of assistance; deserving; desire to reform; desire to support themselves; desiring to amend life; desiring to lead better lives; desiring to reform; dishonorable; erred; erring; exposed to the temptations; fair character; good; fallen; falling into criminal ways; falling; feeling the need of reformation and protection; good moral character; have not lived vicious lives; idle; immoral; in danger of falling; in need of protection; industrious; innocent; menace; misstep; moral; needing protection or help; needing protection; not lived vicious lives; obscene; of good conduct; of reform institutions; references regarding character; reformatory cases; reputable; respectable; responsible; risk; sin; temptation; tempted; unexceptional reference as to character; unfaithful; unprotected; vice; vicious surroundings; virtue; virtuous; who desire to learn; who desire to reform; who wish to reform; wish to reform; worthy; self-respecting.

TABLE 8-1—*(continued)*

POOR: beg; beggar; begging; destitute of the means of support; destitute; destitution; formerly living in the almshouses; formerly living in the poorhouses; from state almshouses; in need of assistance; indigent; mendicant; neccesitous; needy; of city almshouses; of the almshouse; of town almshouses; pauper; poor; poorer; poorest; residents of almshouses; too poor to pay; without means or friends who can support them; without means or friends who can support; without means or relatives able to pay.

SICK: accident; ailment; are recovering from acute illness; beyond the need of constant attention from a physician; bones; cancer; cannot pay for the services of the trained nurse; charity patients; consumption; consumptive; contagious; convalescent; convalescing; cutaneous; diptheria; disease; ear; erysipelas; eye; fever; free patients; from the city hospitals; from the orthopaedic wards; glands; gynecological; health breaks down; heart cases; hip; ill; illness; in hospitals; in need of a vacation; in need of medical treatment; in need of recuperation; in need of rest from overwork; in need of rest; incurable; infectious; injured; joint; laryngeal; leper; lung; lupus; maimed; malady; measles; medical; need 2 weeks care and rest after illness; need rest; needing a few days rest; needing rest; non-contagious; nose; not ill enough to be admitted to a regular; not ill enough to be admitted; nourishment; opthalmia; orthopaedic; patient; pthisis; recovering from an acute illness; recovering from; recovering; recuperate; recuperating; reported to the department by the attending physician; require rest; requiring care of a physician; requiring hospital care; rest after illness; rest; resting; ruptured; sick; sickness; skin; small-pox; so far recovered from illness; spine; surgery; surgical; teeth; throat; tubercular; tuberculosis; typhus; unable to pay for either physician or medicine; unable to procure proper medical assistance; vacation; venereal; visited by the summer corps of physicians; ward patients; who are recovering from acute illness; who need care nursing and rest; who need fresh air rest and medical care; who need rest; wounded; wounds.

UNEMPLOYED: are without employment; awaiting permanent employment; desiring jobs; employment; employments; looking for employment; no means of gaining a livelihood; not lawfully employed; out of employment; out of work; seeking employment; seeking permanent employment; seeking work; unable to obtain employment; unemployed; want of employment; who desire situations; without employment.

of employment (UNEMPLOYED), being in need of housing or shelter (HOMELESS), or being in need of treatment for drug or alcohol abuse (IN-TEMPERATE). The specific classifications used for this analysis are listed in Table 8–1.[11]

Analyses

If social welfare institutions during the Progressive Era applied the same sort of two-tiered treatments to men and women as Fraser has described with reference to the contemporary American welfare state, then we can expect to find evidence of that fact in the varied ways in which male and female identities were classified by social welfare organizations during these years. The earlier discussion about the difference between men's and women's social welfare programs suggests some hypotheses about how the discourse on social relief may have differed for men and women during the Progressive Era.

For example, Fraser argues that women are less likely to be individualized and more likely to be "familialized." By this she means that women were more likely to be identified as a member of a household, and thus their needs were more likely to be viewed in terms of the needs of the household, the needs of their family, and the needs that emerge out of their role as parents. The other striking characteristic about feminized social welfare programs, according to Fraser, is the extent to which they construe women as being in need of moral supervision. Whether we're describing the food stamp program in which relief applicants are not trusted to make responsible consumer choices, or the AFDC program in which relief recipients' sexuality is the object of scrutiny, feminized social welfare programs tend to view women as being in need of close moral supervision.

In like fashion, if we assume that men's needs were constructed in the same way that Fraser has described them with reference to the contemporary welfare state, then we would presume that the discourse around men's needs would be oriented toward their status as members of the workforce. Consequently, we would expect the discourse on men's needs to emphasize problems associated with job training, unemployment, and retirement from the active workforce.

Table 8–2 describes the prevalence of various categories of needs for male and female identities. I have arranged this table so that the variables are clustered according to whichever gendered identity was most likely to be associated with each type of need. The far right column indicates whether the difference between male and female distributions are significantly different from one another. Notice that a good many of these identities were

TABLE 8–2. Frequency With Which Female and Male Identities Are
Associated with 8 Categories of Needs, New York City Charity
Directories, 1888–1917.

	Female/Ids		Male/Ids		Sig.[†]
	N	%	N	%	
Poor	460	16.0	128	9.3	***
Sick	200	7.0	60	4.4	***
Domestic	448	15.6	20	1.5	***
Moral	313	10.9	86	6.3	***
Homeless	81	2.8	68	5.0	***
Intemperate	29	1.0	38	2.8	***
Disabled	51	1.8	32	2.3	—
Unemployed	39	1.4	15	1.1	—

[†] Difference as measured by chi-square test, *** $P \leq .001$

not classified according to any of the eight categories of need listed here
(more than 54 percent of the female and 68 percent of the male identities
were not associated with any of these categories of need). This is because
they either were classified according to other types of needs not included in
this table or, more frequently, they were linked to services by virtue of some
status claim without also being classified according to their needs.

Perhaps the most striking feature of this table is the extent to which
it reveals the nonsignificance of unemployment as a recognized and acknowledged social need for either men or women. Just over 1 percent of both male
and female identities were explicitly associated with their need for employment. This suggests that during the Progressive Era, social rights, to the extent that they existed at all, were far more likely to be linked to various status claims or to the more general problem of impoverishment. Notice, for
example, that for both male and female identities, poverty was the most frequently invoked category of need. For women, domestic needs were invoked
nearly as frequently, however, lending support to the notion that women were
constituted as "familialized" social subjects by the social welfare system
during the Progressive Era just as they are today. And, quite interestingly,
for both men and women the next most frequent category of needs were
those that had to do with issues of morality. Aside from the already noted
gender difference around family-associated needs, men and women differed
most noticeably in the greater probability that males would be identified with
the problems of homelessness and intemperance.

While these differences are instructive, they do not yet convey the manner in which these classifications are embedded within a system of discursive meanings regarding the needs of social welfare clients. In other words, we may notice differences in prevalence, but that doesn't tell us whether, for example, moral needs were construed in the same way for men and women or whether the meaning of poverty, in the discourse that was employed by social welfare professionals, differed by gender. To explore this question we must examine the data differently. If we assume that meaningfulness is constituted out of the juxtaposition of different categories within the same general classification system, then we can begin to consider the ways in which poverty meant different things (in this discourse system) for men and for women by looking at how men's and women's needs were formally differentiated in the organizational system of social welfare services. In other words, we can look at how organizations tended to bring together men with various kinds of needs for treatment inside the same organization and see how that system of juxtapositions compared to the ways in which organizations that treated women tended to combine different kinds of needs. To do this I have divided organizations into two groups—those that treat women and those that treat men. I have then constructed an 8x8 matrix for each group of organizations, with the eight different need variables in both rows and columns. Each cell of these matrices then contains a count of the total number of different organizations that describe the individuals that they treat by using both sets of need categories.

Table 8–3 contains information about all organizations in all four Charity Directories that listed women as recipients of their services. The diagonal entries contain the total number of these organizations that refer to their clients in terms of each of these eight categories of needs. Notice, for example, that there were 280 of these organizations that described their clients in terms of their domestic needs and 174 of these organizations that referred to the health needs of the women that they treated. There were only 84 of these organizations, however, that referred to their clients in terms of their needs for both health care and domestic issues. When the data is summarized in this fashion it gives a much better sense of the kinds of juxtapositions of needs talk that was carried on by these organizations and, hence, a better sense of the ways in which the meaningfulness of these needs were organized within the institutional system of discourse. My goal in these analyses is to compare the ways in which the juxtapositioning of men's and women's needs were structured in similar, or dissimilar ways.

Table 8–4 contains the same information as Table 8–3 except that I have employed the Jaccard measure (the *similarity ratio*) to compensate for uneven cell sizes.[12] This measure constrains each cell to a value between 0 and 1, where

TABLE 8–3. Frequency of Co-occurrence of References to 8 Categories of Needs by Organizations Serving Women, New York City Charity Directories, 1888–1917.

	Domestic	Sick	Homeless	Disabled	Unemployed	Intemperate	Moral	Poor
Domestic	280							
Sick	84	174						
Homeless	8	9	34					
Disabled	8	11	1	35				
Unemployed	2	4	1	0	16			
Intemperate	5	2	4	1	1	15		
Moral	46	44	14	8	6	9	164	
Poor	128	90	18	24	5	1	97	289

TABLE 8–4. Similarity Between 8 Categories of Needs as Defined by Frequency of Co-occurrence Within Organizations Serving Women, New York City Charity Directories, 1888–1917.

	Domestic	Sick	Homeless	Disabled	Unemployed	Intemperate	Moral	Poor
Domestic	1.000							
Sick	0.227	1.000						
Homeless	0.026	0.045	1.000					
Disabled	0.026	0.056	0.015	1.000				
Unemployed	0.007	0.022	0.020	0.000	1.000			
Intemperate	0.017	0.011	0.089	0.020	0.033	1.000		
Moral	0.116	0.150	0.076	0.042	0.034	0.053	1.000	
Poor	0.290	0.241	0.080	0.080	0.017	0.003	0.272	1.000

TABLE 8–5. Similarity Between 8 Categories of Needs as Defined by Frequency of Co-occurrence Within Organizations Serving Men, New York City Charity Directories, 1888–1917.

	Domestic	Sick	Homeless	Disabled	Unemployed	Intemperate	Moral	Poor
Domestic	1.000	.	.	.	.	.	.	.
Sick	0.000	1.000	.	.	.	.	.	.
Homeless	0.045	0.048	1.000	.	.	.	.	.
Disabled	0.000	0.222	0.000	1.000	.	.	.	.
Unemployed	0.000	0.000	0.200	0.000	1.000	.	.	.
Intemperate	0.273	0.083	0.056	0.000	0.000	1.000	.	.
Moral	0.250	0.000	0.143	0.000	0.034	0.107	1.000	.
Poor	0.031	0.143	0.407	0.038	0.036	0.036	0.282	1.000

a value of 0 indicates a complete absence of co-occurrences of two need classifications within the same organization and a value of 1 indicates a perfect co-occurrence—that is, every time one need is invoked, the other is as well. Table 8–5 contains the same information for male identities.[13]

To facilitate the interpretation of these tables I have used them as inputs to a multidimensional scaling analysis.[14] This type of analysis translates the similarities among each pair of needs into a comparable Euclidean distance. To do this the scaling program locates all the variables in a two-dimensional space in such a way as to simultaneously maximize (across all pairs) the goodness of fit between the measure of similarity for each pair of variables (as is captured in the table) and their distance from one another in the scaling plot. So, two types of needs that appear to be very similar in Table 8–2 (impoverishment and domestic needs, for example) should also be very close to one another in the multidimensional scaling plot. Conversely, two variables that are quite dissimilar in Table 8–2 (such as unemployed and disabled) should

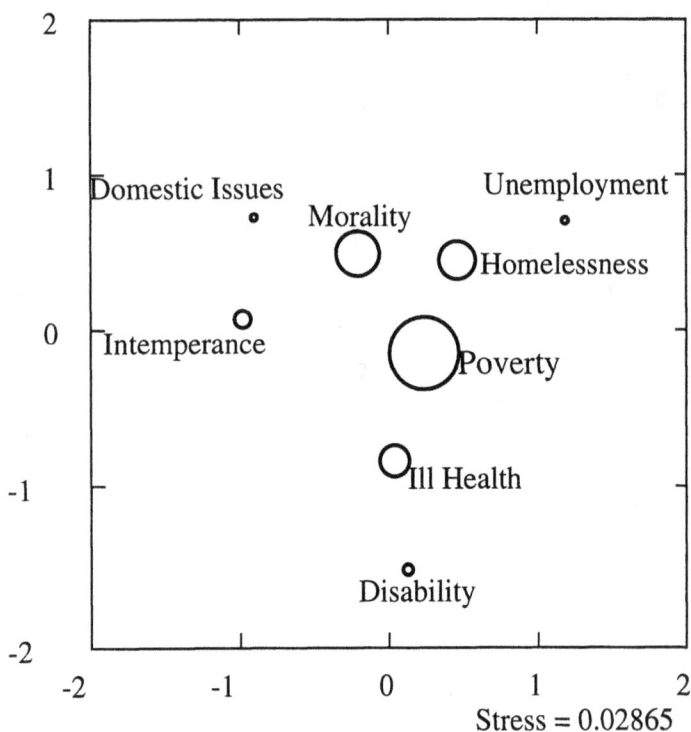

Figure 8–1. Social Needs Discourse as Defined by Organizations Serving Men, New York City, 1888–1917.

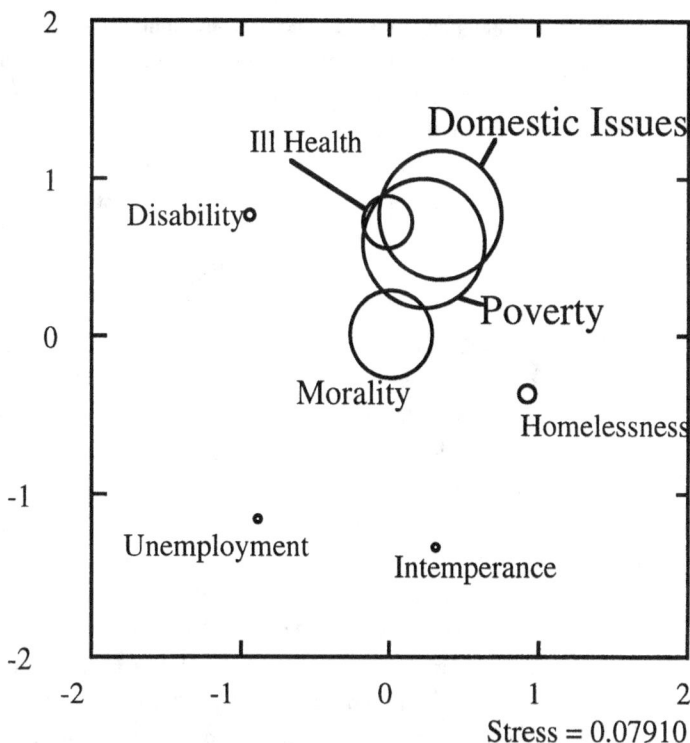

Figure 8–2. Social Needs Discourse as Defined by Organizations Serving Women, New York City, 1888–1917.

be located a large distance from one another in the plot. Figure 8–1 contains the information on the discourse regarding men's needs. Figure 8–2 contains the information regarding women. In these plots I have set the size of the point for each variable to a scale that reflects the frequency with which each category of social needs occurs within the identity level database.[15]

Consider first the plot representing the discourse of needs for male identities in the Charity Directories. This plot suggests several interesting features of the meanings of men's needs. First, notice that the problem of impoverishment is the most centrally located concept in the meaning space. This suggests that poverty, and not unemployment, was the central organizing concept in the discourse of needs for men. This is also reflected by the frequency with which terms indicating impoverishment occurred, as indicated by the larger circle for the concept of poverty. In contrast to what we had expected, unemployment is nowhere near the center of the discourse space. Neither is unemployment closely linked to poverty in this plot, suggesting that the problem of unemployment was no more likely to be associated with men's poverty than any of the other needs assessed in this analysis. On the contrary, in the system of meanings that is represented here, unemployment for men was most closely associated with the problem of homelessness. This is worth reflecting on for a moment.

The work of numerous historians has suggested that up through the turn of the century the problem of unemployment was not generally recognized as a structural problem of society so much as an individual problem indicating an unwillingness to work (Keyssar 1986; Ringenbach 1973; Sautter 1992). Moreover, the problem of unemployment was closely linked in the minds of social welfare professionals to the tramp problem (Katz 1983). It thus should come as no surprise that homelessness and unemployment occur very near one another in the discourse space of men's needs. At the same time, however, notice that homelessness is almost equidistant from the needs of unemployment, poverty, and morality. In a sense, we can *interpret* the meaning of homelessness as it was applied to men who were identified according to this condition as a social identity that was composed of equal parts of immorality, poverty, and unemployment. Similar interpretations can be made of other categories of need. Notice, for example, that intemperance was a need that was closely identified with both domestic problems and immorality. The problem of disability, on the other hand, apparently had a certain legitimacy as an acceptable category of need, as it is the one category which is located the furthest away in the discourse space from problems of morality.

Figure 8–2 contains the plot containing the structure of discourse concerning women's needs. Once again, there are several distinctive features which reveal a good deal about the way in which the meanings regarding women's needs were organized. First, it is striking to see the very central location of problems of morality in this discourse space. Apparently women's needs were all associated with morally charged issues and while poverty, sickness, and domestic needs were generally somewhat closer to problems of morality, on the whole, there was not a great difference between any of these categories of need with respect to their distance from moral concerns.[16] This, then, suggests that questions concerning morality figured very prominently in all corners of the social welfare discourse regarding women's needs during the Progressive Era.

Notice also the close association here between the problem of impoverishment and the needs that women were construed to have in their role as parents. Here, again, we see further evidence that the meanings associated with women's needs were organized in a fashion which is very reminiscent of Fraser's suggestions regarding the "familialized" character of women within the social welfare sector.

All of this suggests that the discourse of needs was in fact gendered during these years—men's needs were perceived to be rather different than women's needs. Moreover, there is evidence here which suggests that Barbara Nelson was at least partially correct. The ways in which women's needs were interpreted during the Progressive Era do bear certain similarities to the ways in which Fraser has described the cultural assumptions of the contemporary two-tiered American welfare state. Then and now, women's poverty was tightly coupled to their identities as mothers and the discourse regarding women's needs was clearly centered around their perceived need for moral supervision and evaluation. Of course, men's needs were also embedded in a moral discourse during these years, but problems of morality appear to have played a more tangential role for men during the Progressive Era, just as they do today.

More generally, by focusing on the way in which assumptions about needs were embedded in the categories used by social welfare organizations to refer to their clientele, I have sought to show that we can begin to gain access to the classificatory logic which served to organize this system of social welfare. Moreover, by treating this type of "needs talk" as data I have tried to demonstrate one way that we can make use of formal analytic techniques to contribute to an interpretive analysis of these types of institutional arrangements.

DISCUSSION

I began this chapter by asserting that an important component of citizenship was the way in which the relationship between states and citizens leads to their constitution as subjects within various discursive domains. Specifically, I noted that in claims made upon the state for their social rights, citizens enter into bureaucratic encounters in which they are necessarily subjected to the classificatory logic of social welfare agencies which locate them within a set of predefined identities. Although historians and more traditional institutional analysts have always seemed to be concerned with the ways in which these kinds of relationships are premised upon a complex and contested system of meanings which both condition the nature of citizenship and lead to changes in the structure of welfare states, I suggested that the shift that occurred towards the use of formal analysis in the comparative and macro-institutional research literature a generation ago led to an abandonment of this more interpretive component. I also suggested that much of the research trajectory since that time has involved a systematic reclaiming of more nuanced ways of measuring welfare states, and that this had led to an increasingly sophisticated interpretive analysis. From an initial tendency to operationalize welfare states in formal analyses as gross level of expenditures, we have seen a careful respecification of measures reflecting variations in services, types of claims, and, with the feminists, a focus on types of needs.

In this chapter my aim has been to suggest that we are now well positioned to take a further step. I have proposed that we begin to think about the ways in which we can make use of methods of formal analysis that will allow us to capture the classificatory logics of social welfare systems. I have argued that systems of this sort are constructed out of a repertoire of recognized social identities which are differentiated one from another on the basis of three (mutually constitutive) classificatory projects—regarding claims, needs, and solutions. In proposing this definition my aim has been to emphasize that classificatory logics are ways in which systems of meanings are anchored in the institutional practices of welfare states.

In my empirical example I sought to demonstrate one way in which formal analysis can be used to recapture the systems of meanings that operate within welfare states. In this procedure I focused on how discourses regarding the needs of social identities are embedded within the classificatory activities of social welfare agencies. While informative, this approach represents only a partial solution to the problem. A full appreciation of these systems of meanings requires that we attend to more than one dimension at a time. In other words, rather than merely measuring the way in which meanings are embedded within the discourse of needs, we must also look to understand how the relief practices (solutions) of welfare agencies and the classificatory structure of status claims are organized into meaningful narratives about the social rights of these same identities.

More than this, I suggested earlier that these three classificatory projects were mutually constitutive. By this I meant to emphasize that the discourse on needs is tightly coupled to the discourse on solutions. Unemployment is a problem for which job training is a type of solution. Thus, these two classificatory projects have to be seen as complementary—as mutually constitutive. The same could be said for the relationship between claims and needs or between claims and solutions. In other words, a full accounting of the classificatory logic in which these identities are embedded would require that we find a way to analyze the interaction of all three discursive dimensions simultaneously.

Vincent Duquenne and I (Mohr and Duquenne 1997) have sought to address this problem by mapping out these types of mutually constitutive relationships with Galois lattices. This is a procedure which emphasizes a nondeterminative duality of two dimensions of such a classificatory logic.

Elsewhere (Mohr, forthcoming [b]) I have argued that techniques such as this which make use of various types of discrete mathematics rather than more traditional types of probability based models may hold the solution to thinking about these kinds of interpretive problems.

Another route that can be pursued, however, is to focus on the ways in which these types of classificatory logics are materially inscribed within the institutionalization of specific organizational forms. A field of organizational forms (containing "insane asylums," "government unemployment offices," "social security bureaus," etc.) represent another level of aggregation within these types of classification systems. Like an identity, an organizational form in the social welfare sector may be defined by the particular constellation of services that are provided to individuals identified as having specified needs and particular types of claims upon the social welfare system. In other work, Francesca Guerra-Pearson and I have been able to map out the institutional structure of outdoor (Mohr and Guerra-Pearson, forthcoming) and indoor (Mohr 1995) social welfare organizations from the Progressive Era. By looking at how these organizations are positioned vis-à-vis one another within the system of discourse, we have sought to develop an understanding of how service niches are organized within social welfare systems.

More generally, my intention has been to propose that these types of projects represent a rather different sort of rapprochement between the goal of using formal methodologies to compare welfare states across time and country and the ambitions of feminist scholars to develop an interpretive analysis of social welfare institutions. Ideally, projects such as I have demonstrated here might be developed into a broader research agenda in which the formal analysis of welfare states can be advanced without necessarily relegating the meaningful character of these practices to the status of dependent variables which are perceived to play little or no substantive role in the developmental logic of welfare states and social rights. In short, a focus on classificatory logics pushes us to more fully confront the ways in which meanings are both produced by and are essential to the production of systems of social welfare.

Notes

An early version of this paper was presented at the 1992 annual meeting of the American Sociological Association, in Pittsburgh, PA. Thanks to Andrew Abbott, Bill Bielby, Lisa Brush, Paul DiMaggio, John Foran, Noah Friedkin, Roger Friedland, Barbara Hobson, Connie McNeely, Charles Perrow, Josep Rodriguez, Margaret Somers, John Sonquist, John Sutton, and the members of the UCSB Comparative Institutions Seminar, the UCSB Social Networks Seminar and the Yale University Complex Organizations Workshop for useful comments on earlier drafts. Research support on this project has been provided by the Nonprofit Sector Research Fund of the Aspen Institute, UCSB Academic Senate Research Grants, and by the ASA Advancement of the Discipline NSF Small Grant Program.

1. *See*, for example, Shalev (1983), Skocpol and Amenta (1986), Hasenfeld, Rafferty, and Zald (1987), Esping-Anderson and van Kersbergen (1992).

2. I include within this broadly defined feminist paradigm the scholars whose work tends to privilege the role of gender in developing an understanding of social welfare institutions. Examples of this type of work can be found in the following collections: Gordon (1990b), Bock and Thane (1991), Koven and Michel (1993), Sainsbury (1994). As will be clear from the discussion, I have defined the formal comparativists as a very broad category in which I include scholars such as Harold Wilensky, Francis Castles, Michael Shalev, as well as Walter Korpi and Gøsta Esping-Anderson. Of course, these are necessarily somewhat arbitrary classifications, especially considering that there is another large and differentiated group of state theorists and comparativists whose work is included in volumes such as Flora and Heidenheimer (1981) and Weir, Orloff, and Skocpol (1988). In reality, the boundaries between these scholars and the two "paradigms" I have identified in the text are not hard and fast. Thus, for example, many that I am identifying as members of the feminist paradigm could just as easily be located within this third grouping and, likewise, the boundary between the formal comparativists and this third group is by no means solid.

3. Among institutionalist and world system variants, independent variables include features of the global social order and a particular country's relationship to that order. *See*, for example the work collected in Thomas, Meyer, Ramirez, and Boli (1987) as well as the essays collected in this volume.

4. Wilensky (1975) identifies other factors—the degree of governmental centralization, rates of social mobility and the political organization of the working class— which account for other more complex variations among developed welfare states.

5. Wilensky (1975) used overall expenditures for Social Security programs compared to GNP and overall military expenditures.

6. Esping-Anderson's colleague and sometimes co-author Walter Korpi should also be credited for this innovation. *See*, for example, Korpi (1989).

7. It is important to note that formal comparativists have also been interested in categories of needs which confront individuals, but they have traditionally been far more likely to suppose that these are less a matter for interpretation than an expression of natural and universal categories of human needs which possess a kind of transparent obviousness. Thus, while acknowledging the role of cultural norms in modifying expectations for a certain "quality of life," Wilensky and Lebeaux (1958) argued that the basic needs which social welfare programs were intended to address were more or less predefined and largely incontestable.

8. Bourdieu's theory of institutional fields is especially useful for understanding social welfare institutions. A particularly relevant discussion can be found in Bourdieu (1987). *Also see* Mohr (forthcoming[a]) and Swartz (forthcoming).

9. For details on the dataset and procedures used for coding these identities, *see* Mohr (1992, 1994).

10. I aggregated a large number of text strings to generate these eight inclusive categories of needs. Still, there were other statements of needs (needs for spiritual uplift, for recreation, for legal aid, etc.) that were excluded here. I used two criteria for inclusion. First, I included all types of needs that were especially prevalent in the Directories. Second, I made an effort to include those categories of needs that seemed to be especially appropriate to match Fraser's theorization of the types of needs that would be relevant to identifying the existence of the two-channel welfare state.

11. Plural forms of these text strings were also used in the search procedures. I have not generally included plural forms in this table.

12. The Jaccard measure corrects for uneven cell sizes by dividing the number of matches by the total number of non-zero occurrences. In other words,
If:

$$a=(\text{Case } 1 = 1 \text{ and Case } 2 = 1),$$
$$b=(\text{Case } 1 = 1 \text{ and Case } 2 = 0),$$
$$c=(\text{Case } 1 = 0 \text{ and Case } 2 = 1), \text{ and}$$
$$d=(\text{Case } 1 = 0 \text{ and Case } 2 = 0)$$

Then, for x and y,
$$\text{Jaccard }(x,y) = \frac{a}{a+b+c}$$

13. The table for male identities contains a high proportion of 0 entries (39%). This is largely a reflection of the fact that there were fewer organizations which specialized in serving male clients. The high percentage of empty cells makes the interpretation of the multidimensional scaling plot less robust and all findings should take that fact into consideration.

14. I used the multidimensional scaling module in Systat (Kruskal's stress formula 1).

15. Specifically, each point is scaled to represent .5 multiplied by the percentage of identity-level observations that are described by each category of need.

16. Recall that the proper measurement here is the distance from the centers of each circle.

REFERENCES

Abramovitz, Mimi. 1988. *Regulating the Lives of Women: Social Welfare Policy from Colonial Times to the Present*. Boston: South End Press.

Alber, J. 1981. "Government Responses to the Challenge of Unemployment: The Development of Unemployment Insurance in Western Europe." Pp. 151–183 in *The Development of Welfare States in Europe and America*, edited by Peter Flora and Arnold Heidenheimer. New York: Transaction Books.

Bock, Gisela, and Pat Thane, eds. 1991. *Maternity and Gender Policies: Women and the Rise of the European Welfare States, 1880s–1950s*. New York: Routledge.

Bourdieu, Pierre. 1987. "The Force of Law: Toward a Sociology of the Juridical Field." *Hastings Journal of Law* 38:209–248.

Bourdieu, Pierre, and Loïc J. D. Wacquant. 1992. *An Invitation to Reflexive Sociology*. Chicago: University of Chicago Press.

Bussemaker, Jet, and Kees van Kersbergen. 1994. "Gender and Welfare States: Some Theoretical Reflections." Pp. 8–25 in *Gendering Welfare States*, edited by Diane Sainsbury. Thousand Oaks, CA: Sage.

Coughlin, R. M., and P. K. Armour. 1983. "Sectoral Differentiation in Social Security Spending in the OECD Nations. *Comparative Social Research* 6:175–199.

Daly, Mary. 1994. "Comparing Welfare States: Towards a Gender Friendly Approach." Pp. 101–117 in *Gendering Welfare States*, edited by Diane Sainsbury. Thousand Oaks, CA: Sage.

D'Andrade, Roy G. 1995. *The Development of Cognitive Anthropology*. Cambridge: Cambridge University Press.

Douglas, Mary. 1986. *How Institutions Think*. Syracuse, NY: Syracuse University Press.

Durkheim, Emile, and Marcel Mauss. 1963 [1903]. *Primitive Classification*. Chicago: University of Chicago Press.

Esping-Anderson, Gøsta. 1990. *The Three Worlds of Welfare Capitalism*. Princeton, NJ: Princeton University Press.

Esping-Anderson, Gøsta, and Walter Korpi. 1984. "Social Policy as Class Politics in Post-War Capitalism: Scandinavia, Austria, and Germany." Pp. 179–208 in

Order and Conflict in Contemporary Capitalism, edited by J.H. Goldthorpe. Oxford: Oxford University Press.

Esping-Anderson, Gøsta, and Kees van Kersbergen. 1992. "Contemporary Research on Social Democracy." *Annual Review of Sociology* 18:187–208.

Flora, Peter, and Arnold Heidenheimer, eds. 1981. *The Development of Welfare States in Europe and America,* edited by Peter Flora and Arnold Heidenheimer. New York: Transaction Books.

Franzosi, Roberto, and John W. Mohr. 1997. "New Directions in Formalization and Historical Analysis." *Theory and Society* 26(2–3):133–160.

Fraser, Nancy. 1989. *Unruly Practices: Power, Discourse and Gender in Contemporary Social Theory.* Minneapolis: University of Minnesota Press.

Gordon, Linda. 1990a. "The New Feminist Scholarship on the Welfare State." Pp. 9–35 in *Women, the State and Welfare,* edited by Linda Gordon. Madison: University of Wisconsin Press.

Gordon, Linda, ed. 1990b. *Women, the State and Welfare.* Madison: University of Wisconsin Press.

Griffin, L.J., J. Devine, and M. Wallace. 1983. "On the Economic and Political Determinants of Welfare Spending in the Post-World War II Era." *Politics and Society* 12:331–372.

Hasenfeld, Yeheskel, Jane A. Rafferty, and Mayer N. Zald. 1987. "The Welfare State, Citizenship and Bureaucratic Encounters." *Annual Review of Sociology* 13: 387–415.

Hobson, Barbara. 1994. "Solo Mothers, Social Policy Regimes, and the Logics of Gender." Pp. 170–187 in *Gendering Welfare States,* edited by Diane Sainsbury. Thousand Oaks, CA: Sage.

Katz, Michael B. 1983. *Poverty and Policy in American History.* New York: Academic Press.

Keyssar, Alexander. 1986. *Out of Work: The First Century of Unemployment in Massachusetts.* Cambridge: Cambridge University Press.

Korpi, Walter. 1978. *The Working Class in Welfare Capitalism: Work, Unions and Politics in Sweden.* London: Routledge & Kegan Paul.

Korpi, Walter. 1989. "Power, Politics, and State Autonomy in the Development of Social Citizenship." *American Sociological Review* 54:309–328.

Koven, Seth, and Sonya Michel, eds. 1993. *Mothers of a New World: Maternalist Politics and the Origins of Welfare States.* London: Routledge.

Lipsky, Michael. 1980. *Street-Level Bureaucracy: Dilemmas of the Individual in Public Services.* New York: Russell Sage Foundation.

Marshall, Thomas H. 1964. "Citizenship and Social Class." Pps. 65–122 in *Class, Citizenship and Social Development.* Garden City, NY: Doubleday and Co.

Mashaw, Jerry L. 1983. *Bureaucratic Justice: Managing Social Security Disability Claims.* New Haven: Yale University Press.

Mohr, John W. 1992. "Community, Bureaucracy and Social Relief: An Institutional Analysis of Organizational Forms in New York City, 1888–1917." Dissertation. Department of Sociology, Yale University.

Mohr, John W. 1994. "Soldiers, Mothers, Tramps and Others: Discourse Roles in the 1907 New York City Charity Directory." *Poetics: Journal of Empirical Research on Literature, the Media, and the Arts* 22:327–357.

Mohr, John W. 1995. "Reinventing Asylums: Transformations in the Niche Structure of Progressive Era Custodial Institutions." Presented at the meeting of the American Sociological Association, Washington, DC.

Mohr, John W. Forthcoming(a). "Implicit Terrains: The Role of Spatial Metaphors in the Theorization of Organizational Environments." In *Constructing Industries and Markets,* edited by Joseph Porac and Marc Ventresca. New York: Elsevier.

Mohr, John W. Forthcoming(b). "Measuring Meaning Structures." *Annual Review of Sociology* 24.

Mohr, John W., and Krista Paulsen. 1996. "Locating the Origins of America's Two-Channel Welfare State: Evidence from New York City's Relief Organizations, 1888–1917." Unpublished manuscript.

Mohr, John W., and Vincent Duquenne. 1997. "The Duality of Culture and Practice: Poverty Relief in New York City, 1888–1917." *Theory and Society* 26(2–3): 305–356.

Mohr, John W., and Francesca Guerra-Pearson. Forthcoming. "The Differentiation of Institutional Space: Organizational Forms in the New York Social Welfare Sector." In *Bending the Bars of the Iron Cage: Institutional Dynamics and Processes*, edited by W. Powell and D. Jones. Chicago: University of Chicago Press.

Murray, Charles. 1984. *Losing Ground: American Social Policy, 1950–1980*. New York: Basic Books.

Nelson, Barbara J. 1990. "The Origins of the Two-Channel Welfare State: Workmen's Compensation and Mother's Aid." Pp. 123–151 in *Women, the State and Welfare*, edited by Linda Gordon. Madison: University of Wisconsin Press.

O'Connor, James. 1973. *The Fiscal Crisis of the State*. New York: St. Martin's Press.

Orloff, Ann Shola. 1991. "Gender in Early U.S. Social Policy." *Journal of Policy History* 3:249–281.

Orloff, Ann Shola. 1993. "Gender and the Social Rights of Citizenship." *American Sociological Review* 58:303–328.

Polanyi, Karl. 1957 [1944]. *The Great Transformation: The Political and Economic Origins of Our Time*. Boston: Beacon Press.

Ragin, Charles. 1994. "A Qualitative Comparative Analysis of Pension Systems." Pp. 320–345 in *The Comparative Political Economy of the Welfare State*, edited by Thomas Janoski and Alexander M. Hicks. Cambridge: Cambridge University Press

Ringenbach, Paul T. 1973. *Tramps and Reformers: The Discovery of Unemployment in New York, 1873–1916*. Westport, CT.: Greenwood Press.

Rosch, Eleanor. 1978. "The Principles of Categorization." In *Cognition and Categorization*, edited by Eleanor Rosch and B. Lloyd. Hillsdale, NJ: Erlbaum.

Sainsbury, Diane, ed. 1994. *Gendering Welfare States*. Thousand Oaks, CA: Sage.

Sautter, Udo. 1992. *Three Cheers for the Unemployed: Government and Unemployment before the New Deal*. New York: Cambridge University Press.

Shalev, Michael. 1983. "The Social Democratic Model and Beyond: Two Generations of Comparative Research on the Welfare State." *Comparative Social Research* 6:315–351.

Skocpol, Theda. 1992. *Protecting Mothers and Soldiers: The Political Origins of Social Policy in the United States*. Cambridge, MA.: Harvard University Press.

Skocpol, Theda, and Edwin Amenta. 1986. "States and Social Policies." *Annual Review of Sociology* 12:131–157.

Skocpol, Theda, and John Ikenberry. 1983. "The Political Formation of the American Welfare State in Historical and Comparative Perspective." *Comparative Social Research* 6:87–148.

Starr, Paul. 1992. "Social Categories and Claims in the Liberal State." *Social Research* 59(2):263–295.

Swartz, David. Forthcoming. *Culture and Power: The Sociology of Pierre Bourdieu*. Chicago: University of Chicago Press.

Thomas, George M., John W. Meyer, Francisco O. Ramirez, and John Boli. 1987. *Institutional Structure: Constituting State, Society and the Individual*. Beverly Hills, CA: Sage.

Weir, Margaret, Ann Orloff, and Theda Skocpol, eds. 1988. *The Politics of Social Policy in the United States*. Princeton: Princeton University Press.

Wilensky, Harold L. 1975. *The Welfare State and Equality*. Berkeley: University of California Press.

Wilensky, Harold L., and Charles N. Lebeaux. 1965 [1958]. *Industrial Society and*

Social Welfare: The Impact of Industrialization on the Supply and Organization of Social Welfare Services in the United States. New York: Free Press.

Wilson, Elizabeth. 1977. *Women and the Welfare State.* London: Tavistock.

9 GENDERING THE ANALYSIS OF WELFARE STATES

(WITH EXAMPLES FROM AUSTRALIA AND THE UNITED STATES)

Ann Shola Orloff

No one who listens to contemporary social policy debates—for example, about what is the proper balance between work and parenting for sole mothers receiving state pensions ("welfare mothers," in American parlance)—could doubt the importance of gender in the welfare state. While disagreement continues about the root cause of women's oppression, few would deny that the character of welfare states affects men's and women's material situations, shapes gender relationships, structures political conflict and participation, and contributes to the formation and mobilization of gendered identities and interests.

The recognition of the gendered character of state social provision and social politics is an important corrective to the generally gender-blind mainstream literature on the welfare state. However, most feminist research on the welfare state has not been systematically comparative, and much of it tends to assume that state social provision functions to reproduce male dominance. Thus, there has not been much attention to the ways in which states vary qualitatively in their effects on gender relations, or have varied over time. We need conversations across analytic perspectives to develop conceptual frameworks to guide comparative research sensitive to the importance of gender relations.[1]

In this article, I offer some critical reflections on the analytic categories that have informed mainstream comparative and historical research on the welfare state and offer an alternative, feminist conceptual scheme, illustrated with material from Australia and the United States.[2] I begin with the framework employed by the influential "power resources" school of analysis, which has developed a useful framework for evaluating *qualitative* variation across welfare states. Because it is premised on the idea that legislated social rights have the potential to enhance the political and material situations of working classes, it provides a good bridge to some recent feminist work on the welfare state, which increasingly has been concerned with the possible "woman-friendliness" of social provision (to use Hernes' [1988] phrase; *see* e.g., Koven and Michel 1993; Orloff 1991, 1993; Piven 1985; Skocpol 1992). Both emphasize the potential of social provision in democratic states to work in ways that contradict the market, male-dominant family or other relations and institutions of domination, even as they acknowledge that this potential is far from being uniformly realized in actual welfare states.

I first describe the power resources analytic framework, then propose an alternative scheme for evaluating and categorizing state social provision that can capture both class and gender effects—and that can serve as a beginning for developing a model that will also encompass racial and ethnic effects. My proposal is threefold. First, we should start from the premises that citizenship is gendered and that men and women do not necessarily have access to the same quality of civil and political rights. Second, I reconstruct the three dimensions of qualitative variation suggested by the power resources analysts to incorporate gender: (1) the *state-market relations dimension* is extended to consider the ways countries organize the provision of welfare through families as well as through states and markets; it is then termed the *state-market-family relations dimension*; (2) the *stratification dimension* is expanded to consider the effects of social provision by the state on gender relations, especially the treatment of paid and unpaid labor; (3) the *social citizenship rights/decommodification dimension* is criticized for implicit assumptions about the sexual division of caring and domestic labor and for ignoring the differential effects on men and women of benefits that decommodify labor. Third, I propose two additional dimensions to capture the effects of state social provision on gender relations: *access to paid work* and *capacity to form and maintain an autonomous household*.

THE POWER RESOURCES PERSPECTIVE
On Citizenship

Power resources analysts, such as Gøsta Esping-Andersen (1990) and Walter Korpi (1989), build on T.H. Marshall's work (1950) on the civil, political, and social rights of citizenship, linking it to a sociological analysis of the distribution of different types of power resources. Capitalists have greater resources within the market, whereas workers—because of their numbers—have greater resources in the polity, given that the right to vote and organize for collective action are equally distributed in a democracy. Wage earners, they argue, will be interested in using political resources to extend social rights—benefits and services that may be claimed on the basis of citizenship status. As Korpi puts it, "The establishment of legislated social rights decreases the scope of markets and changes the basis of distribution in these areas from market power to political resources" (1989:313). For individual wage earners, by providing income outside the market these rights strengthen their market capacities and weaken "the whip of the market" (Palme 1990:8); they also help to build working-class political solidarities. Capitalists will fight to have market-based processes determine welfare outcomes and to limit the extent of social rights.

The Dimensions of Welfare State Regimes

Esping-Andersen and Korpi propose three dimensions as characterizing the content of welfare states. These dimensions may be considered in their own right as ways to describe welfare states, or one may consider clustering of systems along these dimensions as defining what Esping-Andersen calls the "three worlds of welfare capitalism"—liberal, conservative-corporatist, and social-democratic regime-types. (1) *State-Market Relations* concerns the "range, or domain, of human needs that are satisfied by [state] social policy" as opposed to the market. (2) *Stratification* concerns the stratifying effects of social provision. While it is a common view that "welfare states" generally promote greater equality, they actually have variable stratifying effects: some may promote cross-class solidarity and the minimization of economic differences, but others may create, maintain, or strengthen class, status, and/or occupational differentiation. (3) *Social Rights and the Decommodification of Labor* concerns the character of social citizenship—eligibility criteria and the generosity and duration of benefits, and their effect upon class relations. Esping-Andersen is interested in whether social rights lead to what he calls the decommodification of labor, defined as the "degree to which the individual's typical life situation is freed from dependence on the labor market" (Esping-Andersen and Korpi 1987:40). These rights affect the class balance of power by insulating workers to some extent from market pressure.

Social-democratic policy regimes are interventionist, universalistic, and redistributive, fostering solidarity as the entire citizenry is united in dependence on some form of social provision. By offering many generous benefits on a universal basis, they do the most to promote decommodification. Conservative-corporatist regimes offer state protection to all and the range of state action is relatively wide, but status and occupational differentiation are reinforced with separate provision for different social strata and income-graded benefits. Their contributory, work-related programs tend to reinforce the logic of the market and market-based inequalities. Liberal states roughly correspond to what others have called "residual" regimes (e.g., Titmuss 1958). They do not intervene extensively and limit assistance to the marginal or "truly deserving," encouraging social dualisms between the few, most desperate, who must rely on limited forms of social assistance and the many who rely on the market for welfare (e.g., private pensions, health plans, and the like). Decommodification is limited given their circumscribed work-related programs and stigmatized and inadequate income-tested benefits. Despite the fact that "there is no single pure case," Esping-Andersen argues that the liberal states include the United States, Canada, Australia, and (probably) Great Britain; social-democratic regimes are found among the Nordic countries; and conservative-corporatist regimes include Austria, France, Germany, Italy, and the Netherlands.

A Feminist Conceptual Scheme for Evaluating Welfare States

The power resources perspective has led to valuable insights, and the three-dimensional scheme has helped to give analytic coherence to comparative studies, revealing distinctive clusters of countries based on their systems of social provision—clusters which are not discernible using expenditure data alone. Yet including gender leads to a fundamental revision of this scheme.

Feminism on Citizenship

Feminist scholars raise two key questions for mainstream assumptions about citizenship: Who can be a citizen? and, To what rights do different citizens have access? They point out that much as the independent male householder serves as the ideal-typical citizen in classical liberal analysis, the male worker serves as the ideal-typical citizen in the literature on social rights (Hernes 1988; Pateman 1988:238–239). This gender bias is usually implicit, as mainstream analysts opt for the gender-blind categories of class, citizen, and democracy. Yet in their empirical work, they focus on how social rights affect "average" production workers, who, because of prevailing sex segregation in occupations and household composition, "happen" to be men. The social rights of citizens who are economically dependent, the vast majority of whom are women, are simply not considered. Moreover, there has been little concern with variation in the extent to which equality of civil and political rights, including the legal rights of personhood, has been realized formally or in practice for men and women. (One key issue is who shall have power over women's bodies [Shaver 1993a].) Yet the exercise of these rights is supposed to be the base for enriching social citizenship in the first place.

A Feminist Rethinking of the Dimensions of Welfare States

State-Market-Family Relations

Mainstream analysts generally have given more attention to the way states and markets divide welfare functions than to the role of families in providing welfare. Provision of welfare seems to "count" only when it occurs through the state or the market, while women's unpaid work in the home is ignored, as are differences in men's and women's sources of income. The sexual division of labor within states, markets, and families also goes unnoticed.

Both the United States and Australia are labelled as liberal regimes because of the relatively large scope of the market in providing welfare benefits and services.[3] Yet men and women in these countries are not positioned in the same way relative to market, family, and state. As in all advanced Western countries, married women depend largely on their husbands for income; according to Hobson's (1990) comparative study of economic dependency, the average contribution of husbands to family income ranged from 67 to 80 percent in (listed from lowest to highest contribution) Sweden, the United States, Australia, Canada, Germany, and the United Kingdom. This reflects the traditional division of labor, with husbands "specializing" in market work and wives in the provision of domestic work and child care (studies show they still do most of it—about 75–80 percent in these countries [Baxter 1993; Wright et al., 1992]). Thus, when marriages break up or end in widowhood, mothers are often unprepared for assuming the full burden of providing income and care for their families, while widows have less access to market-based retirement income, and both are likely to have to rely on public provision.

As is the case across the West, U.S. and Australian women of all ages depend on public provision more than do men (Mitchell 1993; Rainwater 1993; Smeeding, Torrey, and Rainwater 1993). Women's greater dependence on the state for income has distinctive consequences given the shape of market-state relations there. Because private provision linked to work status is relatively more important in these liberal regimes, women have less access to many important sources of welfare, such as occupational pensions, than do men or their counterparts in societies where more welfare is state-provided. However, there is some interesting variation in the extent of the state's contribution to family incomes. All types of families with children in Australia receive about twice the proportion of their income from public sources as compared to their American counterparts. Thus, 62 percent of household income comes from public sources for Australian sole-mother families, 23 percent for sole-father families and 10 percent for couple-headed families; for U.S. families, the proportions are 36 percent, 9 percent, and 5 percent, respectively (Mitchell 1993:22).

In his recent book, Esping-Andersen pays a bit of attention to variation across regime-types in relations between states and families, focusing on services that respond to "family needs . . . [and] also allow women to choose work rather than the household" (1990:28). Conservative-corporatist regimes do not provide services that enable mothers (or other primary care-takers) to enter the paid labor force and thus reinforce traditional family relations. Social-democratic regimes, committed to gender equality, attempt to "preemptively socialize the costs of familyhood," and encourage mothers to work for pay by providing daycare and parental leaves. In liberal regimes, "concerns of gender matter less than the sanctity of the market," so services tend to be provided privately and to benefit most those groups which can afford them.

Services are important to women's abilities to enter the paid labor force, but Esping-Andersen's classificatory scheme does not fully reflect differences in how care is provided (e.g., Leira [1992] shows that social-democratic Sweden and Norway differ in their levels of daycare provision and women's labor-force participation; others make a similar point about corporatist-conservative France and Germany). Nor do the regime types and concomitant differences in service provision fully predict women's employment patterns (e.g., levels of part-time work or occupational sex segregation; see O'Connor 1993). Thus, for example, although public child care services in the "liberal" United States and Australia are undeveloped relative to Scandinavia and overall levels of participation in the two do not differ dramatically—about 68 percent of U.S. women and 62 percent of Australian women were in the paid labor force in 1990—other work patterns do differ. For example, Australian women are more likely to work part-time than are Americans—40 percent versus 25 percent (O'Connor 1993:41, using 1990 figures), and are more likely to be totally economically dependent housewives—40 percent versus 30 percent (Hobson 1990:240, using figures from the mid-1980s). Among single mothers, Americans are more likely to be participating in the paid labor force than are Australians—57 percent versus 35 percent (Mitchell 1993:4). Thus, Australian single mothers are more dependent on public provision than are their U.S. counterparts, while married women seem to be somewhat more dependent on their husbands (Mitchell [1993:4] notes that the participation rates of married women with children at home are 53 percent in Australia and 59 percent in the United States). While we cannot rule out the significance of differences in the economies of these countries, it is also likely that—as Leira (1992) argues is the case for Scandinavia—this reflects different "models of motherhood"—beliefs about the appropriateness of public versus private child care, of mothers working for pay, and the like, as institutionalized in public policies. This dimension does not seem to covary with differences in state-market relations.

These analytic inadequacies are related to some of Esping-Andersen's premises, which neglect gender relations and feminist scholarship. He sees women as *choosing* between "work and the household," with work possible for most women only if state services are widely available. Yet women do not choose between paid work and unpaid housewifery (including mothering) as exclusive activities—they can choose to be stay-at-home wives and mothers only or combine paid work with their domestic work. Nowhere in the industrialized West can married women and mothers choose *not* to engage in caring and domestic labor (unless they are wealthy enough to purchase the services of others). The core aspects of the sexual division of labor remain: Women perform most domestic work whether or not they work for pay, while men do very little domestic work. Indeed, there is very little difference across regime types in the extent to which men do housework—men do about 22–25 percent of domestic work according to studies of a number of advanced industrial democracies (Baxter 1993; Wright et al., 1992). The dimension of state-market relations as formulated by Esping-Andersen simply ignores the tremendous amount of unpaid caring labor and housework provided by women—housewives and wage earners alike. All Western welfare states, including those in the U.S. and Australia, depend upon the care to a great extent (Finch and Groves 1983; Taylor-Gooby 1991; Waerness 1984).

Mainstream analysts recognize that the "division of labor" between states and markets in providing welfare is a political question—an issue about which decision rules and which actors will control the distribution of valued welfare resources. They recognize that the market and the division of labor between the market and polity are constructed on the basis of relations of power, but do not extend this insight to the family and the division of labor between family and state in providing incomes and welfare services. They do not discuss power relations within the family, nor do they look at gender power within other realms. Once gender power is considered, one may argue that moving decisions about the distribution of resources from the family to the polity is parallel to the shift from market-based to political decisions. It is a shift from an arena in which resources are disproportionately under the control of men to one in which power is at least potentially more equally distributed between men and women.

STRATIFICATION

Mainstream analysts have focused on the effects of state social provision on social differentiation and class hierarchy, but have ignored its effects on gender differentiation and hierarchies. Their existing scheme could capture gender differences in benefit levels that depend on labor market processes. Women's inferior status in the workforce means that women are disproportionately disadvantaged when benefits reflect market-based inequality and depend on paid work to establish eligibility, as is the case in many social insurance systems. In liberal regimes, because most citizens rely heavily on private provision of services and income, public provision is not generous, an arrangement Esping-Andersen says gives rise to a stratification pattern of dualism. But men and women are not equally affected by dualism, given that women are overrepresented among those depending on public provision. To date, however, researchers have not done even this minimal gender-sensitive analysis. And mainstream analysts have not addressed two significant ways that states affect gender differentiation and hierarchy: (1) by underlining distinctive, gendered identities and interests *(gender differentiation)*, and (2) by privileging full-time paid worker-citizens—mostly men— over citizens who do unpaid work or who combine part-time paid work with domestic and caring labor—almost all women *(gender inequality)*.

Gender Differentiation. Some states have reinforced social divisions through the establishment of separate programs for different groups, as in Germany's pension programs for salaried and waged workers or the separate welfare systems for indigenous peoples run by Australia and the United States (Shaver 1990). Similarly, differentiation in gendered identities and interests can be strengthened by offering different programs for women and men. Feminist analysts, including American scholars such as Nancy Fraser (1989) and Australian analysts such as Sheila Shaver (1987, 1990, 1991, 1993b) have argued that despite the official gender neutrality of systems such as those in the U.S. and Australia, there is a pronounced, and gendered, dualism in these systems of social provision. This is marked, and partially determined, by the differing kinds of claims made by men and women. Men make claims as worker-citizens—they need programs to compensate for failures in the labor market; women make claims as members of families and need programs especially to compensate for family "failures." Thus, Shaver notes that the Australian "income security provision consists very largely of two kinds of benefits, one in which eligibility is tied most closely to workforce statuses and another geared to support for the family unit" (1987:107); Fraser and others make similar claims about the U.S. system. In both countries, women are the vast majority of beneficiaries in family-related programs such as sole parent provision or survivors' insurance, while almost all men are the clients of work-related programs such as provision for unemployment (although as women's participation in the paid labor force increase, more women are making claims as workers) (Australia, Department of Social Security 1990; Orloff 1994; U.S. Social Security Administration 1993).

Gender Hierarchy. It seems that in most systems of social provision, claims based on motherhood or marriage to a covered wage-earner are associated with lower benefit levels or fewer services than work-based claims, and often with more stringent eligibility requirements. Conservative regimes contribute to gender hierarchy through making most programs earnings-related and "rewarding" unpaid labor with lower dependents' benefits; gender inequality, like that based on class, is reinforced. Social-democratic regimes have a number of universal citizenship entitlements which offer equivalent benefits to men and women, but among universal programs, labor market-related programs are fully funded but child care programs are not, and not all who need these services can get them (Hobson 1990; Leira 1992). Thus, "there is a political struggle between men and women to count certain types of unpaid work as a legitimate basis for welfare rights" (Hernes 1988:194), although there are clearly cross-national and historical differences in the extent to which states help to reduce the costs to women for engaging in traditional patterns of participation in paid and unpaid work—in terms of current living standards and pension or other social benefits (e.g., some countries give credits for periods of unpaid childrearing within their contributory old-age insurance programs; the United States does not).

What of the so-called liberal regimes? American scholars have tended to see a direct link between differentiation and inequality, identifying a "two-tier" welfare state with inadequate social assistance programs serving a predominantly female clientele and relatively more generous contributory social insurance targeting a male clientele (*see,* e.g., Nelson 1984, 1990; Pearce 1986). Fraser (1989:152) describes the U.S. system:

> Consider that the "masculine" social-welfare programs are [contributory] social insurance schemes. They include unemployment insurance, Social Security (retirement insurance), Medicare (age-tested health insurance). . . . These programs . . . are administered on a national basis, and benefit levels are uniform across the country. Though bureaucratically organized and administered, they require less, and less demeaning, effort on the part of beneficiaries in qualifying and maintaining eligibility than do "feminine" programs. . . . [I]n most cases [they] lack the dimension of surveillance. . . . In sum, "masculine" social insurance programs position recipients primarily as *rights-bearers.* . . . Neither administrative practice nor popular discourse constitutes them as "on the dole. . . ." [T]he "feminine" sector . . . consists in relief programs, such as AFDC [Aid to Families with Dependent Children], food stamps, Medicaid, and public-housing assis-

tance . . . [which] are not contributory but are financed out of general tax revenues . . . [and] not administered federally but by the states. As a result, benefit levels vary dramatically, . . . though . . . everywhere [are] inadequate. . . . They require considerable work in qualifying and maintaining eligibility, and they have a heavy component of surveillance. These programs do not in any meaningful sense position their subjects as rights-bearers. . . . These recipients are . . . essentially *clients*.[4]

The "two-tier" formulation focuses on the *direct* claims made by men and women. However, many women—a larger number than social assistance clients—are incorporated into the welfare state indirectly, on the basis of their marriage to husbands who have made contributions to social insurance programs. Women claiming old-age insurance benefits based on their marital tie to covered wage-earners receive relatively worse benefits than do men— who claim as wage-earners—within the same program; dependents' benefits are 50 percent of the retired workers' benefit, although survivors inherit 100 percent of the pension (U.S. Social Security Administration 1993:34). Fraser (1989:150–151) calls the Social Security system (i.e., contributory old-age and survivors' insurance) "hermaphroditic," "internally dualized and gendered," in offering benefits to many women as wives and to almost all men as wage-earners. (And she does not deal with the significant proportion of women claiming old-age benefits—currently, just over a third—in their own right, that is, based on their work in the paid labor force and contributions [Orloff 1994].[5]) This is quite true as regards the *basis* of claims— but it is not true with respect to the *treatment* of claims. Women receiving Social Security, as wives or widows with or without children, unlike women receiving social assistance, are still treated as rights-bearers rather than clients—their marital tie to a covered breadwinner entitles them to the same standardized treatment and to nationally-set, inflation-indexed benefits accorded to men under social security. They are therefore considerably better off than those depending upon AFDC.[6]

Some women are bound to the U.S. welfare state *as (needy) mothers*, others *as the wives of covered wage-earners,* although divorce—or the threat of it—may undercut that bond for some women. This distinction is significant politically. Wives and needy mothers are not united merely because both make claims on the basis of "marital or family status," rather than as workers. (And recall that many women *are* making claims as workers.) Indeed, in the United States, the system of social provision divides women in a number of ways; for example, it reinforces differences among single mothers—widows (disproportionately white) rely on social insurance, never-married mothers (disproportionately women of color) and divorced mothers on social assistance. The difference between the two tiers of social insurance and social assistance in the United States—often understood as producing different treatments for men and women—would be better conceptualized as producing different treatment for members of families which are headed by a male breadwinner with an economically dependent wife (and children) on the one hand and families maintained by women who are outside the paid labor force, or on its fringes, on the other (Weir, Orloff, and Skocpol 1988). Indeed, some men—those without attachment to the paid labor force, disproportionately of minority racial or ethnic backgrounds—also rely on the lower, social assistance tier. All of these factors undercut the argument that two-tier systems of social provision generate distinctive interests for all women or all men.

Things look somewhat different from an Antipodean perspective. Australia is cross-nationally unusual in that contributory social insurance is virtually undeveloped (although Medicare requires a small contribution from beneficiaries), while other social programs—benefits for the elderly, sole parents, the unemployed, and others—are income-tested (Shaver 1991:156–158). Thus, according to Shaver (1989:160), the Australian system is

> more unitary than contributory systems, in which gaps and shortfalls in contributory coverage typically have to be filled by means-tested supplements. . . . The two-tier [i.e., social insurance and social assistance] basis creates social and political distinctions between entitlements paid for through contributions, and welfare conceded to the poor. Australia's tax-transfer framework defines access and equity within a single system of revenue and eligibility. While it makes comparatively few distinctions among claimants, the rights of all claims carry the welfarist connotations of means-testing.

Thus, in Australia, there is differentiation in the types of claims men and women make, but the system of social provision does not offer different benefit levels to clients of work-related versus family-related programs—pension levels are set at the same level for the elderly, sole parents, and the unemployed, with the same access to dependents' allowances, and the like, although there are some differences in income and assets tests (Australia, Department of Social Security 1990). Pensions for the elderly, the welfare-state program affecting the largest number of citizens, are noteworthy in that they do not reward wage-earners any more than those who have been principally caregivers. Women (even those who have not worked for pay) qualify for support in their own right as (needy) individuals (Cass 1994:107). This contrasts with the contributory systems in other countries, including the United States, or the proposals for contributory age pensions made by Australian conservatives in the 1930s (Watts 1987), where many married women (and widows) gain access to benefits through their husbands' contributions.

Australian provision was shaped by assumptions about the traditional sexual division of labor, but this was reflected in different institutional arrangements than was the case in the United States and in other "two-tier" systems. Shaver (1989:160) notes that

> the primary vehicle of Labor's patriarchal state was the means test. This embodies the assumptions of the fa mily wage in its family unit basis, measuring eligibility of each partner against the joint resources of the couple. The test effectively precluded one member (usually the wife) from eligibility for benefit when the other (usually the husband) was earning.

Moreover, until very recently, the Australian system of social provision offered support for a distinctively feminine pattern of full-time care for children and lifelong economic dependency for women without husbands through sole parent benefits and the Class B widow's pension; changes made in 1987 (discussed below) have removed these provisions (Cass 1994; Shaver 1993b).

This unitary system of provision does not entrench differences among women as deeply as a "two-tier" system would. For example, once the supporting parents' allowance was initiated with the same benefits as the already-established widows' pensions, the position of widowed mothers was not materially better than that of divorced, deserted, or never-married mothers (Shaver 1987:109). Perhaps there was some political significance to the different programs, particularly in regard to underlining the distinctive identity of different groups of single mothers. With the amalgamation of the former Class A widow's pension and supporting parent's benefit into a single program, sole parent pension, in 1989 (Australia, Department of Social Security 1990:64), even this distinction has been erased (at least officially).

Thus, different gender identites are certainly underlined by the Australian system. But I would agree with Shaver (1987:109) when she contends that the Australian system is "not as deeply gendered as the [U.S.] system Fraser points to." It is largely in the realm of the market that men's relatively higher economic standing is produced in Australia—through private, rather than public, provision (e.g., occupational pensions), and because of men's greater earnings capacities and opportunities.

SOCIAL CITIZENSHIP RIGHTS

Both feminists and mainstream researchers agree that the character of citizenship rights is a critical dimension of state social provision. Here, we must consider two issues: first, how does gender affect citizens' access to state services and benefits, and second, whether the concept of decommodification is adequate for understanding the effects of the welfare state on gender relations.

Gendered Access to State Services and Benefits. Mainstream researchers have been concerned about how rules of access to social benefits undercut or reinforce the market. An important aspect of social benefits as they affect gender relations is the extent to which they individualize or "familize" recipients—is there individual access? or is access mediated by one citizen's relation to another through marriage or familial relationship? For example, in many countries' social insurance programs—including those of the United States (and the U.K.), married women are made eligible for dependent spouses' pensions on the basis of their husbands' contributions and employment history and may face barriers to establishing their own individual claims. Universal citizenship pensions in Sweden and Canada give individual entitlement to men and women, but, interestingly, the (generously) means-tested Australian age pension also offers individual entitlement. In income-tested social assistance programs, the use of household means tests undermines women's abilities to claim benefits as individuals—in the unemployment assistance programs of Australia (and the U.K. and Canada), eligibility is conditioned jointly on the incomes of both spouses in the case of married couples, which effectively disqualifies the second earner, usually the woman, from benefits when her income is interrupted. Women's claims to benefits are also undercut by the "cohabitation rule," present in many countries' social assistance programs for sole parents, including those of the United States and Australia. This presumes that living or sleeping with a man indicates that he is financially supporting his partner. Regulations allowing women independent access to benefits and services arguably are more woman-friendly than those that force dependence on household qualification.

Gendering Decommodification. Esping-Andersen's concept of decommodification is inadequate for understanding the effects of state social provision on all workers because it ignores gender differences in the situations of men and women workers, particularly with reference to domestic and caring labor, and in access to the paid labor force. Decommodification as a dimension of policy regimes must be understood in the context of gender relations and also must be supplemented by a new analytic dimension: the extent to which states guarantee women access to paid employment and services that enable them to balance home and work responsibilities, and the mechanisms and institutions that implement these guarantees.

Power resources analysts implicitly begin with the situation of male workers and ignore the gender division of labor that makes the situations of men and women in the paid workforce different. Benefits that decommodify labor give male workers greater capacity to resist capital and enter the market on their own terms, but unpaid services provided by wives, mothers, daughters also enhance male workers' capacities. Thus, to focus only on decommodification is misleading about male workers' situation. What of women workers? Again, power resources analysis starts from an implicitly male premise: Women have "chosen" between housewifery and paid work, so that once they enter the paid labor force, their domestic responsibilities disappear from the analysis and they become indistinguishable from male workers. Social benefits that decommodify labor affect women and men in different ways because their patterns of participation in paid and unpaid labor differ. For instance, taking parental leave, an example of a benefit that decommodifies labor, may reduce a working woman's earning capacity because continuous service with a single employer often pays off in increased wages. The implicit male standard for "worker" obscures power relations in the family and the conditions under which people do domestic work and provide care for children, the elderly, and the disabled.

ACCESS TO PAID WORK

How does an analysis based on the situation of commodified male workers deal with women working in the home? For many women and others excluded from paid labor, commodification—that is, obtaining a position in the paid labor force—is, in fact, potentially emancipatory. Many women want paid work because it provides independence and enhanced leverage within marriages and patriarchal families. Equal access to paid employment and equal pay has been a consistent—and contested—demand of women's movements over the past century. In marriages (or other family relationships) in which power relations are based largely on economic dependence, access to paid work and to the services that make employment a viable option for mothers (or other caretakers) is as important as—perhaps even more important than—the insulation from market pressures provided by decommodification. We need, then, to supplement the dimension of decommodification with a new analytic dimension that taps into the extent to which states promote or discourage women's paid employment—the right to be commodified, if you will. I call this fourth dimension of welfare-state regimes *access to paid work*. In some countries, men's rights to jobs are promoted through full employment and active labor market policies. Thus, I contend that the extent to which the state ensures access to paid work for different groups and the mechanisms that guarantee jobs are dimensions of all policy regimes. The key issue in investigating states' effects on gender relations is the extent to which women (or subgroups of women) can claim this right.

The historical development of decommodification indicates the importance of access to paid work and social benefits. Expanding social rights was an historically-specific strategy of most male-dominated labor movements and their elite (male) allies in the first half of this century, and is the dominant goal of post–World War II workers' movements. It is worth noticing that this policy strategy was and is premised on a traditional gender division of labor. Some working-class movements have changed in response to the increasing numbers of women in their constituencies and have supported antidiscrimination and comparable worth legislation and services such as day care. Yet in few (if any) instances have such movements embraced an explicit feminist goal of economic independence for women. Rather, their goal usually is to allow married women to combine paid work with family responsibilities—to be secondary earners while continuing to service their husbands. (Single women may fare somewhat better.)

The Capacity to Form and Maintain an Autonomous Household

The concept of decommodification originated in analyses of class relations and class politics. We will need new categories to deal with the effects of state social provision on gender relations. If individuals who carry out caring and domestic work do not enter the labor market, or enter it only as secondary workers, the resulting distribution of income within the family and the availability of other income sources affects their own and their children's well-being. Over the last century or so, the "family wage" supplemented by social rights has provided unevenly for wives and children. Feminists often say that women are "a husband away from poverty"—if you've got a husband and he shares his income with you, you're protected, but if not, you're likely to suffer economically. Most men simply do not share their income with their children after the dissolution of marriage, and although there is some cross-national variation, states do not make up the difference fully (Garfinkel and Wong 1990). Single mothers, who have lower earning capacities relative to men and more responsibility for their children's well-being, exemplify the economic vulnerabilities of all women, which is hidden when women have a secure tie to breadwinners. Indeed, the deprived circumstances of single mothers are sometimes an incentive for women to marry (or to not divorce). Moreover, family income is not always shared equally in marriages (Land 1983; Pahl 1983), and women's economic dependency is a significant basis for men's power advantage in families.

If decommodification is important because it frees wage earners from the compulsion of participating in the market, then we need a parallel dimension that indicates the ability of those who do most of the domestic and caring work—almost all women—to form and maintain autonomous households, that is, to survive and support their children without having to marry to gain access to breadwinners' income.

I see two ways to conceptualize a dimension of social provision that characterizes degrees of family support and the exigencies of marrying. First, we might develop a general dimension of self-determination that would include independence from markets and marriages. The decommodification dimension could be subsumed under a more generic dimension measuring independence or autonomy, that is, it would indicate individuals' freedom from compulsion to enter into potentially oppressive relationships in a number of spheres. States now offer resources to the different parties in relationships of domination, accommodation, and conflict such as markets, families, and interracial relations. These state-provided resources alter the balance of power in these relations and within the polity. Individuals typically participate in many such relationships. Thus, the role of the state cannot be understood in reference to only one relationship—decommodification vis-à-vis the market cannot ignore gender relations in the family or race relations in communities. The total package of resources available from both public and private sources across social locations must be considered. Attention would shift from dimensions tied to only one set of potentially unequal or oppressive relations to an examination of the combined effects of all programs on individuals in specific politically and socially significant groups. This solution would meld the concepts of decommodification and access to an independent income (outside of marriage) into a unitary concept of individual independence, or better yet, a concept of self-determination within webs of interdependencies (complete individual autonomy does not exist). In the end, I prefer that separate dimensions deal with different social relations, but a single dimension that explicitly considers gender as well as class relations would, I think, be an improvement over the decommodification/social rights dimension alone.

Second, we might proceed inductively, and develop a dimension based on the demands of women's movements, just as decommodification represents the aims of male-dominated workers' movements. (This inductive strategy is not innocent of theory, but allows us to use feminists' suggestions about what may be necessary to emancipate women to further clarify the significance of the demands for which social movements have struggled.) I argue that the appropriate dimension is *the capacity to form and maintain an autonomous household* (which can be secured in a number of ways). Women's movements have pursued two principal strategies to gain economic independence: (1) Establishing secure incomes for women who engage in full-time domestic work and caring for their children; and (2) improving access to paid work and establishing services that reduce the burden of caring on individual households.

Some "maternalist" women reformers in the first half of the 20th century proposed state support to widowed or abandoned mothers so they could stay at home to care for their children (Koven and Michel 1993; Lake 1992; Orloff 1991; Skocpol 1992). This contrasted with the relief policy for the poor which refused most single women sufficient support to maintain their families, thus forcing them to relinquish their children to orphanages (*see*, e.g., Vandepol [1982] on the U.S.). Others also fought for an "endowment of motherhood" for all mothers, which would confer political recognition on the work of mothering as well as provide an independent income to mothers (Lake 1992; Pedersen 1989). This general approach did not succeed, except in much shrunken form as children's allowances, which also were harnessed to elites' goals of holding down wages. Most states paid these to mothers, but they never were sufficient to support a woman without a husband. Other benefits and services were restricted to single mothers, usually widows, but sometimes divorced, separated, or unmarried women (e.g., widows' pensions or survivors' insurance). Thus, "maternalist" programs came to be primarily a back-up for the "failures" of the family wage system (Gordon 1988; Skocpol and Ritter 1991). They allowed women and their children to survive without husbands, albeit in relatively deprived circumstances.

Since World War II, and especially since the 1960s, most women's movements have pursued a goal of equal rights that aims at creating conditions enabling everyone—men and women alike—to be economically independent individuals who can also contribute in part to the support of their children (Freeman 1990). Reformers support policies that enhance women's access to employment and increase women's wages and opportunities. Countries vary in whether such opportunities are created through state employment or through state regulation of private employers, in the extent to which they support full-time mothering at all, and in the extent to which they promote full-time or part-time work for mothers. In addition, reformers have advocated programs that require fathers or the state to supplement single mothers' wages with child support funds. Recently, men's wages have eroded and gender gaps in wages persist, so it has come to seem increasingly unrealistic to expect mothers to earn enough in the market to support themselves and their families.

Both strategies would provide women with incomes sufficient to support themselves and their children apart from any claims on breadwinners' income. Indeed, if successful, these strategies would extend to women rights and capacities that are implicitly or explicitly now guaranteed to men (at least those of the dominant race/ethnic group) through private or public employment or state (or state-guaranteed) benefits which allow them to maintain wives and children. The focus on women's independent income for supporting a household and their choices about (at least potentially oppressive) marriage goes beyond the focus of the power resources analysts on "socializing the costs of familyhood" and "allowing women to choose work." The capacity to form and maintain an autonomous household relieves women of the compulsion to enter or stay in a marriage because of economic vulnerability (thus paralleling the effects of the citizen's wage for workers vis-à-vis the market). Following from Albert Hirschman's work (1970), the right and capacity to exit—in this case, to be able to choose *not* to enter or stay in a marriage—should alter the power relations *within* marriages (England and Kilbourne 1990). The state is woman-friendly to the extent that benefits for single mothers directly increase the absolute and relative standards of living of woman-maintained families and indirectly enhance women's leverage within marriage (e.g., giving them the capacity to impose domestic obligations on men).

These strategies have overlapped historically, but the second has emerged as the more important in the "second wave" of feminism. And there are important cross-national variations in the extent to which women's movements have embraced one or the other of these goals. As many feminists have pointed out, tension exists between these two strategies (often understood as protection or difference versus equal treatment or sameness). To some extent, these are alternative rather than complementary, although I would like to believe that there is at least the possibility for synthesis. Yet by considering the example of working-class strategies and regime types, we may reasonably expect that different social policy regimes (including gender, class, and other elements) will be associated with the predominance of different strategies on the part of women's movements, as well as with varying levels of strength of women's movements, different relations between women's and labor movements, and so on. We can still assess the extent of "woman-friendliness" as it is revealed in the extent to which women, like men, have the right to a family—that is, the capacity to form and maintain autonomous households, and in the *form* adopted to secure that aim.[7]

In both the United States and Australia, the state offers benefits that allow single mothers to maintain independent households, although because of disincentives to paid work and low benefit levels, a poverty-level existence is almost assured (using data from the Luxembourg Income Study [circa 1985], Rainwater [1993:5] reports that of single mothers without earnings, fully 96 percent were poor in the United States, and 90 percent in Australia, as compared to 22 percent in the U.K. [although this is rising], or 18 percent in Sweden).[8] Despite the shortcomings of the programs for sole parents, feminists and others have been more likely to defend them as an important social right in the wake of cutbacks (Cass 1994; *see*, e.g., Piven 1985). The Australian system recently has undergone restructuring (the Social Security Review of the late 1980s), and the United States, despite the passage of major changes in social assistance programs in the Family Support Act of 1988, is in the midst of considering yet further changes. Changing gender relations have helped to propel the changes, and shifting assumptions about gender as embodied in the reformed systems will have far-reaching implications for men and women.

Australia is now pursuing a policy of *encouraging* sole parent pensioners to enter the labor force while their children are young, and requiring work after children reach age 16 (when entitlement for the pension ends, forcing parents to work or move to unemployment programs) (Australia, Department of Social Security 1990:64–67; Cass 1994). With the end of the Class B widow's pension (for those whose children had left home but who were too young for the age pensions), the system no longer provides for the traditional woman's pattern of full-time caregiving and housewifery over the entire life cycle. Rather, full-time caregiving will only be supported through the sole parent's pension for a limited period (Cass 1994:109). "As it applies to the provision of basic income support, a gender-neutral model of citizen worker has largely overtaken earlier provisions framed in terms of [gender] difference and a distinctive role for women as dependent on a male breadwinner in Australian social security" (Shaver 1993b:10).

Under the Democratic Clinton administration, the United States is moving to *require* that single mothers receiving AFDC (or "welfare") enter the paid labor force, whatever the age of their children. Under current ("unreformed") regulations—that is, on the basis of the Family Support

Act of 1988 (passed with bipartisan support during Ronald Reagan's administration)—single parents are required to be at work or in training after their youngest child reaches three years of age, and states have the option of requiring work or training for parents of children as young as one year (U.S. Social Security Administration 1993:83–97); however, states are far from fully implementing these provisions—they are more expensive than simply sending checks in the mail. Reforms currently under consideration at both the state and national level propose that AFDC recipients be required to work after two years of benefits; debate is raging over whether public employment should be guaranteed to those whose benefits have run out, whether part-time work should "count" as fulfilling the work requirement for sole parents, and so on.[9] Some states (e.g., New Jersey) have enacted legislation that will deny additional benefits for children born while a beneficiary is on welfare, and others are considering this change. All of these changes will further limit full-time caregiving as an option for poor mothers, already severely circumscribed by the only partially implemented reforms of 1988. The United States, then, is moving in the direction of making AFDC more like unemployment insurance—a short-term benefit to help claimants "get on their feet" after the crisis of job loss, divorce, or birth of a child outside of marriage, but resolutely pushing them to commodification and the labor market through the stick of short benefit duration or benefit cut-off and, in some states, the carrot of job training, day care subsidies, and health insurance guarantees. While (like their Australian counterparts) Clinton administration officials evidence some concern about children's poverty, they have not focused on lessening poverty through raising benefits; rather, they have sought to "make work pay" through tax credits and increasing the minimum wage.

Australia, despite recent changes, still offers single mothers the capacity to maintain an autonomous household without participation in the labor market for a certain period of their children's lives. Indeed, the vast majority—70 percent—of single mothers received a pension (Saunders and Matheson 1990). The United States is moving to require that all who want to maintain a household obtain the means of supporting that household through the market. Already, fewer than half of single mothers rely on AFDC—44 percent in 1986 (Reischauer 1989:15); the majority of the rest must work for pay. This is a fairly significant difference in the character of social rights as it applies to gender relations. While Shaver and Cass are, I think, correct to identify a shift from gender "difference" to "sameness" in the Australian social security system, the shift toward entitlement being based solely on worker status has been far more dramatic—and coercive—in the

United States. I would argue that—at the least—there are different models of motherhood in operation.

What accounts for these differences? I am now carrying out research on this issue, but will hazard the guess that surely the difference relates in large part to the racial characteristics of the clientele of sole-parent programs in the two countries as this has been historically created by the structures of social provision and immigration and settlement patterns. Australian sole-parent pensioners are overwhelmingly white. Until fairly recently, Aboriginal women were often not allowed the "right to a family" or the capacity to form an autonomous household—their children were forcibly removed, while the "white Australia" policy prevented non-Europeans from entering the country. In the United States, single mothers on benefits are disproportionately minority and indeed, a majority of claimants are African-American or Latino; white women are a significant proportion of AFDC recipients, but, not being concentrated in the ghettoes of major metropolises, have less public visibility, and are indeed less likely than minority mothers to be on the program for long periods (Bane 1988; U.S. Department of Health and Human Services Office of Family Assistance 1991:6). Another key difference is the strength of organized labor (which is related to racial and ethnic heterogeneity), which has affected the development of social rights more generally.

BACK TO POLITICS

There remains one critical and problematic issue even if we go "beyond decommodification" to consider womens' capacities to form and maintain autonomous households. This is the question of political power. Even if state provision enables individual women to leave oppressive situations, this does not embody a true social right—as opposed to a social benefit or an unintended consequence of backing up the family wage system—if it is not coupled with women's political participation and power. If women do not participate in policymaking, their concerns are less likely to be reflected in social programs. In this regard, the experience of early women welfare reformers is instructive. The origins of the welfare state were marked by the attempts of feminists and women reformers to valorize caring work and motherhood as a basis for claims to honorable citizenship benefits. Claims based on motherhood were not seen as inferior to claims based on work or "universal" citizenship—they were a claim that women's work, their form of service to the state, *entitled* them to honorable citizenship benefits (Lake 1992; Orloff 1991). It is a measure of their lack of political power that they were unable to make that understanding dominant. The struggle over the value of caring work for making claims on the welfare state continues, and we will need to consider both material or social rights and participatory or political rights to fully understand the effects of the welfare state on gender.

CONCLUSION

A gendered version of the power resources analysts' scheme for assessing social policy regimes would prove a fruitful guide for future research. As more scholars investigate the content of social policy regimes, we will provide a foundation for a more systematic assessment of the effects of state social provision on gender relations and the identification of distinctive gender regimes. This in turn will allow us to focus on the causes of variation in the gendered content and effects of state welfare programs. Incorporating new dimensions of social provision that consider gender relations will make research more complicated, and it may entirely "upset the apple cart"—in other words, newly defined gender regimes may not parallel the regimes identifiable by the social rights attached to the status of citizen-worker, the patterning of stratification among dominant-group men, and state-market relations (Hobson 1990; Lewis 1992; Sainsbury 1993; Taylor-Gooby 1991). There is already evidence that aspects of regimes particularly relevant for gender relations are not uniform within regime types as defined by the power resources analysts; for example, Leira (1992) finds different "models of motherhood," in reference to the need for part-time work or withdrawal from the paid labor force for certain periods of children's lives, across the Nordic states. We will need systematically to compare national systems of social provision with an explicit focus on gender relations to find out. This will be of interest in its own right, but will also be relevant for our larger theoretical concerns with the nature of states, capitalism, and male dominance—and the relations among them.

NOTES

1. The term "welfare state" may assume what must in fact be proved—that states promote the welfare of their citizens through the mechanism of social policy. Generally, the welfare state is conceptualized as a state committed to modifying the play of social or market forces in order to achieve greater equality. It is clear that states intervene in civil society, but I do not judge a priori that all state social interventions are aimed at, or actually produce, greater equality among citizens. One further terminological caveat: using the terms "mainstream" and "feminist" to describe bodies of diverse research does oversimplify things; I simply want to indicate that mainstream work has been almost uniformly blind to gender differences and inequalities, whereas feminist work is premised on the importance of gender in social and political life.

2. *See* Orloff (1993) for a fuller discussion of the conceptual framework here described.

3. *See* Castles and Mitchell (1993) for an argument that Australia represents a radical regime type in contrast to the liberalism of the U.S. policy regime; they point, for example, to the greater income equality in Australia. Castles (1994) has argued that this represents the fruit of the Labor Party's historical and contemporary goals

and political strategies, in which welfare goals are not provided through state benefits and services but by means of state regulation of wages and other aspects of the labor contract, resulting in a "wage-earners' welfare state." This seems to me clear evidence of an important difference between the United States and Australia. And there have been significant partisan differences within both countries in the extent to which residualism and inequality within social provision are supported, yet in neither case has the state ever offered the range of services and benefits as have the welfare regimes of Europe. I am willing to accept the label "liberal" as reasonable given the importance of market-provided welfare in both.

4. Author's emphasis.

5. Actually, almost three-fifths of women are entitled to retired-worker benefits based on their own record as paid workers; however, about 40 percent of this group (or 24 percent of all women receiving social security benefits), is "dually entitled," that is, they are entitled to both a retired-worker benefit and a dependent spouse's benefit. Because their individual benefits are less than the benefit to which they are entitled simply by virtue of their marriage, they receive partial wife's benefits—however, they are counted as retired-worker beneficiaries in offical publications (see Orloff 1994 or Sainsbury 1993 for more detailed commentary).

6. It should be noted that access to maritally-based claims to social insurance is not the same for women in different class and racial or ethnic groups—to state the obvious, one must be married to a man in covered employment to gain access to dependents' benefits; among men, racial or ethnic minorities and all blue-collar workers bear a disproportionate share of the burden of unemployment, both temporary and long-term, with clear implications for those who depend on them for financial support. U.S. men who cannot qualify for social insurance programs—disproportionately ethnic and racial minorities—also depend upon social assistance programs, usually called general assistance, which are not available nationwide, receive no federal funding, and are equally intrusive—and even less generous—than AFDC. (Single women are also ineligible for AFDC.)

7. The notion of a right to a family could form the basis for analyzing the impact of state social provision on racial and ethnic differences, since this right has been unequally available to different races and ethnicities.

8. U.S. single mothers with access to survivors' insurance through Social Security—widows of covered wage-earners—fare much better than other single mothers; their benefits are higher and they may combine them with paid work with no penalty (Garfinkel and McLanahan 1986). However, they make up a relatively small proportion of single mothers.

9. Information about these proposals comes from articles published in the New York *Times* during 1993 and 1994; details available from the author.

REFERENCES

Australia, Department of Social Security. 1990. *Annual Report, 1989–90.* Canberra: Australian Government Publishing Office.

Bane, Mary Jo. 1988. "Politics and Policies of the Feminization of Poverty." Pp.381–396 in *The Politics of Social Policy in the United States,* edited by Margaret Weir, Ann Shola Orloff, and Theda Skocpol. Princeton, NJ: Princeton University Press.

Baxter, Janeen. 1993. "Gender Equality and Men's Participation in Domestic Labour." Paper presented at the Australian Family Research Conference, Sydney, Australia.

Cass, Bettina. 1994. "Citizenship, Work and Welfare: The Dilemma for Australian Women." *Social Politics* 1:106–124.

Castles, Francis. 1994. "The Wage Earners' Welfare State Revisited: Refurbishing the Established Model of Australian Social Protection, 1983–1993." *Australian Journal of Social Issues* (June).

Castles, Francis, and Deborah Mitchell. 1993. "Worlds of Welfare and Families of Nations." In *Families of Nations*, edited by F.G. Castles. Aldershot: Dartmouth.

England, Paula, and Barbara Kilbourne. 1990. "Markets, Marriages, and Other Mates: The Problem of Power." Pp. 163–188 in *Beyond the Marketplace*, edited by R. Friedland and A. F. Robertson. Hawthorne, NY: Aldine de Gruyter.

Esping-Andersen, Gøsta. 1990. *The Three Worlds of Welfare Capitalism*. Princeton, NJ: Princeton University Press.

Esping-Andersen, Gøsta, and Walter Korpi. 1987. "From Poor Relief to Institutional Welfare States: The Development of Scandinavian Social Policy." Pp. 39–74 in *The Scandinavian Model: Welfare States and Welfare Research*, edited by R. Erikson, E. Hansen, S. Ringen, and H. Uusitalo. New York: M. E. Sharpe.

Finch, Janet, and Dulcie Groves. 1983. *A Labour of Love: Women, Work and Caring*. Boston, MA: Routledge and Kegan Paul.

Fraser, Nancy. 1989. "Women, Welfare and the Politics of Need." Pp. 144–160 in *Unruly Practices*. Minneapolis: University of Minnesota Press.

Freeman, Jo. 1990. "From Protection to Equal Opportunity: The Revolution in Women's Legal Status." Pp. 457–481 in *Women, Politics and Change*, edited by L. Tilly and P. Gurin. New York: Russell Sage.

Garfinkel, Irwin, and Sara McLanahan. 1986. *Single Mothers and Their Children: A New American Dilemma*. Washington, DC: Urban Institute.

Garfinkel, Irwin, and Patrick Wong. 1990. "Child Support and Public Policy." Pp.101–126 in *Lone-Parent Families: The Economic Challenge*. Paris: Organization for Economic Cooperation and Development.

Gordon, Linda. 1988. "What Does Welfare Regulate?" *Social Research* 55:609–630.

Hernes, Helga. 1988. "The Welfare State Citizenship of Scandinavian Women." Pp. 187–213 in *The Political Interests of Gender*, edited by K. Jones and A. Jonasdottir. Newbury Park, CA: Sage.

Hirschman, Albert. 1970. *Exit, Voice, and Loyalty*. Cambridge, MA: Harvard University Press.

Hobson, Barbara. 1990. "No Exit, No Voice: Women's Economic Dependency and the Welfare State." *Acta Sociologica* 33:235–250.

Korpi, Walter. 1989. "Power, Politics, and State Autonomy in the Development of Social Citizenship." *American Sociological Review* 54:309–328.

Koven, Seth, and Sonya Michel. 1993. *Mothers of the New World: Maternalist Politics and the Origins of the Welfare State*. New York: Routledge.

Lake, Marilyn. 1992. "Mission Impossible: How Men Gave Birth to the Australian Nation—Nationalism, Gender and Other Seminal Acts." *Gender and History* 4:305–322.

Land, Hilary. 1983. "Poverty and Gender: The Distribution of Resources Within the Family." Pp. 49–71 in *The Structure of Disadvantage*, edited by M. Brown. London: Heinemann.

Leira, Arnlaug. 1992. *Welfare States and Working Mothers: The Scandinavian Experience*. New York: Cambridge University Press.

Lewis, Jane. 1992. "Gender and the Development of Welfare Regimes." *Gender and History* 4:305–322. *Journal of European Social Policy* 3:159–173.

Marshall, T. H. 1950. *Citizenship and Social Class and Other Essays*. Cambridge, England: Cambridge University Press.

Mitchell, Deborah. 1993. "Sole Parents, Work and Welfare: Evidence from the Luxembourg Income Study." Unpublished manuscript, Research School of the Social Sciences, Australian National University.

Nelson, Barbara. 1984. "Women's Poverty and Women's Citizenship: Some Political Consequences of Economic Marginality." *Signs* 10:209–232.

Nelson, Barbara. 1990. "The Origins of the Two-Channel Welfare State: Workmen's Compensation and Mothers' Aid." Pp. 123–151 in *Women, the*

State, and Welfare, edited by L. Gordon. Madison, WI: University of Wisconsin Press.

O'Connor, Julia. 1993. "Labour Market Participation in Liberal Welfare State Regimes." Unpublished manuscript, Department of Sociology, McMaster University, Hamilton, Ontario, Canada.

Orloff, Ann Shola. 1991. "Gender in Early U.S. Social Policy." *Journal of Policy History* 3:249–281.

Orloff, Ann Shola. 1993. "Gender and the Social Rights of Citizenship: The Comparative Analysis of Gender Relations and Welfare States." *American Sociological Review* 58:303–328.

Orloff, Ann Shola. 1994. "Income Security Policies: Gender Differentiation and Gender Inequality." Paper presented at the annual meeting of the American Sociological Association, Los Angeles, CA, August; forthcoming in *States, Markets, Families: Gender, Liberalism and Social Policy in Australia, Canada, the United Kingdom and the United States,* by Julia O'Connor, Ann Shola Orloff, and Sheila Shaver.

Pahl, Jan. 1983. "The Allocation of Money and the Structuring of Inequality Within Marriage." *Sociological Review* 9:313–335.

Palme, Joakim. 1990. *Pension Rights in Welfare Capitalism: The Development of Old-Age Pensions in 18 OECD Countries 1930 to 1985.* Stockholm, Sweden: Swedish Institute for Social Research Dissertation Series, No. 14.

Pateman, Carole. 1988. "The Patriarchal Welfare State." Pp. 231–278 in *Democracy and the State,* edited by A. Gutmann. Princeton, NJ: Princeton University Press.

Pearce, Diana. 1986. "Toil and Trouble: Women Workers and Unemployment Compensation." Pp. 141–162 in *Women and Poverty,* edited by B. Gelpi, N. Hartsock, C. Novak, and M. Strober. Chicago, IL: University of Chicago Press.

Pedersen, Susan. 1989. "The Failure of Feminism in the Making of the British Welfare State." *Radical History Review* No. 43:86–110.

Piven, Frances Fox. 1985. "Women and the State: Ideology, Power, and the Welfare State." Pp. 265–287 in *Gender and the Life Course,* edited by A. Rossi. New York: Aldine.

Rainwater, Lee. 1993. "The Social Wage in the Income Package of Working Parents." Luxembourg Income Study Working Paper #89.

Reischauer, Robert. 1989. "The Welfare Reform Legislation: Directions for the Future." Pp. 10–40 in *Welfare Policy for the 1990s,* edited by Phoebe Cottingham and David Ellwood. Cambridge, MA: Harvard University Press.

Sainsbury, Diane. 1993. "Dual Welfare and Sex Segregation of Access to Social Benefits: Income Maintenance Policies in the UK, the US, the Netherlands and Sweden." *Journal of Social Policy* 22:69–98.

Saunders, Peter, and George Matheson. 1990. "Sole Parent Families in Australia." University of New South Wales, Social Policy Research Centre Discussion Paper No. 23.

Shaver, Sheila. 1987. "Comment on Fraser I." *Thesis Eleven* no. 17:107–110.

Shaver, Sheila. 1989. "Sex and Money in the Fiscal Crisis." Pp. 154–171 in *Australian Welfare: Historical Sociology,* edited by Richard Kennedy. Melbourne: Macmillan.

Shaver, Sheila. 1990. "Gender, Social Policy Regimes and the Welfare State." Paper presented at the annual meeting of the American Sociological Association, Washington, DC.

Shaver, Sheila. 1991. "Gender, Class and the Welfare State: The Case of Income Security in Australia." Pp. 145–163 in *The Sociology of Social Security,* edited by Michael Adler, Colin Bell, Jochen Clasen, and Adrian Sinfield. Edinburgh: Edinburgh University Press.

Shaver, Sheila. 1993a. "Body Rights, Social Rights, and the Liberal Welfare State." *Critical Social Policy.*

Shaver, Sheila. 1993b. "Women and the Australian Social Security System: From Difference Towards Equality." University of New South Wales, Social Policy Research Centre Discussion Paper No. 41.

Skocpol, Theda. 1992. *Protecting Soldiers and Mothers.* Cambridge, MA: Harvard University Press.

Skocpol, Theda, and Gretchen Ritter. 1991. "Gender and the Origins of Modern Social Policies in Britain and the United States." *Studies in American Political Development 5* (Spring):36–93.

Smeeding, Timothy, Barbara Torrey, and Lee Rainwater. 1993. "Going to Extremes: An International Perspective on the Economic Status of the U.S. Aged." Luxembourg Income Study Working Paper #87.

Taylor-Gooby, Peter. 1991. "Welfare State Regimes and Welfare Citizenship." *Journal of European Social Policy* 1:93–105.

Titmuss, R. 1958. "War and Social Policy." Pp. 75–87 in *Essays on the Welfare State.* London: Allen and Unwin.

U.S. Department of Health and Human Services Office of Family Assistance. 1991. *Characteristics and Financial Circumstances of AFDC Recipients, FY 1991.* Washington, DC: U.S. Department of Health and Human Services.

U.S. Social Security Administration. 1993. *Statistical Supplement to the Social Security Bulletin, 1992.* Washington, DC: U.S. Department of Health and Human Services.

Vandepol, Ann. 1982. "Dependent Children, Child Custody and Mothers' Pensions: The Transformation of State-Family Relations in the Early Twentieth Century." *Social Problems* 29:221–235.

Waerness, Kari. 1984. "Caregiving as Women's Work in the Welfare State." In *Patriarchy in a Welfare Society,* edited by Harriet Holter. Oslo, Norway: Universitetsforlaget.

Watts, Robert. 1987. *The Foundations of the National Welfare State.* Sydney: Allen and Unwin.

Weir, Margaret, Ann Shola Orloff, and Theda Skocpol, eds. 1988. *The Politics of Social Policy in the United States.* Princeton, NJ: Princeton University Press.

Wright, Erik Olin, Karen Shire, Shu-ling Hwang, Maureen Dolan, and Janeen Baxter. 1992. "The Non-Effects of Class on the Gender Division of Labor in the Home: A Comparative Study of Sweden and the United States." *Gender and Society* 6:252–282.

10 COLLECTIVE IDENTITIES, WOMEN'S AGENCY, AND THE FRAMING OF CITIZENSHIP

Barbara Hobson

Not too long ago, one would have a hard time imagining a set of debates about the concept of citizenship in gender terms. The contours of citizenship were bounded by notions of universality, envisioned as a person who embodied a bundle of obligations and rights. However, within the universal framework was a gendered inner frame that contained a male citizen: he was the independent, paterfamilias in the liberal state, the male breadwinner and his family in Marshall's (1950) framework of social citizenship, or the Rawlsian just representative of the independent household (1971).[1] Applying a gendered lens to citizenship, the recent wave of feminist research has sought to redefine and extend the conceptual boundaries of citizenship by decoding keywords that form the basis of dominant theories: dependency/ independency; private/public; and needs/rights (Fraser 1989; Gordon 1994; Saraceno 1992, 1997).

In some respects the feminist project to engender citizenship is part of a broad research agenda to extend the conceptual boundaries of the citizenship paradigm. This occurs at a time when citizenship is a highly contested concept with a great deal of currency. In the realm of European policy and politics, one cannot ignore the collapse of the Soviet regime, which has resulted in a recasting of citizenship in post-communist societies, and its corollary outcome, the rise of ethnic and national identity politics and warfare. Not only the breaking apart of nation-states, but the question of citizenship outside national borders is now on the agenda; Eurocitizenship, or world citizenship, or the citizenship within imagined communities among homosexuals, pacifists, environmentalists, or feminists (Jones 1994; Turner 1992). The frame of citizenship has become a strategy among social scientists to rediscover the foundations for theories of rights, social membership, and political participation during a period of welfare state retrenchment and rollbacks (Lister 1996; Turner 1992).

This renewed interest in citizenship among scholars has opened up conceptual space for more dynamic frameworks. Hence the new discourse on citizenship goes beyond the conventional notions of citizenship as a status (formal rights) and more recently as identity (Brubaker 1992). This scholarship has reintroduced the dimension of participatory citizenship rooted in traditions of the Greek democratic forum or Rousseau's idea of civic republicanism (Lister 1993; Mouffe 1992; Turner 1992). These are traditions in which women were consciously left out of the script. But one could also make a case that the framework of participatory citizenship produces a theoretical terrain for recognizing the role of women as social actors in the construction of citizenship (Dietz 1992; Hobson 1996; Lister 1996).

A surge of books and articles in the current wave of gender research has made explicit the need for a theory of women's agency and the parameters of citizenship rights (Hobson 1996; Lister 1996; Siim 1994; Skocpol 1992). In rediscovering the importance of participatory rights and citizenship boundaries, some feminist scholars engaged in the project of engendering citizenship have reclaimed Hanna Arendt (*see* edited collection by Bonnie Honig 1995), though gender as historical category or women as particularized citizens are conspicuously absent in her analysis. Nevertheless, feminist scholars who have been inspired by Arendt's writings on citizenship and democracy have found legitimacy for a revitalized notion of citizenship. Her vision of politics is seen as dynamic, with fluid and open political spaces (Landes 1995). As Arendt rediscovered these contested moments or "lost stories" in the creation of democratic societies, feminists seek to rediscover a women's politics and moments when women as social actors were visible.

It is understandable that Arendt's radical notion of politics is a seductive package for feminist scholars, since it represents a departure from the narrow field of formal politics and national political parties, in which women are rarely key actors. Yet in the quest for theories of women's agency and the construction of citizenship, Arendt's formulation can take us just so far. She shades out large areas of women's lives in her denial of the social or "private" spaces as legitimate areas of politics (Landes 1995). Arendt's theorizing provides little leverage for a crucial issue that has emerged in feminist writings on citizenship: the links between participation and access to politics is highly dependent on social rights. Hence, women who are economically dependent on their husband's income cannot make claims in the family over time to participate in spheres outside the home. More often than not, they are isolated from networks and organizations in which politics are devised and implemented.

Here it is logical to turn to T.H. Marshall's (1950) analysis of social rights. Citizens in Marshall's community, as is true of Arendt, are disembodied individuals who do not bear children, care for family members, or experience exclusion from participation in the full heritage of social and political life in the community on the basis of gender. Marshall recognized the linkages between political rights and social rights; social rights followed political rights in his sequence of civil, political, and social rights. However, how to link political and social citizenship is problematic in Marshall if one considers his assumption that the "normal method of establishing social rights is by the exercise of power," in which he means exercising one's vote or veto, that is, representation in the state apparatus through political parties. It is difficult to imagine politics from below and spheres of participatory democracy, social movements, and new forms of power articulation that take in the broad sphere of politics from which women as social actors have made claims upon the welfare state.[2]

Parties representing a women's constituency, and women's parties, have not been a force in electoral politics, with the exception of the women's party in Iceland. Historically, women have been marginalized from worker's organizations and even today rarely wield power in unions. Therefore, to understand how women's collectivities have extended citizenship rights, one must develop alternative models and different modes of power articulation. In effect, this implies a new theorizing around the practice of citizenship (Jones 1994; Phillips 1991; Siim 1994), through neighborhoods, workplaces, political institutions, and social movements.

The practice of citizenship is bound up with collective identity formation. This is a crucial component for developing a theory of women's agency in the framework of citizenship, which is referred to throughout this chapter as *composing constituency*. To compose literally means to come together in a place (translated from its Latin and Old English roots), and when applied to movements to extend citizen rights this usage encompasses the process of creating shared meanings and consciousness among individual members of a social group, the framing of grievances and goals in a social movement, and the representation of that constituency in public arenas. In coining the term composing constituency (1996), I sought to highlight the importance of social actors and the dynamic processes of identity formation, historical contingencies, and unexpected political opportunities. I am not using constituencies in the narrow sense of voting constituencies, but more broadly as the representation of social groups in discursive arenas, in texts aimed at a general audience, and in politics within and across parties (Hobson 1996).

To understand how collectivities compose constituencies and practice citizenship, one has to take a step back in time and theoretical space to the prefigurative and formative stages in the making of gendered identities. Beginning with a prefigurative phase in the composing of constituency offers a way out of the dilemma posed in debates on citizenship and gender, that is, the dilemma of differentiated versus universal citizenship, sometimes cast as the equality and difference dilemma. A process-oriented model of identity formation (the composing of constituency), provides a framework for recognition of (1) multiple identities in the category of women and (2) the convergence of beliefs and visions that are expressed in the practice of citizenship. Thinking about the making and remaking of women's collectivities offers a way out of the conceptual entropy surrounding theories of gendered identities.[3] It is subversive to the notion of gender as a primordial category.[4]

How leaders of social movements compose constituencies not only involves locating a core set of issues or grievances, but finding a frame that resonates among the members of a collectivity. I have characterized this process of collective identity formation as cognitive framing, which can be viewed as the DNA of movements in which cultural coding and information is reproduced in the various organizational settings of movements: public meetings, journal articles, and discussions within groups (Hobson 1996). In social movement theory, cognitive framing is a concept that reflects the process of linking the belief system or world view of the individual participant with the ideological frame of the movement organization (Snow and Benford 1986, 1992).[5]

Building upon earlier research on women's power resources in welfare states (Hobson 1993, 1996), I suggest that cognitive framing is a useful analytical tool for understanding how collectivities articulate claims in welfare states. I posit that (1) cognitive framing is a crucial phase in the making of collective identities and mobilizing constituencies. The process involves locating grievances, interpreting them, and representing them in public debate in ways that increase cohesion—which in the case of women's collectivities implies finding a vocabulary that creates loyalty among diverse groups of women. (2) Cognitive framing shapes the discursive and organizational resources of social groups. In this respect, feminist struggles for citizenship rights are in fact recognition struggles and their success is dependent upon their ability to represent themselves as a constituency. (3) Cognitive framing shapes the boundaries for future mobilization and claim making.

In this article I concentrate on two main frames, or vocabularies, of citizenship that mirror various strands of feminist mobilization in the first decades of this century: women as mothers and women as citizens, which feminist scholars have conceptualized as maternalism and participatory citizenship.

Though there are varied definitions and scholarly uses of maternalism, which I outline below, most researchers who have employed this concept would agree that maternalism embodied these basic shared values: (1) women's identity revolved around care for children and the vast majority of women believed that this was their contribution to society and that it was valued; and (2) that, because of their unique capacity for care, women were responsible for all families in their roles as social mothers (Gordon 1994; Ladd-Taylor 1994; Michel 1996).

The main premise in the participatory citizenship frame is that women have been denied participatory rights in democratic societies. Thus feminist organizations argued that women as a group lacked a political voice or representation in political, legal, and economic institutions. Although questions around motherhood were incorporated into a cognitive frame of participatory citizenship, the basis for women's activism was not bound by a maternalist world view that women had unique political identities based upon their motherly roles or gender difference, but rather a perception that women as a constituency with varied social roles as workers, mothers, and citizens needed to have their interests and needs represented.

In the following section, I focus on these two frames that were central to the mobilization of women's collectivities during the first decades of the 20th century. First I consider the varied contexts of the maternalist frame in women's movements at the beginning of this century by revealing its different contexts. Then I map out the contours of women's collective identity formation in one political landscape, Sweden, where participatory citizenship was the dominant frame for composing a women's constituency. I concentrate on the Swedish case to provide a detailed analysis of a participatory citizenship frame because it is rarely featured in comparative studies of women's agency and the origins of welfare states.[6] Moreover, it is a case that has been characterized as feminism without feminists, in which women were objects and not subjects of policymaking. But this value-laden account of what constitutes feminism does not take into account different forms of mobilization and cognitive framing that have been expressed in Scandinavian feminist movements.

MATERNALIST FRAMES

Much of the scholarship on feminist movements in the first decades of the 20th century has adopted the term "maternalist" to express women's activism that sprung from a recognition of women's interests as mothers. This is a problematic concept for several reasons. First, it is used in many different senses: as an ideology that "extolled the values of domesticity and simultaneously legitimated women's public relationships to politics, the state, and the workplace" (Koven and Michel 1993), as a women's movement (Ladd-Taylor 1994), and as a type of welfare state (Skocpol 1992). Second, there are many subtexts in the mobilization and constructed political identities around motherhood.

To analyze the variations in construction of political identities around motherhood, we need to begin to unpack maternalism as a framework. Consider the varied ways in which motherhood was framed by women's collectivities in the first decades of the 20th century as a service, as wages for carework, as a social function, as the replacement for a male breadwinner wage.

In Australia, where women were granted political rights in 1902, feminists campaigned for the endowment of motherhood as a citizenship right based on their service to the state as mothers disconnected from their wifely service. The cognitive frame in the Australian women's movement for mother's endowment was the independent mother-citizen who embodied both the state's recognition of women's service to the state equivalent to men's military service, as well as the right to act as independent citizens with their own wages. Feminists demanded the state pay them for their service to society, and argued that women's dependent status as wives was denial of citizenship (Lake 1994). As one feminist active in the Australian labor party bluntly put it: "A man who controls a woman's purse controls her actions and consequently her essential freedom as a citizen" (quoted in Lake 1996: 200). A maternity allowance, lobbied for by women's groups from the housewives association to the labor women, came into effect in 1912 and was seen as the first installment of maternal rights.[7] However, though child benefits were won, a social wage for motherhood never became a reality.

Similar to the Australian case, the British feminist campaign for the endowment of motherhood framed their claims for mother's rights as a way of redressing the imbalance of power in the family. Wages paid directly to mothers also would insure that the family needs would be met if a husband squandered his wages (Lewis 1991, 1993) and would protect wives from a husband's tyranny. To represent a mother's benefit as wages for work clearly threatened male unionists' campaigns for male breadwinner wages. British union resistance to mother's benefits and child allowances paid directly to mothers was resisted by labor unions, who joined forces with conservatives to protest the endowment for motherhood as a threat to the family (Pedersen 1993).

Maternalism in the American context reflected a different set of assumptions about the role of the state to intervene in questions relating to power and dependency in families. Rather than rights for a mother's service to society or wages for mother work, mother needs and protection for vulnerable mothers was the main frame of the feminist campaigns in the decades after suffrage was won.[8] American feminists who successfully campaigned for mother's pensions, maternal health care, and protective labor legislation, did not challenge the male breadwinner wage ideology, but sought protection from the loss of male breadwinner. Not mothers, but vulnerable mothers—widows and abandoned wives—were to receive benefits for caring for their children at home.

That French women's collectivities mobilized around the interests of mothers is not surprising in light of the centrality of the population decline after the First World War. Both confessional and republican women's groups valorized motherhood as a social function, campaigned for maternal and child benefits, and embraced the icon of motherhood. For confessional women's groups, mothers were the preservers of social order and stability of society, as well as reproducers of the French population (Jensen and Sineau 1995; Pedersen 1993). Republican feminists articulated their claims for mother's contribution to society, but unlike confessional feminists did not view the family as a harmonious unit. Nevertheless, they did not campaign against child allowances that were paid to the father nor claim rights redress that would have challenged the principle of male breadwinner wages (Pedersen 1994). For Republican feminists, motherhood was a frame that gave them a discursive space to claim rights for maternal leaves and daycare for mothers in paid work.

Motherhood was a main frame for mobilizing women's constituencies in the first decades of the 20th century, but it took on board various meanings and it was fitted into different landscapes. Maternalism did not, however, fit the ways in which feminists in Scandinavia mobilized women's collectivities. They constructed another framework: citizenship and participatory democracy became the principal cognitive frame for feminist movements in Sweden and other Scandinavian countries.[9] Swedish feminists articulated their versions of women's multiple identities as citizens, as workers, as mothers, as builders of social democracy.

A maternalist tradition existed in Swedish feminism and its main protagonist was Ellen Key, who claimed that a woman's power derived from her maternal role and female consciousness. However, this stance that embodied a view of essential gender difference lost ground in the 1930s.[10] Beginning in the 1920s and throughout the 1930s, Swedish feminists constructed a political identity around concepts of citizenship and democratic participation in government. In effect, they affirmed that there were no special women's issues: everything concerns women and what women think concerns everyone (Eskillsson 1991).

Like so many European feminist movements during the first decades of the 20th century, Swedish women's groups were divided by class, political loyalties, and ideological disagreements around protection and rights. Class and party cleavages were reactivated and intensified after the enactment of suffrage. For Swedish women's groups, the fractures around ideological positions cut more deeply because of long-standing class antagonisms. The citizenship frame shored up the fractures among various feminist groups and was the basis for composing a new political identity for women's groups.

Swedish feminist groups defined their goals and legitimated their activism through the frame of citizenship and participatory democracy. Facing a general lack of involvement among women in the political realm—a significant proportion of women did not even exercise their right to vote—leaders of women's organizations waged a campaign to engage women in the sphere of politics. Politics was meant in the broadest sense of civicness—to be an informed and engaged citizen in the making of new politics. Kerstin Hesselgren, first woman factory inspector and the first female member of parliament, maintained that women's voices were essential for maintaining a democratic society. Implicit in this frame of citizenship were obligations and rights: "Our democracy of the future must be supported by enlightened women's elective. The uneducated, the passive female citizen is a direct threat to our democracy" (in Thorell 1969:2).

Cross-party and cross-class alliances resulted in new innovative practices of citizenship. In 1936, 25 women's organizations signed a public letter calling on women to work for increased political representation on the part of women. This collaborative letter, entitled "A Call To Swedish Women," was signed by women's organizations ranging from the Organization of Female Postal Workers to the Organization of Swedish Christian Young Women (*Arbetets Kvinnor* 1936:221–222). It was published in both women's trade union journals and bourgeois women's journals and urged women to contribute to the advancement of women by joining a party and actively campaigning for female politicians. Its stated goals sought to transcend political party lines: "Make Sweden's women worthy citizens of society. Push for equality between men and women, socially and economically. Protect the new rights that women have won. Strengthen solidarity among women" (Svenska Kvinnors Medborgarsforbund 1931:23).

A dramatic surge in women's organizations came about in the 1930s. Beyond the actual numbers within organizations,[11] there was a networking and crosstalk among feminists in different organizations which represented women with varied social backgrounds, political orientations, and specific reform agendas. They spoke at each other's meetings, published in each other's journals, and cooperated around a range of issues.

ARTICULATION OF GRIEVANCES AND CLAIMS

The struggle over meanings is a critical site in which the boundaries of citizenship are contested. Not only who is entitled to what, but at stake are the basic values and policy frameworks that form the criteria for what constitutes a right and the right to have rights. Lacking durable institutional bases or reservoirs for articulating claims, women's activism has been highly dependent on discursive resources for actualizing policy goals (Fraser 1989). Through the frame of citizenship, Swedish feminists were able to reclaim the traditional cultural narrative in Swedish society, the Folkhem or People's Home.

For feminists the Folkhem provided discursive space that allowed them to articulate their demands for more participatory rights and policy influence. It enabled them to couple the social and everyday experiences of care work and childrearing to political spheres and public debate. The separation of public and private domains of social life that formed the basis of liberal theories of citizenship were linked together symbolically in the metaphor of the Folkhem, and women found public space for claim making that extended the realm of citizenship to questions of abortion and contraception, mother's health, daycare, and rights of working mothers to remain in the labor market after they married and had children.

Because of Alva and Gunnar Myrdal's famous book, *Kris i Befolkningsfrågan* (Crisis in the Population Question), the Swedish population debate is well known. In the book they warned that Swedes were not reproducing themselves and concluded that the way to increase Sweden's population was through social reforms and the redistribution of resources (Myrdal and Myrdal 1935). Leading the feminist campaign for married women's right to work, Alva Myrdal transformed a potentially conservative discourse around population concerns and encased it in a frame of citizenship rights and participatory democracy. The right of mothers to work and to have families was in essence the right to participate as mothers, workers, and citizens in a democratic society (Myrdal 1945).

The citizenship frame empowered Swedish women's groups to respond unilaterally to the threat to women's right to work that loomed on the horizon in many industrialized countries during the depression era. In Sweden, the right to work represented a core principle of Social Democracy. To deny women that right represented a threat to their claims for recognition as citizens.

Some Swedish women had a practical stake in maintaining the right to employment (married women comprised 10 percent of the female labor force), yet many more realized the symbolic significance of defending it as a basic citizenship right. The whole spectrum of women's organizations, including the National Housewives Association, defended women's right to work on the basis that it was a citizenship right. Though the preference of the National Housewives Association was for mothers to be at home, even their spokespersons came out against a proposal to offer married women early retirement with some severance pay. Within the citizenship frame, the right to gainful employment was cast as a right to "contribute to society" (Kock 1935), to participate in different spheres of life as workers, mothers, and active citizens.

Swedish women's organizations during this period not only prevented the assault on married women's right to work,[12] they in fact achieved legislation that increased women's rights as workers in a depression decade when women throughout Europe and North America were losing that right. A law passed in 1938 prohibited the firing of women who were married, pregnant, or solo mothers.

Cognitive framing in social movements is important for locating grievances and interpreting them so that they build solidarity and loyalty. Women's collectivities that appear fractured lose a critical resource, their ability to make claims on behalf of women's interests. Finally, cognitive frames can open up political space for women's collectivities or delimit the parameters of what can be claimed as representing a constituency's interests. If we turn to another case during the same period, we can see that the framing of women's collectivities based on caregiving and childbearing roles weakened the feminist campaign to protect women's rights as workers.

During the 1930s in the U.S., there were public denunciations of married women's employment, and national and local laws were passed barring married women from working in the public sector jobs. The Economy Act, a national law passed during the Depression Era, forbade employing two persons from the same household in the civil service. Numerous communities enacted laws that led to wholesale firing of married teachers (Hobson 1993). Feminist groups were unified in their opposition to the marriage bar, and in their campaign to defeat it, were unified across earlier ideological cleavages among those who affirmed women's maternalist identities and supported protective labor legislation, and those who asserted women's equal opportunity and introduced the Equal Rights Amendment (Hobson 1993).

However, the discursive resources of American feminists were limited by earlier framing of women's maternal interests beyond the domains of home and for roles other than carers for children and family members. Motherhood was the idiom for mobilizing a women's constituency, and women's groups articulated claims for new policies based on women's roles as childbearers and caregivers. Throughout the 1920s, American feminists who operated within a maternalist frame were able to gain benefits for women through special legislation for mothers: widows pensions, maternal health, protections for mothers at workplaces, restrictions on hours and types of work (Ladd-Taylor 1994; Skocpol 1992). However, the maternalist frame that had brought so much success a decade earlier during the depression era inhibited women's groups seeking to mobilize around the right to work as a citizenship right.

It is misleading to suggest that maternalism was a cognitive frame that reflected only a middle-class world view. Working-class feminist groups also mobilized around women's caregiving roles. The campaigns for the endowment of motherhood in England and Australia are cases in point (Lake 1994; Lewis 1991). Nevertheless, one could imagine why Swedish feminists placed women's interests within an embracing theme of citizenship. A cognitive frame that revolved around women's role as mother and caregiver would not have appealed to the Swedish Social Democratic women who cast women's citizenship in broad terms: as mothers, workers, and democratic citizens. The majority of Social Democratic women in the 1930s, however, not only recognized that many women had to work for economic survival, they viewed work as a basic citizenship right in a political configuration in which citizen and worker were bound together (Lewis and Ostner 1994).

Swedish women's organizations found a common vocabulary and a core of issues that enabled them to build a coalition among a broad spectrum of women's groups. Moreover, that working-class women's organizations were key actors in the construction of Swedish women's political identities during this formative period meant that the policy agendas that emerged in Sweden took into account the experiences and needs of working-class women. One can only imagine that a coalition that included Swedish Social Democratic women would have protested vigorously against the invidious distinction that was perpetuated and institutionalized in Roosevelt's New Deal: the distinction between "worthy" widows who were entitled to benefits as wives and unmarried or divorced mothers who were given benefits on the basis of "moral character" and economic needs, which came to be known as welfare in the American context (Gordon 1994).

The French case offers another example of the opportunities and constraints imposed by the maternalist frame. In many respects, women's collective identity formation in France can be seen as the epitome of maternalist movements, since feminists of every stripe, from republican feminists to confessional or social Catholic women's groups themselves, were included within that framework (Pedersen 1994). In framing women's interests in strictly maternal terms, French women reaped benefits as family members (with high child allowances, paid mandatory maternal leaves) and places for breast-feeding babies in workplaces. But a cognitive frame that circumscribed women's social function to motherhood inhibited women's groups from presenting a counterdiscourse to the illiberal vision of women's roles and the narrow pronatalist goals manifested in Vichy France. It also did not open up discursive space for claims made based on political citizenship and participatory rights. No mass movement in the sphere of political and participatory rights emerged after the war and women's suffrage was enacted in France in the 1940s despite the lack of women's mobilization. The legacies of maternalism linger in modern day France; in Mitterand's France, participatory citizenship (equality policy) was disconnected from social citizenship (family policies). Mitterand created a minister for women 's equality in response to feminist activism, but also appointed a minister of family affairs to address pronatalist concerns. However, in a short period, family policies and maternal interests gained prominence in the Mitterand cabinet (Jensen and Sineau 1995).

CONCLUSION

As these historical cases reveal, the composing constituency and the formation of political identities is a central node in the practice of citizenship. In focusing mainly on the Swedish case, I am not suggesting Sweden as the normative case for women's citizenship. Rather, my purpose is to reveal the dynamic processes of how and when women's agency shapes the contours of citizenship in welfare states. Cognitive framing of citizenship among women's collectivities in different political landscapes illustrates the interdependencies in composing constituencies and articulating claims (as shown in Figure 10–1). Cognitive frames conjoin with the discursive lines in the larger society and facilitate organization building and networking. Finally, organizational strength and recognition as a constituency open up political opportunities that positively influence policy outcomes.

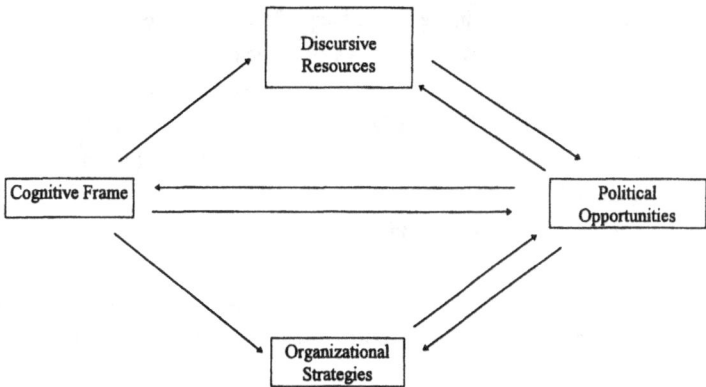

Figure 10–1. Interdependencies in Composing Constituencies, Political Opportunities, and Articulation of Citizenship Rights. (This model is derived from Hobson's [1995, 1996] research on gender and citizenship.)

The 1930s was a golden age of Swedish women's activism and the flowering of women's political organizations. In many respects, it was an exceptional period for feminist mobilization, a period of open political space where a revitalized form of women's citizenship could emerge, what Hanna Arendt would call a "lost treasure of democracy." It was also a period when welfare states were developing and expanding; there was room for social groups to articulate new claims for extending citizenship rights. Finally, it was a period in Swedish political life when political parties did not have huge majorities, and the long tenure of the Social Democratic party was not assured.

During the 1930s Swedish women's groups were successful in pushing through policies that were to become the core of women's citizenship in the Swedish welfare state: maternity leaves and job security; protection of married women's right to work; income maintenance for single mothers; and universal maternal healthcare. A mother's benefit based on needs was also enacted, but it was nearly universal in that it included the vast majority of mothers (Ohlander 1992).[13] Although in terms of actual spending, unemployment and pensions involved greater expenditures, nevertheless, the measures enacted and many of the debates on women's citizenship represented an extension of the welfare state into new terrain, which increased women's social rights—benefits were given directly to women and were structured in such a way that they could form autonomous households (Hobson 1990; Orloff 1993). These policy initiatives and debates laid the foundation for a set of policy initiatives that came to offer generous parental leave benefits, and developed a state-supported daycare and elderly care system that provided women jobs in the public sector. The contours of women's citizenship can be traced to this period, in which participatory citizenship came to mean participation in the spheres of politics, paid work, and family work. The aspects of citizenship framed in this period are visible in current Swedish patterns of dual family earners: the high proportion of mothers with young children in the Swedish labor market and the large proportions of mothers who work part time, an indication that the goal for social and economic equality between men and women formulated in the collaborative letter, "A Call To Swedish Women," has not been achieved. But another legacy from this period, the highest proportions of women in parliament among Western democracies, reveals the importance of participatory citizenship as a mobilizing force in Swedish politics.

The cognitive framing of citizenship also imposes constraints on the universe of political discourse and the possibilities for articulating claims in the future. From this perspective, one can say that there is a path dependency in the framing of citizenship rights, with the caveat that mobilizing constituencies are dynamic processes dependent on historical contingencies and new political actors.

The limits of the maternalist framing of women's citizenship are implied in the historical examples that I have presented. To compose constituencies of women around mother roles and mother work circumscribed the discursive and policymaking universe of women's groups. Outside the circle were issues of employment, rights to work, and equal pay. Perhaps most problematic in the constructions of maternalism was the decoupling of social citizenship from political citizenship. The inclusion of women as full citizens presupposes that they are to be both subjects and objects in the making of policies—in the making of welfare states. Protecting motherhood, wages for mother work, or even motherhood as service to the state, were cognitive frames that tended to reinforce the notion of separate spheres and steered women's activism away from more active roles in politics.

The legacies of the citizenship frame are obvious when we consider the visible and vocal presence of women in the political sphere (between 40 and 45 percent). Its limitations and constraints are also visible, as seen in the lack of articulation of conflicts around power in the family and, until recently, the invisibility of public discussions addressing sexual violence in the home and sexual harrassment in the workplace. In the citizenship frame, we find the other side of the dilemma of difference implicit in the maternalist framing of women's interests: how to define a differentiated citizenship that allows for full participation in the community, but at the same time recognizes women's disadvantage as a result of the gendered divisions of paid and unpaid work, and recognizes care work as a crucial dimension of welfare states. Women's collectivities continue to articulate claims and grievances within the framework of participatory democracy. One example is the mobilization against welfare state retrenchment in which cuts in care services are represented as undermining women's citizenship rights to participate fully in workplaces and work organizations. Another is the challenge to the European Community as an undemocratic forum in which Swedish feminist politics and policymakers have little or no influence.

Whereas Marshallian logic would presume that the inclusion of new groups results in the extension and broadening of citizenship rights (Barbalet 1988), the basic premise in this study is that the process of composing constituencies (the practice of citizenship) is the missing middle term in that construction. For groups which do not have institutional bases in unions or political parties, such as women's collectivities, the practice of citizenship is an essential part of the analysis. Here I suggest two keys for analyzing when and how women's collectivities have shaped the contours of citizenship: (1) the ability of social groups to extend citizenship rights is incumbent upon their inclusion in political spheres, not merely as individual voters but as collectivities articulating claims and representing a constituency; (2) contests around social rights involve both distributional conflicts over resources (that are concerned with income inequalities) and recognition struggles (that assert the disadvantaged position of groups based upon cultural, sexual, and social categories other than class).

These perspectives on the practice of citizenship shed light on some of the current discussions of citizenship in the new democracies in Eastern and Central Europe. Scholars from both Eastern and Western Europe and the United States have raised the perplexing question of why a women's movement has not emerged to respond to the dramatic loss of social and civil rights (Feree 1995; Gal 1996; Smejkalova-Strickland 1994). Loss of reproductive rights, loss of social services, discriminatory employment practices, and the decrease in political representation are reflections of the gendered dimensions of citizenship in the transition to democracy in these societies. Gender equality was part of the Soviet rhetoric and women were accorded many social rights. However, with the collapse of that regime it has become clear that women were not viewed as a constituency, nor did they view themselves as a group with a shared identity and common interests. Unstable parties and permeable political boundaries constitute opportunity structures for mobilized groups in many of these countries, but for feminists the mobilization costs are extremely high. The task of mobilizing women politically implies more than finding a grievance—and there are many, such as repressive laws against abortion and contraception. The challenge begins with how to elaborate a cognitive frame that can forge a shared identity among women who have not considered themselves as a group with common interests in the past. In societies under the veneer of equality between the sexes in the official rhetoric are layers of essentialist ideologies of women's nature and gender difference (Gal 1996; Smejkalova-Strickland 1994). These are the layers that are now appearing in the cultural narratives in many Eastern European countries, one that harkens back to an era of church authority and traditional family roles.

For East German feminists, finding a cognitive frame to mobilize a women's constituency appears most problematic, since it entails locating a set of shared meanings and interpretations of past and present, East and West, male and female interests, family and individual interests. As recent surveys of attitudes among East German women suggest, the search for a political identity involves more than a simple rejection of the past or nostalgia for the security of the old regime (Stolle 1995). On the one side, East German women do not see the family as an expression of patriarchy (Western style feminism), but as a site of resistance against state patriarchy. On the other side, East German women reject the housewife role assigned to them through policies inherited from West Germany after unification. As recent surveys suggest (Stolle 1995), labor market work constitutes a core of East German women's identity and the majority of women view employment and family as equally meaningful for their happiness.[14]

However, a cognitive frame that was built around women's identities as workers would have the stigma of the old regime. Furthermore, given that the unemployment rate for East German women is twice that of men and is increasing, a women's collectivity built around the worker citizen would have to come to terms with the unequal gender power relations in the family, market, and politics. Implicit in the earlier discussions of collective identity formation is that representing grievances is part of the framing process. For East German women, this would entail a rejection of values and practices of family members as units of resistance against authoritarianism.

Myra Marx Feree (1995) in her discussion of feminist identities makes the astute observation that collective identity is neither simply a reflection of the past nor independent of it, but a shared history actively constructed and interpreted. To compose a women's constituency, feminists in Eastern Europe have to imagine citizenship frames that are neither tainted by associations with the old regime of worker citizens nor by replicas of Western-style feminism.

1. There is a vast literature on gender scripting within citizenship frameworks: *see* Pateman's (1988) pathbreaking work on classic texts; for an analysis of gender neutral concepts in Marshall, *see* Fraser (1989), Gordon (1994), Hobson (1994), Orloff (1993), and Pedersen (1994); Okin (1989) provides an insightful critique of Rawls.

2. For the power resource theorists, such as Walter Korpi (1989) and Gøsta Esping-Andersen (1990), Marshall's legacy can be seen in the analysis of the politics of numbers; mobilized workers invest their power resources into leftist parties.

3. This theoretical stance goes against the grain within a body of feminist literature that maintains that there are women's interests beyond the political context, either an essentialized notion of motherhood or care (Gilligan 1982) or a view of relational feminism based upon women's distinct spheres: *see* Elshstain (1981) and Offen (1988).

4. De-essentializing gender has been a crucial contribution of the postmodernist project: *see* Fraser (1989); Butler and Scott (1992). It is a point of departure for analyzing sites of convergence among fragmented and multiple identities in the practice of citizenship.

5. Here I acknowledge my debt to the social movement literature that has brought to light the role of cultural meanings in the mobilization process: *see* Morris and Mueller (1992); Melucci (1995); Snow and Benford (1992); Snow et al. (1986).

6. Many researchers have used the Scandinavian welfare state as model or exemplar of a women-friendly state. This term was coined by Helga Hernes (1987) who maintained that gendered citizenship has been followed by a gendered mobilization in Scandinavia. Women were mobilized through interaction with public policies. In this chapter, I reveal that policies are also a reflection of the success of women's groups to represent themselves as a constituency.

7. Marilyn Lake (1996), writing about feminist groups in the post-suffrage era, calls this period the golden age of feminist citizenship.

8. Wendy Sarvasy (1992) argues that service was a mobilizing frame among feminists, but this is not a dominant view in American feminist activism around maternalism; *see* Michel (1996).

9. Norway is the exception, since maternalist issues formed the basis of feminist activism there; *see* Leira (1992).

10. Ellen Key (1912) can be seen as the ultimate maternalist: she was highly critical of all feminist movements that sought influence in male domains of politics and the labor market.

11. Sweden's Social Democratic Women's Union increased their membership from 7,302 in 1930 to 26,882 in 1940. The National Association of Housewives mailing list grew steadily during this decade: 10,000 newsletters were sent in 1930, and by 1940, over 23,550 women received newsletters (Lindholm 1990:88, 99). This is remarkable if one considers that these figures showed that almost twice the number of women were now organized compared to those in the suffrage campaign (Losman 1987:199).

12. It was common practice for some factories to fire women when they married and standard procedure for insurance companies and banks to dismiss women five months after marriage (Wikander 1992).

13. Also discussed in this period was extending public provision of child care. This measure had to wait for the pressure of women's movements in the 1960s and 1970s.

14. A striking finding from a 1993 survey in Germany is that a much higher proportion of East German women than East German men (or men and women from the West) indicated that they would like to be employed even if they did not need the money (Stolle 1994).

REFERENCES

Arbetets Kvinnor. 1932. "Utredning om Gift Kvinnas Statsjanst." March:4–5.

Barbalet, J. M. 1988. *Citizenship.* Buckingham: The Open University Press.

Brubaker, W. R. 1992. *Citizenship and Nationhood in France and Germany.* Cambridge, MA: Harvard University Press.

Butler, Judith, and Joan W. Scott. 1992. *Feminists Theorize the Political.* London: Routledge.

Dietz, Mary. 1992. "Context is All: Feminism and Theories of Citizenship." In *Dimensions of Radical Democracy: Pluralism, Citizenship, and Community,* edited by Chantal Mouffe. London: Verso.

Eisenstein, Hester. 1995. "The Australian Femocrat Experiment: A Feminist Case for Bureaucracy." In *Feminist Organizations: Harvest of the New Women's Movement,* edited by Myra Marx Feree and Patricia Y. Martin. Philadelphia: Temple University Press.

Elshtain, Jean Bethke. 1981. *Public Man, Private Woman: Women in Social and Political Thought.* Princeton, NJ: Princeton University Press.

Eskillsson, Lena. 1991. *Drommen om Kamratsamhallet.* Stockholm: Carlssons.

Esping-Andersen, Gøsta. 1990. *The Three Worlds of Welfare Capitalism.* Princeton, NJ: Princeton University Press.

Feree, Myra Marx. 1995. "Patriarchies and Feminisms: The Two Women's Movements of Post-Unification Germany." *Social Politics: International Studies of Gender, State, and Society* 2(3):10–24.

Fraser, Nancy. 1989. *Unruly Practices, Power Discourse, and Gender in Contemporary Social Theory.* Minneapolis: University of Minnesota Press.

Gal, Susan. 1996. "Feminism in Civil Society: Some Reflections on Eastern Europe." In *Transitions: Global Feminism,* edited by Joan Scott and Cora Kaplan. London: Routledge.

Gelb, Joyce. 1989. *Feminism and Politics: A Comparative Perspective.* Berkeley, CA: University of California Press.

Gilligan, Carol. 1982. *In a Different Voice: Pyschological Theory and Women's Development.* Cambridge, MA: Harvard University Press.

Gordon, Linda. 1994. *Pitied But Not Entitled: Single Mothers and the History of Welfare.* New York: The Free Press.

Hernes, Helga. 1987. *Welfare State and Woman Power: Essays in State Feminism.* Oslo: Norwegian University Press.

Hirdman, Yvonne. 1989. *Att Lagga Livet till Ratta: Studier I Sventsk Folkhems Politik.* Stockholm: Norstedts Forlag.

Hobson, Barbara. 1990. "No Exit, No Voice: Women's Economic Dependency and the Welfare State." *Acta Sociologica* 3:235–250.

Hobson, Barbara. 1993. "Feminist Strategies and Gendered Discourses in Welfare States: Married Women's Right to Work in the U.S. and Sweden During the 1930s." Pp. 396–429 in *Mothers of a New World: Maternalist Politics and the Origins of Welfare States,* edited by Seth Koven and Sonya Michel. New York: Routledge and Kegan Paul.

Hobson, Barbara. 1994. "Solo Mothers, Policy Regimes, and the Logics of Gender." In *Gendering Welfare Regimes,* edited by Diane Sainsbury. London: Sage.

Hobson, Barbara. 1996. "Gendered Identities, Women's Agency, and the Practice of Citizenship." *Feministche Studien.*

Honig, Bonnie, ed. 1995. *Feminist Interpretations of Hannah Arendt.* University Park, PA: Pennsylvania State University Press.

Jensen, Jane. 1987. "Changing Discourse, Changing Agendas: Political Rights and Reproductive Policies in France." Pp.64–88 in *The Women's Movements of the United States and Europe: Consciousness, Political Opportunity, and Public Policy,* edited by Mary Katzenstein and Carol Mueller. Philadelphia:

Temple University Press.

Jensen, Jane, and Mariette Sineau. 1995. "Family Policy and Women's Citizenship in Mitterand's France." *Social Politics: International Studies of Gender, State, and Society* 3(2):244–269.

Jones, Kathleen B. 1994. "Identity, Action, and Locale. *Social Politics: International Studies in Gender, State, and Society* 1(3):256–271.

Key, Ellen. 1912. *The Woman Movement*. New York: Putnam.

Kock, Karin. 1935. "Kris i Befolkningsfragan." *Husmodersforbundets Medlemsblad* (February): 1, 4, 5.

Korpi, Walter. 1989. "Power Politics and State Autonomy in the Development of Social Citizenship." *American Sociological Review* 54:309–328.

Koven, Seth, and Sonya Michel, eds. 1993. "Mothers of a New World: Maternalist Politics," in *Mothers of a New World: Maternalist Politics and the Origins of Welfare States*. New York: Routledge and Kegan Paul.

Koven, Seth, and Sonya Michel. 1990. "Womanly Duties: Maternalist Politics and the Origins of Welfare States in France, Germany, Great Britain and the United States, 1820–1920." *The American Historical Review* 1076–1108.

Ladd-Taylor, M. 1994. *Mother-Work: Women, Child Welfare, and the State, 1890–1930*. Urbana: University of Illinois Press.

Lake, Marilyn. 1994. "Personality, Individuality, Nationality: Feminist Conceptions of Citizenship, 1902–1940." *Australian Feminist Studies* 19:25–38.

Lake, Marilyn. 1996. "The Inviolable Woman: Feminist Conceptions of Citizenship in Australia, 1900–1925." *Gender and History* 8(2): 192–211.

Landes, Joan B. 1995. "Novus Ordo Saeclorum: Gender and Public Space in Arendt's Revolutionary France." In *Feminist Interpretations of Hanna Arendt*, edited by Bonnie Honnig. University Park, PA: Pennsylvania State University Press.

Leira, Arnlaug. 1992. *Welfare States and Working Mothers*. Cambridge, England: Cambridge University Press.

Lewis, Jane. 1993. *Women and Social Policies in Europe: Work, Family and State*, edited by Jane Lewis. Aldershot, England: Edward Elgar.

Lewis, Jane. 1991. "The Politics of Motherhood: Child and Maternal Welfare in England." In *Maternity & Gender Policies: Women and the Rise of the European Welfare States, 1880s–1950s*, edited by Gisela Bock and Pat Thane. London: Routledge.

Lewis, J., and E. Ostner. 1994. "Gender and the Evolution of Social Policies." ZES Arbeitspaper, Nr. 4/94. Bremen: Centre for Social Policy Research.

Lindholm, Margaretha. 1990. *Talet Om Det Kvinnliga*. University of Gothenberg.

Lindholm, Margaretha. 1992. *Elin Wagner och Alva Myrdal*. Uddevalla: Anamma Forlag.

Lister, Ruth. 1996. "Dilemmas in Engendering Citizenship." *Economy and Society* 24(1):1–40.

Lister, Ruth. 1993. "Tracing the Contours of Women's Citizenship." *Policy and Politics* 21(1).

Lösman, Beata. 1987. "Kvinnoorganisering och Kvinnororelser i Sverige." In *Handbak i Svensk Kvinnohistoria*, edited by G. Kyle. Stockholm: Carlssons.

Marshall, T.H. 1950. "Citizenship and Social Class and Other Essays." Cambridge, England: Cambridge University Press.

Melucci, Alberto. 1995. "A Strange Kind of Newness: What's New in New Social Movements." In *New Social Movements: From Ideology to Identity*, edited by Enrique Larana, Hank Johnston, and Joseph Gusfield. Philadelphia: Temple University Press.

Michel, Sonya. 1996. *Children's Interests/Mothers' Rights*. Princeton, NJ: Princeton University Press.

Morris, Aldon, and Carol Mueller. 1992. *Frontiers in Social Movement Theory.* New Haven: Yale University Press.

Mouffe, Chantal. 1992. "Feminism, Citizenship, and Radical Democratic Politics in the Return of the Political." In *Feminists Theorize in the Political*, edited by Judith Butler and Joan Scott. New York: Routledge.

Myrdal, Alva. 1936. "Fackforeningsfolket och Befolkningspolitiken." *Fackforeningsrorelsen* 293–299.

Myrdal, Alva. 1945. *Nation and Family.* London: Kegan Paul, Trench, Trubner, and Co.

Myrdal, Alva, and Gunnar Myrdal. 1935. *Kris i Befolkningsfrågan.* Stockholm: Bonnier.

Myrdal, Gunnar. 1935. "Befolkningsfrågan och Kvinnofrågan." *Hertha*, April: 81–82.

Offen, Karen. 1988. "Defining Feminism: A Comparative and Historical Approach." *Signs* 14:157–199.

Ohlander, Ann-Sofie. 1992. "The Invisible Child: The Struggle Over Social Democratic Family Policy." Pp. 213–236 in *Creating Social Democracy: A Century of the Social Democratic Party in Sweden*, edited by Klaus Misgeld, Karl Molin, and Klas Amark. University Park, PA: Pennsylvania State University Press.

Okin, S.M. 1989. *Justice, Gender, and the Family.* New York: Basic Books.

Orloff, Ann Shola. 1993. "Gender and the Social Rights of Citizenship: The Comparative Analysis of State Policies and Gender Relations." *American Sociological Review* 5:303–328.

Pateman, Carole. 1989. *The Disorder of Women: Democracy, Feminism and Political Theory.* Stanford, CA: Stanford University Press.

Pedersen, Susan. 1993. "Catholicism, Feminism, and the Politics of the Family during the Late Third Republic." In *Mothers of a New World: Maternalist Politics and the Origins of Welfare States*, edited by Seth Koven and Sonya Michel. New York: Routledge.

Pedersen, Susan. 1994. *Family, Dependence, and the Origins of the Welfare State: Britain and France, 1914–1945.* Cambridge, England: Cambridge University Press.

Phillips, Anne. 1991. *Engendering Democracy.* Cambridge, England: Basil Blackwell.

Rawls, J. 1971. *A Theory of Justice.* Cambridge: Belknap of Harvard University Press.

Saraceno, C. 1992. *Trends in the Structure of the Family from 1950 to the Present.* Florence: UNICEF.

Saraceno, C. 1997. "Reply: Citizenship is Context Specific." *International Labor and Working Class History* (Fall/52).

Sarvasy, Wendy. 1992. "Postsuffrage Feminism, Citizenship, and the Quest for a Feminist Welfare State." *Signs* 17:329–362.

Siim, Birte. 1994. "Engendering Democracy: Social Citizenship and Political Participation for Women in Scandinavia." *Social Politics: International Studies in Gender, State, and Society.*

Skocpol, Theda. 1992. *Protecting Soldiers and Mothers.* Cambridge, MA: Harvard University Press.

Smejkalova-Strickland, Jirina. 1994. "Do Czech Women Need Feminism? Perspectives on Feminist Theories and Practices in Czechoslovakia." *Women's Studies International Forum* 17(2/3):277–283.

Snow, David A., and Robert D. Benford. 1992. "Master Frames and Cycles of Protest." Pp. 133–155 in *Frontiers in Social Movement Theory*, edited by A.D. Morris and C.M. Mueller. New Haven: Yale University Press.

Snow, David A., E. Burke Rochford, Jr., Steven K. Worden, and Robert D. Benford. 1986. "Frame Alignment and Mobilization." *American Sociological Review* 51: 464–481).

Stolle, Dietlind. 1995. "The Impact of German Unification of the Identity of East

German Women." Paper presented at the Hampshire Symposium, Conway, June 23–29.

Svenska Kvinnors Medborgarforbund. 1931. *Kort Berattelse om Dess Forsta Tio Ar, 1921–1931.* Stockholm: J.R. Karlson.

Thorell, Ruth Hamrin. 1969. "Ruth Hamrin Thorell i Riksdagen." *Hertha* (February): 23–24.

Thorell, Ruth Hamrin, Ulla Lindstrom, and Gunborg Stenberg. 1969. *Kvinnors Rost och Ratt.* Stockholm: Allmanna Forlaget.

Tingsten, Herbert. 1973. *The Swedish Social Democrats: Their Ideological Development.* Translated by Greta Frankel and Patricia Howard-Rosen. Totowa, NJ: Bedminster Press.

Turner, Bryan. 1992. "Outline of a Theory of Citizenship." In *Dimensions of Radical Democracy: Pluralism, Citizenship, and Community,* edited by Chantal Mouffe. London: Verso.

Wikander, Ulla. 1992. "Kvinnorna i den Tidiga Industrialiseringen." In *Kvinnhistoria.* Stockholm: Utbildningsradion.

11 SUBSTANTIATING A WORKER'S RIGHT TO COMPENSATION

T. Ryken Grattet

The relevance of critical sociolegal studies rarely has been more apparent than in the previous decade of debates over the political utility of "rights" discourse. At stake in such debates is the principal strategy of modern social reform movements, which have relied heavily on rights claiming as a method for aiding oppressed groups and taken for granted the moral correctness of expanding rights. The conservative and communitarian critique is that the present preoccupation with assigning rights to everything has severed the meaning of the term from its constitutional basis and that the proliferation of rights engenders conflict between groups, accentuates the selfish-individualist strand of American culture, and signals the decline of community. While this critique views the denigration of rights discourse as recent phenomena, a second critique sees rights, like all other legal concepts, as incoherent, indeterminate, and internally contradictory because, for example, policies expanding rights sometimes contain contradictory goals, such as simultaneously promising liberty and state "protection" (Minow 1987: 1864). According to this perspective,

> Rights are too contingent to be relied upon. Even small changes in setting or circumstances modify or minimize the meaning of rights. Thus, rights are neither inherent nor generalizable. The consequences of rights are indeterminate. There is nothing there. (Milner 1991:259)

As a response to these critiques a reconstruction of rights discourse has emerged.

THE RECONSTRUCTION OF RIGHTS DISCOURSE

This reconstructed rights discourse accepts much of the initial criticisms, but contends that abstract concepts like rights are not entirely indeterminate but instead take on specific meaning only within local contexts and within "interpretive communities" (Geertz 1983; Minow 1987). While the meanings of rights lack a foundation in pure logic or nature, they are anchored in the cultures of local communities, people who agree about the meaning of rights. Contrary to the initial critique, which sees rights discourse as accelerating the disintegration of community, rights discourse is understood as an important mechanism by which communities are formed. When groups assert rights they are marking out an identity, defining the relations between themselves and other groups in society, and defining the relationship between themselves and the formal institutions of governance (Schneider 1986). Thus, the meaning members of an interpretive community attach to rights is contingent upon the experiences and practical activities of that community.[1] As yet, little empirical research has been done on the local production of rights claims. Bearing in mind the critique of rights and its attempted reconstruction, this chapter describes the ways in which workers compensation reformers sought to implement social insurance for industrial accidents. In particular, I examine the ways in which compensation activists mobilized and attached context-specific meaning to the concept of rights, and what (if any) relationship rights claiming has to the formation of interpretive communities.[2]

Mobilizing for Compensation Reform

There is a dual sense in which movements for social reform are all about organizing. First, and most obviously, some of the basic problems confronting would-be reformers are solved by "organizing." Activists require ways of making connections with other like-minded activists, circulating information about their cause, mobilizing mass participation, and accumulating material resources (Jenkins 1983). In the modern West, formal organizations are widely understood as the most effective means of accomplishing these goals (Thomas et al. 1987). A second sense in which social movements are all about organizing is that a central product of social movements are new ways of organizing social practices. In other words, movements promote "frames" or "designs" for social practice that include the construction of new identities and reorganized relations between social groups. Even after specific instrumental goals of social reform fail, the lasting impacts of movements can be novel meaning constructions (McAdam 1994: 48–52; McCann 1991).

The question of how the second of these by-products of social movements is created has been the concern of two largely separate fields of inquiry. The first is social movement theory emphasizing "framing" processes

(Snow et al.1986; Snow and Benford 1988). "Framing" denotes the process by which movement "organizers seek to join the cognitive orientations of individuals with those of social movement organizations . . . framing efforts can be thought of as acts of cultural appropriation, with movement leaders seeking to tap highly resonant ideational strains in mainstream society as a way of galvanizing activism" (McAdam 1994: 32–33). For the present purpose, the central premise of this perspective is that movement objectives and legitimating frames are constructed from appropriated cultural materials, such as long-standing cultural symbols and the frames of prior movements. These elements form a "tool kit" (Swidler 1986) for movement organizers, who use them to piece together distinctive frames to garner support for their movement. Cultural "tool kits" therefore provide both opportunities for and constraints on movement work.

A second research tradition is work on "legal mobilization" (Zemans 1983). This group of scholars focuses more directly on movements that view law as a vehicle to promote social reform. According to this perspective, legal culture represents an extremely salient part of the cultural "tool kit" of reformers. Law is understood not simply as a cluster of formal institutions which can be used as instruments to pursue movement goals. Rather law is understood as an "identifiable tradition of symbolic practice" (McCann 1991: 227) through which reformers' goals are constituted. Law's symbols, however, do not provide reformers with fixed and determinant meanings. Legal concepts, such as rights, are given substance within the local context of their use. In other words, reformers add meaning to—or "substantiate"— legal constructs in particular struggles. This, for example, accounts for the variety of ways in which rights have been employed by social movements.

Combining the insights from both "framing" and "legal mobilization" analyses I examine the substantiation of rights claims within the movement for workers' compensation. I find three key insights of these perspectives. First, both perspectives suggest that rights claims can foster the formation of an interpretive community (McCann 1991; Minow 1987) or, in the language of the framing literature, can elicit participation by creating opportunities for social actors to identify with the grievances and goals of the movement (Snow et al. 1986). Both focus specifically on the process by which the individuals whose struggles are the focal concern for the movement come to share identification with a community of similarly situated agents. As aptly posed by Milner (1991: 269), the questions are: "What is the process through which these communities are formed? Do rights act as a common ground? Do rights in fact invite participation? By whom and with what results?" Such questions are designed to yield insight into the precise ways that rights claiming is connected to the formation of interpretive communities.

Second, the framing and legal mobilization perspectives view cultural materials as providing both opportunities and constraints for the construction of movement products. Both perspectives stress that users of "master" frames (Snow and Benford 1988) and abstract legal concepts like rights have latitude in how they deploy them. As Merry (1990: 6) notes, legal cultures provide symbols which can be manipulated by their members for strategic goals. Likewise, central to the "tool kit" model of culture-in-action is the idea that cultural elements can be placed together in "varying configurations to solve different kinds of problems" (Swidler 1986: 273). Both perspectives indicate that rights will be substantiated in strategic ways and stress innovation (Jenness 1995; Jenness and Broad 1994) and the flexibility of cultural materials. However, they also invite attention to the ways legal and movement cultures can place limits on the ability of reformers to imagine truly revolutionary changes.

A final insight relates to a common way that rights are substantiated. Schneider (1986) suggests that rights are mobilized by "exploiting the conflict between already settled rights claims and practices violating those rights; by exploiting implicit contradictions within settled discursive logics of rights; or by developing logical extensions or new practical applications of settled rights claims" (paraphrased by Milner 1991: 233). In other words, rights are substantiated by situating the right of workers to adequate compensation within established conventions of legal thought. A speaker's strategy is to link the present with the past by describing the continuity of the specific interpretation of rights with more long-standing legal concepts and logic.

This chapter investigates the usefulness of these three insights in explaining the form and consequences of reformers' claims that compensation was a worker's right. First, however, I offer a brief description of necessary background and the methods that guide this investigation.

Background and Methods

Although social insurance principles were understood by a handful of elites and policymakers during the 1890s, it was not until 1909 that a social movement to reform the procedures for dealing with industrial accidents emerged. The 19th century system took the stern view that, for the most part, the costs of industrial accidents were to be borne by the worker. The only circumstance in which employers owed compensation to injured workers was when employers were directly at fault for the accident. Since employers were rarely present during the production process, the chances that they would have caused an accident directly were small. Some changes took place in the law from the mid-18th century, but these reforms took the form of minor alterations of the existing system rather than a wholesale dismissal or change. Workers' compensation, the idea that the costs of industrial accidents should be passed on to society through social insurance, emerged in Germany during the 1880s and swept across Europe during the following decades. By 1905 the United States was the only major industrial power that had not switched the way it dealt with industrial accidents over to a social insurance scheme.

One impediment to reform in the United States was that American progressives viewed state governments as the principle sites of reform. Mounting a state-level reform campaign was a daunting task for legislators, especially in the area of industrial policy, because legislators believed that costly reforms in one state might drive industry to neighboring states. Most reformers believed that compensation would result in higher prices for products, since the financial burden of insurance would be passed on to consumers. Thus, reforms must be undertaken cautiously with an eye constantly on what your neighbor was doing. Reforms accomplished in European countries at the national level had to be coordinated across many states to have a comparable effect (i.e., nationwide).

Compensation reformers confronted this need to orchestrate reform across state lines by discussing and debating industrial problems within national-level organizations. Although compensation was discussed in national meetings ranging from the American Federation of Labor to the American Association for Labor Legislation to the National Association of Manufacturers, only two organizations held conferences that were exclusively devoted to the subject. The first was an organization formed by individuals associated with state commissions in Minnesota, New York, and Wisconsin (other states participated as well). This organization was known by two different names during its life course, the National Conference on Workmen's Compensation for Industrial Accidents and the Conference of Commissions on Compensation for Industrial Accidents. Its initial meeting in Atlantic City in 1909 was followed by meetings in Washington, DC in January 1910, Chicago in June 1910, and Chicago in November 1910. Complete transcripts exist for the first and fourth of these meetings. The second organization that devoted meetings specifically to the issue of industrial accidents was the National Civic Federation. The NCF was a unique organization devoted to fostering cooperation between industrial and labor leaders on pressing social problems (Green 1973). The NCF meetings in 1909 and NCF 1911 both concerned the issue of industrial accidents.

I selected two conferences from the National Conference of Commissioners (1909, 1910) and two from the National Civic Federation (1909, 1911) to examine closely for evidence of reformers' rights-claiming strategies. The national conferences sponsored by these organizations occurred during the most intensive period of activity on the industrial accident problem and therefore provide evidence of the meaning key actors in the reform network attached to both compensation alternatives and the prior system. The men and women who participated in these conferences were the leading figures in the movement for compensation, several authored important texts on the subject, and others helped to craft legislation for their home states. The proceedings of the four conferences total 1,200 pages and include 91 speeches. I selected these conferences because they were the central arenas for the national movement for compensation reform.

The present analysis focuses on the ways in which reformers constructed rights claims within the four national conferences. The basic theoretical constructs used in this analysis were developed through a combination of induction and application of existing theoretical materials, most specifically T.H. Marshall's (1950) typology of citizenship rights. Conference texts were closely read, and constructs were provisionally operationalized for the major variants of rights discourse. As evidence was gathered, construct definitions became more focused and delimited. Employing these constructs three elements of each speech were coded and tabulated. In this way, grouping of fragments of text under general constructs is balanced with a more traditional interpretive approach of trying to understand the diversity of meanings reformers associate with general cultural categories.

The unit of analysis for the tabulations is the speech. First, I coded the form of rights discourse speakers employed in their justification of compensation. It is important to note that not all speakers employed rights arguments and that several speakers employed multiple forms of rights discourse. The other forms of justification used on behalf of compensation will be addressed in future work. Second, I identified the speaker's occupational background in order to determine whether members of common occupational groups used rights discourse in similar ways. The major categories are labor, employers, legal, and professional (*see* Table 11–1 for definitions). If rights claims do facilitate interpretive community formation based upon shared status or social location, we might expect that speakers with similar occupational backgrounds employ similar forms of rights discourse. The final element coded is the particular form of compensation the speaker advocated. This allows an analysis of whether or not particular forms of rights discourse are used to support specific reform proposals and not others. If

TABLE 11–1. Occupational Background Classification Scheme

Labor:	Includes union officials, state labor bureau officials, labor lawyers, and academics working on labor issues. (Labor encompasses not only those who work for organized labor but those whose sympathies most likely overlap with those of labor. In truth, only a few participants in the conferences were trade union representatives.)
Employers:	Includes employers and members of employers associations.
Legal:	Includes judges, lawyers, legislators, and law professors.
Professionals:	Includes representatives of other professions: social workers, academics, insurance experts, state bureaucrats. (Those individuals classified as having a Legal background would not be counted as Professionals unless they had a second occupational association, such as a state bureaucrat or academic.)

Note: When this scheme was applied to the speakers at the conferences, many speakers had dual or multiple affiliations. For example, a lawyer who worked for an insurance company would be classified as a lawyer and a professional. Thus, both occupational affiliations were captured. Also, occupational data could not be found for 21 of 91 conference participants.

rights are determinant or constraining constructs to reformers, then they may lead to specific solutions and rule out others. On the other hand, if speakers use similar kinds of rights arguments to justify very different sorts of compensation models, then it suggests that rights are more flexible indeterminate constructs that can be employed in multiple, perhaps even contradictory ways.

The discussion of the analysis proceeds in two phases. First, I describe the multiple meanings attached to rights within compensation reformers' speeches. The focus is on the idiosyncrasies of reformers' constructions and usages of rights. It is a focus on details. The second phase involves a summary of the general forms that rights took within the compensation movement. The purpose is to identify commonalities between reformers' use of rights and to assess the usefulness of the theoretical approaches described earlier.

RIGHTS TO COMPENSATION

Conference speakers incorporated rights claims into their arguments about the industrial accident problem in a variety of ways. The multiple meanings attached to the concept support the interpretivist understanding of law as consisting of "a complex repertoire of meanings and categories understood differently by people depending upon their experience with and knowledge of the law" (Merry 1990: 5). First, a few speakers used rights language in consciously broad and unspecific ways, such as justifying compensation as an "entitlement" of workers, the "duty or obligation" of employers or simply announcing it as a "right" without providing further specification. For example,

> Now, what is the basis of this act? The intention is to provide that every workman injured while working for an employer shall be *entitled* to receive compensation for loss of wages through such injury. (NCF 1910: 9, emphasis added)

Does this speaker mean that such a right is sustained by law or that there exists a broader moral basis for compensation? Perhaps both. Rights, entitlements, and duties are all only partly legal concepts (Milner 1989: 648). Although rights are defined by law and entitlements legally protected, speakers occasionally employ them as though they are rooted in broad nonlegal norms. Which does the speaker mean to signify with the deployment of the term "entitled"? Quite likely, it is precisely this ambiguity that the abstraction of rights relies upon for its force. Vaguely defining something as a "right" implies both that it is an inherent possession of all humans and also supported by the state. While obscuring the exact basis for compensation-as-right, the unsubstantiated use of rights seems crafted to capitalize on the rhetorical power of simply announcing something as a "right" (*see* Williams 1991).

Even as they added substance to the concept of rights, speakers differed with regard to whether they described the right as an inherent property of all humans or whether it was a legal construction. For example, law, more specifically the Constitution, was described as an impediment to the fulfillment of a right.

> . . . that which stands as the palladium of human liberties can be so construed as to deprive the greater portion of the people a right that is inherently theirs . . . (NCF 1910: 189)

In other words, there is an inherent right to compensation that is currently rendered unattainable by the very document designed to express basic rights of citizens. Law as an impediment to the fulfillment of rights can be contrasted with an image of law as the "rights-giver"—rights are legal constructions.

Under employer's liability a man must bring a lawsuit and fight his employer for the purpose of ascertaining whether he is entitled to anything. He does not know his rights until the verdict is in. Under workmen's compensation a man injured is entitled to a payment, ascertained before he is injured and fixed according to the severity of the injury. . . . Under workmen's compensation, rights are previously determined. (NCF 1910: 29–30)

To another speaker, compensation advocates were "furnishing a new right" (CCCIA 1910: 271). The legal constructedness of such a right is evident in that it is "furnished," not claimed. Such contradictory understandings of the origins of rights did not impede the reform process, nor did they make reformers hesitant to utilize rights arguments with one another. Admittedly, most of the rights claiming by compensation reformers were less vague and contradictory than this abstracted form. However, it is important to address it because it shows that the actors themselves make use of the abstractness of the concept and also, from the researchers' standpoint, it demonstrates that textual data cannot always be easily interpreted.

Reformers added substance to the concept of rights in two general ways, which correspond to two elements of T.H. Marshall's typology of rights (1950). On the one hand, they justified a new response to industrial accidents in terms of established civil rights, specifically contractual rights. This led them to see the issue largely as a matter of contractual equality and liberty of contract. According to this view, a change in the law was needed to equalize the employment relation, but at the same time, changing the law to compensation could not impede workers' and employers' ability to freely contract the conditions of the employment relation. Thus, civil rights, mainly in the form of contractual rights, was one interpretive framework through which reformers analyzed the issue. On the other hand, they employed the rationale of the less well-established idea of social rights, which meant that compensation was required to "provide a modicum of economic welfare and security" (Marshall 1950: 10).

Contractual Rights

First is Marshall's (1950: 10) notion of civil rights, which includes "rights necessary for individual freedom—liberty of the person, freedom of speech, thought, and faith, the right to own property and to conclude valid contracts, and the right to justice." The most salient element of these rights for the question of industrial accidents is the right of contract. Accordingly, the basic issue at the center of the "accident problem" was that there were inequalities between workers and employers that rendered the contractual logic of the old employer's liability and common law system an inappropriate, inefficient, and an injust method for dealing with the matter. Reform of the old system was required to eliminate those elements of the law which prevented equitable relations between workers and employers. Without equality, other elements of the employment contract, particularly the presumption of uncoerced agency (liberty), could not hold true. Speakers that used this form of rights argument did not wish to eliminate the metaphor of the contract as the symbol for employment relation. Instead, their idea was to make that contract truly equal through reform.

Let us turn to the specific ways that contractual rights were substantiated. A lawyer for the Minnesota Employer's Liability Commission argues for the restoration of basic prerequisites for contracts this way:

> I simply want to suggest that, so far as my personal views are concerned, I understand that the fundamental reason for all this legislation is that in dangerous employments the employer and employee do not stand on an equality as to ability to contract respecting the danger (CCCIA 1910: 179).

Under the present system, workers were disadvantaged in their relationship to employers. This inequality was cause for change. Whereas compensation promised equality to workers, employers would be given a system that would eliminate the irrationality of the old system. Many employers viewed the old system as an annoyance mainly because it was unpredictable. Although in most cases the common law and employer's liability doctrines enabled employers to escape liability for accidents, occasionally a jury, moved by sympathy, might grant a large verdict in favor of the injured worker: "... we all know that human sympathy of juries and their desire to relieve the unfortunate is always on the side of the employee." A selling point for compensation was that it enabled employers to plan more rationally for the costs associated with irregular jury awards. This fact "points to the possibility of a changed system, more equitable toward the laborer and more scientific and definite for the employer" (ACCWCA 1909: 283). At the same time, organizing accident compensation as an insurance issue also meant that employers would not be blamed for the accidents. Escaping blame protected the public image of the company.

> The term 'industrial insurance' has been propped, and the term 'social insurance' has been adopted to emphasize the idea that this is not

a question of penalizing the employer: it is a question of getting an equitable social condition. (CCCIA 1910: 43)

Thus, promoting equality between workers and employers was connected to other issues like enabling employers to plan more rationally for the costs associated with accidents and saving employers the embarrassment of individual responsibility.

A common historical narrative accompanied the argument about contractual equality, according to which over the last few decades technological changes occurring within industry resulted in more hazardous working conditions. These new conditions dictated an expansion of the responsibilities employers owed workers.

> I have been in the business as a—well, I will use a familiar term which is not obsolete yet—a labor agitator long enough to realize how much the chasm between the two has narrowed with the last few years and how the agencies which bridge it are developing a spirit on the part of the employer that he is willing to recognize the obligation that lies upon him year by year in greater degree. (NCF 1910: 190–191)

This was not only a narrative that workers and their representatives utilized to request greater employer duties. Employers used it to congratulate themselves for at long last coming to recognize fully their duties and obligations to workers (NCF 1910). Increased employer obligations were not purely the offspring of mechanization, but were supposedly part of a rising "awareness" of the duties employers owed workers. One employer described the equalization using terms like "fellowship" and "partnership." For example,

> before an employer can bring himself to the full discharge of his duty and obligation in the matter of safeguarding dangerous machinery, he must come to regard his workmen in a light new to many employers, but which happily is coming to be more and more the common view of the best employers in the land. . . . He cannot adequately discharge this duty while he regards the relationship as that merely of master and man, with no sense of moral obligation for the welfare of the man; but only as it is borne in upon him that his workman is his *partner,* contributing his valuable part to the success of the enterprise. (NCF 1910: 59)

The image of equality was not a foreign concept to employment relations. The employment "contract," which contained ideas about liberty of contract and contractual equality, had for many years signified the basic legal construction of worker and employer relations. Thus, the legal construction of the employment contract provided a powerful standard upon which to measure the justness of the industrial accident system. To justify altering the system, reformers merely needed to find a way of showing it did not measure up to that standard. Thus, rather than challenging the fundamental bases of the employment relation, reformers sought merely to hold it up to its original standards.[3]

In addition, the meaning of the employment contract was frequently modified in reformers' discourse. It was not just an arrangement between worker and employer, but one in which society itself had a role. It was still a contract, but now the relationship consisted of a broad "societal contract" which stressed the obligations of society to workmen. Workers were not merely servants of employers and owners, but toiled for the general benefit of society. According to American Federation of Labor president Samuel Gompers (NCF 1910: 49),

> All we can hope to do is . . . accomplish the desired result and establish some semblance of justice that, for the service which the workers perform to society, the assumption of risk shall not be all their own, but that either industry or society in the interest of humanity shall bear the burden.

This understanding of the employment relation as containing duties and obligations society owed workers fit nicely with the historical narrative about the increasing awareness—now attributed to society, not just employers— that workers were entitled to more than they were getting under the employer's liability system.

> The steel worker, on modern high structures, is compelled to take chances never before demanded of labor. Yet men must do this work. It is part of our civilization. Society depends upon their daring, but it is tardily learning to appreciate its obligation to them. (NCF 1910: 107)

Thus, workers' entitlement to compensation derives not solely from their service to particular employers but from the service they provide to society in general. In a sense, society was a party to the employment contract. Obligations and duties were owed not just by employers but by all of society. This argument leads directly to social insurance as a solution to the accident problem. In theory, if compensation to injured workers was organized as a solution, the costs of accidents could be figured into the general operating expenses of the company and passed on to consumers in the form of slightly higher prices. In other words, society would assume the burden for compensation by paying more for the products of industry.

> Unquestionably, it is a sounder doctrine that it is better for the public to bear, in some shape of an increased cost of product, the burden resulting from compensation to the injured employee rather than to bear the burden of the accident in the shape of support of paupers who are created by accidents. It is much better to prevent pauperism than to undertake to relieve pauperism after such has occurred. (NCF 1910: 218)

This reconstruction of the contractual logic of the employment relation provided a basis for the "social rights" discourse I will turn to in a moment. Suffice it to say that by broadening the metaphor of the contract, reformers neatly connected the past and the future of the law of industrial accidents.

In summary, contractual rights provided a means for reformers to criticize the old system and a basis upon which to construct a new system. Measuring contractual equality contained in the old law of industrial accidents against the ideal of the employment contract, reformers sought to demonstrate that the old system placed workers and employers on an unequal footing. Inequality in the employment relation meant that law needed to be changed to conform to the legal premises of the employment contract. Furthermore, compensation combined the promise of greater equality for workers with a system that freed employers from any blame for causing accidents. This made change less costly for employers, because it meant that reforming the system would not be accomplished by shifting blame from employees to employers. Finally, although interpreting the issue in terms of contract meant that other power inequities within the employment relation were rendered invisible, it was not necessarily a constraint. Reformers expanded the idea of contract, investing it with novel meaning as a broad societal contract. Thus, contractual duties and obligations served as a basic metaphor justifying increasing societal obligations to workers.

Social Rights

The second way reformers added substance to the concept of rights was to justify a worker's entitlement to compensation in terms of "social rights"

(Marshall 1950: 46), the right of all citizens to be free of destitution, starvation, and misery. However, in 1909 social rights were a relatively new basis for justifying change of the law.[4] In contrast to the contractual rights framework which already formed the backbone of the law of the employment relation, the argument that the state has an obligation to provide for the welfare and security of economically marginalized individuals had to be invented.[5] Reformers relied upon two general strategies. First, they linked reform to preexisting legal concepts, prior governmental traditions, and accepted norms of state practice. Such justifications involved piecing together elements of state and legal culture to construct a foundation for reform. Second, they based reform on an amalgam of extralegal cultural elements from theories of poverty from the emerging profession of social work and actuarial theories of social risk. By arranging elements from these varied sources, reformers claimed that shifting the burden of industrial accidents from individuals to society was part of a new social compact in which society—or its proxy, the state—was obliged to protect its most vulnerable elements from pauperization.

The first general way speakers linked social rights to accident law reform was to portray reform as consistent with prior governmental traditions and norms of state practice. One way speakers accomplished this was to argue that throughout history the governments of just and humane civilizations recognized their obligation to care for their weakest members. Without providing specific examples, one labor union representative argued that America was departing from established norms of proper government role by neglecting the poor.

> It has been recognized from time immemorial and under all of the older forms of government, that the obligation rested inherently on the State to care for its non-productive members, whether through invalidity, from accident, sickness, or otherwise, that obligation was inherent. (NCF 1910: 187)

Another labor spokesman gave a more direct indictment.

> It seems to me that in our mad rush for wealth and power, for idleness and leisure, we are not properly regardful of the interests and the happiness of our neighbors. It seems to me that no country is really and truly great that is not concerned about the welfare of the humblest of its citizens or the least of the little children in the factories. (NCF 1910: 342)

Such quotes connect the extension of social rights to the construction of a "great" society and affirm national identity and distinctiveness.[6] State action on poverty was an important, although recently neglected, part of the national project. Economic strength was not sufficient to propel the nation into greatness. As it was put by one speaker, the welfare of the laborer is "essential to the welfare of the nation" (NCF 1910: 185). Thus, the state was held accountable for fulfilling the broader social purpose of preserving the health and welfare of its citizens.

Within such an understanding, a powerful motive for reform was that state practices were shown actually to contribute to poverty. The problem was worse than benign neglect, because state practices, in fact, caused injured workers to enter the ranks of the poor. For example,

> The large bulk of pauperism is primarily due to the bad environment of the individual, and is a result in part of our so-called employer's liability legislation. (ACCWCA 1909: 46–47)

Where the law contributed to pauperization there was the greatest need for reform. In this way, criticism of the old laws was founded on the premise that the state should work to reduce poverty and it should start by eliminating programs and policies that unintentionally contribute to it (*see also* ACCWCA 1909: 40).

The next strategy reformers used to legitimate social rights in terms of established legal and state cultures was to link social rights to contractual rights. In other words, reformers justified social rights in terms of contractual rights. For example, J.H. Boyd, an Ohio Employer's Liability Commission member and the subsequent author of *Workmen's Compensation* (1913), argued in favor of compulsory compensation.

> You are furnishing a new right, a new remedy. And, as has been pointed out by Mr. Bailey, it is in the nature of an equitable right. And for that reason it should be obligatory on both parties. It comes back to that. And for the same reason it is a national necessity, and for the same reason that compulsory educational scheme is required for children from six years to fourteen years of age to go to school, regardless of whether their parents want them to go or not, so this is a national necessity for the general benefit of society. (CCCIA 1910: 271)

Boyd begins by arguing that a logical consequence of the contractual rights view of compensation is that it should be compulsory, that is, "obligatory on both parties." However, he continues by describing reform as a "national necessity" much like another social right, compulsory education. In other words, what starts off as a justification based upon the equality between employers and workers winds up being a benefit for the nation in general. While Boyd does not say specifically that reducing poverty is his goal, he draws a parallel with compulsory education, a policy he claims was enacted for the general welfare of society—especially its weakest members. Boyd knows that compulsory education is a social right that enjoys widespread support. Thus, he rather compactly demonstrates that compulsory compensation is consistent with both pre-existing notions of contractual equality and established policies aimed at improving the health and welfare of the nation. Thus, in trying to justify compulsory compensation, Boyd constructed an argument that fused contractual rights with a social rights framework.

The strategy of justifying compensation by describing its similarity to other kinds of policies, like compulsory education, represents another way that reformers drew upon elements of state and legal culture to advance compensation. For example, a speaker draws a parallel between care of the mentally ill and victims of industrial accidents.

> We do not have any scruples about taking care of society's mental wrecks. The state provides institutions for their care; perhaps largely because they may become a menace to society, dangerous to its citizens. Why should we show any scruples about taking care of the physical wrecks of society? I believe that industry ought to bear the burden of own accidents. (ACCWCA 1909: 264)

Other speakers drew parallels between compensation and Roosevelt's conservation policies, arguing that compensation represented a "conservation" of human resources (NCF 1910: 109, 343). This approach identifies compensation as consistent with prior governmental policy commitments. Such linkages were crucial given that one concern compensation advocates shared was whether or not policymakers and judges would perceive compensation to be incompatible with traditional functions of American government.

These examples demonstrate that one way reformers sought to create a foundation for social rights was by drawing upon elements of state and legal culture. They emphasized that social rights were consistent with "well-established" norms of governmental practice, arguing that state efforts toward reducing poverty were an indicator of a just and humane civilization. Where existing state practices contributed to pauperization, speakers argued that there was a glaring and immediate reason for reform. They put forward an argument that rooted social rights on the more well-established contractual rights. They pointed to other areas of state policy that embodied a social rights logic, such as compulsory education and mental health policy; they developed arguments based simultaneously on contractual rights and social rights. All of these strategies reflect a common element, use of some element of the received culture of the state to justify a social rights initiative.

Another way speakers substantiated social rights claims was by linking compensation to extralegal sources of legitimacy. These sources allowed speakers to justify the need for compensation in much broader terms. In other words, the social rights claims used to justify compensation were not only founded upon prior legal and governmental traditions, but also upon other institutions and other sources of received wisdom. In particular, compensation was aligned with two extralegal institutions: actuarial theories associated with the growing insurance industries and social theories of poverty linked to the profession of social work.

The influence of social work theory was evident in the remarks of a number of speakers, none more than Lee Frankel, a government actuary who conducted research and co-authored an important volume on the European laws (Frankel and Dawson 1910).

> The poor are not responsible for their condition. If there is any theory that has been exploded in the last ten or fifteen years in the treatment of those who have become impoverished, in the relation of charitable organizations to their beneficiaries,—if there is one fact that has been brought out prominently, it is, that the large bulk of those who become recipients of charitable aid are the creatures of their environment, and that they are not so because of any shortcoming, carelessness, or other inferiority in themselves. (ACCWCA 1909: 46)

The distinctive feature of professional social work theories of poverty was the shift of blame from the victims of poverty to the environment. Social workers offered this theory to counter the moralistic view of poverty that governed the response of private charitable organizations (Rothman 1980). Social work theory complemented the motives of compensation reformers who wanted to remove the investigation of individual fault from industrial accident case processing. In this view, victims of accidents were not to be pitied or given support based upon charity. Rather, compensation was their right, a matter of justice. In one speaker's view, the idea was to substitute "justice for charity" (NCF 1910: 110). Charity was regularly criticized as a motive for reform.

We must admit now that it is not *just* to place on the back of the workmen injured, the financial as well as the physical burden of the accidents that to-day are the inevitable result of trade hazard. Nor can we to-day proceed as if public policy is subserved by relegating the injured workingman or his family to charity, under an employer's liability system, when the whole world under workmen's compensation regards the financial burden of the industrial accident as part of the expense of production. (NCF 1910: 28)

Despite occasional lapses into heartfelt humanistic pleas for changing the system, reformers wanted to define compensation as a right, as justice for services rendered. Defining relief of poverty as a right meant removing from private hands and placing under state control. In other words, reformers understood that charity is a matter for private community institutions, whereas rights and justice are the concern of governments.

Actuarial theories provided another set of concepts upon which to construct compensation. Actuarial theory meant seeing accidents as essentially faultless.

An accident would not be an accident if it could be foreseen, predicted, avoided or prevented. How, then, can anybody be responsible and liable for it? The accident is an inevitable incident of the trade. It is not due, legally speaking, to the carelessness of the employee. It just happens. It can only be put to the imperfections of the trade. Therefore, the only logical and just way to compensate for the injuries done is by *insurance*." (NCF 1910: 18)

This view of accident does not seek to shift blame over to employers (*see also* NCF 1910: 322). In principle, an insurance system relieves both workers and employers from fault.

The term "industrial insurance" has been propped, and the term "social insurance" has been adopted to emphasize that this is not a question of penalizing the employer: it is a question of getting an equitable solution. (CCCIA 1910: 75)

The displacement of fault is comparable to the social work principle that paupers are not responsible for their condition. The actuarial approach, however, extends this even further by not only relieving the injured workers from blame, but also employers. However, while social work ideology points toward a broadly therapeutic response to social problems, it does not contain a clear organization model for a new system. The actuarial perspective, on the other hand, contains a specific plan for organizing compensation. Such a plan involves the creation of an insurance mechanism that would distribute the costs of accidents across an entire industry, employers pay premiums to the insurer, the costs of those premiums are then passed on to the consumer in the form of higher prices for the industry's product, injured workers must file a claim to receive compensation, and the system places caps on the amounts that can be recovered. There were remaining issues, such as whether or not the state should be the insurer or private stock insurance companies or whether companies could insure themselves, but the basic organizational features of the system are easily defined once the issue is understood as an actuarial problem.

In summary, reformers substantiated social rights with two general strategies. The first involved showing how the extension of social rights in the area of industrial accidents was consistent with prior legal and governmental traditions. They sought to define compensation as compatible with norms of humane governance, combined arguments containing a social rights logic with those of the more well-established contractual rights, and drew parallels between compensation reform and other accepted policies. All of these strategies are attempts to substantiate social rights by founding them upon pre-established elements of state and legal culture. The second strategy involves substantiating social rights by linking them to professional theories of social work and the actuarial field. These two professions contain partially overlapping patterns of thought, specifically with relation to questions of individual agency and fault. However, they also complement one another—social work theory offers a general theory of poverty and the actuarial perspective provides an organizational template for compensation systems.

DISCUSSION

The preceding section described the diverse deployments of rights discourse within the movement for worker's compensation. Here, I return to and assess the three propositions from the framing and legal mobilization perspectives.

Rights and Intrepretive Communities

The first proposition is that rights discourse contributes to the formation of an interpretive community or, in the language of framing analysts, is employed to mobilize movement participants. What evidence exists to support or refute the idea that rights are used to forge interpretive communities? Unlike women's rights, the movements for rights for the physically disabled, homeless rights, or most any other kind of rights movement, declaring the right of compensation was not designed to mobilize participation from the victims of industrial accidents, nor was it designed to mobilize workers. More specifically, the legal mobilization perspective contains a "bottom-up" imagery of how rights are substantiated—collectives of actors are unified by common definitions of their situation. Rights claims, so this argument goes, have a unifying effect because they are given context-specific meaning from the everyday life experiences of the participants. While this imagery is appealing for explaining the rights campaigns for the physically disabled, women, and gays and lesbians, it works less well for campaigns in which proxies, like the professionals involved in the present case, employ rights discourse on behalf of a third party. In other words, the rights deployment within the compensation movement does not fit the image supplied by the first proposition. Mobilization of participants or the formation of an interpretive community among those affected by the social problem is not the goal of these reformers. As a result, the particular forms of rights discourse are not constructed from the everyday experiences of accident victims.

But the image of rights deployment as a mechanism to facilitate the creation of interpretive communities can not be completely dismissed. A slightly revised version of this idea involves understanding that many social reform movements are not principally concerned with mass mobilization or the formation of interpretive communities of the aggrieved. Such movements consist of collective actors who serve as proxies, who perhaps attempt to be sensitive to the needs of the groups of actors whose conditions they seek to change, but at the same time have their own interests to pursue. When such collective actors substantiate rights it often reflects more about their own lifeworlds than those of the aggrieved. Compensation reformers fit this revised image of the relation between interpretive community formation and rights usage. To more thoroughly demonstrate this, further evidence can be introduced on the general ways interest groups surrounding the industrial accident problem employed rights claims.

Using the occupational background coding classifications in Table 11–1, Table 11–2 shows the distribution of rights claims across major interest groups. Focusing first on occupation, the largest portion of the conference participants (38.5%) were associated with professional occupations. Labor representatives constituted the next biggest contingent (22%), followed closely by employers (18.7%), and, finally, representatives of the legal profession (13.2%). Relative to their overall level of participation in the conferences, some

TABLE 11–2. Number of Social or Contractual Rights Claims by Speaker's Occupational Background (N = 91).

	Labor	Employers	Legal	Professional	Total
Speakers	20	17	12	35	
	(22%)	(18.7%)	(13.2%)	(38.5%)	
Social Rights Claims	9	5	3	18	27
Contractual Rights Claims	6	3	2	8	15

groups were more likely to use rights arguments than others. The cell percentages show that both labor and professionals were more likely to describe the issue in terms of both variants of rights discourse. Employers might be less likely to employ rights discourse because they feared that emphasizing employees rights would weaken their ability to control the terms of the employment relation. In their view, justifying reform on the basis of worker's rights might result in workers asserting an avalanche of rights-based claims. Lawyers' reluctance to use rights-based arguments is perplexing, given that lawyers default ways of thinking about questions like this were probably more influenced by legal language and symbols. But having more technical or legalistic definitions of rights might actually make lawyers more reluctant to employ rights in the broad metaphorical way that the other groups do.

Examination of the right marginals reveals that out of all 91 participants 27 employed the social rights arguments and 15 contractual rights arguments.[7] The difference in the totals, however, is mainly accounted for by professionals' proclivity for social rights arguments—the other groups use both arguments with similar frequency. Why do professionals employ rights arguments more frequently than other groups? If there was any group of actors that was trying to construct an interpretive community through compensation reform, it was professionals. However, their use of social rights arguments is not designed to elicit participation.[8] Instead, it is oriented toward building alliances with other professions. As the discussion presented in the prior section indicates, all of the social rights arguments are designed to parallel the arguments of other professions: social workers, actuaries, and, albeit abstractly, legal professionals. Because social rights are given meaning from cultural materials from other professions, they can be understood as substantiated out of the everyday worlds compensation reformers occupy. Thus, while interpretive communities of the aggrieved do not provide the basis for the movement for compensation, and while participant mobilization does not appear to be the principle purpose of rights deployment, the interpretive community idea is not completely irrelevant to this case. Compensation reformers used social rights arguments to align themselves with similar professional movements. Furthermore, they substantiated social rights through their everyday life experiences, as members of an emerging professional class.

Determinacy of Rights

The second proposition is that while cultural materials, such rights frames, have no determinant meaning—speakers take them to mean a variety of different things—they still place constraints on reform products. The diverse meanings attached to rights described in the previous section serves as one example of the flexibility of the legal concepts. A method of examining the constraints that rhetorical forms place on movement products is available in Table 11–3. The forms of rights claims are cross-classified with the reform solutions favored by speakers. The most important aspects of this table for demonstrating the relations between forms of rights discourse and support for forms of compensation are the cells showing that social rights and contract rights are used with similar frequencies by speakers offering general support for compensation, and for those advocating optional or compulsory systems. Thus, the table shows that the kind of rights argument a speaker uses does not influence the kind of reform solution he offers. Employing a particular form of rights argument does not constrain one to support a singular policy route. In summary, while rights are clearly used in a multiplicity of ways, they do not wind up being particularly consequential for the kinds of policy options reformers choose.

Building New Rights upon Established Rights

The final proposition refers to the general process by which social movement actors create rights claims. The characteristic features are that speakers construct rights claims by contrasting existing social and legal practices with already settled rights; they use established rights as the metric against which a present issue is compared; they identify contradictions within established rights, and/or they develop "logical" extensions of settled rights. Compensation reformers rights-claiming fits this depiction of the process of rights extension in two major ways. First, several reformers interpreted the issue in terms of right of contract, which represents an indisputably legitimate way of understanding the issue, since it formed the basis of the old system. In the contractual view, compensation was justified as a method for more equitably dividing the costs of industrial accidents between worker and employer. Contractual equality became a standard upon which the old system could be judged. Where reformers could show that it failed to meet those

TABLE 11-3. Numbers Expressing Support for Various Forms of Compensation in Response to Different Rights Claims by Speakers (N = 91).

	Social Rights	Contractual Rights	Did Not Use Rights	N
No Clear Stance Taken	6	3	17	24 (26%)
General Support	11	6	18	31 (34%)
Advocating Optional Compensation	5	3	11	16 (18%)
Advocating Compulsory Compensation	5	3	11	18 (20%)
N	27 (30%)	15 (17%)	56 (62%)	

standards, they implicitly created grounds for changing the system. Reformers who employed contractual rights discourse were not articulating a new basis for the laws, they were simply holding it accountable to its own premises.

Second, several speakers who employed social rights arguments found ways of linking them to pre-existing rights. Some speakers actually fused together contractual rights arguments with social rights, as if to say that a broad social contract exists involving not only the employer and employee, but also society. With the involvement of society in the employment contract, through its proxy the state, the nature of obligation shifted—society was obliged to provide security for workers who might fall into poverty as a result of industrial accidents. Another speaker, in the same sentence, declared the importance of equality in the employment relation while simultaneously stating defining compensation as a "national necessity." In doing so, he merged contractual and social rights, capitalizing on the legitimacy of the former to advance the latter. Finally, a more concrete method reformers used was to describe compensation as consistent with other state policy practices that are based upon social rights, such as the treatment of the mentally ill, conservation policy, or compulsory education.

Thus, this last proposition is borne out in the experience of compensation reformers. More generally, this proposition suggests that an important requirement for social movement organizing is that movement actors find ways of linking the past to the future. They must cast the movement product in relation to tradition, and demonstrate its consistency with history and convention. This process serves a broader purpose than participant mobilization; it satisfies movement actors' own cognitive sense that the reform "fits" into the institutional structure of American society. Rights appear to be handy tools for accomplishing this fitting. Defining something as a right means adding it to a cluster of other items that have historically been protected by the most powerful institution in society.

CONCLUSION

As used by workers compensation reformers, rights are highly flexible constructs. They are abstract concepts that serve to represent social reform as continuous with prior governmental traditions, yet do not impose any particular constraints on reform. Rights do not necessarily facilitate participant mobilization, nor are they used narrowly for that purpose. When professional experts employ rights, the particular forms of rights discourse they create reflect more about their own social location, culture, and experiences than those of the aggrieved. Not surprisingly, the kinds of policy solutions they devise also reflect more about the culture of professionalism than anything else. In short, the cautioning by critics of rights and those who wish to reconstruct them seems well-placed. It cannot be taken for granted that rights expansion will promote the interests of marginalized groups. Attention must be give to which historical agents gain ownership of a particular issue, and how their own positioning influences the construction of rights discourse.

NOTES

I would like to thank Valerie Jenness, Katherine Donato, and Connie L. McNeely for their helpful comments.

1. Criticisms and reconstructions of rights discourse are much more complex than described here. For example, the critique of rights and its attempted rescue are connected to the broader influences of deconstruction, as well as critical and interpretivist approaches to sociolegal studies. For more nuanced accounts of this debate *see* Tushnet 1984, Milner 1989, 1991, Minow 1987, McCann 1991, Villamoare 1991. For a general discussion on the development of critical and interpretivist sociolegal studies *see* Silbey and Sarat (1987), Trubek and Esser (1990), and Harrington and Yngvesson (1990) .

2. Regardless of whether or not rights discourse is a useful political strategy, the quandary over rights provides an opportunity for rolling back many of the state policies that were justified by them. One area in which state policy is currently in jeopardy of receding is what T.H. Marshall (1950) refers to as "social rights." Contemporary national and state conflicts over such issues as educational choice, when people should be thrown off welfare, national health care, homelessness, and the reform of social security signal a reordering and reconstitution of social rights, defining rights in limited rather than expansive ways. It may be an opportune moment to look backward across historical time to examine how social rights were conceived and employed to legitimate such policies in the first place.

3. I am not suggesting that the change to worker's compensation actually increased equality between workers and employers. As Marx and Engels (1978 [1845]) so eloquently described, formal equality tends to be a way in which inequalities between labor and capital are legitimated and obscured.

4. In Marshall's (1950) classification scheme compulsory education is included as a social right. Although compulsory education was established in the United States prior to the 20th century, few other social rights existed prior to worker's compensation.

5. Somers (chapter 7, this volume) makes the case that social rights, in fact, existed in premodern England, but receded in the centuries prior to the 20th century. Nineteenth century relief of the poor in America followed English Poor Laws, which defined relief not as a right, but a charitable response to individuals who fell into poverty because of their own moral inadequacies.

6. Several speakers alluded to the commendable efforts of the European nations on matters of social insurance and industrial accident compensation. A common technique was to show that the American methods were less "advanced" than those of the Europeans. By portraying America as a backwater nation, out of step with world opinion, compensation became an important means of signaling that America had joined the community of just and humane civilizations (CCCIA 1910; NCF 1910, 1911).

7. Although it is not displayed in the present table (see Table 11–3), 56 speakers (62%) never employed either variant of rights discourse. Thus, it is difficult to maintain the argument that these discussions were dominated by the use of rights discourse, although for a sizable number of participants it did represent a way of understanding the accident problem. This is an important reminder that although rights discourse can be important, it is often only one of several possible ways of apprehending an issue.

8. Professions do not gain power and authority by gaining membership. Actually, the opposite is often true. They gain power, prestige, and authority by controlling entry into the profession (Abel 1989) and by defining a narrow professional role.

REFERENCES

Abel, Richard. 1989. *American Lawyers*. New York. Oxford University Press.
Atlantic City Conference on Workmen's Compensation Acts (ACCWCA). 1909. Report, July 29–31. Atlantic City, NJ.
Boyd, J.H. 1913. *Workmen's Compensation*. Indianapolis: Bobbs-Merrill.
Conference of Commissions on Compensation for Industrial Accidents (CCCIA). 1910. Proceedings. Chicago, November 10–12, 1910. Boston: George H. Ellis.
Frankel, Lee K., and Miles M. Dawson. 1910. *Workingmen's Insurance in Europe*. New York. Russell Sage Foundation.
Geertz, Clifford. 1983. *Local Knowledge: Further Essays in Interpretive Anthropology*. New York: Basic Books.
Green, Marguerite. 1973. The National Civic Federation and the American Labor Movement, 1900–1925. Westport, CT: Greenwood Press.
Harrington, Christine, and Barbara Yngvesson. 1900. "Interpretive Social Research." *Law and Social Inquiry* 15: 135.
Jenkins, Craig. 1983. "Resource Mobilization Theory and the Study of Social Movements." *Annual Review of Sociology* 9: 527–553.
Jenness, Valerie. 1995. "Social Movement Growth, Domain Expansion, and Framing Processes: The Gay/Lesbian Movement and Violence Against Gays and Lesbians as a Social Problem." *Social Problems* 42 (1): 145–169.
Jenness, Valerie, and Kendall Broad. 1994. "Antiviolence Activism and the (In)Visibility of Gender in the Gay/Lesbian and Women's Movements." *Gender and Society* 8 (3): 402–423.
Marshall, T.H. 1950. *Citizenship and Social Class and Other Essays*. Cambridge, England. Cambridge University Press.

Marx, K., and F. Engels. 1978 [1845]. "The German Ideology." Pp. 146–200 in *The Marx-Engels Reader*, edited by R.C. Tucker. New York: W.W. Norton.

McAdam, Doug. 1994. "Culture and Social Movements." Pp. 36–57 in Enrique Larana, Hank Johnston, and Joseph R. Gusfield (eds.), *New Social Movements: From Ideology to Identity*. Philadelphia, PA: Temple University Press.

McCann, Michael. 1991. "Legal Mobilization and Social Reform Movements: Notes on Theory and its Application." *Studies in Law, Politics, and Society* 11: 225–254.

Merry, Sally Engle. 1990. *Getting Justice and Getting Even: Legal Consciousness Among Working-Class Americans*. Chicago: University of Chicago Press.

Milner, Neal. 1989. "The Denigration of Rights and the Persistence of Rights Talk: A Cultural Portrait." *Law and Social Inquiry* 14: 631.

Milner, Neal. 1991. "Rights, Politics, Faith, and Judgement: Limits of Interpretive Legal Scholarship." *Studies in Law, Politics, and Society* 11: 255–283.

Minow, Martha. 1987. "Interpreting Rights: An Essay for Robert Cover." *Yale Law Journal* 96: 1860.

National Civic Federation (NCF). 1910. Proceedings of the Tenth Annual Meetings. New York, November 22–23, 1909. New York: National Civic Federation.

National Civic Federation (NCF). 1911. Proceedings of Department of Compensation for Industrial Accidents and Their Prevention. Winter Meeting, December 8, 1911. New York: National Civic Federation.

Rothman, David. 1980. *Conscience and Conenvience: The Asylum and its Alternatives in Progressive America*. Boston: Little, Brown.

Schneider, Elizabeth M. 1986. "The 'Dialectic' of Rights and Politics: Perspective From the Women's Movement." *New York University Law Review* 61: 589.

Silbey, Susan, and Austin Sarat. 1987. "Critical Traditions in Law and Society Research." *Law and Society Review* 21: 167.

Snow, David, E. Burke Rocheford, Jr., Steven K. Worden, and Robert D. Benford. 1986. "Frame Alignment Processes, Micromobilization, and Movement Participation." *American Sociological Review* 51: 761–775.

Snow, David, and Robert D. Benford. 1988. "Ideology, Frame Resonance, and Participant Mobilization." In *From Structure to Action*, edited by Bert Klandermans, Hanspeter Kriesi, and Sidney Tarrow. Vol. 1 of *International Social Movement Research*. Greenwich, CT: JAI Press.

Swidler, Ann. 1986. "Culture in Action: Symbols and Strategies." *American Sociological Review* 51: 273–286.

Thomas, George M., John W. Meyer, Francisco O. Ramirez, and John Boli. 1987. *Institutional Structure: Constituting State, Society, and the Individual*. Newbury Park, CA: Sage.

Trubek, David, and John Esser. 1989. "'Critical Empiricism' in American Legal Studies: Paradox, Program, or Pandora's Box?" *Law and Social Inquiry* 14(1): 3–52.

Tushnet, Mark. 1984. "An Essay on Rights." *Texas Law Review* 65: 101.

Villamoare, Adelaide. 1991. "Women, Differences, and Rights as Practices: An Interpretive Essay and a Proposal." *Law and Society Review* 25(2): 385–410.

Williams, Patricia. 1991. "On Being the Object of Property." Pp. 165–180 in *Feminist Legal Theory*, edited by Katherine T. Bartlett and Rosanne Kennedy. Boulder, CO: Westview.

Zemans, Frances. 1983. "Legal Mobilization: The Neglected Role of the Law in the Political System." *American Political Science Review* 77: 690.

12 CITIZENSHIP AND RIGHTS

WORKER PROTECTION IN GERMANY AND THE UNITED STATES

Dula J. Espinosa

World and domestic changes are forcing modern nation-states to reconsider the role of national governments in allocating worker protections. Concerns are high even in major world economic powers, such as Germany and the United States. Although their laws on worker protection differ greatly, both of these nation-states are trying to grapple with soaring costs resulting from economic, social, and political change. In Germany, where worker protections are defined as citizenship entitlements, the government has begun to reduce labor-associated costs by reducing entitlement amounts. In the United States, where benefits are mostly job-related, businesses have begun to lower costs by shifting workers away from high-benefit jobs. This chapter examines these changes and their implications for citizenship rights, nation-state welfare systems, and legal cultures in the context of a declining global economy.

Background

Although both Germany and the United States (U.S.) are now considered democratic countries, the state welfare system is much older and stronger in Germany (Currie 1994:5–24). Indeed, Germany has long been considered the originator of the modern social welfare system (Mitchell and Rojot 1993:160; Shlaes 1994:110). The tradition dates back to 1881 when Kaiser Wilhelm I issued the first social insurance laws in Germany (Windschild 1991:92–93). The Weimar Republic later expanded that tradition by granting limited social welfare and the right to a public education (Currie 1994:5–6). Citizenship rights continued to expand in later years with the granting of mine-worker insurance in 1923, general unemployment insurance in 1927 and, under Hitler's reign of Nazi terror, the granting of craft-worker insurance in 1938 (Windschild 1991:92). It was also during this period that German workers were first granted the right to participate in the economic and political decision-making processes of larger firms through the newly created Works Councils (U.S. Department of Labor 1995:19).

Following the fall of the Nazi regime in 1945, Germany was split into two parts with one part coming under the control of the Allied Powers. The Allied Powers appointed local administrators to run the day-to-day activities of the defeated country and to draft a new Constitution. Although the Constitution of the Federal Republic of Germany (West Germany) was considered "provisional," it became official in 1949 and was later applied to all of Germany as a result of unification in 1990 (Jacobi, Keller, and Muller-Jentsch 1992:225; U.S. Department of Labor 1995:5–6). The new regime is simply referred to as "United Germany" or as the "United Federal Republic of Germany" (U.S. Department of Labor 1995:6).

The Constitution of 1949, as Table 12–1 shows, committed the Federal Republic of Germany to an expanded social welfare system (U.S. Department of Labor 1995:5–7; Windschild 1991). The Constitution declared the form of government to be "democratic and social" (Article 20). It also banned government infringement on human dignity (Article 1) and mandated special state "protection" of marriage and the family, mothers, and illegitimate children (Article 6). The Constitution also gave German workers the right to choose their work, the location of their work, and the location of their training (Article 12), and "to form associations to safeguard and improve working and economic conditions" (Article 9).

Other citizenship rights granted by the German Constitution included the guarantee of certain individual liberties. As Table 12–1 shows, Germans were granted freedom of religion (Article 4), speech (Article 5), movement (Article 11), and assembly (Article 8). Also granted was the right to hold and bequeath property (Article 14) and to be equal "before the law" (Article 3). Equality on the basis of gender was specifically mentioned, as was the banning of special treatment due to ascribed characteristics such as sex and race or because of political or religious views (Article 3). Also granted by the German Constitution was the right to vote by Article 38, as amended in 1970, to all citizens aged 18 and over (Currie 1994:358).

The same range of citizenship rights was not, however, present in the Constitution of the United States, which was written more than 160 years earlier. As Currie notes (1994:21), social welfare was mentioned only twice in the U.S. Constitution. While the Preamble committed the new government to "promote the general welfare," Article 1, section 8 authorized Congress to "provide for the common defense and general welfare of the United States." In other words, the U.S. Constitution committed itself and Congress to the nation's welfare, but never defined the terms of that provision.

TABLE 12–1. Selected Portions of the German Constitution

Article 1	(1)	Human dignity is inviolable. To respect and protect it is the duty of all state authority.
Article 3	(1)	All persons are equal before the law.
	(2)	Men and women shall have equal rights.
	(3)	No one may be disadvantaged or favored because of his sex, his parentage, his race, his language, his homeland and origin, his faith, or his religious or political opinions.
Article 4	(1)	Freedom of faith and of conscience, and freedom to profess a religion or a particular philosophy, are inviolable.
Article 5	(1)	Everyone has the right freely to express and disseminate his opinion in speech, writing, and pictures and freely to inform himself from generally accessible sources.
Article 6	(1)	Marriage and family enjoy the special protection of the state.
	(4)	Every mother is entitled to the protection and care of the community.
	(5)	Illegitimate children shall be provided by legislation with the same opportunities for their physical and mental development and for their place in society as are enjoyed by legitimate children.
Article 8	(1)	All Germans have the right to assemble peaceably and unarmed without prior notification or permission.
Article 9	(3)	The right to form associations to safeguard and improve working and economic conditions is guaranteed to everyone and to all occupations.
Article 11	(1)	All Germans shall enjoy freedom of movement throughout the federal territory.
Article 12	(1)	All Germans have the right freely to choose their trade, occupation, or profession, their place of work, and their place of training.
Article 14	(1)	Property and right of inheritance are guaranteed.
Article 20	(1)	The Federal Republic of Germany is a democratic and social federal state.
Article 38	(1)	Anyone who has attained the age of eighteen years is entitled to vote; anyone who has attained majority is eligible for election as amended in 1970.

Source: Basic Law of the Federal Republic of Germany (1949)

Even though the U.S. Constitution did not confer what Marshall terms "social citizenship," it did confer what Marshall terms "civil citizenship" by granting certain individual liberties (Crompton 1993:140–148). Most of these rights were added through the Bill of Rights adopted in 1791—four years after the U.S. Constitution was first signed. The First Amendment, for example, granted U.S. citizens some of the same rights conferred to German citizens such as freedom of speech, freedom of religion, and freedom of assembly (Amendment 1). Also included in the Bill of Rights were other personal liberty guarantees including the right against self-incrimination in criminal trials (Amendment V), trial by jury (Amendment VI), and protection "against unreasonable searches and seizures" (Amendment IV).

The German Constitution and the U.S. Constitution also originally differed on what Marshall terms "political citizenship" (Crompton 1993:140–148). Unlike the 20th century German Constitution, the 18th century U.S. Constitution did not specify who could become a citizen or who could vote. Both decisions were essentially left to individual states which singled out, almost exclusively, whites for citizenship and wealthy white males for citizenship rights such as voting (*see* Elk v. Wilkins 1884; Minor v. Happersett 1875; Scott v. Sandford 1856).[1] As a result, the battle over who qualified for U.S. citizenship and for U.S. citizenship rights lasted for decades and was won at different times by different groups of individuals. Blacks, for example, did not qualify for citizenship until 1868 when the Fourteenth Amendment was added to the U.S. Constitution, and were not granted voting rights until 1870 when the Fifteenth Amendment was added. Native Americans similarly did not qualify for U.S. citizenship or U.S. voting rights until Congress passed the Indian Citizenship Act of 1924, more than 130 years after the Constitution was first signed. Even white women, who were considered citizens at the time the Constitution was first adopted, were not allowed to vote until 1920. Responsible was the Nineteenth Amendment, which also granted minority female citizens the same right to vote. The last change in federally conferred voting rights occurred in 1971 when the Twenty-Sixth Amendment was passed granting suffrage rights to citizens aged 18 and over.

In sum, Germany and the United States differ in four important respects in their orientations toward citizen protections. First, only Germany has a long tradition as a welfare state in which citizens are granted economic caretaking by the government as a constitutional right. Second, only the German Constitution originally granted citizenship rights to all citizens regardless of gender and race—a battle that was fought before and after the Second World War in the United States. Third, only Germany attempts to exert state control over the economy to improve working conditions and to ensure the social security of its citizens. Most important, however, is the fact that only the German Constitution grants special protections to workers, including the right to form unions.

WORKER PROTECTIONS

Although the U.S. Constitution never granted citizens special worker protections, federal employment laws did eventually arise, especially in response to the Depression of the 1930s. Most U.S. employees, for example, became entitled to old-age pension and unemployment insurance through the Social Security Act of 1935 and to minimum wage through the Fair Labor Standards Act of 1938.[2] Other examples of U.S. federal worker-protection laws are listed in Table 12–2. Workers are, for example, protected from gender and race discrimination by Title VII of the 1964 Civil Rights Act, protected from age discrimination if aged 40 or older by the Age Discrimination in Employment Act of 1967, and protected from disability discrimination by the 1990 Americans with Disabilities Act. Also important are the Equal Pay Act of 1963 which mandates equal pay for equal work performed by men and women and the 1993 Family and Medical Leave Act which gives unpaid leaves for family-related purposes such as the birth or adoption of a child.

As expected, given the constitutional differences, German federal law goes far beyond U.S. federal law in regulating employment conditions and benefits. Although Germans are accorded many of the same benefits as U.S. workers such as unemployment and retirement pay (U.S. Department of Labor 1995:14–16), many German laws have no U.S. equivalent, as Table 12–3 shows. For example, employers who wish to fire salaried workers must comply with the Act of 1926, and employers who wish to fire workers with six or more months of tenure must comply with the Termination Protection Act of 1969. German workers are also entitled to employment pay during illness by the Sick Pay Act of 1969, to 18 days of paid leave, excluding holidays and Sundays, by the Vacation Act of 1963, and, if female, to maternity pay by the Mother Protection Act of 1968. Employment disputes are also covered by German federal employment law with company-level decisions regulated by the Labor-Management Relations Act of 1972 and third-party decisions guaranteed by the Labor Court Act of 1979. German workers also have the right to be represented on the supervisory boards of larger companies by the Labor-Management Act of 1952. Even stronger is the right given to German workers to have greater input into the decision-making processes of larger companies by the Co-Determination Act of 1979.

TABLE 12–2. Selected U.S. Federal Employment Laws

Age Discrimination in Employment Act, 1967 as amended	Applies to private employers with 20 or more workers, state and local governments, and employment agencies
	Prohibits age discrimination against any worker aged 40 and over
Affirmative Action (Revised Order No. 4) as amended	Requires organizations to make good faith efforts to hire & promote women & minorities in job groups in which they are underrepresented
	Applies to federal government agencies, state and local governments, and private firms with 50 or more employees that have federal contracts worth $50,000 or more
Americans with Disabilites Act of 1990	Prohibits discrimination against qualified workers with disabilities and also requires that employers reasonably accommodate known disabilities
	Applies to private employers with 15 or more employees, state and local governments, and employment agencies
Equal Pay Act, 1963	Requires that an employer pay a man and a woman the same pay rate when they are performing the same work
	As part of the Fair Labor Standards Act, the Equal Pay Act applies to all organizations required, for example, to pay federal minimum wage including many private employers, state and local governments, and the federal government except for uniformed military personnel and Congressional employees

TABLE 12-2 (continued)

Family and Medical Leave Act, 1993	Among other provisions, it entitles employees to take medical leave for family-related purposes such as the birth or adoption of a child and to care for a child, spouse, or parent with a serious medical condition
	Applies to federal, state, and local governments, and any person that employs 50 or more workers within 75 miles of the employment site
Title VII of the Civil Rights Act of 1964 as amended	Prohibits discrimination against employees or applicants for employment on the basis of race, color, religion, sex, or national origin
	Applies to private employers that have 15 or more employees, and to state, federal, and local governments, and to employment agencies that refer workers to covered employers

TABLE 12-3. Selected German Federal Employment Laws

Law	Description
Act Regarding the Periods of Notice of Termination of Salaried Employees of 1926	Mandates the conditions under which a salaried employee may be terminated
Labor Management Relations Act of 1952 as amended	Mandates that one third of the supervisory board of a stock corporation or a partnership limited by shares shall consist of employee-elected worker representatives
Federal Vacation Act of 1963 as amended	Mandates 18 working days of vacation excluding holidays and Sundays for workers employed six or more months
Mother Protection Act promulgated in 1968 as amended	Protects expectant and nursing mothers by, for example: Requiring employers to take necessary precautions with regard to machinery, tools, and work administration Requiring employers to give expectant or nursing mothers short breaks and to provide rooms in which these mothers may lie down for short times Banning the employment of mothers in jobs deemed to have health risks such as exposure to excessive heat and noise Mandating paid maternity leave Banning the termination of the mother up to four months after delivery

(TABLE 12–3 (continued)

Sick Pay Act of 1969 as amended	Entitles workers to employment pay during illness even if the employer terminates the relationship because of inability to work
Termination Protection Act of 1969 as amended	Mandates the conditions under which employees with six or more months of tenure may be terminated
Labor Management Relations Act of 1972 as amended	Establishes, among other things, the Works Council which consists of elected group of workers that meets regularly with the employer to settle labor disputes at the company level
Co-Determination Act of 1976	Grants workers the right to co-determination through supervisory boards which consist of workers and union representatives in companies meeting certain requirements
Labor Court Act of 1979 as amended	Gives exclusive jurisdiction over collective bargaining and other employer-employee disputes to labor courts

Source: Gres and Jung (1983)

A comparison of these laws reveals that even when there are seeming U.S. equivalents, the U.S. laws are generally weaker and less universal than the German laws. For example, the U.S. Family and Medical Leave Act of 1993 (*see* Table 12–2) and the German Mother Protection Act of 1968 (*see* Table 12–3) both allow mothers and mothers-to-be to take a maternity leave for the birth of a child. The U.S. Act gives a woman meeting these conditions the right to take an unpaid leave if she is a public sector worker or if her private sector employer employs 50 or more workers at or within 75 miles of her worksite. The German Act, on the other hand, applies to almost all mothers-to-be, granting them paid maternity leave as well as other protections, including short breaks during the working day, protection from termination up to four months after delivery, and safe working conditions. In other words, female workers do not have to meet job-related criteria, as they do in the U.S., to qualify for federal employment maternity and maternity-related protections.[3]

The net effects of these laws is presented in Table 12–4, which shows the levels of federal government social insurance coverage provided by both nation-states. The table shows, for example, that only Germans qualify for federally guaranteed sick pay when employed, paid maternity leave, cash payments for the birth of each child, monthly child benefit payments, and comprehensive health care.[4] The German system, which provides virtually all Germans with state-of-the-art medical care, has few out-of-pocket costs (U.S. General Accounting Office 1993:3; U.S. Department of Labor 1995:16, 33–34). Covered by the German health plan are such expenses as: "ambulatory and hospital care; maternity, dental, physical therapy, and preventive care; drugs; family planning; rehabilitation; eyeglasses; medical appliances; home health care; and fitness tests and work therapy, including spa visits as part of work therapy" (U.S. General Accounting Office 1993:3).

The difference in coverage is also large even when both nation-states address the same issues, as Table 12–4 shows. For example, although federal law grants women in both nation-states the right to take a maternity leave, U.S. women are not federally guaranteed paid leaves as are German women. Also greater in Germany is unemployment insurance which is set to 68 percent, 63 percent if single, of after-tax earnings for just over two years compared to 50 percent of earnings in the U.S. for up to 39 weeks in especially depressed regions. Different still are the upper limits placed on U.S. retirement and disability pensions—limits missing in German law. Family maintenance benefits are also more generous in Germany, since they are tied to unemployment assistance rather than to poverty criteria as they are in the United States. In other words, families in Germany do not have to wait un-

TABLE 12-4. Comparison of Selected U.S. and German Federal Employment Protections

	United States	Germany
Unemployment	About 50% of earnings for (approx.) 1–26 weeks in most states plus up to 13 weeks more in selected regions	68% of after-tax earnings, 63% if single, payable from first day for 78–832 weekdays or more
Sickness	No federal program; but 5 states and Puerto Rico provide proportion of earnings, others provide none	100% of earnings for 6 weeks with up to 80% thereafter for up to 78 weeks in 3 years
Old-Age Pension	Based on earnings after 1950 or age 21 if later, no minimum for age 62 retirees after 1981 and maximum of $1,228 per month for age 65 retirees in 1993	1.5% of worker's assessed last 3 year earnings times years of coverage
Invalidity; Disability	No minimun for workers disabled after 1981, maximum of $1,228 per month for workers disabled in 1993	General disability 1.5%, Occupational disability 1%, of earnings times years of insurance
Healthcare	No comprehensive system; aged and poor are covered for most doctor, drug, and lab fees	Comprehensive medical and dental coverage; copayments for some items such as drugs
Maternity	Unpaid medical leave for family related purposes; 5 states plus Puerto Rico provide proportion of earnings, others provide none	100% of earnings for 6 weeks and 8 weeks after confinement plus a cash payment of DM 150 (about $94) or more for each birth

(continued on next page)

TABLE 12-4 (continued)

	United States	Germany
Family and Income Maintenance		
Child Benefits	None	Monthly payments in the following amounts: First child: DM 70 (about $44); Second child: DM 70–130 (about $44–82; Third child: DM 140–220 (about $88–138) Others: DM 140–240 (about $88–150)
Other Programs	Means tested benefits for single-parent households plus food stamps	Means tested unemployment assistance of indefinte duration at 58%, 56% if single, of previous earnings with annual qualifying exams required

Source: Department of Health and Human Services (1994).

til most or all of their resources are depleted before receiving government aid as they do in the United States.

The main difference between German and U.S. worker protections, however, concerns the question of universality. While German employment protection laws are granted as a matter of citizenship, the ability to qualify for U.S. federal employment protection laws depends on job-related factors. Table 12–5 shows one of the most important of those factors: employment status. The table repeats the U.S. federal employment laws presented in Table 12–2 and then shows which laws a given firm would have to abide by for a given status of worker. The table assumes that the firm under discussion has already met the other qualifying criteria of each law, such as number of employees and job sector location.

In essence, Table 12–5 shows that not all workers employed within the geographical boundaries of a given firm would qualify for the same types of federal employment protection. While all full-time workers in permanent positions would qualify for all the laws listed, workers in other categories would not. For example, permanent part-time workers would not qualify for Affirmative Action protection, and directly hired temporary workers would not qualify for either Affirmative Action or Equal Pay protection. Most telling, however, are the temporary-agency, leased, and independent-contractor workers who would not qualify at their worksite for any of the federal employment protections listed. Indicative of the lack of federal protection for the contingent workforce is a recent federal court decision that dismissed an age discrimination claim brought by an independent contractor (Sotos 1994). The case was dismissed because federal age discrimination law applies only to directly hired employees.[5]

The fact that "benefits are attached to a particular employer" (Mitchell and Rojot 1993:128) in the United States is made especially clear in Table 12–6. The table shows the percentage of full-time employees in U.S. private business, by number of employees, that receive German-type benefits paid in part or in full by the employer. A comparison of the firms by number of employees reveals that workers in the larger firms are much more likely to receive the following benefits: paid vacations, sick leave, unpaid maternity, hospital room and board, inpatient surgery, all the insurances listed, and the retirement plans. Occupational disparity also exists, with professionals being more likely to receive a wider range of benefits than clerical and production workers in both large and small firms.

Thus, even though both the United States and Germany offer worker protections, they differ on how and to what extent these protections are offered. In Germany, worker protections are viewed as citizenship entitlements

TABLE 12–5. U.S. Federal Employment Law Applicability by Employee Status Within a Given Firm

	Employee Status Within a Given Firm					
Must the Firm abide by . . . ?	*Full-time Permanent*	*Part-time Permanent*	*Temporary Employee*	*Temporary Agency Employee*	*Leased Worker*	*Independent Contractor*
Age Discrimination in Employment Act, 1967, as amended	yes	yes	yes	no	no	no
Affirmative Action (Revised Order No. 4), as amended	yes	no	no	no	no	no
Americans with Disabilities Act of 1990	yes	yes	yes	no	no	no
Equal Pay Act, 1963	yes	yes	no	no	no	no
Family and Medical Leave Act, 1993	yes	yes	yes	no	no	no
Title VII of the Civil Rights Act of 1964, as amended	yes	yes	yes	no	no	no

TABLE 12-6. Percent of Full-Time Employees in U.S. Private Businesses Receiving Selected Benefits Paid in Part or Full by the Employer.*

	Private Firms with < 100 employees				Private Firms with ≥ 100 employees			
	All	Professional	Clerical	Production	All	Professional	Clerical	Blue Collar
Paid Leaves								
Vacations	96	97	98	95	88	94	94	81
Holidays	92	93	94	90	82	94	90	74
Sick	67	87	82	48	53	74	70	35
Maternity	2	3	2	1	2	3	2	1
(Unpaid Maternity)	37	43	38	33	18	27	20	13
Insurance								
Medical	83	85	81	84	71	83	78	61
Noncontributory Medical	41	38	35	46	37	43	40	34
Hospital/Room and Board	83	85	81	84	71	83	78	61
Inpatient Surgery	83	85	81	84	71	83	78	61
Life	94	98	95	92	64	77	73	53
Accident/Sickness	45	32	35	57	26	24	27	27
Dental	60	67	60	57	33	43	37	27
Long-term Disability	40	61	49	24	23	43	31	10
Noncontributory Long Term Disability	31	46	38	20	18	38	26	6
Retirement Plans								
Defined Contribution	48	57	53	39	33	43	38	26
Defined Benefit Pension	59	60	56	59	22	21	25	20

*Note: "Professional" includes technical and related fields; "Clerical" includes sales; "Production" and "Blue Collar" include services.
Source: U.S. Bureau of the Census (1994).

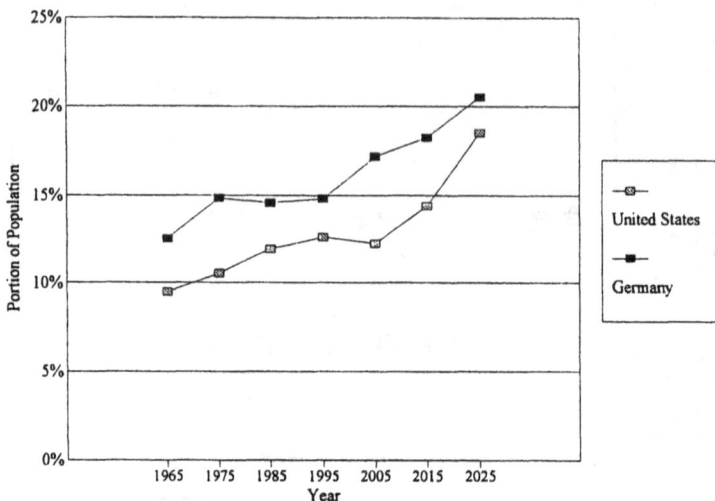

Figure 12–1. Estimated Portion of Population Age 65 or Over, 1965–2025.
Source: U.N. Department of Economic and Social Development (1993).

and are, therefore, broader in scope, more generous in conditions, and generally more universally applied than in the United States. In the United States, there is less federal protection for workers and that which does exist limits protection mostly to workers with full-time positions who are employed in certain sectors of the labor market. In short, while citizenship is generally enough to qualify for worker protections in Germany, access to worker protections in the United States is more likely to be granted as a job-attached benefit rather than as a matter of federal law.

WORLD AND DOMESTIC CHANGES

Despite their differences, changes in the international and domestic systems are beginning to increase the costs associated with employee benefits in both Germany and the United States. On the domestic front, both nation-states are expected to experience increases in their elderly population which are expected to further increase costs associated with retirement and health. As Figure 12–1 shows, by the year 2025, the proportion of the population aged 65 years and older is predicted to account for 18 percent of the total U.S. population and 21 percent of the total German population (U.N. Department of Economic and Social Development 1993:380–381; 190–191). These estimates represent increases in the elderly population since 1965 of 8 percent for Germany and 9 percent for the United States.

Industrial restructuring is also occurring in Germany and the United States (Godbout 1993; U.N. Economic Commission for Europe, 1994:41).

As Figure 12–2 shows, between 1970 and 1990, employment in both nation-states increased in services, decreased in agriculture, and dramatically decreased in industry and manufacturing. Employment in industry and manufacturing decreased by 8 percent and 8.4 percent in the U.S. and by 9.7 percent and 8.9 percent in Germany, respectively. Also indicative of the massive shift was the manufacturing share of the gross national product which decreased, from 1980 to 1990, by 1.7 percent in Germany and 3.6 percent in the United States (U.N. Industrial Development Organization 1993:A-46, A-107). The situation is likely to worsen for Germany, as it currently employs a higher proportion of workers in manufacturing than do other nations, including the United States and Japan (U.S. Department of Labor 1995:11).

According to the United Nations (U.N.) Economic Commission for Europe (1994:41), the trend towards more "long-term structural unemployment in the western industrial countries" is likely to continue as industry and manufacturing jobs decline. Contributing to the problem is the slowed economic growth in high-wage countries that include the United States and Germany (van Liemt 1992). Labor costs per hour in 1993 show, for example, that German workers average $25 and that U.S. workers average $15.5, compared to $3 for Mexican workers and $2.5 for Malaysians (Shlaes 1994:112). In essence, the lower labor costs of Asian and other transitional nations is likely to further decrease the already declining manufacturing and industrial bases of the German and U.S. economies.

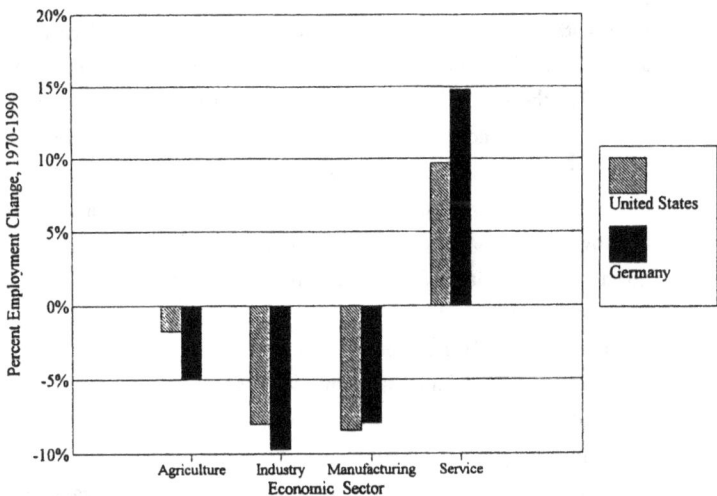

Figure 12–2. Change in Employment by Economic Sector, 1970–1990.
Source: Godbout (1993).

Also problematic in both modern nation-states is rising health care costs. While Germany has managed to keep health costs to an average 8.3 percent of the gross domestic product from 1989 to 1991 (U.S. Bureau of the Census, 1994:859), the costs of health care are high and expected to grow even higher (U.S. General Accounting Office, 1993:47; U.S. Department of Labor, 1995:33–34). Although much of the concern is on the rising costs of pharmaceuticals, the cost of nursing homes is considered most problematic, given its rising costs and the aging German population (U.S. General Accounting Office, 1993:47; U.S. Department of Labor, 1995:32).

Health-care costs are also rising in the United States. The health care expenditure share of the gross domestic product grew from 9.2 percent in 1980 to 13.4 percent in 1991 (U.S. Bureau of the Census 1994:859). Also indicative of the rising costs of health care is the Consumer Price Index, which grew from 1960 to 1993 by 396.6 percent, while its medical component rose by 836.7 percent (Karsten 1995). In fact, federal and state spending now account for almost half of all spending on U.S. health care, with the federal share nearly doubling since 1980 (Clinton 1995:42–44).

Germany, a country that now spends an estimated 84 DM in social insurance for every 100 DM paid to employees in wages (Shlaes 1994), is also faced with problems resulting from its 1990 unification (Jacobi et al. 1992:225; U.S. Department of Labor 1995:25–26). In effect, 17 million former East Germans can now lay claim to unified Germany's state welfare benefits even though they have never paid into the social system (Peel 1994). Another outcome of unification is unemployment, which is high and rising (Peel 1994; U.S. Department of Labor 1995:25–26). Unification was also faced with a former East Germany that is economically suffering (Jacobi et al. 1992:225–227; Soskice and Schettkat 1993; Windschild 1991:98). It no longer has the Soviet Union as a main trading partner (Soskice and Schettkat 1993:121–122) and is in need of vast modernization of its infrastructure and its low-paid, lower-skilled workforce (Jacobi et al. 992:225–227).

U.S. employers also cite other reasons besides health care for rising employment costs. Among the most popular is the high cost of enforcing government mandates designed to protect workers. Another reason is the liability that employers are increasingly assuming in the workplace (Green and Reibstein 1992). The concern over increased liability and greater enforcement costs in light of a tight job market may not be exaggerated. A recent study of more than 1,000 applications found that about one-third of the applicants had written false information on their resumes (Brown 1993).

In sum, although Germany and the United States vary greatly on worker protection laws, international and domestic system changes are beginning to increase labor costs. Plaguing both nations are slowed economies, aging domestic populations, and rising health-care costs. Also problematic for Germany is unification, which linked a highly industrialized major economic power to a nation-state with an outdated infrastructure and a lower-skilled workforce. Cited as contributing factors to increased labor costs by U.S. employers are increased employer liability and the costs of enforcing worker protection laws.

Responses

Largely because of the differences in the source of employee benefits, differences exist in the solutions used to reduce these costs in Germany and the United States. In the United States, businesses have responded by shifting workers away from traditional high benefit full-time positions. The shift has occurred to such a large extent that one researcher is literally questioning the future of these positions (Bridges 1994). Workers are, instead, increasingly being hired for positions that offer less job security and lower benefits, such as part-time, temporary, and leased agency positions.[6]

The growth in the U.S. contingent workforce has been phenomenal. Between 1980 and 1991 temporary work increased by 225 percent, part-time by 24.5 percent, and self-employed by 21.2 percent (Parker 1994:31). By 1988, 81 percent of surveyed businesses had reported using part-timers, 59 percent their own temporary workers, 84 percent temporary agencies, and 57 percent independent contractors (Lewis and Molloy 1991:114–115). The case of independent contractors is, however, less clear, as there are no government statistics tracking their employment, even though all are self-employed (Carre 1992:68). What is clear from Census reports is that the number of self-employed workers has increased from just over 7 million in 1970 to almost 10.5 million by 1993 (U.S. Bureau of the Census 1994:404).

In essence, by 1988, nearly 23 percent of all U.S. workers were employed outside the permanent full-time workforce (reported in duRivage 1992:89). Much of the growth was due, and continues to be due, to the direct and indirect use of temporary workers and to the use of leased-agency workers. The National Association of Temporary Services recently reported, for example, that businesses in 1989 employed over one million temporary workers per day at a cost of more than $16 billion (Lewis and Molloy 1991:1). The amount of business conducted by personnel-supply services similarly grew by $15.8 billion from 1985 to 1992 with employment agencies alone accounting for $4.2 billion of that growth (U.S. Bureau of the Census 1994:799). Also increasing was the number of leased workers, which grew by 30 percent to 700,000 employees from 1988 to 1989 (Feldman

1990). The process of leasing generally involves the firing of most or all of a given workforce which is then rehired by the original employer through a leasing firm (Nye 1988:55–56).

The trend towards a greater U.S. contingent workforce continues. Between 1993 and 1994, for example, the proportion of full-time workers increased by 1.4 percent compared to an 11.6 percent increase in part-time workers (U.S. Bureau of Labor Statistics 1995:18). Especially growing are the number of "part-time workers who would prefer full-time hours" (Tilly 1992:15). Indeed, the proportion of so-called "involuntary" part-timers grew from 1970 to 1990 by 121 percent compared to a 69 percent increase in the number of voluntary part-timers and a 54 percent increase in all workers (Parker 1994:11). In fact, the increase in part-timers from July 1990 to January 1992 was entirely due to an increase in involuntary part-timers which now amounted to just about 21 percent of all part-timers (Appelbaum 1992:1–2).

As duRivage (1992:91–94) points out, businesses are increasingly using part-time, temporary and subcontracted workers to reduce labor costs due to the lower pay and benefit levels. In 1993, for example, the median hourly pay of part-time workers was $5.55 compared to $8.89 for full-time workers (U.S. Bureau of the Census 1994:432). Part-timers are also less likely to receive holidays, sick pay, vacation days, health insurance, or retirement pension and are less likely to be promoted (Parker 1994:146; Tilly 1992:20–25). Temporary workers are even less likely to receive benefits provided by the leasing agency or any other employer, because they are generally not employed long enough to qualify, since qualification tends to depend on number of hours worked (Parker 1994:99). Most vulnerable, however, are independent contractors, who generally work for one company with no benefits and "no guarantee of work" (Carre 1992:68).[7]

Also relevant to the discussion of benefits under U.S. law is the fact that even when contingent workers are covered by federal laws, minimum number of hours per week or per year are generally required to receive that protection. The U.S. Family and Medical Leave Act, for example, applies to part-time and temporary workers only if they regularly work 20 or more hours per week or work a total of 1000 hours per year (duRivage 1992:111–112). The fact that many workers have trouble meeting these hour requirements means that many contingent workers do not receive protections for which they ostensibly qualify (Williams 1989:5–6). The problem, as Carre (1992:83) notes, is that U.S. federal employment laws generally assume that "employment should be full-time, year-round, and with a single employer."

The push to lower worker costs in the United States has also begun to alter access to health care in a more direct manner. A 1992 U.S. Supreme Court decision has put U.S. workers at greater risk of losing medical benefits even if those benefits were granted as a condition of hiring (Gostin and Widiss 1993). The Court let stand a lower-court decision that allowed an employer to lower the lifetime coverage of an HIV-positive man from $1 million to $5000 (Gostin and Widiss 1993:2527–2532). The case is particularly important because benefits were not curtailed until four months after the worker told the employer about his illness (McGann v. H & H Music Company 1992). By refusing to hear the case, the U.S. Supreme Court has, in effect, granted employers the right to retroactively alter the conditions under which employees are originally hired (Turner 1992).

Concern over the plight of uninsured workers has prompted much discussion at the federal level. One of the most comprehensive bills, proposed by Representative Pat Schroeder in 1992, would have provided part-time and temporary workers with health and pension benefits (Carre 1992:82). Although Schroeder's bill failed to pass, the question of providing contingent employees with health insurance has recently resurfaced with Senator Edward Kennedy. His proposal calls for employers to pay half of the insurance costs of full-time workers until 1998 and 20 percent of their costs after 1998, when part-time workers would be added to the coverage (Kosterlitz 1994).

The question of health care is also being reframed as a citizenship right by President Clinton, who has offered a comprehensive health plan for all Americans. Although the proposal failed in large part due to the lack of big business support (Martin 1995), the President returned to the issue of health care in 1995 (Clinton 1995). Cited as problematic were the vulnerability of workers to health-coverage loss when leaving or changing jobs, the high proportion of health care paid by tax dollars, and the ever-increasing costs of health care as currently administered (Clinton 1995:42–27).[8] Concern over health care is so high that one researcher recently commented: "The basic question no longer is whether the U.S. should have universal health care insurance but what specific health care policy the country should adopt in order to strengthen the market system and to maximize social welfare as effectively as possible" (Karsten 1995:129).

Like businesses in the United States, the German government has also begun to respond to rising employee benefit costs. In 1992, it agreed to curb retirement costs. New regulations have now limited annual retirement-pension increases to net growth of earnings in the prior year and have gradually begun to alter age conditions (U.S. Department of Labor 1995:14–15). The German retirement age will be gradually increased and benefits will be tied to that age. In essence, by the year 2012, male and female retirement will be set at 65 years of age with reduced benefits for those who retire earlier and increased benefits for those who retire later (U.S. Department of Labor 1995:15).

In addition to curbing retirement costs, Germany is also reconsidering the viability of its generous welfare system (Peel 1994; Shlaes 1994:122–124; Windschild 1991). In 1993, for example, the German government announced that it would "prune" unemployment and welfare payments by about $45.2 billion dollars over a three-year period (Protzman, 1993). It was also in 1993 that Germany passed the Health Care Structure Reform Act aimed at saving about "6 percent of the total 1992 sickness fund expenditures" (U.S. General Accounting Office 1993:9). The savings are supposed to be accomplished by a series of measures that include, for example, greater charges to patients and mandatory spending limits on "physician, hospital, dental services, and prescription drugs" (U.S. General Accounting Office 1993:9). The 1993 Act is just one of a series of legislative steps taken by the German government to curb health costs (U.S. Department of Labor 1995:33; U.S. General Accounting Office 1993:37–39).

While the more recent measures have focused on rising health care costs, earlier cost-cutting measures altered working conditions. The Employment Protection Act of 1985, for example, has already abolished protection against dismissal and lengthened fixed term contracts from 6 to 18 months (Jacobi et al. 1992:240). Also amended was the Work Promotion Act to end benefits to employees who were indirectly "affected by industrial action in the same industry, but in another bargaining district" (Jacobi et al. 1992:241). In 1989 it amended the Works Constitution Act even though the changes could "weaken the works council as a unitary representative of the employees" (Jacobi et al. 1992:240). In addition, since 1987 there has been discussion of a new Working Time Act to replace an act in 1938. The new act "would allow greater flexibility on the part of employers in determining daily and weekly working-time, ending the principle of the normal working day" (1992:241).

Other proposals are also being considered. Among the most debated is the proposed mandatory nursing home insurance program. The cost of nursing home care is now so high that it has already depleted the personal funds of nearly one-third of the 1.65 million Germans that needed such care (U.S. Department of Labor 1995:32). One solution being discussed by the German government is whether workers should give up a national holiday in order to pay for a mandatory nursing home insurance program (U.S. Department of Labor 1995:32). Another proposal being discussed would pay for nursing homes by increasing the tax paid by employers and workers by "up to 1.7 percent of pay" (U.S. Department of Labor 1995:32).

The changes in the employment laws of Germany and the United States have different implications for citizens, citizenship rights, and nation states. In the United States, where the state is usually separated from the economy, it is largely the marketplace that defines employee status and worker rights. The lack of constitutional protection for workers has, in the era of a declining global economy, led to a reduction of labor costs at the worksite. The reductions are being accomplished by the changing of workers from full-time to part-time and from permanent to temporary. Although legal protections have thus far remained untouched in the United States, federal lawmakers are considering changes in worker-protection laws to aid part-time and temporary workers and to provide health coverage to all.

In Germany, a corporatist welfare state in which unions are accorded special constitutionally granted rights, the economy and state are less separated. As a result, changes in worker rights, designed to reduce labor costs, have been accomplished through a redefinition of citizenship and citizenship rights. Since there is not the same separation of economy from polity in Germany as in the United States, the reduction of worker rights has evoked a political crisis. Change is not, as in the United States, left to the market but decided instead at the highest levels of government. Thus far, Germany has reduced its social protection costs by limiting allocation amounts and raising taxes.

These changes have strong implications for the notions of citizenship and welfare states in the context of a declining global economy. Among the most important of these changes are the aging of populations, the shift away from manufacturing and industrial jobs, and increasing labor costs. The response in Germany has been to reevaluate the orientation to social citizenship by reducing worker-protection entitlements even as the nation-state remains committed to the welfare of its citizenry. In the United States, the shifting of workers from high-benefit jobs to lower labor costs has prompted government officials to reconsider the question of social citizenship. In sum, these changes call into question the commitment of the German government to its long tradition of welfare insurance and calls further into question the ability and willingness of U.S. businesses to grant social entitlements to citizens.

The question of health care for all Americans, however, raises other questions. Of particular concern is the lowered costs of contingent workers that is now attracting businesses. Contingent workers are less likely to be as attractive to businesses should the federal government require health insurance for them. Also raised is the question of who would pay for the universal health coverage, since the tax base would be lowered due to the lower number of the generally higher-paid full-time permanent workers. Relying on employers to pick up the costs is likely to further increase labor costs and to prompt employers to sacrifice other workers and other benefits to remaining workers in order to carry the new financial burden. A third question raised is whether the U.S. government will consider granting other social insurance beyond health care, such as expanded retirement pensions. Since many contingent workers are likely to receive little or no retirement pensions per se, the question of increased public welfare for senior citizens is likely to be an ever-increasing problem as the contingent workforce faces retirement with little or no employer-paid retirement savings.

In Germany, the decision to reduce entitlement amounts calls into question the viability of social citizenship. The cutbacks initiated by the German government in response to increased costs suggests that other cuts are likely to occur as the world economy continues to decline. German workers are likely to be less protected at the very time that the protection is most needed, given their shifts from higher paying to lower paying jobs and the increasing aging population. The solutions proposed to date curb the very rights that have been long held by German citizens.

Given these changes, it is highly unlikely that these trends will be modified or reversed. In short, workers in the United States will undoubtedly continue to be displaced and shifted, while in Germany citizenship rights will continue to be reduced. Despite their differences, the outcome is likely to be the same—workers in both the United States and Germany, who are already seeing protections erode, will continue to see even greater erosion in those protections in future years.

NOTES

1. The Uniform Rule of Naturalization, passed by Congress in 1790, limited naturalized citizenship consideration to whites only and gave states the right to "proscribe" citizenship. As a result, state-set criteria was used to confer U.S. citizenship until 1856 when the U.S. Supreme Court revoked the practice in the Scott v. Sandford case.

2. Although Germany does not have a minimum wage law, it does have the highest wages in the world, which are due mostly to collective bargaining agreements (U.S. Department of Labor 1995:4).

3. The U.S. Family and Medical Leave Act is, however, more universal in that men are also allowed to take an unpaid leave for family related purposes such as the birth of a child—a provision not accorded German men under the Mother Protection Act.

4. Although not included in Table 12–4, German families with children are also entitled to tax cuts and to paid parental leave without fear of termination for up to five years (U.S. Department of Labor 1995:17–18).

5. The fact that independent contractors are not currently considered employees under federal law is, however, becoming more questionable. A person who was believed by himself, and by the person who had contracted with him for his services, to be an independent contractor was recently ruled an employee for tax and benefit purposes by the Michigan Supreme Court (Herr v. McCormick Grain 1993).

6. The structural shifts reported in Figure 12–2 have also resulted in decreased employee costs. The 1993 per hour costs of services averaged $11.34 in wages and $4.17 in total benefits compared to manufacuturing which averaged $6.74 in wages and $13.35 in total benefits (U.S. Bureau of the Census 1994:433). In other words, the shifting of workers from manufacturing to services saved U.S. businesses a total of $4.58 per hour.

7. Changes in federal tax laws are now making the use of leased workers less profitable. For example, the Tax Reform Act of 1986 altered retirement rules to benefit leased workers at the expense of the worksite employer. A worksite employer is now required to include leased workers on company retirement plans if 20 percent or more of all the workers employed at the worksite are leased (Nye 1988:58–59).

8. U.S. health costs have dramatically risen in the past three decades. Total costs from 1960 to 1991 rose from $27.1 billion to $751.8 billion with the public share rising from $5.7 billion to $315.9 billion (U.S. Bureau of the Census 1994:109).

REFERENCES

Appelbaum, Eileen. 1992. "Structural Change and the Growth of Part-Time and Temporary Employment." Pp. 1–14 in *New Policies for the Part-Time and Contingent Workforce*, edited by Virginia duRivage. Armonk, NY: M.E. Sharpe.

Bridges, William. 1994. *Jobshift: How to Prosper in a Workplace Without Jobs.* Reading, MA: Addison-Wesley.

Brown, Marlene. 1993. "Checking the Facts on a Resume." *Personnel Journal* 72 (1, supplement):6–7.

Carre, Francoise J. 1992. "Temporary Employment in the Eighties." Pp. 45–87 in *New Policies for the Part-Time and Contingent Workforce*, edited by Virginia duRivage. Armonk, NY: M.E. Sharpe.

Clinton, William J. 1995. *The Economic Report of the President Transmitted to Congress.* Washington, DC: U.S. Government Printing Office.

Crompton, Rosemary. 1993. *Class and Stratification: An Introduction to Current Debates.* Cambridge, England: Polity Press.

Currie, David P. 1994. *The Constitution of the Federal Republic of Germany.* Chicago, IL: University of Chicago Press.

duRivage, Virginia L. 1992. "New Policies for the Part-Time and Contingent Workforce." Pp. 89–121 in *New Policies for the Part-Time and Contingent Workforce,* edited by Virginia duRivage. Armonk, NY: M.E. Sharpe.

Elk v. Wilkins. 1884. *Supreme Court Reporter* 5:41–56.

Feldman, Stuart. 1990. "Companies Buy into Employee Leasing Plans." *Personnel* 67(10):1–2.

Godbout, Todd M. 1993. "Employment Change and Sectoral Distribution in 10 Countries, 1970–90." *Monthly Labor Review* 116(10):3–20.

Gostin, Lawrence O., and Alan I. Widiss. 1993. "What's Wrong with the ERISA Vacuum? Employers' Freedom to Limit Health Care Coverage Provided by Risk Retention Plans." *Journal of the American Medical Association* 269(19):2527–2332.

Green, Ronald M., and Richard J. Reibstein. 1992. *Employer's Guide to Workplace*

Torts: Negligent Hiring, Fraud, Defamation, and Other Emerging Areas of Employer Liability. Washington, DC: BNA Books.

Gres, Joachim, and Harald Jung. 1983. Handbook of German Employment Law. Frankfurt, Germany: Alfred Metzner Verlag.

Herr v. McCormick Grain. 1993. Federal Supplement 841:1500–1522.

Jacobi, Otto, Berndt Keller, and Walther Muller-Jentsch. 1992. "Germany: Codetermining the Future." Pp. 218–269 in Industrial Relations in the New Europe, edited by Anthony Ferner and Richard Hyman. Oxford, England: Blackwell Business Publishers.

Karsten, Siegfried G. 1995. "Health Care: Private Good vs. Public Good." American Journal of Economics and Sociology 54(2):129–144.

Kosterlitz, Julie. 1994. "A 50 per cent solution?" National Journal 26(30):1748.

Lewis, William, and Nancy H. Molloy. 1991. How to Choose and Use Temporary Services. New York: American Management Association.

Martin, Cathie Jo. 1995. "Stuck in Neutral: Big Business and the Politics of National Health Reform." Journal of Health Politics, Policy and Law 20(2):431–436.

McGann v. H & H Music Company. 1992. Federal Reporter 946:401–408.

Minor v. Happersett. 1875. United States Reports 88:162–178.

Mitchell, Daniel J. B., and Jacques Rojot. 1993. "Employee Benefits in the Single Market." Pp. 128–166 in Labor and an Integrated Europe, edited by Lloyd Ulman, Barry Eichengreen, and William T. Dickens. Washington, DC: The Brookings Institution.

Nye, David. 1988. Alternative Staffing Strategies. Washington, DC: The Bureau of National Affairs.

Parker, Robert E. 1994. Flesh Peddlers and Warm Bodies: The Temporary Help Industry and its Workers. New Brunswick, NJ: Rutgers University Press.

Peel, Quentin. 1994. "Germans in a Bind: The Limits of Policy." World Press Review 41(1):10–11.

Protzman, Ferdinand. 1993. "Germany Moves to Make First Cut in its Generous Social Safety Net." The New York Times 142:A1(N).

Scott v. Sandford. 1856. United States Reports 60:393–633.

Shlaes, Amity. 1994. "Germany's Chained Economy." Foreign Affairs 73(5):109–124.

Soskice, David, and Ronald Schettkat. 1993. "West German Labor Market Institutions and East German Transformation." Pp. 102–127 in Labor and an Integrated Europe, edited by Lloyd Ulman, Barry Eichengreen, and William T. Dickens. Washington, DC: The Brookings Institution.

Sotos, James B. 1994. "Independent Contractor's Age Bias Suit Rejected." Chicago Daily Law Bulletin 140(14):6.

Tilly, Chris. 1992. "Short Hours, Short Shrift: The Causes and Consequences of Part-Time Employment." Pp. 15–44 in New Policies for the Part-Time and Contingent Workforce, edited by Virginia duRivage. Armonk, NY: M.E. Sharpe.

Turner, Ronald. 1992. "ERISA and Employer Capping of Medical Benefits for Treatment of AIDS and Related Illness." AIDS and Public Policy Journal 7(2):89–91.

U.N. Economic Commission For Europe. 1994. Economic Survey of Europe in 1993–94. New York: United Nations.

U.N. Department of Economic and Social Development. 1993. The Sex and Age Distribution of the World Populations. The 1992 Edition. New York: United Nations.

U.N. Industrial Development Organization. 1993. Industry and Development: Global Report. New York: United Nations.

U.S. Bureau of the Census. 1994. Statistical Abstract of the United States: 1994. 114th edition. Washington, DC: U.S. Government Printing Office.

U.S. Bureau of Labor Statistics. 1995. Employment and Earnings: January 1995. Washington, DC: U.S. Government Printing Office.

U.S. Department of Health and Human Services. 1994. *Social Security Programs Throughout the World*. Washington, DC: U.S. Government Printing Office.

U.S. Department of Labor. 1995. *Foreign Labor Trends Report, Germany: 1991–92*. Washington, DC: U.S. Government Printing Office.

U.S. General Accounting Office. 1993. *German Health Care Reforms: New Cost Control Initiatives*. Report to the Chairman, Committee on Governmental Affairs, U.S. Senate (GAO-HRD-93-103), Washington, DC.

van Liemt, Gijsbert. 1992. "Economic Globalization: Labour Options and Business Strategies in High Labour Cost Countries." *International Labour Review* 131(4–5):453–470.

Williams, Harry B. 1989. "What Temporary Workers Earn: Findings from New BLS Survey." *Monthly Labor Review* 112(3):3–6.

Windschild, Gunther. 1991. "The Social Component of the Market Economy." Pp. 89–99 in *Meet United Germany*, edited by Susan Stern. Frankfurt am Main: Frankfurter Allgemeine Zeitung GmbH Informationsdienste.

13 CONTESTED CITIZENSHIP

THE DYNAMICS OF RACIAL IDENTITY
AND SOCIAL MOVEMENTS*

Anthony W. Marx

While scholarly discussions of citizenship, social movements, and racial identity-formation have generally remained distinct, these social institutions and processes are intimately connected. Official policies of exclusion from citizenship according to race have drawn boundaries solidifying subordinated racial identity, which then forms the basis for collective action in response to shifting state policies. Forms of domination are thus two-edged; exclusion of officially specified groups has the unintended consequence of defining, legitimating and provoking group identity and mobilization, forging struggles for inclusion between state agents and emerging political actors. This dynamic has generally been overlooked by those theorists of social movements who have focused on relative deprivation, resource mobilization, and responses to political opportunities, without explaining the related process of identity formation.

Defining the "who" of social mobilization must logically and (to some degree) temporally precede the logic by which a group responds to its economic and political situation, with the definitional issues shaping how such situations or opportunities are perceived and acted upon. In Karl Marx's (1977:214) terms, a group must be conscious of existing "in itself" before it can engage in collective action "for itself."[1] The "object" of a self-conscious group must be evident before it can act in response to its situation. I believe that the state plays a leading role in so defining a collective object, and in doing so both constrains and facilitates the terms by which deprivation, resources, and opportunities are understood, resisted, or embraced. Indeed, opportunities for mobilization according to race are defined as such and pursued, depending on whether and how such identity has developed in the first place. Social categories of identity thus shape social outcomes.

To clarify this argument as it applies to race, it is useful first to review recent developments in theoretical work. I will then proceed to examine the actual dynamics in three cases: South Africa, the United States, and Brazil with their majority, minority, and roughly equal mix of African descendants, respectively. Combining these three disparate cases will prove particularly useful for comparative purposes, in that any explanation of racial exclusion, identity, and mobilization in South Africa and the United States must be consistent with the relative lack of such dynamics in Brazil. Finally, albeit briefly, it will be possible to suggest the implications of these dynamics for other forms of identity and social movements.

One of the classic explanations of social movements argues that "relative deprivation" provokes mobilization (Gurr 1970). Theorists concerned with race and ethnicity have followed this argument in suggesting that increased economic competition, "split labor markets," or job replacement by immigrants, provoke protest by displaced blacks (Bonacich 1972; Olzak 1992; Van den Berghe 1967). On empirical grounds, this argument cannot account for extended periods of heightened relative deprivation which failed to produce mobilization, such as during the first half of this century in the United States and South Africa. As Sidney Tarrow concludes, "outbreaks of collective action cannot be derived from the level of deprivation that people suffer" (1994:81). This explanation also ignores the extent to which mobilization, when it does occur, is often more directed at gaining social and political rights than economic advancement per se. Even more profoundly, the relative deprivation analysis cannot account for whether, how, or when blacks might come to develop an "awareness of their deprived status as a group" (Murray and Vedlitz 1977:1070). Deprivation may be experienced and perceived by individuals, who may not see themselves as part of a group so deprived, with or without resources to combat their deprivation. The shift to group solidarity and action remains to be explained.

The resource mobilization approach developed largely in response to the relative deprivation school's empirical deficiencies, if not its omission of the prior issue of identity. According to the resource mobilization theorists, more or less constant economic deprivation and related grievances do not provoke mobilization in the absence of a critical mass of supporters benefiting from allies and organizational resources (McCarthy and Zald 1977; Morris and Mueller 1992:3).[2] Critics have argued that this approach places undue emphasis on external and elite actors, for instance largely ignoring the "indigenous" resources provided by urban networks, churches, colleges and other associations which were centrally involved in mobilization of the Civil Rights movement in the United States (McAdam 1982; McAdam et al. 1988:702; Morris 1984). In addition, the resource mobilization school generally ignored the role of the state as a provider of external resources, and the importance of divisions within the ranks of the ruling elite (Hechter 1987:48; Tarrow 1994:88). Again, these empirical deficiencies ignore the more fundamental question of whether, why, and how group identity emerges to build and take advantage of either external or indigenous resources.[3] Resources become relevant only if there is a collective actor that perceives them as such and acts upon them.

More recently, theorists of "political opportunity structures" have made a significant contribution in explaining why mobilization occurs during particular historical periods. According to this approach, the state emerges as a central actor, for as the modern state increasingly penetrates society its actions provoke and serve as a target of mobilization (Tarrow 1994:31, 61–62).[4] Protest, elite division, economic and international pressures may make the state increasingly responsive or vulnerable to pressure, inviting further mobilization by increasing the likelihood of reform (Chong 1991; McAdam 1982; Tarrow 1983; Tilly 1992). Groups then organize to take advantage of such opportunities, following the schedule of shifts in state policy, and pursuing "repertoires" of collective action designed to take advantage of such political opportunities (Wilson 1973:61; Tilly 1992; McAdam 1983). But as useful as this approach is for explaining the timing of mobilization as a response to state policy, it still does not directly address the prior question of how a group identity is formed which can perceive or act upon such opportunities. Nor does it address how opportunities are themselves shaped or interpreted according to the emergence of such identities.

By the mid-1980s, theorists had finally begun to focus on the question of identity formation. Establishing "who" mobilizes is constitutive of, if not prior to, considering how and when a social movement emerges (Cohen 1985).[5] As such, the identity-formation approach well described by Jean Cohen moved beyond a focus on individual economic rationality or resource availability applied to an unspecified group.[6] Further theoretical advances were suggested by Charles Tilly's (1985) discussion of the importance of "cateness and netness," referring to identifying categories and networks as building blocks of movements. But as much as this approach broke new ground in recognizing the significance of identity formation, it generally abstracted the actual processes which would explain the emergence and boundaries of a particular identity as a social actor. More recent scholarship has addressed this issue, focusing on the role of "frames," inequality, and identities as motivating factors in social mobilization, thereby demonstrating the connection between identity formation and previous discussions of deprivation, resources, and opportunities (Morris and Mueller 1992).

In order to specify further the process of identity formation, it is useful to pursue earlier insights as to the role of the state. Clearly, states and social movements interact, for most modern movements are aimed at altering state policy and shaped by the opportunities for such reform. In a general sense, "it is impossible to understand the history of the powerless without understanding the history of the powerful" (Viotta da Costa 1985:xvii). More precisely, we have already seen that strong states that penetrate civil society tend to provoke equally strong nation-wide mobilization (Birnbaum 1988; Tilly 1974). The "structure of domination" would then somehow seem to shape the structure of resistance (Oberschall 1978). Following Weber, if public policy by the state provides some "transparency of the connections between the causes and consequences" of domination, then it should be possible to so specify this process (Gerth and Mills 1958:184). If indeed the type of movement is "perhaps determined primarily by the type of state to which it was opposed" (Birnbaum 1988:73), then we should be able to explain the process of identity formation as an outcome of state policy, prior to and determining of forms of mobilization. Of course, not all identities or social movements emerge from this dynamic, for instance with "new social movements" distinguished by their greater autonomy from the state. But given that many movements are shaped by and respond to the state, this dynamic deserves further analysis.

States shape civil society, *inter alia,* by establishing boundaries for inclusion or exclusion in the polity, through the process of "social closure" (Morris and Mueller 1992; Parkin 1979; Parkin 1982). The key mechanism for such "closure" is via the establishment of rules for citizenship, described by T.H. Marshall (1992) as selectively providing distinct civil, political, and economic rights. By defining and specifying "others" outside of the citizenry, states seek to unify those included in the nation as citizens. In the process, states provide a clear definition of those excluded, with the policies of such exclusion inadvertently serving as a unifying target of mobilization for "inclusion in the polity" (Shklar 1991:62).

Citizenship thus creates the "social construct" of relevant identities, with "oppositional consciousness" forged in reaction to the frame of domination (Morris and Mueller 1992). Group exclusion defines subordinate identity and provokes a struggle for inclusion defined by the terms of citizenship, which often results in the further extension of such rights until they become "universal" (Bendix 1964:3; Shklar 1991:15). The historical expansion of "citizenship emerged through a rough dialectic between movements—actual and feared—and the national state" (Tarrow 1994:76). This process of gradual inclusion involves protracted contestation, with contestants defined by exclusion and motivated by their "aspirations for public standing," or "rewards" gained only by inclusion in the political system (Calhoun 1994; Lipsky 1968; Shklar 1991). Gaining citizenship rights thus serves as a "frame" for mobilization, with exclusion defining and shaping opportunities for collective action aimed at inclusion legitimated as citizenship (Morris and Mueller 1992). Building on Hirschman's (1970) classic analysis, groups defined by their formal exclusion must use their "voice" to overcome their enforced and defining "exit" from the polity. Citizenship thus appears to be crucial in setting the boundaries of group identity as a basis for mobilization directed at overcoming exclusion and gaining citizenship, the central aspiration of the populace in the era of the nation-state. Deprivation, resources and opportunities are perceived and acted upon within this context of emerging group identity and solidarity.

If this argument about the potential consequences of state policies of citizenship exclusion is to prove robust, it must not only explain identity formation but also variations in mobilization by groups so defined. There is an established literature describing shifts in "repertoires" of contention as responses to changing forms of domination (Bright and Harding 1984; Tarrow 1994). Both heightened repression and reforms can invite mobilization by excluded groups angered or encouraged by shifts of policy, with mobilizing groups seeking to learn from previous experience and to build on earlier successes at moving toward inclusion (Hardin 1982; Muller and Opp 1986). Thus, social movements are shaped both by the "push" of their own internal development and by the "pull of a common target" defined by exclusion (Tarrow 1994). In this sense, the identity and strategy of movements are linked, both as directly related to state policy (Escobar and Alvarez 1992). Exclusion defines the group and "political opportunities" for overcoming such exclusion, and influences the timing and form of such efforts. And as T.H. Marshall (1992) suggested, such efforts are directed at winning civil political and social rights, often in that order.

Based on this theoretical discussion, it is now possible to put forward a more informed thesis of racial identity formation and mobilization. States reinforce racial identity among those excluded from citizenship according to official boundaries referring to physical differences of skin color. Such exclusion then provides a unifying target for mobilization aimed at overcoming exclusion and at winning civil, political, and economic rights. Reinforced exclusion provokes more militant action or separatism, and reforms invite more moderate forms of mobilization, often for integration. The "who" and the "how" of mobilization are thus established by the focal point of the polity, with the form of domination and exclusion having the unintended consequence of setting the terms for its own opposition. As social movements in the modern nation-state are generally aimed at winning concessions and acceptance from the state, the state defines the dynamic of this process. Explicitly racial domination thus is two-edged, inviting racial identity formation and providing opportunities for mobilization, in turn. States create and legitimate racial categories through exclusion, with subsequent state policies providing resources and shaping opportunities for mobilization aimed at overcoming such exclusion so defined. Exclusion defines and unifies "who" are subordinated, and invites pressure for inclusion; identity formation and opportunity structures are thus connected. Ironically, categorical exclusion punishes the excluded in the short term, but provides them with bases for mobilization pressing for redress in the long run; lack of categorical exclusion is beneficial in the short term, but inhibits mobilization in the long run.

Constructing an abstract theory of identity formation and mobilization is one thing; testing such a theory against historical experience is another. But these two approaches must be connected. Accordingly, I will now proceed to examine the three cases of South Africa, the United States, and Brazil, to see whether the dynamics of racial identity and mobilization follow the general pattern thus far described. If so, then the highly elaborated form of racial domination in South Africa should have provoked considerable subordinated racial identity and mobilization, the lack of such official racism in Brazil should have produced less racial identity consolidation and protest, and the United States can be expected to fall between these two cases but, given Jim Crow, closer to the South African pattern. In exploring this comparison, it is useful to acknowledge up front the difficulty of including "identity" in any such analysis, given that specifying individual and group consciousness is always problematic. That social science cannot "read minds" should not preclude consideration of the mental states of identity as relevant to social outcomes. To address this issue, I will necessarily rely on elite pronouncements and evidence of collective action as indicators of identity formation, cognizant of the limits of this approach.

SOUTH AFRICA: MOBILIZATION AGAINST EXCLUSION

South Africa presents the quintessential case of racial identity and mobilization shaped in response to state policies of exclusion. Unification of the South African state was achieved by official discrimination against the indigenous black majority, consolidating racially defined opposition in response and provoking early forms of protest. As long as formal discrimination appeared fluid and open to reform, mobilization was muted and moderate. Reinforced discrimination provoked a more militant, mass-based response.

When discrimination was further systematized under apartheid repression, collective action was stymied. With the emergence of divisions within "the ruling bloc," mobilization reemerged. Throughout this process, the form of protest reflected shifts in state policy; reinforced racial exclusion provoked black separatism, reforms prompted a shift to "nonracialism," and the state's initiation of negotiations encouraged opposition compromise. In short, the emergence and development of black South African identity and collective action is intimately connected with the dynamics of official racial domination.

The first thing to note is that during the 19th century, before the emergence of a unitary South African state imposing uniform racial exclusion, "black" racial identity or mobilization remained largely inchoate. British "indirect rule" over the Cape and Natal provoked sometimes violent resistance by local groups responding to localized policies, most notably with the defeat of a British regiment by the Zulus in 1879. Colonial policies of playing "tribal" rulers and factions off against each other encouraged "tribal" responses, generally predating the emergence of a unified racial consciousness.[7] In addition, "coloureds" and "Indians," as they came to be categorized, remained largely complacent; the coloureds' "African Political Organization" and Gandhi's mobilization of the Indian community developed only after the turn of the century (Walshe 1971:15–16). In short, neither identity or collective action by race per se developed in the absence of explicitly and fully elaborated formal domination, despite considerable deprivation, oppression, and early discrimination.

Uniform, legal racial domination and resulting protest only emerged with the formation of a unified South African state. In fact, such racial dynamics were encoded in the very founding of that state. As the British High Commissioner, Sir Alfred Milner, understood as early as 1897, unified "self government . . . and colonial loyalty . . . [required] the abandonment of the black races" (Le May 1965:11–12). Milner's expectation proved to be self-fulfilling, with the resolution of the bloody Boer War (1899–1902) between Britain and Afrikaners achieved only on "the Boers' terms," excluding the majority from the polity. Milner's first draft of the 1902 peace treaty included a clause promising extension of the franchise to "the natives." Boer Generals Smuts and Hertzog crossed out this clause, replacing it with a vague commitment to later discussions of this issue, a formulation to which the British agreed (Kestell and van Velden 1912). For the British, peace between them and the Afrikaners, allowing for the consolidation of a single state, proved more important than the protection of native rights, which were accordingly abandoned. The Afrikaners had proved themselves a viable threat to the emerging nation-state and had to be appeased with subordination of the black majority, which had historically been more divided and contained. Racial exclusion became the "founding flaw" of the South African state.

With the formal establishment of a unified South African state in 1910, "an avalanche of segregatory (sic) legislation and discriminatory policies . . . descended upon blacks," setting the terms for subsequent mobilization (Lewis 1987:64).[8] In 1912 what became the African National Congress (ANC) was formed, with the goal of overcoming "tribal" divisions in order to press for "a uniform Native policy" (Seme 1972). The "common destiny" of the African people suffering from political exclusion and segregation was portrayed as the basis for united action in response. According to the ANC's founding president, "the white people of this country have formed what is known as the Union of South Africa—a union in which we have no voice. . . . We have called you therefore to this Conference . . . for the purpose of creating national unity and defending our rights and privileges" (Walshe 1971:34). By 1920, the ANC recognized that "the Union Act of 1910 unites only the white races and that as against the blacks; for the colour bar struck the death-knell of Native confidence in what used to be called British fair play. That cow of Great Britain has gone dry" (Jabavu 1972:120). Accordingly, the ANC abandoned its polite petitioning of the British government, shifting its focus to limited domestic lobbying against the racially exclusive form of South African citizenship.

From the 1920s through the mid-1940s, the South African state wavered in its application of racial segregation, provoking continued but still limited protest by blacks. General Smuts' government proposed to relax the color bar in the early 1920s, with this policy reversed by Hertzog after 1924. In response, the Industrial and Commercial Workers' Union (ICU) organized strikes and adopted Garveyite rhetoric, with the ICU's leader proclaiming that "we natives . . . are dealing with rascals—the Europeans are rascals" (Karis and Carter 1972; Lodge 1983:9; Walshe 1971). Reforms during the 1930s served as a "palliative," bringing the ANC to "the nadir" of its influence (Lodge 1983; Thompson 1991). By 1936, the growth of a small black middle class bolstered by industrialization but still excluded from the polity, inspired calls for "common citizenship" (Karis and Carter 1972). Perhaps most significantly, after 1933 and culminating 10 years later, the South African government abandoned its commitment to specified rights for "coloureds," provoking leaders of that community "to seek closer cooperation with Africans" (Karis and Carter 1972; Lewis 1987:177–211; Marks and Trapido 1987). Consolidation of formal racial discrimination pushed

Coloureds and Africans toward a common identity and mobilization on the basis of their common exclusion from citizenship.

With the National Party victory in 1948 and the reinforcement of segregation as apartheid, the terms for heightened protest were clearly set. The ANC was revitalized by its Youth League, committed to "Africanism" and to encouraging "national consciousness and unity opposed to white racial domination" (Karis and Carter 1972). Massive defiance followed the formalization of apartheid, bringing together Africans, Coloureds, and Indians as common victims of racially defined exclusion, who interpreted this explicit exclusion as an opportunity for advocating its reversal. The distinctions between these groups did not disappear, but a common platform emerged in the Freedom Charter of 1955, adopted by the ANC. Four years later the even more militant Pan Africanist Congress (PAC) was founded, with further protest culminating in the 1960 Sharpeville massacre. Recognizing that its exclusionary policies had reinforced opposition, the South African state moved quickly to ban the ANC and PAC, ushering in a decade of relative quiescence imposed by repression.

The 1970s and 1980s saw a resurgence of opposition, united by apartheid and bolstered by resources and opportunities presented thereby, as I have described elsewhere (Marx 1992). By the late 1960s and early 1970s, demand for more skilled labor brought black students together in segregated schools and universities, including those located in the newly formed separate black homelands. Led by Steve Biko, many of these students came together in the Black Consciousness movement, significantly unifying Africans, Coloureds, and Indians all as "black" victims of heightened racial discrimination. Apartheid had forged a unified racial identity among the excluded, expressed in the 1976 Soweto uprising. Faced with such massive unrest, the South African state began to reform, legalizing trade unions and by 1983 proposing a new constitution offering limited citizenship rights to Coloureds and Indians. The United Democratic Front (UDF) implicitly aligned with the formally exiled ANC, took advantage of the opportunity of this reopening of the issue of citizenship, calling for massive protests against the continued exclusion of the African majority. Official efforts to sideline Africans into citizenship of the homelands were rejected; according to one squatter, "the government is telling us we are not South Africans, but we were born here."[9] When the state clamped down on the UDF with a State of Emergency in the mid-1980s the trade union movements kept up the momentum of pressure, contributing to the initiation of negotiations in 1990.

What emerges from this summary is the degree to which black racial identity was forged in response to official state discrimination. State policies unintentionally provided resources and opportunities for mobilization around emergent black identity. Segregation and apartheid forced together its victims, whose direct experiences informed their common identity as blacks and provoked protest. While full-scale repression curtailed mobilization, as during the 1960s, both reinforced and relaxed oppression provoked increasingly massive protest, in a curvilinear process. Heightened segregation encouraged black separatism, and reforms encouraged "nonracial" efforts at integration. Throughout, official exclusion and segregation provided the crucial ingredient of a common identity, complemented by the resources provided by increased industrialization and urbanization, and the opportunities provided by anger at repression, and space opened by reform. All in all, racial identity and mobilization were closely tied to the dynamics of state policy.

This argument is further validated by recent developments. As the South African state in 1990 began to shift away from formal racial exclusion and segregation, toward "nonracial" democracy, racial identity and mobilization has lost some of its salience. In its place, political entrepreneurs have increasingly relied on "ethnic" identities as the basis of mobilization, as indicated by Zulu nationalism and "coloured" fears of African domination under the ANC. As the glue of official racial domination has dissolved, so has the salience of racial identity and mobilization begun to fade, with reconfigured "earlier" forms of identity reemerging. Earlier state policies, for instance to divide blacks by reinforcing ethnic distinctions, ensured that such divisions would remain "available" for manipulation by political entrepreneurs once unifying racial domination was officially abandoned.

What is also notable from this summary is the primacy of political over economic issues. As long as black South Africans were excluded from the polity and economically disadvantaged as such, it was the former that was more often the target of mobilization. The mainstream opposition, headed by the ANC, explicitly focused on achieving "national democratic liberation," purposefully postponing demands for economic redistribution until a "second stage of struggle." Achieving civil and political rights, as an aspect of nation-building, was seen as prior to addressing social or economic redress.[10] The obvious exception to this priority has been the trade union movement, but even the unions have often subordinated broader economic demands while pursuing the interests of their membership. Given the divergent interests of white workers supporting racial exclusion, economistic mobilization by a unified working class was simply not a viable option. The quest for civil and political forms of citizenship for blacks has taken precedence over related social demands, consistent with the South African state's official focus on political exclusion and with T.H. Marshall's general argument.

In sum, political exclusion and segregation according to race shaped a collective black South African identity accordingly, provoking mobilization in response to available resources and opportunities. Identity formation occurred in response to state policy, logically and temporally prior to the dynamics of social mobilization described by theorists of deprivation resource mobilization and political opportunity. Indeed, these dynamics of collective action were determined by the process of identity formation; exclusion solidified subordinate identity and implicitly created the opportunity for mobilization demanding inclusion.

UNITED STATES: THE QUEST FOR CITIZENSHIP

The issue of whether and how to include blacks in the American polity, and African-American struggles for full citizenship, are as old as the republic (Shklar 1991). Pre-Civil War compromises over the maintenance and extension of slavery were central to the process of state-building, with revolts and abolitionism focused on slavery rather than racial discrimination per se. Explicitly racial identity remained quotidian, and as long as this remained the case, mobilization according to race was constrained. To the extent that post-abolition race relations were considered at all before the Civil War, the prevailing trend among whites and many blacks was for recolonization back to Africa. During the 19th century, more than 13,000 former slaves were "repatriated," with federal financial support (Redky 1969). Abraham Lincoln and black activists such as Martin Delaney supported the colonization efforts. Delaney himself reversed his position, loyally supporting the North's efforts at abolition by joining the Union army during the Civil War, and then again advocating a return to Africa once Reconstruction was abandoned (Moses 1978).

Delaney's own shifting position reflects a general trend among the black elite of moderate patriotism during periods of reform and separatism in response to official betrayal. While Frederick Douglass never supported colonization, he also shifted between support for the Union, pessimism after Reconstruction, and then acceptance of a federal posting in Haiti (Foner 1970; Hamilton 1986; McCartney 1992). Like many others, Douglass believed that effectively "slavery is not abolished until the black man has the ballot," and that militant assertion toward that end would only come with gradually increased socioeconomic status (Du Bois 1965; Marx 1969; Shklar 1991:52). Booker T. Washington accordingly abandoned political assertiveness in favor of separate economic advancement, encouraged by his influence over federal patronage for Southern blacks (Williamson 1986). While W.E.B. Du Bois in the North advocated greater political agitation, he remained ambivalently drawn between loyalty for America and for his race, tortured by "his double self" (Du Bois 1965:215). The unresolved place of blacks in the post–Civil War era, when Jim Crow segregation was beginning to be applied, left African-American intellectuals struggling with this dilemma, seeking to reinforce racial identity as a basis for mobilization once resources and opportunities emerged.

Jim Crow was a local boy, unevenly enforced by states with the grudging complicity of federal authority more concerned with healing the wounds of the Civil War and Reconstruction than with enforcing justice. As a result, the target against which nationwide racial identity could be formed remained less fixed than in South Africa, where segregation was imposed on the majority from the center, albeit for similar purposes of white reconciliation and unity. And where Jim Crow was firmly established with repressive force, mobilization was muted, as it was during periods of extreme repression in South Africa. Civil and political rights remained elusive, as did social advancement. Black racial identity remained caught in Du Bois' "dual striving," provoked by local official exclusion and segregation, but dampened by loyalty and belief in "the American creed" of equality promised more than delivered (Myrdal 1944). America's ambivalence in regard to race provided a still uncertain foundation on which to build a unified black identity or movement.

Full citizenship would only come from federal reforms and mobilization united by common identity and dependent on resources, all of which were in short supply until the mid-20th century. The most notable earlier attempt to forge such mass identity and mobilization was led by Marcus Garvey, who combined Washington's focus on economic advancement with calls for colonization "back to Africa," and for "racial unity" (Bracey et al., 1970; Garrow 1988; Hall 1977). Not surprisingly, Garvey's support was based in the North, where blacks had more resources and were less subject to repression, but Garvey remained controversial and his movement foundered after he was imprisoned by federal authorities (Hamilton 1973).

After Garvey and until the 1950s, the absence of opportunities and resources was reflected in the relative lack of mass mobilization. The Urban League did manage to assist blacks migrating to the North, with federal and corporate support (Parsons and Clark 1965; Weiss 1989). The interracially led NAACP gained a mass following only in the years of economic growth during World War II (Marable 1991; Parsons and Clark 1966). Believing that the government was always the key, and that before 1960 only the judicial branch was "operating" in regard to civil rights, the NAACP focused on obtaining judicial relief.[11] As such, the NAACP was dependent on official sympathy or white allies, and remained skeptical of disruptive mass protest. The relative absence of such protest during the first half of this century reflected not only incomplete identity formation, but also the small size of the black middle class and incomplete consolidation of urbanized black concentrations.

The greatest test of any theory of social movements applied to African-Americans is to account for the dramatic rise of the civil rights movement in the 1950s and 1960s. Theorists of relative deprivation have argued that heightened inequality produced the movement,[12] but such arguments fail to account for why pervasive deprivation provoked mobilization only in the 1950s, and initially in the South. Resource mobilization theorists have generally focused on the rise of white elite allies supporting the rise of the civil rights movement, but they cannot account for why such support developed. In addition, recent studies have shown that the most active civil rights organizations initially received relatively little outside support, and that such support generally followed rather than preceded activism (Jenkins and Eckert 1986; McAdam 1982). Aldon Morris has corrected the resource mobilization approach by demonstrating the greater importance of "indigenous" resources, including the networks of previously conservative black churches and organizations such as the NAACP and the Congress of Racial Equality (Morris 1984; Morris and Herring 1987; Morris and Mueller 1992).

Consistent with this argument, the emergence of the movement coincided with the rising size, urbanization, and expectations of the black middle class as crucial movement actors with resources at their disposal (Carmichael and Hamilton 1967; Landry 1987; Pettigrew 1971; Wilson 1978). It was this group that played a central role in consolidating a collective black identity and group consciousness. The black middle class, particularly in the South, experienced formal racial segregation which precluded them from advancing beyond their imposed category. In response, this black elite saw their fate as tied to blacks as a whole, and recognized the need for collective action. By the 1950s, this elite finally had the resources needed to act more effectively. All that was missing was federal intervention which would provide a nationally unifying spark for collective action, giving impetus to emergent collective identity. Initially among the black middle class, a consolidated black identity emerged to take advantage of opportunities when they arose.

The timing of the emergence of the civil rights movement has been best explained by the opening of "political opportunities" in the form of federal responsiveness (Chong 1991; McAdam 1982). No less an authority than Martin Luther King, Jr. cited the importance of governmental concessions in explaining the rise and moderate form of the movement (Garrow 1988). Building on earlier decisions, the strongest "spark" for the movement came from the Supreme Court's "Brown vs. Board of Education" decision in support of school desegregation, which had the effect of encouraging "moderate" leadership (Carson 1981; Killian 1968). "For the first time since Reconstruction they felt the federal government was actually on their side" (Durr 1990). Further evidence of federal support was provided by the reluctant decision of President Eisenhower to send the army to support desegregation in Little Rock in 1957, "the first such commitment of federal troops since Reconstruction" (Brisbane 1974:31; McAdam 1988). John F. Kennedy's election with decisive black support made black leaders even "more hopeful," despite Kennedy's failure to fulfill his civil rights campaign promises immediately.[13] By 1963, Kennedy had begun to shift away from his reluctance to interfere in "state's rights," declaring that "the time has come for this nation to fulfill its promise" to blacks (Carson et al. 1991:161; Marshall 1964). By then, a consolidated black identity was in place to take advantage of this opening; such solidarity was a vital part of the process of mobilization consistent with the political opportunity thesis, though largely ignored by it.

The causes of the federal government's increased responsiveness were multiple. The trend toward federal intervention to redress social inequality had begun with the New Deal (Parsons and Clark 1965). "Fighting against racism over yonder" during World War II had increased concern about racism at home, among whites and especially black veterans who had been "given a chance to compete" but returned home to segregation.[14] In the aftermath of the war, the United States had emerged as a superpower, determined to defeat Communism and win over allies to the West. Once the paranoia of the McCarthyite period subsided, the federal government became increasingly concerned with the difficulties posed by domestic segregation for winning over African allies. This concern was reflected in the "Brown" decision, and is evident in the quick publicity of that decision in international propaganda over the Voice of America (Kluger 1977). By the late 1950s and early 1960s, the federal government had both the capacity and interest to exert its authority in pushing for civil rights reforms in what Kennedy termed the "second Reconstruction." Early mobilization emerged in the South, where official segregation helped to unify a collective black identity and where protests were aimed at provoking intervention by receptive federal authorities. A more direct or provocative expression of increased "political opportunity" is difficult to imagine.

The emergence of black identity, based on the experiences of official discrimination, segregation, and urbanization, provided a collective actor ready to push for and take advantage of emerging opportunities. Indeed, such solidarity helped to create the opportunity for action and certainly made for a collectivity to take up those opportunities. For instance, pressure from increased black voting in the North among recent migrants from the South pushed the central government toward civil rights intervention. But partisan concern about the black vote only emerged once black identity had developed to the point of solidifying an active voting block concerned with both domestic and international issues. And in the South concern about the black vote would emerge only after civil rights reforms provided for the franchise. But with the opening of reforms, the black collectivity was primed to push further, much beyond what the federal authorities had intended. The emergence of racial identity, based on the experience of segregation, in effect pushed upon the opportunity for collective action, bringing further reforms which reinforced racial identity, in an escalating cycle.

Both the shift of federal policy and the consolidation of nation-wide black identity were influenced by the spread of the mass media. For example, "when the fire hoses were brought down to a church and put on TV, even middle class whites were incensed."[15] According to activist Willie Ricks, "television urbanized the rural folks" and brought them into the movement despite their lack of organizational resources.[16] But the effect was even more pervasive, contributing to the emergence of mobilization also in the North, where (the former) Stokely Carmichael notes that "people . . . saw us being beaten up, building up their own sense of frustration."[17] According to Burke Marshall, the senior civil rights official in Kennedy's Justice Department, "television and communications technology educated the rest of the country to what was an intolerable situation, and that is an important part of what makes the political system run."[18] In other words, black mobilization provoked in the South by local discrimination and encouraged by federal responsiveness, then created images spread by the media which pushed the federal government toward further reforms, inspired wider black solidarity, and helped to provoke later mobilization in the North.

Northern militancy and riots in the 1960s have been described as a signal of the decline of the civil rights movement, but they are better understood as a different form of mobilization provoked by the closing of political opportunities. The Northern riots and Black Power movement of the mid- to late 1960s were aimed, in part, at forcing further federal intervention

during a period of decreasing governmental responsiveness. Success in winning legislative reforms which failed to change harsh conditions on the
ground in the North sparked riots, as symbolized by the Watts riots explod-
ing days after the passage of the Voting Rights Act. Rioters and militant activists were inspired by the Southern movement, reinforcing national solidarity; "the riots came out of what we saw happening in the South. Spirits
were stirred. There was a contagion."[19] Northern blacks were also angered
by the retreat from the exaggerated promises of the Great Society programs
depleted by the rising costs of the Vietnam War (Brink and Harris 1966;
Moynihan 1969; Wofford 1980). Northern blacks in particular watched in
dismay as federal responsiveness to civil rights was replaced by concern for
"law and order" (Button 1978; Calhoun 1994; Tarrow 1994). Richard
Nixon's "Southern strategy," consistent with his policy of "benign neglect"
toward black concerns, symbolized the rightward shift. Again, mobilization
followed a shift of federal policy, this time in the opposite direction from
that which had encouraged the more integrationist civil rights movement.

Analysis of African-American mobilization since the 1950s would
clearly be incomplete without consideration of identity formation. Certainly
the common experience of segregation after the Civil War had gradually reinforced black solidarity, much as early segregation had encouraged solidarity
among black South Africans. At the same time, the localized nature of Jim
Crow had reinforced regional distinctions among blacks, with Northerners
having different experiences and forming distinct early movements. With the
postwar black migration North, this regional divide started to diminish. But
it was the rise of central authority responsiveness and televised activism on
civil rights which finally consolidated a common national black identity,
provoking Northern mobilization linked to Southern activism (Morris and
Mueller 1992; Tarrow 1994). According to one former activist, "it was the
Southern experience which enraged us. . . . I saw kids on TV who looked
like me. I identified with them as heroes. . . . People were coming up from
the South and telling their stories. . . . By 1964 segregation had fallen. Then
we could see the system; we saw it was not just about Southern segregation,
but really more national."[20]

Rising nationwide culture, spread by the media, came together with
the shift of federal policy from noninterference in Jim Crow to purposeful
intervention on behalf of civil rights. Only once the central authority had
the capacity to so exert itself did such intervention reinforce a truly nationwide black identity poised to seize opportunities for further reforms. The
central U.S. state could not and did not exert a uniform racial policy of reform until the middle of this century, no doubt in part because the black

minority was perceived to be a less pressing concern than was unifying regional divisions and gaining electoral support from the white majority. Consolidated black identity formation and mass mobilization emerged fully only once the central state had the capacity to act more forcefully to reform, much as a comparable degree of racial identity and mobilization emerged in South Africa with the consolidation of repressive apartheid in 1948.

Whereas South African mass mobilization was provoked by heightened repression under apartheid, civil rights activism in the United States emerged in response to reforms, with a more militant response emerging in reaction to the reversal of such reforms and urban inequality. By the mid-1960s, most African-Americans had been united in the view that "black people have not suffered as individuals but as members of a group; therefore their liberation lies in group action" (Carmichael and Hamilton 1967:54). Such group solidarity was expressed in Black Nationalism, cultural forums, and in continuing racial mobilization in local and national elections, with group solidarity as a necessary precondition to blacks perceiving and acting upon opportunities (Cole 1976; van Deburg 1992). Throughout these developments, mobilization in response to shifting state policy reinforced a nationwide identity among blacks united by their exclusion from full citizenship. Central state action in regard to racial exclusion and segregation reinforced black identity formation and then mobilization in response to opportunities, with unforeseen consequences. Once such pervasive racial identity had been clearly consolidated, it emerged as a mainstay of American politics, remaining salient even after formal exclusion and segregation had ended.

BRAZILIAN "EXCEPTIONALISM"

South Africa and the United States provide examples of how a state-enforced ideology of racial domination has the unintended consequence of consolidating oppositional identity according to race. Mobilization was then provoked by shifts of state policy, with mass protest in South Africa sparked by heightened repression, and in the United States by reform. The implication is that racial identity and varying mobilization are responses to shifting state capacity and policy, more than they are effects of relative deprivation or resource availability, which become relevant only once they are perceived by a self-conscious group. Exclusive citizenship sets the boundaries which reinforce group solidarity among the excluded, who then use the opportunities of shifting public space to demand inclusion in that space as equal citizens.

If the analysis presented thus far is to prove robust, it must also explain an instance of a relative lack of racial identity and mobilization. Brazil provides such a negative test. Since slavery, the Brazilian state has projected and enforced an inclusive form of citizenship purportedly embracing Brazilians of all color and class. Instead of racial domination, Brazil has projected an image of "racial democracy" purposefully aimed at unifying popular support. This inclusiveness provided a political veneer of equality overlaying vast inequalities between rich "whites" and poorer Afro-Brazilians. The relative lack of racial mobilization in Brazil suggests that such inequality alone is not sufficient to provoke mobilization in the absence of the target of an explicit, official racial ideology. In contrast to Brazil, official racial domination elsewhere has reinforced racial identity among a group able then to take advantage of opportunities and resources for protest, so defined.

The historical developments which led to Brazil's lack of explicit racial order can only be briefly summarized here. Portuguese colonialism imposed on Brazil a more unified central authority than was the case in South Africa or the United States. Emerging nationalism and tensions within Brazil were further muted by the arrival in 1808 of the Portuguese court, forced to flee from Napoleon. The relatively low level of economic development provided little impetus for conflicts that might otherwise have undermined state consolidation and capacity. "Clientalist" and "patrimonial" rule was preserved, and effectively never seriously challenged.[21] A "prefabricated" central state was in place when the winds of modernity hit. As a result, "Brazil is famous for its 'white,' or peaceful revolutions," finessing its transitions from empire to republic, and from slavery to abolition, in 1888–1889 (Freyre 1945:120). With no cataclysmic ethnic or regional conflict, civil war, or reconstruction comparable to that of the United States or South Africa, there was no need for the sort of reconciliation elsewhere achieved through an explicit ideology of racial domination.[22] In place of a nationalism unifying whites as dominant over a common black "enemy," the Brazilian state eschewed legal discrimination and encouraged nationalism which unified all Brazilians of any color (and including native "Indians"). Potential racial conflict was submerged under the myth of "racial democracy" and images of an inclusive nation and corporatist state.[23] The relative lack of ethnic or regional conflict made possible an apparently more "tolerant" racial order.

We must be careful not to slip into taking Brazil's "racial democracy" at face value, for racial inequalities have remained evident in Brazil. During and immediately after abolition, Brazil encouraged European and blocked African immigration, as part of a general project of trying to "whiten" the population (do Nascimento 1979; Franklin 1968; Morner 1970; Skidmore 1974; Toplin 1974). Afro-Brazilians continued to fill subordinate economic roles, reinforcing significant inequalities.[24] By the mid-1970s, more than half of non-white workers received the minimum wage or less, as compared to less than a quarter of white workers (Hasenbalg 1983:10). While it is an exaggeration to conclude that as a result of such inequality, "Brazil has no black middle class," it is fair to note that this black middle class remains small, not bound by legal discrimination to fellow Afro-Brazilians, and resistant to identifying itself with poor blacks.[25] As a result, the small black Brazilian elite did not play a role comparable to the African-American or black South African middle class in helping to forge a collective racial identity.

Though social and economic inequality remains evident, the lack of official racial discrimination was more consequential in muting the prospects for racial identity formation or mass protest. Inequality and informal discrimination were not sufficient to provoke such responses on a large scale. According to leading black activists, Afro-Brazilians face "no legal limits, only practical limits," encouraging blacks to seek advancement through incorporation rather than by racial assertion and collective action.[26] "Racism is camouflaged by the myth of racial democracy. [Most people believe our problems are because] we are poor, not because we are black."[27] The myth of racial democracy "has the power of confusing the Afro-Brazilian people, doping them, numbing them inside or barring almost definitively any possibility of their self-affirmation, integrity or identity" (do Nascimento 1979:2). The result has been a dramatically low level of racial identity consolidation or mass protest according to race, despite inequality, despite a rich history of slave revolts, and despite the exclusion from voting until 1988 by many blacks barred as illiterate. As such exclusion from full citizenship was not explicitly based on race, it provided no identifying category or target for racial mobilization. Nor did efforts at such mobilization garner resources from white allies; "since whites say there is no racism, they give no support to black movements," helping to account for why no black movement organization has lasted even 10 years.[28] As a result, those movements that did emerge remained "limited, not mass movements, and as such they did not touch the consciousness of elites."[29] Even the most sympathetic of analysts have had to conclude that Afro-Brazilian mobilization has remained "quotidian" (Hanchard 1994).

While the inescapable overall conclusion is that Brazil's lack of explicit racial domination has discouraged racial identity-formation and provoked relatively little protest, the limited mobilization which did emerge has followed the patterns suggested above. Only in moments of crisis or transition in the form of state rule, has black protest emerged. Shifts of state policy have provoked what little mobilization did develop, with reforms encouraging a more moderate response and repression provoking greater militancy. For instance, the corporatist regime of Getulio Vargas, begun in the 1930s, initially encouraged black mobilization by "creating a climate of a general opening," including support for expressions of African culture (Levine 1970; Raphael 1981).[30] Established in 1931, the Frente Negra sought to take advantage of this opening, though it remained relatively small, elitist, and distinctly loyal to the regime and to the myth of racial democracy right up until it was banned by Vargas in 1937 (Andrews 1991; de Azevedo 1988; Gonzalez and Hasenbalg 1982; Moura 1989). The post-1964 military regime enacted a volatile mix of explicitly banning any discussion of race and then opening up the space for mobilization in a lengthy *abertura* (do Nascimento 1979; Kennedy 1986; Lovell 1989; Stepan 1989). In response, the Movimento Negro Unificado (MNU) emerged in 1978 "when the traditional system was being challenged with a new momentum, as a part of a general contestation."[31] The MNU was relatively militant, challenging the regime to live up to the image of racial democracy," and organizing local *centros du luto,* but the Movimento also remained small, elitist, and factionalized (dos Santos 1985; Fontaine 1981; Moura 1983; Movimento Negro Unificado 1988).

Since the reestablishment of democracy in Brazil, racial mobilization has remained muted, despite assertions by activists and sympathetic analysts to the contrary. The 1988 constitution declares that "the practice of racism constitutes a crime," clearly maintaining the state's rejection of any ideology of racial domination (Skidmore 1992). At the same time, the central and regional governments have established numerous new offices to coordinate Afro-Brazilian affairs, encouraged limited political activism around race, and supported celebrations of the centennial of abolition in 1988 (IBASE 1989). Progressive political parties have nominated black candidates for electoral office, though often these candidates have themselves downplayed the issue of race (Commisao de Religiosos Seminaristas e Padres Negros 1989; Gonzalez and Hasenbalg 1982; Valente 1986). Activists have complained that party platforms also generally fail to give prominence to the issue of racial discrimination. For instance, the MNU (1991:11) has complained that "according to the left, we are paranoid, fighting an enemy that does not exist."[32] According to one veteran activist, such constraints reflect the popular bias against race rhetoric: "all the politicians are afraid to use race. The great part of blacks don't want a racial discourse. The number of conscious people is very small."[33] The ingrained legacy of the myth of racial democracy has clearly limited the salience of race issues, explaining little popular responsiveness even now that there are no official constraints against addressing the issue of race.

Despite limited efforts at collective action, Brazil's lack of an explicit ideology or practice of racial domination has left Afro-Brazilians without the key initial ingredient for mobilization. With no clear target against which to organize, no unifying Afro-Brazilian political identity has emerged on a broad scale to take advantage of resources or opportunities for mobilization, despite the efforts of black activists. Since there has been no official racial limit on mobility, most blacks have accepted the ideology of racial democracy, seeing their path to advancement through the "whitening" process of miscegenation or passing. According to one veteran activist, "every black wants to be white."[34] As a result, "our biggest problem remains the fundamental lack of united identity,"[35] for without such group solidarity encouraged by official exclusion the possibilities of collective action are not even so perceived, let alone widely pursued. Opportunities for collective action have not been interpreted or acted upon as race specific, because the myth of racial democracy has camouflaged the racial component of subordination and thereby deflected identity formation. Thus, while Brazil appears to be an "exception" to the logic of racial identity formation and mobilization, it actually fits that logic by demonstrating that the relative lack of relevant causes produces an absence of race-specific consequences.

CONCLUSION

A comparison of the dynamics of racial identity formation and mobilization in South Africa, the United States, and Brazil is useful as much for the similarities revealed, as for the differences. By examining three cases of divergent political and economic development with varying demographic mixes of ancestry, it is possible to look for patterns linking such variation with similarity and difference of outcomes. The overarching pattern which does emerge is the similarity between South Africa and the United States in terms of official racial exclusion, identity formation, and mobilization, as contrasted with their relative absence in Brazil. What then do these patterns tell us about the dynamics of identity formation and mobilization?

First, neither relative deprivation or resource availability in themselves explain racial identity and mobilization. Put simply, deprivation and resource availability have heightened and diminished in South Africa and the United States without mobilization following the timing of these trends. Nor have deprivation and resources in Brazil brought comparable levels of mobilization. And these dynamics cannot explain the development of a collective identity of blacks as logically prior to such a group acting in response to its deprivation or resources.

A three-case comparison has demonstrated the central role of the state in shaping collective racial identity. For their own purposes, the South African and American state drew racially defined boundaries of exclusion from full citizenship, which had the unintended consequence of reinforcing a subordinated racial identity among blacks. Once such an identity was consolidated in response to official policy, then a collective actor self-consciously existed to interpret and respond to shifting political opportunities, economic conditions, and resources, defined accordingly. Full-scale repression often dampened mobilization, but variations in racial domination, either toward greater suppression or reform, invited mobilization. Change on the side of the state has provoked corresponding movement by subordinates. At midcentury, the South African state reinforced uniform segregation as apartheid, and the United States imposed reforms of localized Jim Crow. Racial identity was further consolidated by these processes, constructing a collective actor then able to take advantage of opportunities for mobilization. The Brazil case negatively reaffirms this pattern, in that the lack of explicit, official racial ideology and practices of racial domination have deprived Afro-Brazilians of a clear target against which their identity could be consolidated. Afro-Brazilian mobilization has remained muted in the relative absence of such identity consolidation, with limited mobilization following the general pattern of the other two cases. Opportunities for mobilization existed, but were not generally interpreted along racial lines and not pursued as such, demonstrating that the logic of opportunity structures is applicable only according to prior identity formation.

The implication of this argument is that the explicit form of state domination is two-edged in setting the grounds on which social movements emerge in response to official policy. This logic of identity formation is necessarily prior to the dynamics of social movement variation, and must be incorporated into such analysis. Not only race, but other forms of identity may emerge from similar dynamics. States often construct identities other than race for their own purposes, through explicit policies of exclusion and also inclusion, and in doing so set the boundaries and incentives for collective action. Therefore, analysis of ethnic, class, regional, or gender mobilization would be well served by further exploring the role of state policy in establishing the definitions and "life chances" of such groups, which then interpret and use resources and opportunities for their own ends. For example, corporatist arrangements of functionally classified citizenship often encourage class identity and trade union mobilization, and ethnically defined exclusion from the nation often provokes counter-ethnic solidarity and protest. A prominent example of such dynamics would be the way in which Stalin ratified ethnic and national categories, which then encouraged such identification and mobilization after the breakup of the Soviet Union. Similar patterns of Hapsburg or Ottoman imperial policies encouraging protonationalism, reinforcing such identities and mobilization accordingly during imperial breakdown, are now being more fully explored. This approach then suggests how analysts can bring together studies of nation-state formation, citizenship, identity, and social movements as interrelated, building upon the insights of earlier theoretical and empirical studies.

In more general terms, the analysis presented here is suggestive of an interaction between institutions and identities. Nation-state consolidation and rules of citizenship construct or reinforce categories of identity, which may then be embraced by those so identified as a basis for mobilization to alter such institutional arrangements. The interaction effects may thus be more iterated than generally understood; institutions shape identities, but mobilization around such identities also reshape institutions. Institutional rules of citizenship thus evolve over time, provoking and reconfigured through contestation.

NOTES

* This chapter previously appeared in *International Review of Social History* 40, Supplement 3 (1995):159–184. Reprinted by permission of Cambridge University Press.
1. *See also* Thompson (1966).
2. *See also* Oliver et al. (1985).
3. *See* Cohen 1985.
4. *See also* Tilly (1975:34, 80, 572); Birnbaum (1988).
5. *See also* Calhoun (1994).
6. *See* Tarrow (1988); Hardin (1982); Morris and Mueller (1992:57).
7. *See* Davenport (1977), Vail (1991).
8. *See also* Ashforth (1990).
9. Interview at Tekoza Squatter Camp, April 1988.
10. *See* Nolutshungu (1993).
11. Interview with Gloster Current, March 1993; Wofford 1980.
12. *See,* for instance, Pettigrew (1971).
13. Interview with Congressman John Lewis, 5 May 1993.
14. Interview with James Farmer, 6 May 1993; Interview with Congressman Charles Rangel, 8 April 1993; Forman 1972:93.
15. Interview with Wayne Greenshaw, 26 April 1993.
16. Interview with Willie Ricks, 28 April 1993.
17. Interview with Kwame Ture (a.k.a. Stokely Carmichael), 19 March 1993.
18. Interview with Burke Marshall, 23 March 1994.
19. Interview with Roger Wilkins, 5 May 1993. *See* Tarrow (1994:5).
20. Interview with Barbara Omalade, 10 March 1993.
21. *See* Roett (1984).
22. *See,* for example, Pierson (1942:335).
23. *See, inter alia,* Skidmore (1974); Fontaine (1985).
24. *See,* for example, Hasenbalg (1977); Wagley (1952); Wood and de Carvalho (1988).
25. Interview with Jao Jorge Santos Rodrigues, 15 June 1993; Fernandes 1969.
26. Interview with Jao Jorge Santos Rodrigues, 15 June 1993.

27. Interview with Benedita da Silva, 20 July 1993.
28. Interview with Januario Garcia, 21 July 1993; Knight 1974:90.
29. Interview with Carlos Alberto Medeiros, 14 July 1993.
30. Interview with Abdias do Nascimento, 28 July 1993.
31. Interview with Carlos Alberto Medeiros, 14 July 1993.
32. *See also* do Valle Silva and Hasenbalg (1992:160).
33. Interview with Abdias do Nascimento, 28 July 1993.
34. Interview with Januario Garcia, 21 July 1993.
35. Interview with Clovis Moura, 8 July 1993.

REFERENCES

Andrews, George Ried. 1991. *Blacks and Whites in Sao Paulo Brazil, 1888–1988.* Madison: University of Wisconsin Press.

Ashforth, Adam. 1990. *The Politics of Official Discourse in Twentieth Century South Africa.* Oxford: Clarendon Press.

Bendix, Reinhard. 1964. *Nation-Building and Citizenship.* Berkeley: University of California Press.

Birnbaum, Pierre. 1988. *States and Collective Action.* Cambridge: Cambridge University Press.

Bonacich, Edna. 1972. "A Theory of Ethnic Antagonism: The Split Labor Market." *American Sociological Review* 37:547–559.

Bracey, Jr., John H., August Meier, and Elliott Rudwick, eds. 1970. *Black Nationalism in America.* Indianapolis: Bobbs-Merrill.

Bright, C., and S. Harding. 1984. *Statemaking and Social Movements.* Ann Arbor: University of Michigan Press.

Brink, William, and Louis Harris. 1966. *Black and White.* New York: Simon and Schuster.

Brisbane, Robert H. 1974. *Black Activism.* Valley Forge, PA: Judson Press.

Button, James W. 1978. *Black Violence.* Princeton: Princeton University Press.

Calhoun, Craig, ed. 1994. *Social Theory and the Politics of Identity.* Cambridge, MA: Blackwell.

Carmichael, Stokely, and Charles V. Hamilton. 1967. *Black Power.* New York: Random House.

Carson, Clayborne. 1981. *In Struggle.* Cambridge: Harvard University Press.

Carson, Clayborne, et al., eds. 1991. *The Eyes on the Prize.* New York: Penguin Books.

Cell, John. 1982. *The Highest Stage of White Supremacy.* New York: Cambridge University Press.

Chong, Dennis. 1991. *Collective Action and the Civil Rights Movement.* Chicago: University of Chicago Press.

Cohen, Jean. 1985. "Strategy or Identity." *Social Research* 52:663–716.

Cole, L.A. 1976. *Blacks in Power: A Comparative Study of Black and White Elected Officials.* Princeton, NJ: Princeton University Press.

Commisao de Religiosos Seminaristas e Padres Negros. 1989. *O Povo Negro e as Eleicoes de 1988.* Rio de Janeiro: Vozes.

Davenport, T.R.H. 1977. *South Africa: A Modern History.* Toronto: University of Toronto Press.

de Azevedo, Celia Maria Marinho. 1988. "Sinal Fechado Para os Negros na Rua da Liberdade." *Humanidades* 5:ILL.

do Nascimento, Abdias. 1979. *Brazil: Mixture or Massacre?* Dover, MA: Majority Press.

do Valle Silva, Nelson, and Carlos Hasenbalg. 1992. *Relacoes Raciais no Brasil Contemporaneo.* Rio de Janeiro: Rio Fundo Editorio.

dos Santos, Joel Rufino. 1985. "O Movimento Negro." *Politica e Administracao.* 11:287–309.

Du Bois, W.E.B. 1965. "The Souls of Black Folk." In *Three Negro Classics*. New York: Avon Books.

Durr, Virginia Foster. 1990. *Outside the Magic Circle*. Montgomery, AL: University of Alabama Press.

Escobar, Arturo, and Sonia Alvarez. 1992. *The Making of Social Movements in Latin America*. Boulder, CO: Westview Press.

Fernandes, Florestan. 1969. *The Negro in Brazilian Society*. New York: Columbia University Press.

Foner, Eric. 1970. *Free Soil, Free Labor, Free Men*. Oxford: Oxford University Press.

Fontaine, Pierre-Michel. 1981. "Transnational Relations and Racial Mobilization." In *Ethnic Identities in a Transnational World*, edited by John F. Stack, Jr. Westport, CT: Greenwood Press.

Fontaine, Pierre-Michel, ed. 1985. *Race, Class and Power in Brazil*. New York: Oxford University Press.

Forman, James. 1972. *The Making of Black Revolutionaries*. New York: Macmillan.

Franklin, John Hope. 1968. *Color and Race*. Boston: Houghton Mifflin.

Freyre, Gilberto. 1945. *Brazil: An Interpretation*. New York: Knopf.

Garrow, David J. 1988. *Bearing the Cross*. New York: Vintage Books.

Gavin, Lewis. 1987. *Between the Wire and the Wall*. Cape Town: St. Martin's Press.

Gerth, H.H., and C. Wright Mills, eds. 1958. *From Max Weber*. New York: Oxford University Press.

Gonzalez, Lelia, and Carlos Hasenbalg. 1982. *Lugar de Negro*. Rio de Janeiro: Editora Marco Zero.

Gurr, Ted Robert. 1970. *Why Men Rebel*. Princeton, NJ: Princeton University Press.

Hall, Raymond L., ed. 1977. *Black Separatism and Social Reality*. New York: Pergamon Press.

Hamilton, Charles V. 1973. *The Black Experience in American Politics*. New York: Putnam.

Hamilton, Charles V. 1986. "Social Policy and the Welfare of Black Americans." *Political Science Quarterly* 101:239–256.

Hanchard, Michael. 1994. *Orpheus and Power*. Princeton: Princeton University Press.

Hardin, Russell. 1982. *Collective Action*. Baltimore: Johns Hopkins University Press.

Hasenbalg, Carlos. 1977. "Desigualdades Raciais no Brasil." *Dados* XIV:7–33.

Hasenbalg, Carlos. 1983. "Race and Socio-Economic Inequality in Brazil." Rio de Janeiro: Institute Universitario de Pesquisa do Rio de Janeiro.

Hechter, Michael. 1987. *Principles of Group Solidarity*. Berkeley: University of California Press.

Hirschman, Albert O. 1970. *Exit, Voice and Loyalty*. Cambridge: Harvard University Press.

Instituto Brasileiro de Analises Sociaes e Economicas (IBASE). 1989. *Negros no Brasil: Dados da Realidade*. Petropolis:Vozes em co-ediacao com Instituto Brasileiro de Analises Sociais e Economicas.

Jabavu, J.D.T. 1972. "Native Unrest." In *From Protest to Challenge*, edited by Thomas Karis and Gwendolyn Carter. Stanford, CA: Hoover Institution Press.

Jenkins, J. Craig, and Craig M. Eckert. 1986. "Channeling Black Insurgency." *American Sociological Review* 51:812–829.

Karis, Thomas, and Gwendolyn Carter, eds. 1972. *From Protest to Challenge*. Stanford, CA: Hoover Institution Press.

Kennedy, James H. 1986. "Political Liberalization, Black Consciousness and Recent Afro-Brazilian Literature." *Phylon* XL:199–209.

Kestell, J.D., and D.E. van Velden. 1912. *The Peace Negotiations*. London: Clay.

Killian, Lewis M. 1968. *The Impossible Revolution?* New York: Random House.

Kluger, Richard. 1977. *Simple Justice*. New York: Vintage Books.

Knight, Franklin W. 1974. *The African Dimension of Latin American Societies*. New York: Macmillan.

Landry, Bart. 1987. *The New Black Middle Class*. Berkeley: University of California Press.

Le May, G.H.L. 1965. *British Supremacy in South Africa, 1899–1907*. Oxford: Clarendon Press.

Levine, Robert M. 1970. *The Vargas Regime*. New York: Columbia University Press.

Lewis, D.L. 1987. *The Race to Fashoda*. New York: Weidenfeld and Nicolson.

Lipsky, Michael. 1968. "Protest as a Political Resource." *American Political Science Review* 42:1144–1159.

Lodge, Tom. 1983. *Black Politics in South Africa Since 1945*. Johannesburg: Ravan Press.

Lovell, Peggy Ann. 1989. "Racial Inequality and the Brazilian Labor Market." Ph.D. Dissertation, Department of Sociology, University of Florida.

Marable, Manning. 1991. *Race, Reform ant Rebellion*. Jackson: University Press of Mississippi.

Marks, Shula, and Stanley Trapido. 1987. *The Politics of Race, Class and Nationalism in Twentieth Century South Africa*. New York: Longman.

Marshall, Burke. 1964. *Federalism and Civil Rights*. New York: Columbia University Press.

Marshall, T.H. 1992. *Citizenship and Social Class*. London: Pluto Press.

Marx, Anthony W. 1992. *Lessons of Struggle*. New York: Oxford University Press.

Marx, Gary T. 1969. *Protest and Prejudice*. New York: Harper and Row.

Marx, Karl. 1977. "The Poverty of Philosophy." In *Karl Marx: Selected Writings*, edited by David McLellan. Oxford: Oxford University Press.

McAdam, Doug. 1988. *Freedom Summer*. New York: Oxford University Press.

McAdam, Doug. 1982. *Political Process and the Development of Black Insurgency, 1930–1970*. Chicago: University of Chicago Press.

McAdam, Doug. 1983. "Tactical Innovation and the Pace of Insurgency." *American Sociological Review* 48:735–754.

McAdam, Doug, J.D. McCarthy, and M.N. Zald. "Social Movements." In *The Handbook of Sociology*, edited by N. Smelser. Newbury Park, CA: Sage.

McCarthy, John D., and Mayer N. Zald. 1977. "Resource Mobilization and Social Movements." *American Journal of Sociology* 82:1212–1241.

McCartney, John T. 1992. *Black Power Ideologies*. Philadelphia: Temple University Press.

Morner, Magnus. 1970. *Race and Class in America*. New York: Columbia University Press.

Morris, A., and C. McClurg Mueller, eds. 1992. *Frontiers in Social Movement Theory*. New Haven, CT: Yale University Press.

Morris, Aldon, and Cedric Herring. 1987. "Theory and Research in Social Movements: A Critical Review." *Annual Review of Political Science* 2:137–195.

Morris, Aldon. 1984. *The Origins of the Civil Rights Movement*. New York: Free Press.

Moses, Wilson Jeremiah. 1978. *The Golden Age of Black Nationalism*. New York: Archon Books.

Moura, Clovis. 1983. *Brasil: Raizes do Protesto Negro*. Sao Paulo: Global Editora.

Moura, Clovis. 1989. *Historia do Negro Brasileiro*. Sao Paulo: Editora Atica.

Movimento Negro Unificado. 1988. *1978–1988: 10 Anos de Luta Contra o Racismo*. Salvador, BA: O Movimento.

Movimento Negro Unificado. 1991. "MNU e as Ideologias Brancas." *MNU Journal* 18.

Moynihan, Daniel Patrick. 1969. *Maximum Feasible Misunderstanding*. New York: Free Press.

Muller, Edward N., and Karl-Dieter Opp. 1986. "Rational Choice and Rebellious Collective Action." *American Political Science Review* 80:471–488.

Murray, Richard, and A. Vedlitz. 1977. "Race, Socio-economic Status, and Voter Participation in Large Southern Cities." *Journal of Politics* 39:1064–1071.

Myrdal, Gunnar. 1944. *An American Dilemma.* New Haven: Yale University Press.

Nolutshungu, Sam C. 1993. "Reflections on National Unity in South Africa." *Third World Quarterly* 13:607–625.

Oberschall, Anthony. 1978. "Theories of Social Conflict." *Annual Review of Sociology* 4:291–315.

Oliver, Pamela, Gerald Marwell, and Ralph Prahl. 1985. "A Theory of Critical Mass." *American Journal of Sociology* 91:522–586.

Olzak, Susan. 1992. *The Dynamics of Ethnic Competition and Conflict.* Stanford: Stanford University Press.

Parkin, Frank. 1979. *Marxism and Class Theory: A Bourgeois Critique.* New York: Columbia University Press.

Parkin, Frank. 1982. *Max Weber.* London: Tavistock Publications.

Parsons, Talcott, and Kenneth B. Clark, eds. 1966. *The Negro American.* Boston: Houghton, Mifflin.

Pettigrew, Thomas F. 1971. *Racially Separate or Together?* New York: McGraw-Hill.

Pierson, Donald. 1942. *Negroes in Brazil.* Chicago: University of Chicago Press.

Raphael, Alison. 1981. " Samba and Social Control." Ph.D. Dissertation, Department of History, Columbia University, New York.

Redky, Edwin S. 1969. *Black Exodus.* New Haven: Yale University Press.

Roett, Riordan. 1984. *Brazil: Politics in a Patrimonial Social.* New York: Praeger.

Seme, Pixley ka Isaka. 1972. "Native Union." In *From Protest to Challenge,* edited by Thomas Karis and Gwendolen Carter. Stanford, CA: Hoover Institution Press.

Shklar, Judith N. 1991. *American Citizenship: The Quest for Inclusion.* Cambridge: Harvard University Press.

Skidmore, Thomas E. 1974. *Black into White: Race and Nationality in Brazilian Thought.* New York: Oxford University Press.

Skidmore, Thomas E. 1992. "Fact and Myth: An Overview of Afro-Brazilian Studies in Brazil." Kellogg Working Paper 1.

Stepan, Alfred. 1989. *Democratizing Brazil.* New York: Oxford University Press.

Tarrow, Sidney. 1983. "Struggling to Reform." Ithaca, NY: Cornell University, Western Societies Program Working Paper No. 15.

Tarrow, Sidney. 1988. "National Politics and Collective Action." *Annual Review of Sociology* 14:421–440.

Tarrow, Sidney. 1994. *Power in Movement.* Cambridge: Cambridge University Press.

Thompson, E. P. 1966. *The Making of the English Working Class.* New York: Vintage Books.

Thompson, Leonard. 1991. *A History of South Africa.* New Haven: Yale University Press.

Tilly, Charles. 1974. "Social Movements and National Politics." In *Statemaking and Social Movements,* edited by Charles Bright and Susan Harding. Ann Arbor: University of Michigan Press.

Tilly, Charles, ed. 1975. *The Formation of National States in Western Europe.* Princeton: Princeton University Press.

Tilly, Charles. 1985. "Models and Realities of Popular Collective Action." *Social Research* 52:717–748.

Tilly, Charles. 1992. "How to Detect, Describe and Explain Repertoires of Contention." New York: Center for the Study of Social Change, New School.

Toplin, Robert Brent. 1974. *Slaver and Race Relations in Latin America.* Westport, CT: Greenwood Press.

Vail, Leroy, ed. 1991. The *Creation of Tribalism in Southern Africa.* Berkeley: University of California Press.

Valente, Ana Lucia E. F. 1986. *Politica e Relacoes Raciais: Os Negros e as Eleicoes Paulistas de 1982.* Sao Paulo: FFLCH-USP.

Van Deburg, William L. 1992. *New Day in Babylon.* Chicago: University of Chicago Press.

Van den Berghe, Pierre L. 1967. *Race and Racism*. New York: Wiley.

Viotta di Costa, Emilia. 1985. *The Brazilian Empire*. Chicago: University of Chicago Press.

Wagley, Charles, ed. 1952. *Race and Class in Rural Brazil*. Paris: UNESCO.

Walshe, Peter. 1971. *The Rise of African Nationalism in South Africa*. Berkeley: University of California Press.

Weiss, Nancy. 1989. *Whitney Young Jr. and the Struggle for Civil Rights*. Princeton: Princeton University Press.

Williamson, Joel. 1986. *A Rage for Order*. New York: Oxford University Press.

Wilson, William Julius. 1973. *Power, Racism and Privilege*. New York: Macmillan.

Wilson, William Julius. 1978. *The Declining Significance of Race*. Chicago: University of Chicago Press.

Wofford, Harris Jr. 1980. *Of Kennedys and Kings*. New York: Farrar, Strauss, Giroux.

Wood, Charles H., and Jose A.M. de Carvalho. 1988. *The Demography of Inequality in Brazil*. Cambridge: Cambridge University Press.

PART IV
CONCLUSION

14 RIGHTS AND RULES

CONSTITUTING WORLD CITIZENS

John Boli

> If there is a universal moral code of law which is superior and exists prior to the solidification of the authority of the state, then the individual must be conceived as having some obligation to that law; and it is an obligation which, at least hypothetically, takes precedence over state law. Moreover, the undermining of that universal law in one place endangers the whole moral code and must be resisted by all who can.[1]

The contemporary world, increasingly conceptualized and organized as a distinct social entity with an identifiable cultural system (Boulding 1990; Featherstone 1990; Robertson 1992), is full of puzzles. Why do states routinely grant noncitizens many or most of the rights and privileges enjoyed by their citizens (Jacobson 1996; Soysal 1994)? What has made it possible for the global women's movement to induce states to create ministries to promote women's equality and advancement (Berkovitch 1997)? Why is the business of setting global technical standards left almost entirely to engineers, technicians, and scientists who expressly ignore national interests in developing standards documents (Loya and Boli 1997)? How could a handful of nongovernmental organizations induce the most powerful countries on earth to declare Antarctica a sort of world park where mining operations would not be permitted (Kimball 1988)? How could whales and rain forests come to be seen as endowed with rights against exploitation or destruction?

In this final chapter, I suggest that we can better solve these and other such puzzles by taking seriously the concept of world citizenship. Leave it to moral philosophers and political partisans to argue among themselves as to whether world citizenship is possible, desirable, utopian, necessary, or absurd. By setting world citizenship in its proper context of structures of authority, levels of social organization, theories of sovereignty, and ideologies of rights and duties, we can get good purchase on many aspects of global change that are otherwise inexplicable. World citizenship's engine is already running, its wheels are turning. We have difficulty recognizing it only because of its unusual form and mode of operations.

Most discussions of citizenship content themselves with analyzing what has become its overwhelmingly dominant form: national citizenship (Turner 1993; van Steenbergen 1994). This form is far more highly codified, rationalized, structured, and contested than any other, now or in the past. But most of the enormous literature on national citizenship adopts a peculiarly narrow focus on the relationship between states and individuals, with citizen rights vis-à-vis states consuming an extraordinary amount of paper. Too little analytical effort is devoted to the collective nature of citizenship as an institution operating at distinct but interconnected levels of social reality. Correspondingly, too little attention is paid to forms of citizenship operating via logics of authority that do not fit the conventional understanding of citizenship as a property of national polities governed by formally sovereign states. World citizenship is just such a form, and its consequences for global and national development are considerably more extensive than analysts are wont to admit.

CITIZENSHIP IN ACTION

Citizenship is status, a condition of being and of doing. As a condition of being, citizenship is the rules defining membership in a collectivity: who is in and who is out. It is also the rules defining the nature of the citizen, that is, the properties common to all who are in rather than out. These properties are fictions, that is, they are not descriptive generalizations about the actual citizens of an actual polity but, rather, moral prescriptions about how citizens should be constituted: loyal, informed, committed, tolerant, reasonable, law-abiding, and so on. The "good" citizen is the model to which actual citizens should aspire, and it has become remarkably uniformly constructed around the world (Boli 1987).

As a condition of doing, citizenship is the rules defining prescribed, permitted, and prohibited actions within the collectivity. Citizenship is therefore a conception of the properly behaving actor. Citizens can and should vote, collect social security payments, seek housing subsidies; they can and should start businesses, choose lifestyles, raise children who in turn will be good citizens. All this is not simply normatively valued; it is also supported by theories of action that depict such behavior as the secret to success, both for the individual citizen and for society as a whole. Citizenship is therefore central to the general political culture of society (Jepperson et al. 1996), holding out a vision of the model individual whose actions as model citizen will contribute directly both to the citizen's personal well-being and to the creation and sustenance of the model society.

Seen in this broad vision, citizenship entails not only formal rules, written and codified and systematized in constitutions, legislation, and court rulings, but also a host of informal rules, many of which may rarely be acknowledged. In no case can citizenship be reduced to a distinct set of documents or codifications; neither can its contents be definitively stated by any authority or analyst, not least because it is constantly undergoing elaboration. Citizenship is, thus, an institution, and like all institutions it is subject to complex processes of self-reproduction and modification involving its interrelations with other institutions and various processes of social change.

Because, at its core, citizenship concerns the relationship between individuals and the state, a major set of processes that both reproduce and modify citizenship are those shaping the reach and responsibilities of the state. The expansion of the state's agenda, the proliferation of state programs, the increasing complexity of social life that is in part fomented by the state and in any case is gradually incorporated into the nexus of state legislation and adjudication—all this complicates the rights and rules of citizenship enormously. It also makes of citizenship much more than a political construct. As the chapters in this book demonstrate, citizenship entails assumptions about being and doing right across the spectrum of social sectors— economic, familial, sexual, religious, educational, recreational. With this elaboration, and the increasing interpenetration of state and society (Habermas's [1989] "refeudalization" process), the concept of the state broadens as well. The state becomes not simply the organizational apparatus of the various branches of government, but a loosely-defined complex of authority relations regarding the centralized management of society. These relations are themselves more or less formal, with varying scope and inclusiveness. I develop this theme further below.

Besides its expansion, citizenship has also become peculiarly principled. In her chapter in this volume, Somers rightly takes Marshall (1950) to task for failing to recognize the roots of his neatly encapsulated civil, political, and social rights in bitter political struggles since medieval times. Yet, despite her historical tour de force reviewing efforts by subordinate groups to improve their standing and life chances, she seems to have overlooked the key aspect of modern conceptions of citizen rights: They proclaim themselves as abstract, universalistic principles of extraordinary egalitarianism. Rights are not simply codified summaries of the outcomes of cases brought by peasants seeking protection from encroaching landlords or woolen workers turning to the courts to enforce labor market regulations. They are rationalized principles grounded in moral philosophical positions regarding justice and propriety in the constitution of the polity and its citizenry (Kalberg 1993). When freedom of religious conscience, which is often described as the first right to take principled form, began to appear in constitutions and basic laws, it was not a matter of a particular Dissenter group in 17th-century England or Baptist congregation in 19th-century Denmark having the right to worship as it pleased. Rather, it was a principle that reflected a vision of the citizen qua citizen as inherently imbued with spirituality and ultimately responsible for his or her soul. All citizens shared this fundamental nature and were entitled to express and develop it, just as all citizens were entitled not to be pressed into any particular religious mold by the state.

Somers recognizes the principled nature of the issues at hand in her discussion of court adjudication of specific struggles, but the generalized disembodiment of specific struggles via their translation into abstract doctrines of rights—a development above all of the 18th and 19th centuries, and so a partial vindication of Marshall—escapes her notice. What rights doctrines do, in essence, is call a halt to particularist struggles, particularly foundational struggles about legal standing and judicial access. They settle such matters in favor of a remarkably universal and egalitarian conception of citizens, all of whom have standing and judicial access by right rather than by power or influence. Struggles then revolve around issues of the meaning and application of rights, and they can no longer be particularist because they are framed precisely as matters of principle and doctrine.

These two central aspects of modern citizenship—its effusive expansion and resolutely principled form—provide prerequisites, as it were, for the development and organization of world citizenship. The working out of the institution of national citizenship, a process very far along by the latter part of the 19th century when global economic, cultural, and organizational processes converged to produce a recognizable world polity and social system, provided a prominent platform upon which world citizenship could be constructed. The form of that construction would depart significantly from the form of national citizenship, however, not least because national citizenship was so well institutionalized as the relationship between state and citizen. Those who promoted, consciously or unconsciously, a more inclusive vision of the being and doing of membership were compelled to find another way.

POLITIES AND FORMS OF AUTHORITY
National Sovereignty and National Citizenship

States reign supreme in their national polities. They exercise, in Weber's terms, legal-rational authority or domination; in the language of political theory, they are sovereign powers. States are "constitutionally independent" (James 1986), "not subject without consent to external . . . control by any like authority" (Fawcett 1971), empowered to "act externally with a freedom that is limited only by voluntarily-accepted constraints" (Reynolds 1975). No higher authority than states exists, in this doctrine. States may be subject to influence from many sources, but they owe obedience to no one. They have exclusive jurisdiction over their associated territories, and any limits on that jurisdiction may not be imposed against their volition.

But states are not in and of themselves sovereign (Nettl 1968). Sovereignty is essentially a theory about the location of ultimate authority (Boli 1993), and that authority, in the modern conceit, lies in the hands of "the people," not in the state itself. Democratic ideology, arguably now the only legitimate political doctrine everywhere in the world polity, holds that all power derives from the people. Democratic institutions, that is, mechanisms whereby executives and legislators are elected (however indirectly) and serve "at the pleasure" of the people (however unpleasant the electoral process may be), are specified in almost all constitutions and are absolutely essential elements of the moral order of the contemporary world. Any regime that promulgates a polity of autocracy, military dictatorship, oligarchy, or inner-party control faces both external reprobation and internal unrest.[2]

What democratic theory accomplishes is the fiction of the sovereign citizen as the foundation of societal (and, hence, state) authority. This citizen is human, singular, and uniform; all the earlier, highly varied forms of the citizen, differentiated and partial and exclusive as they were, have given way to a theory of citizenship as universal and entirely egalitarian. Everyone is eligible for citizen participation on strictly equal terms: one person, one vote, regardless of any and all distinctions among persons (Ramirez and McEneaney 1996); any citizen, any office, subject to the barest minimum of qualifications. No one is formally more equal than others.

The form of authority implicit in modern citizenship, this fiction of the sovereign citizen, is based in legal-rational instruments. National constitutions spell out the largely uniform and expanding set of citizen rights (Boli 1987) whose content and practical import are adjudicated in legislation and court decisions. Similarly, definitions of citizenship emerge in legislation and fundamental documents specifying the conditions under which individuals are eligible to exercise these rights, in whole or in part. The complex nature of citizenship is given by a formally rationalized bundle of proscriptions and empowerments of great prominence and motive force in the politics of every national polity.

While national citizenship is a highly rationalized and deeply institutionalized ideological construct, many of the chapters in this volume demonstrate that its basic form, the one-individual, one-state model, seems to be eroding. States grant many or most of the same rights to noncitizens (those who do not meet the formal criteria for citizenship or have not undergone the ritual of naturalization) as to citizens. States behave as if they were obligated to protect and empower everyone within their jurisdictions, regardless of nationality or passport, even with respect to such major undertakings as health care, income support, education, and unemployment insurance. Noncitizens, meanwhile, resist efforts to restrict rights and subsidies to citizens. They also behave as if the state that controls the territory in which they find themselves were indeed obligated to protect and empower them, lacking though they may be in allegiance to the state and polity upon which that obligation rests.

Where do national polities draw the line in this blurring of the state-citizen link? What rights and duties are reserved for citizens, making the distinction between citizen and resident noncitizen meaningful? Above all, the noncitizen cannot claim the unconditional right to remain in the country. The noncitizen's presence depends on student status or familial relationships or continued employment in a particular type of job. As long as those conditions are met, however, the noncitizen generally is distinguished primarily by limitations in two domains: political participation and military service. Typically, the noncitizen may neither vote nor hold office, a signal of the noncitizen's ineligibility to act as one of "the people" who are the source of sovereignty. In some countries, even this restriction applies only to participation in national elections (Soysal 1994), the noncitizen's compelling interest in local politics justifying voting rights at the local level. The noncitizen may also be excluded from the military, which is charged with ensuring the integrity of the national polity and assumes the imperative of loyalty to the national polity. In many other respects, however, the noncitizen has the same rights and obligations as the citizen.

Universalization of Sovereignty

Why this peculiar empowerment of noncitizens? On what basis do they deem state policies excluding them from systems of health care, welfare support, employment, or education as unjust, discriminatory, unfair? While one can imagine a variety of instrumental reasons for states to accord expanded rights to noncitizens, ultimately at work is a powerful moral imperative: every person, as a human being, has inherent worth and dignity that are to be respected on a fundamentally egalitarian basis. Every person, that is, is a member of the one grand collectivity of complete inclusiveness, humanity as a whole. Every human has common and equal rights that every other human, and especially every state, should acknowledge and respect.

This doctrine of universal human rights has a long pedigree. It is evident in the early declarations of rights of the 18th century, including the Virginia bill of rights that served as the model for the first ten amendments to the United States constitution, and in the French Declaration of the Rights of Man and Citizen from the revolutionary period. These documents, in turn, built on the universalism of evangelizing Christianity, with its insistence on the ubiquity of the human soul and the unbounded promise of salvation to whosoever should believe in the redeeming messiah.[3] Products of the universalizing ethos of Enlightenment reasoning, the early declarations treat rights as "self-evident" attributes of citizens and, despite their implicit biases in favor of white males, clearly point to the generalizability of their doctrines to all citizens in all countries.

The codification of human rights ideology as explicitly transnational doctrine came much later, of course, with the various United Nations documents (the Universal Declaration of Human Rights and the covenants on political, social, and economic rights) of the postwar period. Since that time we have seen the emergence of a remarkably diverse and active human rights "regime" (Krasner 1983) devoted to reifying and further legitimating human rights doctrine and taking states to task for not living up to the standards specified in these documents (Gaer 1996). Discussions of the human rights sector are, however, typically too narrow. They focus on rights to political freedoms (expression, assembly, organization) and formal equality (for women, minorities, indigenous peoples), but miss the extraordinary range of movements in support of the full spectrum of rationalized rights.

Hence, for example, little notice is taken of the fact that the plethora of organizations in the international development sector operate largely in the name of universal economic rights (Chabbott 1997): the right of all to a minimal level of material comfort, to the gainful employment required to secure that level of comfort, and to basic amenities that are seen as requisites for a decent human existence (including running water, electricity, adequate shelter, mass media access, and so on). Similarly, world-level organizations (led by UNESCO) vigorously promote the right to education for all, increasingly at the secondary level as primary education has become widely available. World health and medicine bodies promote notions of universal health care rights, specifically focusing on access to physicians and hospitals, maternity care, immunizations, disease eradication, and basic hygiene facilities. Environmental organizations activate principles of rights to a healthful and pollution-free environment (Frank et al. 1997); family planning agencies assume rights to birth control technology and choice of family size; charity and relief organizations are motivated by notions of rights to sustenance and shelter when natural or political disasters strike; world peace and world federation bodies even propose a sort of universal right to harmonious relations among countries and peoples.

What is so striking about all of these global movements is precisely the universality of their claims and endeavors. Particular governments may be viewed as illegitimate pariahs deserving only disapprobation and sanctions, but the people subject to those governments are nonetheless deserving of support and aid. Also striking is the breadth of participation in the various global sectors that, implicitly and ever more explicitly, couch their action in terms of principles of universal rights. They include intergovernmental organizations (IGOs), above all the United Nations and its agencies but also many lesser known ones; thousands of international nongovernmental organizations (INGOs); private national organizations, ranging from churches to research institutes to foundations to relief agencies, that operate in the international arena; even state agencies like the U.S. Centers for Disease Control and Prevention (CDC), which acts as a global firefighter against outbreaks of virulent diseases, and European local government units that sponsor such actions as Bosnian relief campaigns and sister-city development projects in less developed countries. Throughout this vast and complex organizational arena, ideas of basic rights to a decent existence for all people in all places shine through.

World citizenship is much more than glorious-sounding but empty ideology, then. It is embodied in structures, backed up by resources, and translated into specific substance and forms. We can observe its increasingly structured rationalization through the measures habitually applied to evaluate national progress in meeting universal human standards. How do we know if rights to health (that is, the moral imperative that all human beings should have adequate health care) are being satisfied? We examine infant mortality, life expectancy, and infectious disease rates. For economic rights we compile information on GNP per capita, calorie consumption, and income inequality. For the right to education we compare literacy rates and enrollment ratios in primary and secondary schooling. For women's right to equality we rank countries in terms of the proportion of managerial jobs held by women or indices of occupational sex segregation. Even with respect to political rights we produce measurements and rankings, such as the various indices of democratic institutions and processes and the annual reports on human rights (narrowly conceived) produced by such monitoring organizations as Amnesty International and Human Rights Watch.

In every domain, the rankings indicate where progress is being made and where progress is problematic. In every domain, the imperative is clear: health care, education, women's equality, free elections, and a rising standard of material consumption are to be achieved everywhere, for these (along with many others) are the elements of world citizenship, the most fundamental form of citizenship, the inherently valued moral status that overrrides the parochialism of national identity distinctions. States bear the primary responsibility for ensuring that these elements are realized in everyday life precisely because states are the focal points of citizen-based sovereignty; states are charged with managing their national polities to ensure the welfare and development of those under their jurisdiction, citizen and noncitizen alike. No overarching world state has yet formed to assume this responsibility instead.

States have considerable latitude regarding the mode by which they are to promote this multidimensional progress; they can choose among various models that make the state more or less directly involved in the production and distribution of progress (Meyer et al. 1996), but they fail as states if they do not organize gradual improvement in these measures (Meyer 1987). Indeed, state failure to organize improvement consistently and uniformly is one of the major factors leading to mobilization by the many rights-promoting transnational and national organizations that fill the world polity.

The impact of world-level organizations on state policies and programs to promote the welfare of their residents goes well beyond simply making good for the failings of states. To a large extent, world bodies fashion the very substance of world citizenship, elaborating, refining, and arguing about its content, while they also educate states about the implementation of that content. Finnemore (1996) offers an early example (from the 1860s) in her analysis of the newly formed, nongovernmental International Committee of the Red Cross, which managed to convince states that combatants had rights to medical care and decent conditions of imprisonment; later Geneva conventions developed under the auspices of the ICRC spelled out rights of noncombatants and extensive limitations on the means of waging war. Similarly, Barrett and Frank (1997) show that population experts and policy analysts taught states to treat population growth not as an unqualified boon to national power but as a barrier to successful national development, as the latter came to be defined in per capita rather than corporatist terms. This was part of the general redefinition of the purposes of the state away from narrow power politics to concern for the welfare of individuals, and it led states to accept international family planning efforts that pushed the model of rights-based approaches to reproduction control (cf. Ramirez and McEneany 1996). So, too, with environmental organizations, which have helped states understand why they should worry about acid rain and deforestation and fluorocarbon emissions, encouraged them to set up agencies to worry officially about these things, and sometimes even provoked legislatures to write environmental rights into national constitutions.

It is worth repeating the question raised earlier, now in more complete form: Why should states respond positively to this barrage of expanding rights, so decidedly universalistic and egalitarian in form, so heavily moralistic and ideological in presentation? States are sovereign actors, so it is claimed. They are not subject to external compulsion; even the United Nations, the organization that some see as the possible nucleus of an eventual world state, is structured as an essentially voluntary organization whose members are free to leave at any time. Yet states everywhere have sometimes eagerly, sometimes begrudgingly, sometimes organizationally, sometimes only symbolically, acknowledged a greatly expanded set of rights, and these rights are seen increasingly as properties of individuals as human beings regardless of nationality. What makes states respond in this way, given that legal-rational authority rests primarily at the national level?

Rational Voluntaristic Authority

The concept of rational voluntaristic authority is useful for capturing the essence of processes of elaboration and structuration of world citizenship (Boli and Thomas 1997a). Rational voluntarism is the authority ensconced in the doctrine of the sovereignty of the people. The doctrine holds that decisions are proper and binding when the people, acting as reasoning individuals via democratic structures, collectively establish policies they deem beneficial to the pursuit of their goals. The goals may be narrowly self-interested or broadly other-beneficial; in either case, those charged with carrying out the decisions have the authority to do so because they are acting in accordance with the reasoned decisions of the sovereign people.

At the world-polity level, rational voluntaristic authority is virtually the only game in town. States cannot command each other; IGOs cannot command states, for IGOs are only voluntary associations; nongovernmental organizations cannot command even their own members, for they, too, owe their substance entirely to their memberships. But rational voluntarism implies that compliance with the decisions reached by the members of a polity (be it a national polity, a professional association, the World Trade Organization, or the International Judo Federation) is the only reasonable mode of action, for the decisions themselves reflect the will of the members.

Further, rational voluntarism has become the morally supreme mode of policy formation and program development. It combines the wills of those ultimately sacred social entities, individuals; it embodies a highly legitimated theory of equal participation in decision making; it accords with the prevailing moral-philosophical view that fairness can be achieved only through rational action. Rational voluntarism, philosophized to utopian purity by Habermas (1989) and made the keystone of moral justice by Rawls (1971), is indeed the highest form of authority in contemporary world culture, of much greater legitimacy than legal-rational and other forms that imply asymmetric relationships of domination and subordination.

In another place (Boli 1997), I explore the institutional and organizational underpinnings of rational voluntaristic authority in the world polity. Suffice it to say here that this form gives the conceptions of value, right, and rights that are debated, elaborated, and promoted at the global level with peculiarly intense moral force. They put states on the defensive, with the obligation to show why they should not be held accountable when world citizenship rights are violated or neglected. They mobilize world citizens, that is, individuals acting in voluntary concert in the framework of transnational organizations or on behalf of transnational principles, to hold states accountable—to lobby states, harangue them, aid opposition forces within them, organize boycotts against them. And they mobilize national citizens and noncitizens, aware of the global standards that also apply to them, wherever they may be, to insist on their rights, form their movements, and demand their due, no matter how unfeasible that may seem in any given situation.

It is this structure of the moral authority of transcendant world citizenship that underlies Held's (1993:26–27) pertinent questions in this passage from his historical review of democracy:

> Whose consent is necessary and whose participation is justified in decisions concerning, for instance, AIDS, or acid rain, or the use of non-renewable resources? What is the relevant constituency: national, regional, or international? To whom do decision-makers have to justify their decisions? To whom should they be accountable?

The answer, in the ideology of world citizenship, is crystal clear: the consent of everyone is required for decisions at any level, because the decisions have consequences for the rights and welfare of human beings; because, as the quotation with which I opened this essay asserts, any subversion of universal principles is apt to be interpreted as an attack on the "whole moral code" embodied in world citizenship doctrine.

All this is, undeniably and inevitably, highly contested. Varying conceptions of rights prevail in different segments of the world polity, and power jockeying generates all sorts of ideological argumentation. A major dispute currently receiving much attention is that between fundamentalist Islamic movements that decry rights doctrines as Western imperialism and the great majority of world organizations that insist on the universalism of rights (Little et al. 1988; Mayer 1991). While this dispute is less substantial than it seems (Boli 1996), it is indicative of the rancor that world-polity development generates. Similarly, authoritarian states in less developed countries are wont to argue that political rights are secondary when basic needs are not being met, that is, when they are not able to guarantee social and economic rights. Smokescreens for obscuring the efforts by ruling elites to maintain their political domination? Certainly. Yet such smokescreens demonstrate the power of rights doctrines, for no state dares ignore these doctrines completely. Some (e.g., China) are better equipped to limit their application and to prevent mobilization in line with their principles, but the long-term costs of doing so are likely to be considerable. The repeated waves of democratization are adequate testimony to this claim.

World Citizenry

Rights doctrines speak of the rights of individuals, and most theory and organization regarding rights focuses on individuals. Much less attention is given to the implicit collectivity that is the basis of the doctrine, the entity known as "humanity" or the "human race" that consists of a particular class of social actors endowed with these rights. This collectivity is structured as what has variously been called a global "society" (Burton 1972; Landheer et al. 1971), "community" (Cobb and Elder 1970), even "village" (McLuhan and Powers 1989). Whatever the term, recent decades have brought an acute sense of all human beings interacting in a single social unit marked by both sweeping commonalities and deep divergencies. The "family of man," this peculiar species capable of so much constructive activity and so much destruction, is become one.

Let us call this collectivity, taken to mean its billions of individual members, world citizenry. Soysal (1994) resists the notion of world citizenship as claiming too much; she is content to speak of postnational citizenship, inspecific though the term may be, to indicate the supercession of national citizenship by something else. But world citizenry is already a well-formed conception, sometimes invoked explicitly (*see* references in Falk [1994]), more often unnamed but nonetheless operative. We can appreciate the degree to which it has been reified by considering two dimensions in which it has become the object of exercises in conceptual delimitation and contestation: debates regarding membership in the collectivity of world citizenry, and dramatic representations of the boundary separating world citizenry from its environment.

WORLD CITIZENRY MEMBERSHIP

If world citizenry comprehends all human beings, what is excluded? On the one hand, other species of living things, animal or vegetable; on the other hand, other entities of social construction, such as associations, corporations, states, and ethnic identity groups. If contestation comes at the margins, we should find disputes concerning membership criteria stated in these terms, and disputes are rampant. Do animals have rights? Which animals? Which rights? What about the rights of plants, or of nature in general? All this is much debated, with general agreement that, though nonhuman rights may be circumscribed, the obligations of world citizens toward nonhuman entities (including "nature" as a whole) are considerable. World citizens owe nonhuman entities respect and protection, not simply because human welfare will thereby be enhanced but as a decidedly moral imperative. Nonhuman entities cannot be full world citizens, because they lack the capacity for rational voluntaristic action, but they are attributed some degree of primordial sacrality that justifies their safeguarding and preservation.

A different kind of contestation concerns human collectivities. Most are generally outside the pale of citizenship conceptions; associations, for example, are constructed as rational voluntaristic assemblages of individuals, so their rights and obligations are entirely derivative of those of their members. Corporations are slightly more problematic in that, while they are expected to behave as "good citizens" (they should respect the rights and needs of individuals wherever they are active), they have quite limited rights (to existence, to judicial adjudication, to protection under the law) because, as rational instruments, they lack human essentialness. They are authorized world citizens in one particular global-organizational domain, that of international industrial and trade groups whose members often are corporations (Boli and Thomas 1997a), but they are excluded from virtually every other global sphere. In the main, corporations are seen as likely infringers of world-citizenship rights (they are exploitative, socially irresponsible, inegalitarian), not as rights-endowed loci of inherent worth.

The more difficult case is that of ethnic and identity groups, concerning which opinions diverge radically. Can an ethnic group be a world citizen, such that its members are entitled to particular rights and considerations that go beyond the rights to which individuals as such are entitled? Do identity groups have rights based on their distinctive history of oppression (by whites, imperialists, men, heterosexuals) or distinctive culture/religion/traditions that make them especially virtuous and therefore deserving of special treatment? Such questions indicate disagreement about the definition of world citizenry as composed solely of individual human beings, but the resistance that collective rights claims engender underscores all the more heavily the strength of this individualistic definition.

WORLD CITIZENRY BOUNDARIES

The concept of world citizenry is reified not only by competing claims about membership but also by processes of boundary definition. If humanity forms a single collectivity, a world polity that nevertheless does not include all that is, how is it demarcated from its enveloping environment? If the Earth is our home, how do we distinguish it from the rest of the universe? My suggestion is that we do so, and vigorously, through the literary genres of science fiction and fantasy. Science itself, that rationalizing disenchanter *par excellence*, tears down all boundaries, proclaiming the nonuniqueness of the sun, the planet, and the planet's life forms. Science's principles are purportedly universalistic in the most literal science, making of the Earth and its global society but an instance of highly general processes. But science fiction and its fantasy cousin dramatize the uniqueness of the human species and the home planet via fictional encounters with other worlds, other civilizations, other social formations distant in time, space, and culture. It hardly seems accidental that these genres also emerged in the late 19th century, when imperialism incorporated the whole globe into the world economy, when INGOs first began to appear in sizeable numbers, when time zones were standardized, when transcontinental cables were first laid.

A second boundary definition process is the pleasant game of attempting to define the uniqueness of the human species and clever attempts on the part of scientific specialists to subvert any such definition. The tool-making animal? But apes break off reeds to make tubes with which to ravage ant colonies. The language animal? But dolphins communicate through a complicated system of high-pitched sounds. The moral animal? But no other species is as savagely immoral as humans in their destructiveness of their own kind.

All this gnawing at the edges of the definition of humanity reifies the collectivity as we cast about almost desperately to establish clarity about the moral order of things. We know that human beings are endowed with inherent rights, but if humans are not unique, to what other species should such rights be extended ("Pets are people too")? If we should encounter some alien species, should its members too be considered rights-bearing entities?

Is this familiar, troubled, wondrous world society that we have wrought truly as distinct from its surroundings as we imagine, or is it only an instance, a case, a potential member of some future galactic federation?

Intense cultural work is involved; the concept of a world citizenry in a world polity is powerful indeed, as indicated by its capacity to evoke so much imaginative invention and scholarly debate. But, again, we need to recognize that it is not simply a concept. It is organization, documentation, mobilization; it is motive and motivation for a great deal of routine action.

WORLD CITIZENSHIP IN PRACTICE

Falk (1994) offers a useful categorization of types ("images") of world citizens in the contemporary world. Two of these are highly prominent in the literature on global social movements: the transnational activist (engaged in human rights, the environment, women's rights, and the like), and the global reformer, the rational elite individual working for improved forms of global politics and governance (a stronger United Nations, a world state or federation, and so on). These types are widely acknowledged as having universalistic concerns that they activate on behalf of a world citizenry organized as an all-inclusive world polity. Falk adds to these several less recognized types, two of which are germane here: the "man or woman of transnational affairs," that is, the global businessperson equally at home everywhere but truly at home nowhere; and the "global management" citizen, a member of the world technical and organizational elite, highly practical in orientation, who is involved in global technical coordination and governance.

These latter types are especially important because they generate the bulk of global organizational activity currently in operation. Most of this activity occurs in one of three forms: transnational corporations (TNCs), intergovernmental organizations, and international nongovernmental organizations. Of these, TNCs and INGOs are by far the most common, the former involving mostly Falk's "men and women of affairs," the latter involving all four types mentioned above. Contrary to the impression given by the media and scholarly literature, however, global management citizens are the most common type within the transnational organizational world because technical and scientific INGOs and IGOs are so much more common than other types of global bodies. Table 14–1 shows the distribution of INGOs (which outnumber IGOs by a factor of ten or more) across social sectors in 1988.

Scientific and technical organizations (medicine, the sciences, and technical organizations) account for over a third of the INGOs, while business and economic bodies (industry and trade plus tertiary economic orga-

TABLE 14-1. Distribution of INGOs by Social Sector, 1988
(N = 4,449)

Sector	Percentage
Industry/trade/industrial groups	17.6
Medicine/health	14.9
Sciences/mathematics/space	11.6
Sports/hobbies/leisure	8.0
Technical/infrastructure/communications	7.4
Tertiary economic/finance/tourism	7.2
Individual rights/welfare	6.3
World-polity oriented*	6.2
Religion/family/cultural identity	6.1
Labor/professions/public administration	6.0
Education/students	4.2
Humanities/arts/philosophy	3.9
Political ideology/party	0.6

Note: Table includes all INGOs in the B, C, and D sections of the *Yearbook of International Organizations* (UIA 1988), as coded by Boli and Thomas (1997a).
*International law, world federation, world peace, environmental, police, and similar organizations

nizations) make up about a quarter. In all, nearly 60 percent of INGOs focus on scientific, technical, or economic matters. Activist and reformer organizations, by contrast, are well under 20 percent of the total (portions of the individual rights/welfare, world-polity oriented, cultural identity, and political INGOs).

Activist and reformer INGOs are certainly much better known than their economic, technical, and scientific counterparts, not least because they engage in direct confrontations with states (especially human and particularist rights groups, environmental organizations, prodemocracy movements, and the like) or are involved in trying to make up for the failures of states in crisis situations (relief and charity organizations). However, most of the global management organizations operate largely outside the domain of states. Scientific bodies organize their respective disciplines and professions; technical groups develop and disseminate standards, manufacturing and assembly methods, and modeling techniques; industry groups develop quality standards, rules of trade, and standards of accounting, all with no or minimal participation of states. In all this they are engaged in developing largely invisible dimensions of global culture and governance. They also, of course, develop ties to IGOs and individual states, as experts, consultants, lobby-ists, and advocates. They form part of what Haas (1992) calls "epistemic communities," combining INGOs, IGOs, state officials, and independent experts in specific domains of global management.

World citizenship in practice thus involves an enormous array of or-ganizations whose participants see the entire globe as their field of action. Rational voluntaristic authority is the dominant mode in INGO operations, in which self-authorized individuals collectively make rational decisions about global management, develop and propagate ideologies regarding the moral nature and practical implications of world citizenship as such, and interact intensely with IGOs and states to translate their visions and practi-cal suggestions into structured forms. IGOs operate in much the same way, as voluntary associations of rationally-oriented states, but their authority is constructed as derivative of the legal-rational authority of the member states. TNCs, meanwhile, rely heavily on state and INGO authority in their op-erations (e.g., the International Chamber of Commerce, an NGO, writes the rules for most technical aspects of international trade; *see* Berman 1988), and their contribution to the development and promotion of world citizen-ship doctrine is quite limited because of their extreme specialization and dubious moral standing as inevitably self-interested parties.

World citizenship is, of course, variably effective. Where state inter-ests are at stake, where TNCs realize that their survival or future profits are in jeopardy, where political leaders fear overthrow or subversion, the moral and organizational authority of world-level organizations, even of IGOs backed by the authority of powerful states, may well be set aside. What is remarkable about the world-citizenship processes that have gathered strength in this century is, nevertheless, their considerable capacity, in some domains, to affect directly the actions of states and other actors (*see* the chapters in Boli and Thomas 1997b), and their capacity to shape the very definition of the state and other actors, especially in terms of how these actors understand their interests and set their agendas for action (Finnemore 1996; Meyer et al. 1996). This sort of cultural-institutional work is perhaps the most im-portant dimension of world citizenship practice at the present time.

World Citizenship and National Citizenship

Does world citizenship entail the decline of national citizenship? Most dis-cussions suggest that it does. We should be wary, however, of such zero-sum thinking. To a large extent, these two forms of citizenship, corresponding to two distinct but highly interrelated levels of social organization, are mu-tually reinforcing rather than contradictory.

Immigration policy provides an excellent example of this mutual reinforcement. Before the 20th century, immigration policy was weak or nonexistent, indicating a relatively weak state-citizen relationship and unsystematic efforts by states to define and control their national boundaries. As the world polity became more integrated and interdependent, states stepped up border surveillance and control; as states expanded their authority and agendas, particularly from the 1930s, the substance of the state-citizen relationship grew denser and more significant in everyday life. Immigration policy became an instrument of national development, building on implicit theories of the types of entrants who would most benefit the nation: human capital theories about economic growth, favoring educated or skilled immigrants; theories of social stability, blacklisting the ideologically deviant; theories of functional needs, favoring low-skilled industrial workers; theories of capital investment, favoring the rich.

All this signals the intensification of national citizenship, but it occurred in the context of, and to a considerable degree in response to, the ever thickening web of transnational economic relationships, interstate relations, global transportation and communications systems, and related developments that were rapidly generating the concepts and organizational structures (TNCs, IGOs, INGOs) that are the primary modes of action of world citizens. In other words, national citizenship and world citizenship are products of the same set of global development forces, and both have strengthened remarkably in this century. Even immigration policy, and the theories by which it is guided, have become quite standard cultural elements in the world polity, activated in similar ways by states operating in highly varied circumstances. What is more, national citizenship seems to be almost a prerequisite for the activation of world citizenship. Boli, Loya, and Loftin (1997) show, for example, that residents of colonies rarely participate in INGOs, but once colonies obtain independence their residents dramatically increase their INGO participation and rapidly approach the participation level of residents of older countries.

That national citizenship is an ingredient of world citizenship is even indicated in the Universal Declaration of Human Rights, one of whose points is that every person has the right to a nationality. Given the primacy of states as loci of formal authority in the world polity, how could it be otherwise? No transnational organization, such as the United Nations, is charged with generally guaranteeing protection and succor to individuals; states have this responsibility. Hence, as a world citizen everyone has the right to be a national citizen, and if one is not a national citizen, one is not a fully constructed actor in the world polity (consider the untenable situation of "stateless" persons).

Finally, it is revealing that the tightening of immigration policy in the developed countries, in the face of high unemployment and a good deal of social unrest related to the uncertain assimilation of their recently expanded immigrant populations, has generally allowed for one major exception: refugees. These are individuals for whom the United Nations and numerous nongovernmental agencies do have first-line responsibility: national citizens whose states so utterly fail in their responsibilities, either to maintain order or to respect the (human) rights of their populations, that they are "thrown on the mercy" of the international community. States are obligated to admit refugees (defined by increasingly rationalized criteria) as a matter of humanitarian principle. Refugees' first right as world citizens is, thus, incipient national citizenship via immigrant status, which can eventually lead to full citizenship.

The mutual reinforcement between global and national levels of organization and ideology has characterized the modern world for centuries, and it operates across a multitude of dimensions (Boli 1993). We may one day see the eclipse of national citizenship by world citizenship, but at this point it seems to make more sense to see both forms as stronger than ever, with the tension between the two providing a good deal of dynamism to the world polity.

Research Directions

The chapters in this book, and such important work on problematic national citizenship as the recent monographs by Soysal (1994) and Jacobson (1996), help us conceptualize world citizenship much more satisfactorily. What is needed most at this point is systematic studies that generate global data relevant to the problems at hand and that enable the testing of competing explanations. To begin with, a cross-national, longitudinal analysis of the extent to which countries differentiate between citizens and noncitizens would help greatly. One could gather data on a set of major dimensions of citizenship, such as voting and holding office (political rights), eligibility for welfare and pension plans and the like (social rights), work and capital investment (economic rights), military service, and so on. Composite indices could then be constructed and trends over time could be identified. These indices could then be analyzed for their relationships with variables reflecting alternative perspectives on citizenship and its place in national and global development.

Such studies likely would find revealing variations that go well beyond the widely discussed transnationalization of citizenship in the European Union. My analysis in this chapter suggests that the trends generally should be in the direction of decreasing distinctions, but dialectical or trade-off effects also seem probable. Some dimensions of citizenship may reveal a blurring of the citizen/noncitizen distinction, while others may move in the opposite direction; the degree of blurring may also vary with national characteristics, links to the world polity, prominence in the world economy, and so on. In any case, it seems likely that boundary-maintenance activity generally has increased, so the logic of the situation may be that of hardening shells around nation-states vis-à-vis the outside world but "softer" citizenship rules inside.

Another fruitful line of investigation could delve into the relationship between world citizenship and national citizenship as matters of individual identity and moral legitimation. We know that many individuals think of themselves as world citizens first and national citizens second (or, even, not at all), but we know next to nothing about how widespread such a global identity is or what factors are related to it. Here again it is important to avoid zero-sum thinking; it may be that strong self-identified world citizens also see themselves as engaged national citizens, or that some minimal level of national identification is necessary for global engagement. Cross-national surveys could help greatly here. They might usefully be combined with studies of moral legitimacy: the relative status and value associated with world figures and phenomena as opposed to their national counterparts. Think of the ubiquity of such designators as "world-class," "world's best," "internationally renowned," "global leader"; these tell us that special value is associated with recognized prominence in the world polity, and they indicate the aspirations of actors in many domains of activity. Longitudinal, comprehensive studies could track the spread and prevalence of such moral constructions, investigate factors that make them more or less prominent, and study their consequences for national status and prestige.

A third type of study could focus on legal systems and the relationship between international and national law. Some constitutions specify adherence to the Universal Declaration of Human Rights; some stipulate that international law takes precedence over domestic law; sometimes domestic court decisions cite precedents from international law or foreign municipal law; the European Court has jurisdiction that supercedes that of its member states with respect to numerous rights-related matters. Systematic, longitudinal data on these issues is, again, lacking; they could tell us much about the interplay between world and national citizenship as this tension translates into juridical structures.

Investigations of these sorts are needed to explore the meaning and structuration of world citizenship in our time. The more energy we devote to such studies, the clearer it will become that world citizenship, having become a major institutional dimension of world culture and organization, has far-reaching implications for the past and future of global development.

NOTES

1. Heater (1990:258)
2. *See* Markoff (1996) on the recurrent waves of democratic social movements and Diamond (1993) on global networks of support for such movements.
3. *See* Berman (1993) on the religious foundations of law and principled rights.

REFERENCES

Barrett, Debbie, and David John Frank. 1997. "Population Control for National Development: From World Discourse to National Policies." In Boli and Thomas (1997b).

Berkovitch, Nitza. 1997. "The Emergence and Transformation of the International Women's Movement." In Boli and Thomas (1997b).

Berman, Harold J. 1993. *Faith and Order: The Reconciliation of Law and Religion.* Atlanta: Scholars Press.

Berman, Harold J. 1988. "The Law of International Commercial Transactions." *Emory Journal of International Dispute Resolution* 2(2), Spring: 235–310.

Boli, John. 1997. "INGO Authority and World Governance." In Boli and Thomas (1997b).

Boli, John. 1996. "World Culture, World Cultures, and Human Rights Ideology: An Islamic Alternative?" Presented at the conference, "Universalizing from Particulars: Islamic Views of the Human and the United Nations Declaration of Human Rights in Comparative Perspective," Princeton University, May 24–26.

Boli, John. 1993. "Sovereignty from a World Polity Perspective." Presented at the annual meeting of the American Sociological Association, Miami Beach, August.

Boli, John. 1987. "World Polity Sources of Expanding State Authority and Organizations, 1870–1970." Pp. 71–91 in Thomas et al. (1987).

Boli, John, and George M. Thomas. 1997a. "World Culture in the World Polity: A Century of International Nongovernmental Organization." *American Sociological Review* 6 (2):171–190.

Boli, John, and George M. Thomas, eds. 1997b. *World Polity Formation Since 1875: World Culture and International Non-Governmental Organizations.* Stanford: Stanford University Press.

Boli, John, Thomas A. Loya, and Teresa Loftin. 1997. "National Participation in World-Polity Organization." In Boli and Thomas (1997b).

Boulding, Elise. 1990. "Building a Global Civic Culture." *Development* 1990(2):37–40.

Burton, John W. 1972. *World Society.* Cambridge: Cambridge University Press.

Chabbott, Colette. 1997. "Defining Development: The Making of the International Development Field, 1945–1990." In Boli and Thomas (1997b).

Cobb, Roger W., and Charles Elder. 1970. *International Community: A Regional and Global Study.* New York: Holt, Rinehart and Winston.

Diamond, Larry. 1993. "The Globalization of Democracy." Ch. 3 in Robert O. Slater, Barry M. Schultz, and Steven R. Dorr, eds., *Global Transformation and the Third World.* Boulder, CO: Lynne Rienner.

Falk, Richard. 1994. "The Making of Global Citizenship." Ch. 10 in Bart van Steenbergen, ed., *The Condition of Citizenship.* London: Sage.

Fawcett, James. 1971. "General Course on Public International Law." Pp. 363 ff. in

Académie de Droit International, Recueil des cours 1971, vol. 1. Leyden: Sijthoff.

Featherstone, Michael. 1990. *Global Culture: Nationalism, Globalization, and Modernity.* Newbury Park, CA: Sage.

Finnemore, Martha. 1996. *National Interests in International Society.* Ithaca: Cornell University Press.

Frank, David John, Ann Hironaka, John W. Meyer, Evan Schofer, and Nancy Brandon Tuma. 1997. "The Rationalization and Organization of Nature in the World Culture." In Boli and Thomas (1997b).

Gaer, Felice D. 1996. "Reality Check: Human Rights NGOs Confront Governments at the United Nations." Ch. 2 in Thomas G. Weiss and Leon Gordenker, eds., *NGOs, the United Nations, and Global Governance.* Boulder, CO: Lynne Rienner.

Haas, Peter M. 1992. "Introduction: Epistemic Communities and International Policy Coordination." *International Organization* 46(1) Winter: 1–35.

Habermas, Jürgen. 1989. *The Structural Transformation of the Public Sphere.* Cambridge, MA: MIT Press.

Heater, Derek. 1990. *World Citizenship and Government.* New York: St. Martin's Press.

Held, David. 1993. "Democracy: From City-States to Cosmopolitan Order?" In David Held, ed., *Prospects for Democracy: North, South, East, West.* Cambridge: Polity Press.

Jacobson, David. 1996. *Rights Across Borders: Immigration and the Decline of Citizenship.* Baltimore: Johns Hopkins University Press.

James, Alan. 1986. *Sovereign Statehood: The Basis of International Society.* London: Allen & Unwin.

Jepperson, Ronald, Alexander Wendt, and Peter Katzenstein. 1996. "Norms, Identity, and Culture in National Security." In Peter Katzenstein, ed., *Culture and Security.* New York: Columbia University Press.

Kalberg, Stephen. 1993. "Cultural Foundations of Modern Citizenship." Ch. 5 in Bryan S. Turner, ed., *Citizenship and Social Theory.* London: Sage.

Kimball, Lee. 1988. "The Role of Nongovernmental Organizations in Antarctic Affairs." Pp. 33–63 in Christopher C. Joyner and Sudhir K. Chopra, eds., *The Antarctic Legal Regime.* Dordrecht: Martinus Nijhoff.

Krasner, Stephen D. , ed. 1983. *International Regimes.* Ithaca: Cornell University Press.

Landheer, B., J. H. M. M. Loenen, and Fred L. Polak, eds. 1971. *World Society: How Is an Effective and Desirable World Order Possible? A Symposium.* The Hague: Martinus Nijhoff.

Little, David, John Kelsay, and Abdulaziz A. Sachedina. 1988. *Human Rights and the Conflict of Cultures: Western and Islamic Perspectives on Religious Liberty.* Columbia, SC: University of South Carolina Press.

Loya, Thomas, and John Boli. 1997. "Standardization in the World Polity: Technical Rationality Over Power." In Boli and Thomas (1997b).

Markoff, John. 1996. *Waves of Democracy: Social Movements and Political Change.* Thousand Oaks, CA: Pine Forge Press.

Marshall, T. H. 1950. *Citizenship and Social Class.* Cambridge: Cambridge University Press.

Mayer, Ann Elizabeth. 1991. *Islam and Human Rights: Tradition and Politics.* Boulder, CO: Westview.

McLuhan, Marshall, and Bruce R. Powers. 1989. *The Global Village: Transformations in World Life and Media in the 21st Century.* New York: Oxford University Press.

Meyer, John W., John Boli, George M. Thomas, and Francisco O. Ramirez. 1996. "World Society and the Nation-State." Department of Sociology, Stanford University, Stanford, CA.

Meyer, John W. 1987. "The World Polity and the Authority of the Nation-State." Pp. 41–70 in Thomas et al. (1987).

Nettl, J. P. 1968. "The State as a Conceptual Variable." *World Politics* XX (4):559–592.

Ramirez, Francisco O., and Elizabeth H. McEneaney. 1996. "From Women's Suffrage to Reproduction Rights? Cross-National Considerations." (To be published in *International Journal of Comparative Sociology.)*

Rawls, John. 1971. *A Theory of Justice.* Cambridge, MA: Harvard University Press.

Reynolds, P. A. 1975. "International Studies: Retrospect and Prospect." *British Journal of International Studies* 1 (April):1–19.

Robertson, Roland. 1992. *Globalization: Social Theory and Global Culture.* London: Sage.

Soysal, Yasemin Nuhoglu. 1994. *Limits of Citizenship: Migrants and Postnational Membership in Europe.* Chicago: University of Chicago Press.

Thomas, George M., John W. Meyer, Francisco O. Ramirez, and John Boli, eds. 1987. *Institutional Structure: Constituting State, Society, and the Individual.* Beverly Hills: Sage.

Turner, Bryan S. 1993. "Outline of the Theory of Human Rights." Ch. 8 in Bryan S. Turner, ed., *Citizenship and Social Theory.* London: Sage.

UIA (Union of International Associations). 1988. *Yearbook of International Organizations,* vol. 25:1988–89. Munich: K. G. Saur.

van Steenbergen, Bart. 1994. "Towards a Global Ecological Citizen." Ch. 11 in Bart van Steenbergen, ed., *The Condition of Citizenship.* London: Sage.

INDEX

M

Maastricht Treaty, 126, 141, 142, 146n.13
Machiavelli, Niccolo, 49
macro relationships, 4, 185
Magna Carta, impact on English guilds, 186
male identities, gendered social needs, 228i, 229–230, 231
man or woman of transnational affairs, world citizenship type, 385
Mann, Michael, 128, 160
manor courts, public sphere and, 169
marital status, women's economic rights, 90
"market man," 51
marriage, women's civil rights and, 69
Marshall, Burke, 355
Marshall, T. H., 154–155
    critique of theories, 157–168, 266–267
    theory of, 10, 11–12, 24, 68, 132, 155–158, 207, 240, 292, 345
Marx, Karl, 341
Marxism, concept of society and, 50
maternalist tradition, 255, 269–271, 278
    France, 271, 276
    Sweden, 271–275
    United States, 271, 275–276
maternity benefits, 323t, 327t, 332
Maternity Convention, The (1919), 97
Maternity Protection Convention (1952), 97
Mattingly, Garrett, 49
McGann v. H. H. Music Company, medical coverage, 333
medieval European society, 42–43
merchant guilds
    citizenship rights and, 188–190
    culture of, 187–188, 189–190
    establishment of English, 185–187
    public sphere and, 170, 183
microrelationships, 4, 185
military services, citizenship and, 131–132
Milner, Alfred, 347
minimum wage
    legislation, 179, 317
    and women's economic rights, 91
Minnesota Employer's Liability Commission, worker's compensation, 296
minority rights, 28
mobilizations
    Brazilian racial, 359–360, 362
    social action, 342, 344–346
    South African, 346–351, 361–362
modernism, master narrative of, 191, 192
monarchy, public sphere and, 170–171
Morris, Aldon, 353
"mother," gendered category, 212

Mother Protection Act (1968), 317, 320t, 322
motherhood, women's economic rights, 87–89, 97–100
Movimento Negro Unificado (MNU), 360
multidimensional scaling analysis, 228
Murray, Charles, 215

N

NAACP, 352–353
nation
    changing citizenship in, 21–22, 31–32, 108, 135
    nature of, 3, 9, 45, 60
Nation-Building and Citizenship, 153
nation-state
    evolution of, 133–136
    global institutionalization perspective, 64–68, 82
    model, Western, 60–61
National Association of Manufactures, worker's compensation, 291
National Association of Temporary Services, 331–332
national citizenship, concept of, 372, 375–376, 387–389. *See also* citizenship
National Civic Federation (NCF), worker's compensation, 291, 292
National Conference on Workmen's Compensation for Industrial Accidents, 291
National Council for the Social Studies (NCSS), Anglophone Africa, 121
National Housewives Association (Sweden), 274
national identity, 3, 7–9
national institutions, citizenship and, 9
National Party (South Africa), 349
national public sphere, English, 161, 169–174
"national will," 48
natural law, 133, 135
natural rights, 92, 163
    Bentham on, 15
need classification, social welfare, 220, 221t–222t, 223
"needs talk," social welfare, 215, 231
Nelson, Barbara, 219
neo-Marxist, on welfare state, 210
New York City Charity Directories, 220
noncitizens
    discrimination against, 30
    rights of, 376
nongovernmental organizations(NGOs), role of, 53–54
North Atlantic Treaty Organization

For Product Safety Concerns and Information please contact our EU
representative GPSR@taylorandfrancis.com
Taylor & Francis Verlag GmbH, Kaufingerstraße 24, 80331 München, Germany